# War in the History of Economic Thought

Even after the experience of WWII and despite the existence of various institutions such as the United Nations to avoid conflict between nations, we have not succeeded in making a world free from war. The Cold War, the Vietnam War, the intervention of the superpowers in local conflicts and the spread of terrorism have made this all too clear.

This volume brings together contributions by leading international scholars of various countries and reconstructs how economists have dealt with issues that have been puzzling them for nearly three centuries: Can a war be 'rational'? Does international commerce complement or substitute war? Who are the real winners and losers of wars? How are military expenses to be funded?

The book offers a refreshing approach to the subject and how we think about the relations between economics and war.

**Yukihiro Ikeda** is Professor of History of Economic Thought at Keio University, Japan.

**Annalisa Rosselli** is Professor of History of Economic Thought at the University of Rome Tor Vergata, Italy.

# Routledge Studies in the History of Economics

For a full list of titles in this series, please visit www.routledge.com/series/SE0341

# War in the History of Economic Thought

## Economists and the Question of War

Edited by
**Yukihiro Ikeda and
Annalisa Rosselli**

Routledge
Taylor & Francis Group

LONDON AND NEW YORK

First published 2018
by Routledge

2 Park Square, Milton Park, Abingdon, Oxfordshire OX14 4RN
52 Vanderbilt Avenue, New York, NY 10017

*Routledge is an imprint of the Taylor & Francis Group, an informa business*

First issued in paperback 2019

*British Library Cataloguing-in-Publication Data*
A catalogue record for this book is available from the British Library

*Library of Congress Cataloging-in-Publication Data*
Names: Ikeda, Yukihiro, 1959– editor. | Rosselli, Annalisa, editor.
Title: War in the history of economic thought : economists and the question of war / edited by Yukihiro Ikeda and Annalisa Rosselli.
Description: Abingdon, Oxon ; New York, NY : Routledge, 2018. | Series: Routledge studies in the history of economics ; 197 | Includes bibliographical references and index.
Identifiers: LCCN 2017014727 | ISBN 9781138244733 (hardback) | ISBN 9781315276656 (ebook)
Subjects: LCSH: War—Economic aspects. | Economics—History. | Economics—Philosophy.
Classification: LCC HB195 .W354 2018 | DDC 330.1509—dc23
LC record available at https://lccn.loc.gov/2017014727

ISBN: 978-1-138-24473-3 (hbk)
ISBN: 978-0-367-35073-4 (pbk)

Typeset in Galliard
by Apex CoVantage, LLC

# Contents

# Illustrations

## Tables

## Map

# Contributors

**Alain Clément** was Professor of History of Economic Thought at the University of Tours, France.

**Daniel Diatkine** is Professor Emeritus of Economics at Evry University. He also directs a research seminar on Hume and Adam Smith at Paris I Panthéon-Sorbonne University, France.

**Raphaël Fèvre** is a PhD student in the Walras Pareto Center at the University of Lausanne, Switzerland.

**Philippe Gillig** is Lecturer in Social Sciences in the *Faculty of Social Sciences* and Researcher affiliated to BETA (Bureau d'Économie Théorique et Appliquée) at the University of Strasbourg, France.

**Tsutomu Hashimoto** is Professor of Economics at the Hokkaido University, Japan.

**Yukihiro Ikeda** is Professor of History of Economic Thought at Keio University, Japan.

**Deniz T. Kılınçoğlu** is Assistant Professor in the Economics Program at Middle East Technical University Northern Cyprus Campus.

**Atsushi Komine** is Professor in the Faculty of Economics at Ryukoku University, Japan.

**Shinji Nohara** is Assistant Professor in the Faculty of Economics at the University of Tokyo.

**Paolo Paesani** is Associate Professor of Economic Policy at the University of Rome Tor Vergata, Italy.

**Annalisa Rosselli** is Professor of History of Economic Thought at the University of Rome Tor Vergata, Italy.

**Nao Saito** is Associate Professor in the Faculty of Economics at Tohoku Gakuin University, Japan.

**Riccardo Soliani** is Associate Professor of History of Economic Thought at the University of Genoa, Italy.

**Philippe Steiner** is Professor of Sociology in Paris-Sorbonne University, France.

**Tadashi Ohtsuki** is part-time Lecturer at the Faculty of Social and Information Studies of Gunma University, Japan.

**Shimpei Yamamoto** is Assistant Professor (Special Appointment) in the Faculty of Economics at Osaka City University, Japan.

# Introduction

*Yukihiro Ikeda and Annalisa Rosselli*

The idea of calling on historians of economic thought to reflect on the relationship between war and economics originated from a specific circumstance and a general feeling. The specific circumstance was the 100th anniversary of WWI, which renewed the interest of researchers in the place of war in our culture, in its many aspects. The general feeling was the impression that the delusion that humanity is progressing towards a totally peacefully era has come to an end. This optimistic view, nurtured by the long absence of gigantic conflicts on a global scale, seemed plausible to the generations born in the richest countries after WWII, who had never experienced war. However, in recent years, ethnic and religious conflicts, millions of refugees, the disintegration of whole states, resurgent nationalisms and the possibility of a new arms race have compelled us to acknowledge the fragility of peace. Unfortunately, war is not an outdated subject.[1]

The economic aspects of war are easy to identify. For centuries war has been a preferred means to acquire wealth, for states and individuals. Analyses of the economic causes of past and present conflicts have always been plentiful. Sometimes they even exaggerate the economic motivations, perhaps in the effort to introduce some rationality into the most irrational of human activities. Wealth has always been not only the aim of wars, but also the necessary condition for their success, be their goal offensive or defensive. Reliance on an adequately fed, trained and equipped army has been a prerequisite for military victory since antiquity. As the historians remind us, the fabulous conquests of Alexander the Great owed as much to his extraordinary leadership as to the gold and silver mines of Macedon (Davies 2002: 82).

It is customary to identify the birth of modern economic science with the recommendations of the merchants to the sovereigns on how to accumulate the treasure necessary for their dominance when the country was not endowed with mines of precious metals. They showed that a trade surplus, achieved through monopolies and protectionist measures, could be less costly than and as effective as the capture of a rich booty. Since then, on the outbreak of war economists have never ceased to offer their advice, usually debating the alternative ways of funding the military effort. They have taken on this role, sometimes with reluctance (like Keynes who famously wrote in 1917, "I work for a Government I despise for ends I think criminal" [Skidelsky 1992: 345]), sometimes in complete agreement with governments, but always as part of their duty towards their country.

However, the present volume does not focus on this aspect of the relationship between economists and war, but on another which we consider equally interesting, albeit controversial. Starting in the 18th century, economic science began to argue that we do not live in a zero-sum society where the enrichment of some must imply the impoverishment of others. What is true for the people of a nation where the division of labour boosts productivity and increases the "necessaries and conveniences of life" for the whole population is also true on a global scale, where trade increases prosperity since it opens up economic opportunities and stimulates growth and industry everywhere. Poverty accompanies isolation. Commercial competition among nations thus has an ambivalent impact on peace: it is a source of conflict over markets and resources, but also leads to interdependence, which makes the interruption of trade far more damaging than in an autarkic system. Since peace is sounder when it is founded on interests rather than passions – to use the terminology of Hirschman's celebrated essay (Hirschman 1977) – the new era of industry and trade had the potential to open the way to a world without wars, with new forms of political organizations. It is this reflection on the opportunities for peace that growing integration of markets and nations could generate which represents, in our view, the most interesting aspect of the relationship between economics and war.

This also seems to be the opinion of the contributors to this volume. We can detect a common thread which endows all the chapters with a certain unity. It lies in the question: What are the rational arguments the economists developed against the irrationality of the sentiments which lie behind wars, for example, the longing for power of sovereigns, the glorification of military prowess, the disdain for death and love of risk displayed by so many youths? What plans have the economists proposed to ground peace on solid foundations?

The volume is divided into three parts, which follow a chronological order. Part I comprises chapters regarding the period from mercantilism to the end of Classical Political Economy with J.S. Mill. Part II focusses on Japan and the cultural background of Japanese economists before and during WWII. Part III is devoted to some of the lessons which economists in the Western world drew from the experience of WWII and their projects for a different economic order.

The volume begins with Alain Clément and Riccardo Soliani's chapter[2] on the "food weapon", that is, the strategic behavior of nations which exploit their dominant position on the foodstuff market deliberately to starve the populations. In focusing on the concept of the food weapon, Clément and Soliani examine the economic and political trends in each period, from mercantilism to the heyday of the British Classical School. They reconstruct the changes in attitude towards the danger of being denied access to foreign markets in times of war or famine. In the 17th century the Mercantilists suggested relying exclusively on self-sufficiency and devoting an adequate part of the labour and resources of the nation to agriculture, fearing dependency on foreign supplies. However, this view was progressively superseded by a new representation of the world based on complementarity, rather than competition, between States (and the food weapon began to be considered, instead, an instrument of control over part of the population). The case of the Netherlands showed that a nation could be rich and powerful without producing its own food, but acquiring it by trade. Clément and Soliani see an echo of this contrast between autarky and free trade in terms of food security in the debate between Ricardo and Malthus on the Corn Laws. According to their original interpretation, Malthus advocated self-sufficiency because he did not trust the "passions" of the foreign countries which could block food supplies to Britain out of selfishness, if they experienced temporary difficulties. Ricardo, by contrast, relied on the interests of the foreign merchants who, he believed, would never miss the opportunity for a handsome profit when the British price of foodstuffs was high enough.

The following two chapters concern the great founders of economics, Adam Smith and his friend David Hume. Both Daniel Diatkine and Shinji Nohara[3] bring to light the differences between these two authors, very close in many other respects, when it comes to analysing the origin of wars. According to Diatkine, Hume devised some of his most famous economic propositions – like the price-specie flow mechanism – to expose the falseness of the mercantilist argument which deemed it possible to finance wars through permanent surpluses of the balance of trade. Under this delusion Britain was tempted to give vent to her desire for power and engage in wars which could ultimately be financed only by public debt. The growth of public debt, repayment of which implied levying heavy taxes on the citizens without their consent, was a threat to constitutional order and could lead to despotism or the end of the nation. Smith, on the contrary, did not blame exacerbated national passions for conflicts like the Seven Years' War, but rather the interests of the merchants, who were able to convince the sovereign and their fellow citizens that what benefited them benefited the whole country. Smith feared that the expansion of the British Empire and disproportionate reliance on colonial trade would force Britain to excessive military efforts, driving her towards tyranny, following the destiny of the Roman Empire.

Nohara sees the relationships between Smith and Hume from a different perspective. Both Hume and Smith rejected Hobbes's notion that the state of nature is a state of war, but sought out different sources of peaceful relations between people and nations. For Smith, the main source is mutual sympathy. However, this sentiment is partial and does not embrace all humankind. It decreases with lack of familiarity and in reaching out beyond the borders of a nation. Wars may come about with a decline in mutual sympathy between people of different nationalities, with different habits, customs, religion and culture. For Hume, "jealousy" of other people's property is the principal cause of war. At the same time, "jealousy" in the sense of commercial competition is a source of economic prosperity. For people who belong to the same nation, Hume thought justice was not natural but based on the rational acknowledgment of a common interest; natural morality was not sufficient for the establishment of social order, and could result in conflict. Thus Hume emphasized the role of the government in maintaining internal security. At the international level, it is much more difficult for peace to rely on the recognition of common interests and justice, there being no international judge to appeal to.

We then turn to France, and again we address Montesquieu's antinomy between "*doux commerce*" and war. Philippe Steiner reconstructs how a political economist (Jean-Baptiste Say), a political theoretician (Benjamin Constant), and a sociologist (Auguste Comte) reflected on the new connections between industrial capitalism and warfare. These three authors developed what may be called the "peaceful industrial society thesis", to the effect that social relations in an industrial society will lead citizens away from war and towards the production and exchange of a growing mass of wealth. This may sound paradoxical considering that Say's views, in particular, were formed while the Napoleonic wars were raging, and a few years before Carl von Clausewitz's theoretical work on the new developments in warfare. Armies of mercenaries were being replaced by the masses moved by political passion for the greatness of their nation – a passion that would orient the art of war in a new and terrible direction. Say, the leading French economist of that time, developed an articulated view of the connection between the new industrial world and the waning of wars. Benjamin Constant, a contemporary political thinker, took up some of Say's ideas in several books published towards the end of the Empire, connecting the economic and political dimensions of the liberal worldview. Industrialism thus became an explicit political philosophy. Finally, Auguste Comte's positive philosophy introduced the thesis of industrial peace to a broad audience, explaining why warfare would fade away in the course of human history.

Say's economics proved influential not only in France and the neighboring nations of Europe, but also in Turkey. Deniz T. Kılınçoğlu examines the influences of Say's economics in the Ottoman Empire, drawing upon an unpublished work by an anonymous author conserved in the Austrian National Library. Addressed to the Ottoman political-military elite in the mid-1830s, who had to face new warfare technologies which required adequate financing, this manuscript constitutes the first-known example of Ottoman-Turkish economic literature. The main objective of the anonymous author was to introduce the new European science of economics to the Ottoman political-military elite as an instrument for the administration of an effective war economy, as well as a guide to bring prosperity to the country. A knowledge of economics, the author believes, is essential for any statesman who wishes to see his country surviving and prospering in the economy-centered modern age. The influence of Say's *Cours complet* is all too evident, although there are no explicit references. Kılınçoğlu's analysis of the text also sheds light on the linguistic and cultural dynamics involved in the transmission of economic ideas to the Ottoman Empire.

Part I concludes with Philippe Gillig's chapter on John Stuart Mill's thought. Those who have read Mill's works are puzzled by the inconsistencies between Mill's liberalism and the advocacy of rather interventionist policies occasionally cropping up in his texts. Gillig tackles this problem with special attention to cases of interference in foreign civil wars, which could appear a clear sign of imperialism. Gillig's conclusion is that Mill is a consistent defender of the non-intervention principle in economic as well as military affairs, but in both cases he considers that this principle should not be applied strictly. The exceptions to the general rule share a common point: the immaturity of the peoples or industries concerned. He argues that intervention in civilized countries is not legitimate because it thwarts the efforts a people must make to assert their freedom, for example against occupation by a foreign power; however, in the case of "barbarous" peoples – that is, people who are still immature – intervention is morally required. Even Mill's defence of Empire still appears to be globally consistent with his commitment to liberalism. White settler colonies, Mill deemed, created conditions for universal peace. His liberalism is reflected in his faith in the peace-promoting virtues of free trade: "It is commerce which is rapidly rendering war obsolete, by strengthening and multiplying the personal interests which are in natural opposition to it" (Mill 1965 [1848]: 594).

Part II is dedicated to the issue of war and the economists in Japan. Since WWII had devastating effects on the country, the chapters of Part II deal mainly with the interwar period and WWII, seeking to reconstruct the cultural environment that led to the conflict. First, Shimpei Yamamoto discusses the importance of "*Shin Jiyushugi*" (New Liberalism), a relatively forgotten monthly magazine published in the interwar period. This publication set out to introduce into Japan the principles of Britain's new liberalism, which integrated social policy within a framework of classical liberalism. Yamamoto emphasizes the lack of a tradition of liberalism in Japan, which the magazine and the various figures associated with it sought to remedy, but without success. Yamamoto argues that the downfall of the group interested in New Liberalism may have been a factor in paving the way to WWII, and the absence of a liberal tradition in Japan held far-reaching implications for Japanese society.

Tadashi Ohtsuki describes how Japanese Higher Commercial Schools and Commercial Universities responded to the war, and especially to the expansion of Japanese imperialism. Ohtsuki fills a gap in the history of Japanese economic thought, for at a distance of nearly 70 years since the end of WWII, studies on this topic remain insufficient. He shows that, with the extension of Japanese colonies in the 1930s, all the institutes of higher education had to reform their curriculums to include the disciplines related to colonization. Theoretical studies in economics decreased as the war progressed, although some economists continued to apply their original academic methods to economic surveys in response to social demand. Others cooperated with the Japanese military administration, whether they approved of it or not. In spite of these departures from academic studies, Ohtsuki clarifies that the developments of post-war economics in Japan owe much to the research carried out in the interwar period, including Okawa's study of the long-term trends of economic quantities.

Part II concludes with Tsutomu Hashimoto's chapter on Takata Yasuma, a Japanese sociologist. Known as an original scholar deeply embedded in the Kyoto tradition, Takata also played an important role in shaping politico-economic thinking during WWII. He was confident that the construction of a political regime in the name of "extended racialism" was a necessary step toward an ideal individualistic society with world government. Takata believed that hybrid races could emerge only through the imperialist expansion of a powerful nation. This unequivocally imperialistic view was taken up to justify Japan's military expansion to the continent. Disentangling the difficult passages penned by Takata, the author follows the sociologist's arguments as expounded during the war and emphasizes the discontinuity with the line he took after it.

Part III is dedicated to the efforts of economists in Western countries to build a long-lasting peace and to reconstruct the economy after the disasters of WWII by stressing the importance of collaboration within and between countries.

Atsushi Komine studies the collaboration between Lionel Robbins and William H. Beveridge and the role they played in shaping British ideas on "how to avoid wars". They were able to assemble eminent scholars including economists in an institution called the Federal Union, established in 1938 – a centre for federalist movements. Robbins worked on the economic aspects of federalism, whereas Beveridge had various roles such as organizing, conceptualizing and publicizing. They had a great influence on federalist movements. Besides political activism, federalism was developed as part of their economic thinking. Robbins attempted to counter Keynes's "insularity" by introducing a clear international dimension into his economic policy. Beveridge, influenced by Robbins, Meade, and Keynes, became convinced that it would be indispensable not only to secure lasting peace but also to maintain full employment in the post-war era. He recognized the need for freedom from want, idleness, and war. The atomic bombing of Hiroshima and Nagasaki prompted further development of his ideas on federalism.

Paolo Paesani and Annalisa Rosselli reconstruct the debate in the Anglo-Saxon world prompted by the success of price control schemes during WWII. This wartime experience taught two main lessons. First, resources could be allocated efficiently and equitably, regulating markets without abolishing them. Second, the success of these regulations depended on mutual accord between workers, producers and governments and, at a higher level, on international cooperation. After the war, the aspiration to set some of the positive outcomes of wartime regulations in terms of price stability, full employment and social justice on a permanent basis, stimulated debate on the pros and cons of extending price controls to peacetime. As a particularly interesting outcome, the debate shows how, after the tragedies of the 1930s and the war, economists were open to explore new roads, even in contrast with some of the tenets of traditional economic theory.

The author of the following chapter, Raphaël Fèvre, approaches the problem from the opposite perspective, confirming that different economic thinking and different experiences in each nation led to different policy implications. Instead of thinking of ways of controlling prices and market mechanisms which could hinder the establishment of the Welfare State, the German Ordoliberals' main problem was to bring the planned economic organization of the Third Reich to an end once and for all. Focussing on a very limited but exceptionally eventful period, namely the early post-war years (1945–1950), Fèvre shows that, from the ordoliberal point of view, the problem "was then seen to lie not so much in the fact that Germany had lost the war as in the perpetuation of an unsustainable economic order" (this volume, p. 218). Perceiving a strict connection between "repressed" inflation and planning activities – one leading to the other – ordoliberal thought began to raise fears about inflation because it affects not only the economic but also the social and political order of a nation as a whole.

The volume concludes, appropriately, with Nao Saito's reflections on liberal economic thought and the commitment of economists against the war. Saito reconstructs the development of the political thought of Kenneth Arrow with special attention to his famous theorem which shows the impossibility of aggregating individual preferences without violating the condition of non-dictatorship. With close scrutiny of the critical response to the theorem and Arrow's reactions, as well as the further developments in his thought, the author casts light on the complexities of the issues surrounding the theorem. It is indeed difficult to respect people's preferences, according to the liberal creed, when they decide to engage in a disastrous war.

All the chapters collected in this volume constitute a selection of those read on the occasion of the 4th ESHET-JSHET joint meeting which took place in Otaru, Japan, from September 11–13, 2015. The title of the conference was "War in the history of economic thought: The economists and the question of war". Scholars from several countries (UK, US, Germany, Switzerland, France, Turkey, Brazil, Italy and Japan) participated, building international academic networks. After all, exchange of ideas, and not only of commodities, is a crucial step towards peace.

## Acknowledgements

We would like to thank the Japanese Society of History of Economic Thought (JSHET) for its generous support in the accommodation of overseas guests at the conference in Otaru, and indeed its support for two Japanese scholars: Nao Saito and Shimpei Yamamoto. Our thanks also go to the European Society for the History of Economic Thought (ESHET) for its financial support to some of the participants from Europe and to the editing of this volume. Special thanks also go to Professor Hideo Tanaka, President of the JSHET, to Professor Susumu Egashira, local organizer of the conference, and to all those who contributed to make such an interesting conference possible.

## Notes

1 For a recent contribution, see Bientinesi and Patalano (2017).
2 A first draft of this chapter was prepared by Clément. After his premature and lamented death in August 2016, Riccardo Soliani, who was friend of Clément and had had frequent conversations with him on the subject, revised and completed the chapter.
3 Throughout the volume, the names of Japanese contributors to this volume appear in Western order: first name followed by surname. However, the names of Japanese historical figures appear in the traditionally Japanese order: surname followed by first name.

# References

Bientinesi, F., and Patalano, R. (Eds.). (2017). *Economists and War: A Heterodox Perspective*, London and New York: Routledge.

Davies, G. (2002). *History of Money: From Ancient Times to the Present Day*, Cardiff: University of Wales Press.

Hirschman, A. (1977). *The Passions and the Interests*, Princeton, NJ: Princeton University Press.

Mill, J. S. (1965 [1848]). *The Principles of Political Economy With Some of Their Applications to Social Philosophy* (J. M. Robson, Ed.). The Collected Works of John Stuart Mill, III. Toronto: University of Toronto Press.

Skidelsky, R. (1992). *John Maynard Keynes: Volume 1: Hopes Betrayed 1883–1920*, London: Macmillan.

# Part I
# Before the two world wars

# 1 The food weapon
## Milestones in the history of a concept (17th–19th centuries)

*Alain Clément and Riccardo Soliani*

Access to food is humankind's most basic need, and the "food weapon" refers to all the means employed to voluntarily starve a population. When a country has an export monopoly on an agricultural food staple or a dominant position on such a foodstuff's market, it can use its management and storage resources to place political pressure on countries importing that product. The food weapon can also be utilized by a central power or a faction, against all or part of a population, in which the pressure that is exerted is an internal one. The different forms of use of the food weapon have been observed countless times in history and, since the middle of the 1970s, contemporary authors interested in development issues have analysed the subject at great length (Ó Gráda 2009; Charlton 1997; Bertrand et al. 1997; Maxwell 1996; Labbé 1994; Macrae and Zwi 1992; Bessis 1985; Wallensteen 1976). The subject of the present chapter is to see how, between the 17th and the 19th centuries, the period when the question of food became of central importance (Clément 1999), the first economists addressed the issue. This analysis will examine the various forms that the food weapon can take, the economic conditions for its implementation, its consequences, and the means of protection against it when countries are threatened by that weapon. The first part of this chapter will study the mercantilist texts that focused largely on questions of food security and self-sufficiency, precisely to reduce – or even neutralize – the potentially dangerous effects that they perceived in the food weapon. The second part will turn to the coverage of the subject during the 18th century. Although less centred on international economic relations, the 18th century attended to the question from a more internal perspective (the food weapon used by leaders or private actors against the people or against a segment of the people). In the third part, the chapter will analyse the 19th century as the period that gave renewed importance to this weapon wielded by and against States at a time when France had orchestrated a continental blockade of the United Kingdom. That analysis will be based primarily on the debates on the Corn Laws, debates that incorporated that "warring" dimension.

## Part I: Multiplicity of "mercantilist" analyses of the food weapon

In respect of the theme of the food weapon, which was addressed in a large number of 16th and 17th century writings, two stages can be identified. The first ranges from Bodin to the first English mercantilists, through the middle of the 17th century, and gives special attention to international economic relations, and to economic conflicts in particular. The second period, which concerns the latter half of the 17th and the beginning of the 18th century, shows little interest in international matters and therefore little interest in the classic food weapon. And yet, the food weapon had not been dismissed from the list of economic concerns. However, it was perceived more as a means of placing economic pressure on a country's citizens.

## 1 The "first" mercantilists and the food weapon

### Economic war vs. military war

In a recent article dedicated to the links between war and trade in mercantilist thought, Shovlin (2014: 305–327) reconsidered the place of war in international relations during the "mercantilist period". Although he observed that war was omnipresent in inter-State relations, it was rarely declared for the purpose of attaining economic goals. However, commercial competition was a form of confrontation between States. Trade was perceived as the new battleground between States, and war was no longer a means of seizing riches. Commercial wars were one of the concrete forms of such clashes: for example, the Second Anglo-Dutch War (1665–1667), with its conflicts along the West Coast of Africa, between the forces of the Dutch East India Company and the forces of the English Company of Royal Adventurers, the latter attempting to break off Dutch trade in gold and slaves (Shovlin 2014: 308–309). This example provided a strong illustration of the new type of warfare between nations. The consequence of this evolution was a desire to establish political power on a solid domestic economic base. Obtaining trade surplus was a priority and became a mean of asserting country's superiority. An illustration of this pursuit of economic power was the quest for national economic independence.

While war had become economic in nature, the food weapon was the favourite armament amongst economic leaders and theorists. This relies first and foremost on a clash between nations' respective agricultural and food powers. But over and above the forces present – somewhat akin to an army of soldiers lined up face-to-face – there was also the use that could be made of the food weapon. Like most of the weapons, the food weapon had two modes, which were clearly perceived by the mercantilists: a defensive dimension and an offensive one.

### Food dependence vs. independence

If a nation's economic power was a new form of political rivalry, its agricultural and food power was one of the methods for achieving that sought-after, proclaimed power. A number of examples taken from French and British texts provide excellent illustrations of how that economic power was viewed. In his *Mémoires des sages et royalles oéconomies*, Sully enthusiastically recalled that

> France is better stocked than any other kingdom in the world (with the exception of Egypt), and those products that consist of grains, vegetables, wines, dyes, oils, cider, salt, hemp, wool, linen, etc., are the cause of all the gold and silver entering France and, consequently, those products are far better that all the silks produced in Sicily, Spain and Italy.
>
> (Sully 1942 [1638]: xvi)

Montchrétien also wrote about the riches of France in glowing terms, with its "five inexhaustible sources of natural wealth [. . .] wheat, wine, salt, woollens, cloths" (Montchrétien 1889 [1615]: 239). Similar analyses emerged in English writings. According to Mun, England was endowed with "great plentie of natural riches, both in the sea for fish, and on the land for wooll, cattle, corne, lead, tin, iron, and many other things for food, rayment and munition" (Mun 1971 [1621]: 50). Thus supplied, the country could survive without the assistance of other nations (Mun 1971 [1621]: 73). In these quotations, it can be seen that one of the forms of a State's political power was based on its ability to feed its people and, conversely, that a country unable to feed its population through its own means was in a position of fragility and vulnerability.

### The defensive weapon, or how the country must feed the country

According to mercantilist analyses, agricultural potential should make it possible to feed the entire population and enable demographic growth, which is a source of military and economic power. It is in the country's interest to preserve that advantage: the policy of self-sufficiency was particularly touted by Montchrétien and Bodin, who mentioned it in *La République*. Food self-sufficiency was given priority over the accumulation of gold and silver earned by trade in those same products. Montchrétien was the first to speak of autarky:

> no society must borrow from elsewhere anything that it holds necessary because, being able to have it only at the mercy of another, it weakens itself accordingly [. . .] there is only the sole necessity that compels the taking from elsewhere of what one has not.
>
> (Montchrétien 1889 [1615]: 66)

This point of view was reinforced by the fact that "in trade, we have as many losses as the foreigner has gains" (Montchrétien 1889 [1615]: 154). Therefore, trade with foreigners should be avoided wherever possible, such that "the country supplies the country" (Montchrétien 1889 [1615]: 112). In parallel, he would not have found it surprising if "the Spanish could also produce wheat to feed themselves, we would be right in complaining that they no longer wanted to buy ours" (Montchrétien 1889 [1615]:155). Mun shared a more moderate version of that point of view. Above all, it appeared important not to be dependent on foreign powers when it came to the procurement of food staples, in particular. The sale of manufactured goods should not be used to satisfy vital needs. It would be useful that

> We may peradventure employ our selves with better safety, plenty, and profit in using more tillage and fishing, than to trust so wholly to the making of cloth; for in times of war, or by other occasions, if some forraign Princes should prohibit the use thereof in their dominions, it might suddenly cause much poverty and dangerous uproars, especially by our poor people.
>
> (Mun 1965 [1664]: 73)

It was essential to prioritize the home nation and trade with other countries as a last resort. This domestic priority placed on food procurement and independence constituted a strength and helped to reinforce one nation's domination over the others: "A kingdom that can supply its own necessities itself is always richer, stronger and more formidable" (Montchrétien 1889 [1615]: 131–132).

### How to develop the defensive weapon?

This policy included two main axes: the encouragement of domestic production on the one hand and the protection and limitation – or even prohibition – of exports of those products on the other. The encouragement of the agricultural sector was due in particular to public figures like Sully, who opposed the development of luxury goods industries.

Controlling the movement of agricultural products toward other countries was the second aspect of this policy. Fulfilling the people's dietary needs at the lowest price possible, not only does it require the development of the agricultural sector, but also a protectionist policy toward foreign countries. This policy was long applied in France and then abandoned during the Restoration; in England, it was instituted at the end of the 14th century and permanently relinquished only in 1846.

According to Bodin, political authorities should allow foreign trade in agricultural products if, and only if, people have sufficient food supply: the institution of export duties should prevent cereals from exiting the country and foster the full satisfaction of all domestic needs, because "France [. . .] has largely enough to feed its people, even during bad years, so long as foreigners do not empty its granaries" (Bodin 1986 [1568]: VI, 432). This policy of domestic priority was also lauded in England for the same reasons. For Mun, for example, "Victuals and munition for war are so pretious in a Commonwealth, that either it seemeth necessary to restrain the exportation altogether, or (if the plenty permits it) to require the return thereof in so much treasure" (Mun 1965 [1664]: 37). Whilst remaining highly favourable to trade and industry, which represented a great source of wealth for his country, he above all wished for his country to be self-sufficient.[1]

*The offensive weapon, or how to weaken others*

Production not only embodies the wealth and power of the members of a national community; it also embodies the power of the nation, measured in relation to the wealth of other countries (Fourquet 1989: 157). This assessment had already been expressed by Bodin. In *La République*, he wrote that a country's wealth was dependent on its agricultural resources: "The greatest treasures will come where there are more of life's necessities, although there are no gold or silver mines, as there are few in this kingdom that nonetheless feeds a large proportion of Europe" (Bodin 1986 [1576]: I, 65). That wealth created a situation of domination: "wine, salt and wheat are three elements on which the life of the foreigner depends, after God" (Bodin 1986 [1568]: VI, 456). This was, for example, the case with Spain, which "owes its life to France" (Bodin 1986 [1568]: VI, 428). Reaping the benefits of this vital advance, France could always apply heavy taxes on export, because demand was relatively inelastic in relation to price, to use a contemporary expression. "It is therefore expedient to similarly raise foreign taxation for goods without which the foreigner cannot live and, by that means, increase finances and relieve the burden of the nation's subjects" (Bodin 1986 [1576]: I, 65–66). This analysis was shared in full by Montchrétien, who considered need as source of weakness and root of possible domination. It is this weakness that Richelieu also wanted to exploit, because

> France is so fertile in wheat [. . .] that Spain, England and all our neighbours must recourse to it. And, so long as we know how to help ourselves to the advantages that nature has given us, we can derive money from those who want our goods that are so necessary to them.
> (Richelieu 1947 [1632–1638]: 418)

For Mun, the possession of the goods necessary for food supply and warfare constituted the highest degree of power for all countries. The existence of large stores of wheat "will make them to be feared abroad" (Mun 1965 [1664]: 70).

*The limitations of the food weapon*

Contemporary historians have underscored the first limitation on this power. International trade in cereals only concerned a small proportion of the products consumed. Braudel estimated that, in the 17th century, European trade in cereals accounted for approximately 6 million quintals, compared to the 240 consumed by Europeans, representing just 2.5 per cent, with maritime trade in wheat being assessed at 1 per cent (Braudel 1979: I, 99–104). The food power was all the more limited to the imported products coming from Poland, Sardinia, Sicily, Sweden, the Ottoman Empire and so forth, that is, from countries that exported foodstuffs to the detriment of their local populations.[2] Although such a trade appeared to be relatively low with respect to the total quantity of cereals consumed, the fact remained that, given the existence of cities and towns that were often on the very limits of survival, that 2 per cent of production could be enough to tip the scale one way or the other (Tilly 1975: 409–412).

The "Dutch model" represented a second limit to the exercise of the food weapon. The Netherlands, a rich and powerful nation, did not produce all its own wheat. And yet, not only was it supplied but it also transported cereals on behalf of other countries. Amsterdam developed into a key depot for North-South trade. International trade showed that it was possible for a country to be dependent on the outside world for its food supply without running any major risk, so long as that country had the financial and technical capacity to contend with that situation. This was Richelieu's point of view: "the opulence of the Dutch [. . .] is an example and proof of the usefulness of trade" (Richelieu 1947 [1632–1638]: 416). Also Mun used trade to explain the wealth and power of the Netherlands (see, e.g., Mun 1965 [1664]: 74).

## 2 The "second" mercantilism rejected the food weapon as a means of pressure on rival nations

### The end of the food weapon, strictly speaking?

During the second half of the 17th century, the strategic dimension of foodstuffs – and their ability to create power dynamics between States – was reconsidered. The primary reason for this was the conception of wealth on the one hand, and the attention paid not to confrontations between nations, but to the complementarity that could be established, even at the risk of allowing a possible food dependency, on the other. Thus the food weapon lost its interest. It did not however disappear completely; instead, it changed its scope of application.

Complementarity, rather than competition, between the States, constituted a new representation of the world, consistent with the gradual dismissal of the notion of a finite world in which "what one gains, the other party loses". The tax policy was successively called into question by Petty (1963 [1662]), Child (1693 [1668]) and Davenant (1771 [1698]). In France, Colbert was more favourable to free foreign trade in wheat, except in the case of famine (Colbert 1861–1882). In England, the increasing awareness of the negative impact of restrictions on international trade was coupled with the perception of the benefits due to the international division of labour. In certain parts of his work, Petty demonstrated that England could give up the idea of producing its own food. Consequently, agriculture, even though it was a source of riches in the "here and now", could be considered as a non-priority activity, and

> it would be the advantage of England to throw up their husbandry, and to make no use of their lands, but for grass horses, milch cows, gardens, and orchards, etc. . . . which if it be so, and if trade and manufacture have increased in England (that is to say) if a greater part of the people, apply themselves to those faculties than there did heretofore, and if the price of

corn be no greater now, than when husbandmen were more numerous, and tradesmen fewer.

(Petty 1963 [1690]: 268)

France, however, which was perceived more as a land-based nation due to its natural inability to become a maritime power, should turn more inward than outward. England, given its geographic layout, could, unlike France, procure food from outside at more advantageous prices (Petty 1963 [1690]: 294).

The authors of the period did not lock themselves into the notion of a world in which food self-sufficiency would be a component of the country's power. The foodstuffs sector was no longer an issue of power, a component of strength or an instrument of pressure because, quite simply, those mercantilists believed that other sectors could better fulfil that role. The control of the sea, especially for Petty, becomes the new power struggle, because "he who holds the sea holds the global networks of economic information, trade, and also industry" (Fourquet 1989: 175). In the eyes of the English mercantilists, the nourishing land was no longer an element of wealth and power.

## *A food weapon against the people?*

Within this new context, the food weapon was applied to a different, domestic space, albeit not entirely unrelated to the situation described earlier. It was used against labourers to incite them to work as much as possible and so to produce more goods and contribute to the nation's wealth. Although the objective of domination had not been dismissed, and economic warfare was still of topical relevance, they were expressed now through heightened international competition, increasingly reliant on the minimization of domestic costs. To simplify, it was necessary to starve the people to push them to work. Indeed authors like Petty and Mandeville considered that workers should be fed "meagrely", relieving their hunger only up to the limits of want. This minimal consumption contributed indirectly to the race toward the country's hegemony and enrichment and therefore its power (less domestic consumption meant more sales abroad and lower living expenses for the workers). Here, the food weapon took the form of an "incentive" designed to drive people to work. None expressed this thought better than Mandeville: "they [*the people*] have nothing to stir them up to be serviceable but their wants, which it is prudence to relieve, but folly to cure" (Mandeville 1924 [1714]: I, 213) and "the only thing then can render the labouring man industrious, is a moderate quantity of money" (Mandeville 1924 [1714]: I, 212–213). The poor had to remain poor, because "wealth consists in a multitude of laborious poor" (Mandeville 1924 [1714]: I, 287). Little food was a more effective incentive than force in encouraging people to work. Maintenance of an inexpensive labour force was a means of producing at lower costs, selling more easily abroad and enriching the nation.

## Part II: Private use of the food weapon by the market's actors during the 18th century

### 1 *The importance of being well fed*

Eighteenth-century France and Great Britain countered the arguments of Petty and Mandeville, developed in previous decades. The physiocrats and anti-physiocrats were highly concerned with satisfying the needs of people. Quesnay and Dupont de Nemours opposed that 17th century conception: "The happiness of the human species consists of a multitude of pleasures" (Dupont de Nemours 1846 [1772]: 369). Both Smith and Steuart adhered to the same concept: each individual must be suitably fed. The first argument was humanitarian and historical: "No society can surely be flourishing and happy, of which the far greater part of the members are poor and miserable" (Smith 1976 [1776]: 96). The second argument was economic: productivity is dependent on feeding the labour force well, because

> [a] plentiful subsistence increases the bodily strength of the labourer, and the comfortable hope of bettering his condition, and of ending his days perhaps in ease and plenty, animates him to exert that strength to the utmost. Where wages are high, accordingly, we shall always find the workmen more active, diligent, and expeditious, than where they are low.
>
> (Smith 1976 [1776]: 99–100)

But are people really protected against the exercise of any form of the food weapon?

### 2 *The anti-liberal fear of strategic basic necessities: a potential risk!*

This fear, founded and transmitted by anti-liberals in respect of use of the food weapon, was primarily based on the very nature of subsistence. Indeed, the main goal of labourer was to provide subsistence for him and his family. Thus, as Abbot Galiani told us in his dialogues – a real bombshell over the course of the highly agitated period of the liberalization of the wheat trade – wheat must be seen as "the material that is the most basic necessity [. . .] and, from that perspective, it belongs to politics and to reasons of State" (Galiani 1984 [1770]: 33–34). As a result, its acquisition could not be delayed. As Abbot Mably put it in his speech on the grain trade:

> If my clothes, my shirts, my stockings and my shoes are worth nothing, I can wait, and never in history has it been written that any insurrection was born of that. But I cannot go a day without bread, without have death pass before my eyes.
>
> (Mably 1794–1795: XIII, 262–263)

Linguet added that it was "an exclusive, daily need", unlike "industrial production, whose use is never essential and whose purchase can always be deferred"

(Linguet 1789: 137). The anti-physiocrat authors first underlined this unpostponable aspect of wheat consumption and the state of dependency that it engenders, in respect of nature and society. Linguet even wrote that there was "no type of food that maintains men more in a state of dependency" – not only physical but also social, because the countries of Europe were "those where the poor are the most effectively enslaved" (Linguet 1789: 27). Was this warning a criticism of the forces underlying the market, a questioning of the trust that we place in it? An expression of fear that people might in turn suffer the effects of the food weapon? On this subject, points of view diverged.

*Liberal faith in the market: a peaceful market!*

For this goal to be attained, all liberal authors placed their faith in market's mechanism and its actors. There should be no State intervention, no constraints on wheat merchants, and no restrictions on the domestic or international trade of cereals. Thanks to merchants, the market is flexible enough to satisfy population's needs and

> regardless of the measure taken, there is only one way to prevent people from starving to death in famine: bringing grain to places where it lacks or putting it aside for bad times; in order to do this, it necessary to take it from where it is abundant, and there must be grain stocks for a later date [. . .] Only free trade can do this at the lowest possible price.
> (Turgot 1913–1923 [1770]: III, 332)

British thinking had the same assessment: Smith did not recommend any intervention by the State, asserting that, since the interests of producers and consumers were not in opposition to one another, the State's intervention could only be disruptive. Smith lamented that merchants formed a category that was strongly loathed by the people, particularly during periods of crisis, when they were (wrongfully, he wrote) accused of inciting price increases. According to Smith, merchants played an essential role in the wheat trade: "After the trade of the farmer, no trade contributes so much to the growing of corn as that of the merchant" (Smith 1976 [1776]: 532). Merchants were perceived as more competent than anybody else to manage insufficient production levels, and the market's mechanism was considered as a source of social peace and harmony. The use of the food weapon was completely neutralized, both in domestic and in international relations. This ideal vision was not unanimously shared. Adversaries of liberalism still fought that viewpoint, seeing market mechanisms as a place of tension and possible economic warfare between consumers, producers and sellers.

## 3 Anti-liberal fear of speculators: the private enemy from within!

Turgot's optimistic vision, shared by the physiocrats, by Condorcet (1774) and by Smith (1976 [1776]), was not shared by the opponents of liberalism and supporters of an administered economy, who dreaded the use of the food weapon by certain players on the market. Those risks were felt on both sides of the Channel. For the opponents to the "all market", the people were at risk of becoming victims of the food weapon, and the main users of it were the masses of traders, wheat merchants and sellers of scraps, rather than the farmers themselves. Many authors singled out the social danger deriving from those who bought and stored the wheat to resell later, when it would be more profitable to them, gaining on the desperation of people. Steuart remarked that, as to the subsistence market, consumers tended to compete more than the merchants, because the former absolutely had to satisfy their needs whilst the latter were motivated by nothing more than the lure of profit (Steuart 1966 [1767]: 153).

Then wheat could serve as a food weapon, engendering criminal behaviours in its sellers, which would be dangerous to consumers. Taking advantage of its pressing nature, they could artificially create scarcity and increase prices in order to swell their profits. Wheat could become an object of speculation, "the more basic and urgent our needs, the more those profit-hungry men will impose their harsh and imperious law upon us", because "greed is the principle, the end goal and the soul of trade" (Mably 1794–1795: XIII, 263 and 288). Linguet offered a similar critique of speculative trade in wheat:

> wheat, along with the weevils that consume it, has produced clever merchants whose task it is to make their fortunes off the price fluctuations that they are able to bring about. From there, I will repeat it, comes the demeaning dependence of the little people, and the inhumane hardening of the great.
>
> (Linguet 1789: 28–29)

In fact, speculation on agricultural products was a behaviour that, although inhumane, was also natural in men fallen prey to the pursuit of their own individual interests (Levine 1980: 113–114).

Galiani also criticized the way in which the cereal markets were regulated, because, according to him, there were malicious players on the market, "monopolists, usurers, monsters [. . .] that pitilessly and mercilessly starve a province by pure greed for profits" (Galiani 1984 [1770]: 162). It would therefore fall to the State to ensure that this food weapon was not turned against the people, because "the Prince is the magazine keeper of foodstuffs for his entire nation" (Galiani 1984 [1770]: 219). He wanted that the weapon were turned against its users. Galiani supported the establishment of a food police that would constitute a defensive weapon against the "monopolizers".

## 4 The anti-liberal fear of speculators: the public enemy from outside!

Galiani also envisaged a potential food weapon that foreign powers could wield against France. To a certain extent, Galiani perpetuated the mercantilist notion of outside risk. To describe and combat that risk, Galiani used the language of war and diplomacy. He spoke of a "treaty" and especially of "reciprocal treatment" between nations, reciprocity that could guarantee outside supply sources in the event of famine, because, generally speaking, "all the kingdoms of Europe disturb and frustrate exportation" (Galiani 1984 [1770]: 262). Galiani suggested to fight the risk of famine and excessive prices through domestic monitoring of the markets and checks on international movements. He did not refuse the entrance or exit of cereals; he wanted to use taxes to regulate cereal movements to and from the outside, as a defensive weapon. He wanted to allow the importation of foreign wheat at a price equivalent to the domestic price, considered as a sort of "natural price", and therefore "foreign wheat will make war on monopolists, and not on farmers" (Galiani 1984 [1770]: 269). It would therefore be the State's responsibility to manage the food supply such that the food weapon would be rendered as harmless as possible.

## 5 How to protect nations against the food weapon without rejecting the market? The physiocratic analysis

Over the course of the 18th century, it was more a question of abundant food than of limitations on it (Clément 2006). However the physiocrats occasionally raise the issue of food dependence and the fears to which it could give rise. Thus, for Quesnay, the position of a country that was dependent on others to feed its people constituted a major risk. He stressed the fact that merchant nations "could only subsist through income from foreigners' property" and "support themselves through the wealth of the foreigner" (Quesnay 2005 [1757]: I, 198), and that "a nation that is reduced to industrial commerce in order to subsist is a precarious and uncertain state [. . .] always reliant and dependent on those who sell it its food staples" (Quesnay 2005 [1757]: I, 200). France, with all its riches, could do without other nations, as any agricultural country does:

> it is quite easy for other nations to do without our fabrics, but less so for them to forego our wines, our grains and all the raw materials that vast cultivation encouraged by the government will have raised to a degree of perfection that may be impossible in any other climate.
> (Grimm in Weulersse 1968 [1910]: I, 250)

This domination was all the more solid, since it was rooted in "fixed, permanent [resources], some of which sheltered, and protected from foreign competition" (Grimm in Weulersse 1968 [1910]: I, 248–249). "The country must feed the country" was the only possible conclusion. Despite stances favourable to free trade, the physiocrats did prefer that the country was not compelled to obtain its food from outside its borders. That point of view is in total agreement with the conception of foreign trade as exchanges of surpluses and with French mercantilist thought.

## 6 James Anderson,[3] or the price of neutralizing the food weapon

James Anderson, who examined agricultural issues, did not suggest that a country should isolate itself from the global market, but instead recommended the maintenance of a degree of protectionism and opposed any repeal of the Corn Laws that would regulate foreign trade in cereals (Anderson 1777; Anderson 1801). For example, if the price of imported grain was lower than the price of grain produced by domestic farmers, competition would discourage the farmers. However, if the import price is set too high, that would artificially encourage the nation's farmers to produce more than necessary. After demonstrating that complete freedom would lead to significant disadvantages, Anderson portrayed the system of subsidies and taxes and deemed it as the lesser evil of the two policies, because of natural constraints and vagaries of production. Freedom would not eliminate the danger of shortages and, in any case, the people would bear the full effects. In a protected system, those effects would be mitigated and divided over a longer period of time, similar to an insurance policy. On the contrary, complete openness to the global market risked ruining domestic agriculture and leading to a state of food dependence. Under those circumstances, the country would be reliant on the good will of others for its supplies. Prices could then rise much higher than they would otherwise have done. Here again, Anderson cast a spotlight on the fear of the food weapon. Anderson's entire analysis was actually based on the necessity for a country to be able to feed itself independently. Despite the challenges inherent to production, any country should be able to feed its people, even in the case of a very large population, account taken of the demographic pressure on food supplies. In reality, the key to Anderson's analyses lay in his trust in technical advancements. Ricardo, however, would derive an entirely different policy from those production challenges. As for Malthus, he would not share Anderson's optimism, rallying instead to a protectionist policy with greater concern for safeguarding the nation's independence.

## Part III: The 19th century, the Corn Laws vs. the food weapon?

Over and above the economic arguments for and against the repeal of the Corn Laws and relating to Great Britain's cereal markets,[4] arguments that were clearly developed in the Ricardo-Malthus debate (Clément 2006), economists gained a renewed interest in the food weapon. The debate, which was raging particularly strongly in the House of Commons and subsequently in public opinion, fed off the very famous context of the continental blockade that Napoleon imposed on Great Britain. It is not the role of this chapter to review the very mixed consequences of that blockade, but rather to examine its related effects on the positions of economists of that era. Between Malthus and Ricardo were two different visions: Malthus's approach stressed the danger of liberalism when applied to domestic food supplies, whilst Ricardo's on the contrary could be summarized as a combination of peace and economic liberalism. This marked a discreet return to

Montesquieu's *doux commerce* (gentle commerce), whereas Malthus's approach could be likened to neo-mercantilist thought.

## 1 A domestic cereal market open to the global marketplace creates the conditions for use of the food weapon

In the absolute for Malthus, the global market would not correct imbalances because the market did not represent a series of attenuating forces, but rather a series of amplifying, contaminating forces for imbalance. This was Malthus's empirical finding in his *Observations on the Effects of the Corn Laws*. That analysis was supplemented by additional reasons, at the root of the market's imbalances, including the behaviour of individuals and States. Thus, a country cannot attempt to procure its food and its food security from the international market. And yet, Malthus noted that "A most perfect freedom of intercourse between different nations in the article of corn, greatly contributes to an equalization of prices" (Malthus 1970 [1814]: 112–113). In fact, he considered that that situation of total freedom could not be more than theoretical, because "It is entirely out of power, even in time of peace, to obtain a free trade in corn" (Malthus 1970 [1815]: 145). The citizens and their governments would prevent a universal balance on the cereal market. The wheat market's operations were not totally mechanical because, to borrow Hodgson's words, economic agents could not be compared to "particles or plants" and, due to "jealousies and fears of nations, respecting their means of subsistence, [the governments] will very rarely allow of a free egress of corn, when it is in any degree scarce" (Malthus 1970 [1815]: 145). Moreover, Malthus considered certain characteristics of human nature that could play a disruptive role in the system: "At the same time it should be observed that we have latterly seen the most striking instances in all quarters, of governments acting from passion rather than interest" (Malthus 1970 [1814]: 116).

Within that debate, the question of food independence was a crucial one. No guarantee of food security could be possible due to the selfishness of nations. A State that counted on outside food sources could face serious difficulties, simply because the supplier country, experiencing temporary difficulties, had to cover its own food needs before those of other countries. Then the country "exposes itself to the risk of having its most essential supplies suddenly fail at the time of its greatest need" (Malthus 1970 [1814]: 115). There can be no doubt that Malthus remained profoundly marked by two major events that justify its relatively cautious position: his trip to Europe at the age of 33[5] and the Napoleonic blockade.[6] W. Spence also rightly recalled that the Napoleonic blockade was an example of what a State may undergo in the event of a conflict with other countries. That episode necessarily drew the attention of political leaders and encouraged them to restrict their liberal fervour (Spence 1991 [1815]: 199–204).

In this way, the cereal markets appeared more like sites of tension between nations, rather than places for peaceful exchanges. The unpredictability of States' positions and behaviours brought the burden of the food weapon (in relation to the advantages that could derive from perfectly free trade) to bear on all nations. It was therefore preferable to produce food at higher prices (that did not penalize employees), but that was safe from competition, than to depend on the global market, foreign nations and their "indolence, industry or caprice" (Malthus 1986 [1803 1826]: III, 397). It followed that self-protection from foreign competition would help feed people within the country, and therefore neutralize the potential consequences of the food weapon.

## 2 A domestic cereal market open to the global market is a powerful balancing tool for peace, which neutralizes the use of the food weapon

To liberals and Ricardo, first and foremost, a cereal market open to international trade would foster, in political terms, a harmonious balance between economic powers. This argument was put forward at a time – 1815 – when peace reigned for the first time in Europe, and most Europeans had only ever known war and political instability. The openness of the marketplace then appeared to be a mark of trust between nations. Free trade was a powerful factor for international peace due to the economic interdependence of nations that have more to gain from commerce than from war. Conversely, a highly protectionist – or even autarkic – policy in this domain would be perceived as a source of strain between nations. A country's withdrawal into its own domestic market would be likely to cause a state of tension in other countries now finding themselves in a place of need. This was the core of the liberal message.

In their counter-attack, supporters of the Corn Laws developed two arguments. The first was based on the tyrannical attitude that a hostile nation can adopt toward the purchasing countries. And yet, for free traders, such a policy would be economically disastrous to the supplying country. There would be overproduction and falling prices, with the inability to immediately reinvest all the capital in other sectors. Ricardo concluded that this was a "distress which no sovereign, or combination of sovereigns, would be willing to inflict on their people; and, if willing, it would be a measure to which probably no people would submit" (Ricardo 1951–1955 [1815]: 28). The very mixed results of the continental blockade of England were undoubtedly a factor underpinning that assessment.[7] In other words, the food weapon was deemed more costly to the party wielding it than to its victim.

The second argument was equally important. It related to what was referred to as "national preference": "When bad seasons occurred abroad, the exporting countries would have, and would exercise, the power of withholding the quantity usually exported to make up for their own deficient supply" (Ricardo 1951–1955 [1815]: IV, 27). That argument appeared to be irrefutable because financial interests were placed before the country's needs. It is more profitable selling wheat abroad at high price, rather than selling cheap on the domestic market:

> Under the circumstances then of bad seasons, the exporting country would content itself with the smallest possible quantity necessary for their own

consumption, and would take advantage of the high price in England, to sell all they could spare, as not only would corn be high, as compared with money, but as compared with all others things.

(Ricardo 1951–1955 [1815]: IV, 30–31)[8]

In all those arguments, particularly the economic ones, the use of the food weapon is put aside in favour of a desire for mutual enrichment, which needs free international trade. To a certain extent, this connects with the theory of *doux commerce*, with commerce replacing war and the food weapon being neutralized by the lure of profit, which was considered as being of much higher priority.

## Conclusion

On the basis of the texts that founded the economic science, it appears that the theme of war, economic war in particular, was highly present, regardless of the period studied. The war could mobilize specific resources (military equipment, soldiers, etc.), but also more common resources of everyday live: foodstuffs. Their production and the use that could be made of them (whether peaceful or aggressive) constituted, each in its own way, a means of waging war: the management of food supplies alone, from production to distribution, could constitute so many acts of war. The mercantilists understood this and differentiated between international uses of the food weapon and possible domestic uses, targeting a fraction of the population. But for those authors, it was primarily the State, or the King, that had access to this formidable weapon. In the 18th century, when there was less interest in international matters, the focus was more on its internal use, on the State's and private actors' capacity to wield that weapon (and the limitations thereon). The 19th century's debate on the Corn Laws returned to the more international aspect, foreshadowing the debates that would begin in the second half of the 20th century concerning the food weapon as an instrument of pressure applied by producing and exporting countries to purchasing countries that were dependent on the market for their food supplies. Although it is now common to discuss the problems raised by the use of the food weapon, let us not forget that the debate today is fuelled by historical forerunner controversies and that it could be further enhanced by a review of those fundamental texts.

## Notes

1 These analyses are in perfect agreement with the agricultural protectionist practices then in effect in all countries. In England, the aim of the first Corn Laws was both to satisfy consumers and to promote domestic agriculture. The oldest law, in the Statute-Book of 1361, prohibited the export of wheat. Although exportation was authorized in 1437, over a certain price point, since in 1534 it required a permit. In 1563, Queen Elizabeth enacted a law designed to increase the pricing threshold above which wheat could be exported (10 shillings per measure). That threshold continued to increase until 1660, when it reached the value of 40 shillings. The policy applied by the Tudors and the Stuarts authorized the exportation of wheat only during periods of abundance, and on condition that its exportation did not give rise to any artificial price increases. A similar policy was in place in France

during that same period. Depending on production levels, exports were sometimes allowed and sometimes prohibited. Despite an attempt at regulation between 1559 and 1571, the policy in practice tended to be more piecemeal.

2  A *Dictionnaire de commerce* (1597), Braudel reports in *Les structures du quotidien*, underscored this curious situation in Poland, where "the Polish only retained such a small proportion of their wheat and rye that one might almost believe that they only harvested them for foreigners. The nobility and the bourgeoisie themselves eat rye bread, and wheat bread is reserved for the tables of great lords" (Braudel 1979: I, 101).

3  James Anderson (1739–1808), a Scottish gentleman-farmer, wrote primarily agricultural texts and became famous for his theory of rent.

4  Wheat duties were mentioned on multiple occasions beginning in 1791. As of that date, free importation was only possible if the quarter of wheat posted a price of at least 54 shillings on the domestic market, compared with the previous 48 s. That scale was raised to 66 s. in 1804 and again to 80 s. in 1815. In reality, that price level was tantamount to a ban on imports (Williamson 1990: 125), a starvation price that could explain the strident discontent developing amongst the industrial class, but also amongst those workers who were primarily concerned with the price of bread (Stevenson 1974: 33–74). The abundance of publications on the subject, at that time, likewise illustrated the crucial impact of that law, passed in 1815, on the economic debate and public opinion. That price was later decreased to 52 s. in 1828. At that point, a new "sliding scale" system was adopted, replacing the absolutely prohibition on imports whenever prices fell below a certain level. That scale essentially meant a slackening in agricultural protectionism. In 1846 the protective scheme was repealed and gradually replaced by a free trade policy.

5  Malthus undertook a trip to the Continent in 1799, but travelled neither to France nor to Italy, as young Englishmen of high society typically preferred to do, instead visiting the Nordic countries, because Europe was at war (2nd Coalition) (see Broc 1984: 147–158).

6  The continental blockade did not, however, have the expected effects (see *infra*, n. 8).

7  Historians have largely confirmed the success of the blockade for England. England gained control of the seas, developed its colonial empire, increased its trade with the United States and neutral countries, and its commerce conquered Germany through Hamburg and dominated the Baltic Sea; and England suffered no worse fate during the later blockade. However, the Napoleonic Wars and the blockade did cause a slowdown in many continental industries, and not just maritime ones, such that the impact was more unfavourable to the Continent than to England, further exacerbating the gap separating the two (Crouzet 1985: 296; Crouzet 1996: 189–209).

8  Torrens drew attention on these matters by putting the then current problem into perspective. He rightly stressed that countries did not import 100 per cent of their food (for England, that percentage was closer to 10 per cent), which meant that the political risk in the event of a conflict with supplier states was extremely low. Along those same lines, he further repeated the usual argument that wheat was a good difficult to transport; the cost of transport was 10 per cent of the price on average. In fact, it was relatively complicated to import because, to be significant and effective, the price difference would have to largely exceed the additional cost of transport, which was not the case with England (Torrens 1815; see also Mill 1967 [1825, 1827]).

## References and further readings

Anderson, J. (1777). *An Enquiry Into the Nature of the Corn Laws; With a View to the New Corn Bill Proposed for Scotland*, Edinburgh: Mrs Mundell.

Anderson, J. (1801). *A Calm Investigation of the Circumstances That Have Led to the Present Scarcity of Grain in Britain*, London: John Cumming.

Bertrand, J-P., et al. (1997). *Le pouvoir alimentaire mondial en question*, Paris: Economica.

Bessis, S. (1985). *L'arme alimentaire*, Paris: La Découverte.

Bodin, J. (1986 [1568]). *Response aux paradoxes de Malestroit touchant l'enrichissement de toutes choses, et le moyen d'y remédier*, Reprint, Paris: Fayard, vol. 6, 411–503.

Bodin, J. (1986 [1576]). *Les six livres de la République*, Reprint, Paris: Fayard, 6 volumes.

Braudel, F. (1979). *Civilisation matérielle, Economie et Capitalisme, XVe–XVIIIe siècle*, Paris: Armand Colin, 3 volumes.

Broc, N. (1984). "Malthus, la géographie et les récits de voyage," in Antoinette Fauve-Chamoux (Ed.), *Malthus, Hier et aujourd'hui*, Paris: CNRS Éditions, 147–158.

Charlton, M. (1997). "Famine and the Food Weapon: Implications for the Global Food Aid Regime," *Journal of Conflict Studies*, 17(1), 28–54.

Child, J. (1693 [1668]). *A New Discourse of Trade*, fourth edition, London: printed for J. Hodges, on London-Bridge.

Clément, A. (1999). *Nourrir le peuple : entre État et marché (XVIe–XIXe siècles)*, Paris: L'Harmattan.

Clément, A. (2006). "L'excès et les contraintes alimentaires vus à travers la pensée économique européenne (XVIe-XIXe siècles)," *Food and History*, 4(2): 187–205.

Colbert, J.B. (1861–1882). *Lettres, Instructions et Mémoires*, Paris: Pierre Clément, 10 volumes.

Condorcet, N. de (1774). *Lettres sur le commerce des grains*, Paris: Couturier Père.

Crouzet, F. (1985). *De la supériorité de l'Angleterre sur la France, L'Économique et l'Imaginaire XVIIe–XXe siècles*, Paris: Librairie Académique Perrin.

Crouzet, F. (1996). *Britain, France and International Commerce: From Louis XIV to Victoria*, London: Variorum.

Davenant, C. (1771 [1698]). "Discourses on the Public Revenues and on the Trade of England in Two Parts, London (1698)," *Works*, 1: 126–388 and 2: 77–162.

de Mandeville, B. (1924 [1714]). *The Fable of Bees: or, Private Vices, Publick Benefits. Containing Several Discourses, to Demonstrate That Human Frailties . . . May Turn'd to the Advantage of the Civil Society, etc.*, Reprint F. B. Kaye, Oxford: Clarendon Press, 2 volumes.

de Montchrétien, A. (1889 [1615]). *Traité de l'Economie Politique*, first edition, Rouen, Reed. Paris: Plon.

de Richelieu, C. 1947 [1632–1638]. *Testament Politique*, Reprint, Paris: Robert Laffont.

Dupont de Nemours, Pierre-Samuel (1846 [1772]). *Abrégé des principes de l'économie politique*, Paris: Eugène Daire (Reed.) (Ed., Intro), *Physiocrates*, Paris: Guillaumin, 2 volumes.

Fourquet, F. (1989). *Richesse et puissance*, Paris: La Découverte.

Galiani, F. (1984 [1770]). *Dialogues sur le commerce des bleds*, London, Reprint, Paris: Fayard.

Labbé, M-H. (1994). *L'arme économique dans les relations internationales*, Paris: PUF.

Levine, D. (1980). *The Ideas and Careers of Simon-Nicolas-Henri Linguet: A Study in Eighteenth-Century French Politics*, Chicago: University of Illinois Press.

Linguet, S.M.H. (1789). *Du commerce des grains, nouvelle édition augmentée d'une lettre à Mr Tissot sur le vrai mérite politique et physique du pain et du bled*, Brussels, publisher not indicated.

Mably, G. (1794–1795). "Du commerce des grains," in *Oeuvres complètes de l'Abbé Mably, Paris l'an III de la République*, 15 volumes, vol. 13 (posthumous), chez Bossange.

Macrae, J., and Zwi, A. B. (1992). "Food as an Instrument of War in Contemporary African Famines: A Review of the Evidence," *Disasters*, 16(4): 299–321.

Malthus, T. (1970 [1814]). *Observations on the Effects of the Corn Laws, and of a Rise or Fall in the Price of Corn on the Agriculture and General Wealth of the Country*, London: J. Johnson, Reprint A. Mc Kelley (Ed.), T. R. Malthus, the Pamphlets, New York, 95–131.

Malthus, T. (1970 [1815]). *The Grounds of an Opinion on the Policy of Restricting the Importation of Foreign Corn; Intended as an Appendix to "Observations on the Corn Laws"*, London: J. Murray and J. Johnson, Reprint A. Mc Kelley (Ed.), T. R. Malthus, the Pamphlets, New York, 137–173.

Malthus, T. (1986 [1803–1826]). *An Essay on the Principle of Population*, London: J. Johnson, Reprint in W. E. Anthony and W. Pickering (Eds.), *The Works of Thomas Robert Malthus*, London, 8 volumes, vols. 2 and 3.

Maxwell, S. (1996). "Food Security: A Post-Modern Perspective," Food Policy, 21(2) (May): 155–170.

Mill, J. S. (1967 [1825]). "The Corn Laws," *Westminster Review*, III, April: 394–420, Reprint in J. M. Robson (Ed.), *Collected Works of John Stuart Mill*, vol. 4, Toronto: University of Toronto Press, Routledge & Kegan Paul.

Mill, J. S. (1967 [1827]). "The New Corn Laws," *Westminster Review*, VII (January): 169–186, Reprint in J. M. Robson (Ed.), *Collected Works of John Stuart Mill*, vol. 4, Toronto: University of Toronto Press, Routledge & Kegan Paul.

Mun, T. (1965 [1664]). *England's Treasure by Forraign Trade*, London, Reprint New York: Augustus Mc Kelley.

Mun, T. (1971 [1621]). *A Discourse of Trade From England Into the East Indies*, London, Reprint New York: Augustus Mc Kelley.

Ó Gráda, C. (2009). *Famine: A Short History*, Princeton, NJ: Princeton University Press.

Petty, W. (1963 [1662]). *A Treatise of Taxes and Contributions*, Reprint, London: Charles H. Hull, "William Petty, The Economics Writtings," 1899, Cambridge: Cambridge University Press, 2 volumes, Reprint New York: Augustus M. Kelley, 1–97.

Petty, W. (1963 [1690]). *Political Arithmetick*, Reprint, London: Charles H. Hull, "William Petty, The Economics Writtings," 1899, Cambridge: Cambridge University Press, 2 volumes, Reprint New York: Augustus M. Kelley, 232–313.

Quesnay, F. (2005). "Grains" (Political Economics), Ms 1757, *Encyclopédie*, VII: 821–831, Reed. C. Théré, L. Charles, J.-C. Perrot, Paris: INED, I, 161–212.

Ricardo, D. (1951–1955 [1815]). *An Essay on the Influence of a Low Price of Corn on the Profits of Stock*, London: J. Murray, Sraffa's edition, IV, 1–41, Cambridge: Cambridge University Press.

Shovlin, J. (2014). "War and Peace: Trade, International Competition, and Political Economy," in P. Stern and C. Wennerlind (Eds.), *Mercantilism Reimagined: Economy in Early Modern Britain and Its Empire*, Oxford: Oxford University Press, 305–327.

Smith, A. (1976 [1776]). *An Inquiry Into the Nature and Causes of the Wealth of Nations*, Reprint in *The Glasgow Edition of the Works and Correspondence of Adam Smith* by R. H. Campbell and A. S. Skinner, Oxford: Oxford University Press, 2 volumes.

Spence, W. (1991 [1815]). *Tracts on Political Economy: The Objections Against the Corn Bill Refuted and This Necessity of the Measure to the Vital Interests of Every Class of Community Demonstrated*, Reprint Bristol: Thoemmes Press.

Steuart, J. (1966 [1767]). *An Inquiry Into the Principle of Political Oeconomy*, Reprint, London: A.S. Skinner, Chicago and Edinburgh: University of Chicago Press and Oliver, 2 volumes.

Stevenson, J. (1974). "Food Riots in England 1792–1818," in R. Quinault and J. Stevenson (Eds.), *Popular Protest and Public Order: Six Studies in British History: 1790–1920*, London: G. Allen & Unwin, 33–74.

Sully, M. de B. (Duke of) (1942 [1638]). *Mémoires des sages et royalles oéconomies d'Estat de Henry le Grand*, Reed. Paris: Gallimard.

Tilly, C. (1975). "Food Supply and Public Order in Modern Europe," in C. Tilly (Ed.), *The Formation of National States in Western Europe*, Princeton, NJ: Princeton University Press, 409–412.

Torrens, R. (1972 [1815]). *An Essay on the External Corn Trade With an Appendix on the Means of Improving the Condition of the Labouring Classes*, London: Longman & al., Reprint New York: Augustus Mc Kelley.

Turgot, A.R.J. (1913–1923 [1770]). "Lettres au contrôleur général, abbé Terray, sur le commerce des grains," Ms., Reed. Schelle, Paris: Felix Alcan, 5 volumes, III, 266–354.

Wallensteen, P. (1976). "Scarce Goods as Political Weapons: The Case of Food," *Journal of Peace Research*, 13: 277–298.

Weulersse, G. (1968 [1910]). *Le mouvement physiocratique en France de 1756 à 1770*, Paris: Felix Alcan, Reprint The Hague: Editions Mouton, 2 volumes.

Williamson, J. (1990). "The Impact of the Corn Laws Just Prior to Repeal," *Explorations in Economic History*, 27: 123–156.

# 2 Why the wars? And how to pay for them?

## A comparison between Hume and Smith

*Daniel Diatkine*

## I

We[1] know that the proximity between David Hume and Adam Smith was great: not only through their bonds of friendship, but also intellectually.[2] However, I would like to suggest studying one point on which the two friends diverge profoundly. I am referring to the origin of the wars, to the means of financing them and to the consequences of this financing.

According to Hume, the wars undertaken by Great Britain (against France, above all) were ruinous, since they were prolonged in an unreasonable manner owing to the aggressive passions of his compatriots, who wanted *to dominate Europe* and thought that the trade surplus could pay the war. Hume sought to demonstrate the illusory character of this reasoning: I will show that the price-specie flow mechanism was invented for this purpose.

Smith's position is very different since it can *name* its enemy. The war was not the effect of an exaggerated *passion*; it conformed to the *interests* of the merchants and manufacturers who *were defending*, in particular, their *colonial monopoly*. It was undertaken by the British government because, under the influence of the specious discourse of the merchants, it confused the interests of the merchants with the interests of the Empire. The final chapter of *The Wealth of Nations* sought to show that this confusion could only – perhaps – be dissipated by a reform of the Empire.

First, I will show how Hume combats the idea whereby the excess of external trade will enable the wars designed to secure British supremacy in Europe to be financed (II).

Next, I will need to evoke certain elements of the historical context in order to show how Smith shifts the playing field. He no longer needs to combat prejudices produced by passions, but interests that use the economic argument to convince legislators that they represent the interests of the Empire (III).

## II

### *Hume, the war, the debt and the currency*[3]

Hume's *Essays* encapsulate a difficulty that, on the one hand, is very well known, and on the other hand, was later to be found in various forms within economic literature. On the one hand, money is neutral, in the sense that a variation both in its quantity or its value must be indifferent to economic agents. On the other hand, an economy in which the circulation of money is scarce is necessarily a poor economy. This difficulty can be summarised using two classic metaphors: on the one hand, money is nothing but the oil in the wheels of trade; on the other hand, money is analogous with the blood that brings to the members of the social body the elements they need. I will show how this difficulty manifests itself in Hume's *Essays* to highlight the fact that it stems *here* from Hume's demonstration of the illusory character of the thesis whereby the trade surplus could finance the public deficit caused by the wars.

While nobody questions the place of David Hume in the history of philosophy, opinions about David Hume as an economist are far more divided. As a matter of fact, Hume's economic writings occupy a minor place in his *oeuvre*. They are mainly to be found in the essays initially published, with other political essays, under the title of *Political Discourses* in 1752. If R. Lucas Jr. (Lucas 1996: 661) had praise in his Nobel Lecture for "David Hume's marvellous essays of 1752, "Of Money and Of Interest", others, including J.A. Schumpeter, were more reluctant to appreciate his thesis concerning the neutrality of money. In the *History of Economic Analysis*, he wrote, for example:

> The genuine quantity theorem that, sometimes in the crudest possible form, became a commonplace for many of the leaders. It is taken for granted by Genovesi, Galiani, Beccaria and Justi, and Hume reasserted it with an emphasis that was hardly necessary.
>
> (Schumpeter 1954: 314–315)

This ambiguous judgment underlines a standard difficulty in Hume's text. On the one hand, Hume shares with Montesquieu and many others the idea of the existence of historical progress. Now this progress is a consequence of the development of commerce. For example, in one of the *Essays Moral, Political and Literary*, "Of the Rise and Progress of the Arts and Sciences", Hume explains "That it is impossible for the arts and sciences to arise, at first, among any people unless that people enjoy the blessing of a free government" (Hume [1742] 1987: I, xiv, 14). And he adds: "That nothing is more favourable to the rise of politeness and learning, than a number of neighbouring and independent states, connected together by commerce and policy" (Hume [1742] 1987: I, xiv, 16). Now it is evident for Hume that trade implies monetary exchange, because barter is contingent, accidental – and consequently is not compatible with general rules. In other words, an economy in which the circulation of money is scarce is necessarily a poor economy. What is true for trade in general is of course true for international trade. In that sense, money seems to be the blood of the social *organism*. On the other hand, Hume wants to state the neutrality of money, which is only the "oil in the wheels" of the economic *mechanism*. How to explain this contradiction between those two propositions?

This difficulty gave rise to an abundant literature that is well described in Wennerlind (2008). It was generally admitted (Rotwein 1955; Wennerlind 2001,

2005; Schabas 1994, 2008) that Hume, along with most of the supporters of the quantity theory of money, accepted the non-neutrality of money in the short term and its neutrality over the long term. Wennerlind (2005) proposes a slightly different interpretation. According to him, Hume opposed an increase in "endogenous" money, the effects of which would be positive on growth and employment, and an increase in "exogenous" money (imported money) that would be neutral. Beyond these debates, we find here one of the major difficulties encountered by the quantity theory of money and that is perhaps why most economists concur (Clower 1969: 17–19 or Lucas 1996: 661) in attributing the paternity of this theory to Hume.

I want to describe here how this issue is born inside Hume's texts, and I will show how this issue is directly linked to the war funding. The neutrality of money is a weapon used by Hume to demonstrate the dangers of the British warmongering politics. As money is neutral, wars can't be financed by foreign trade surplus. Wars can only be financed by and only by public credit which leads necessarily to a political disaster. In the first two essays, "Of Commerce" and "Of Refinement in the Arts", Hume takes a stand in the debate concerning the relationship between increasing wealth and virtue. He opposes the classical tradition that associates wealth and political decadence and that interprets the history of Rome as the story of an interminable abandonment of the virtues – especially martial virtues – that belonged to the ancestors, following the rise in luxury consumption. Hume's thesis is moderate: of course "excessive" luxury may corrupt morals, but under reasonable conditions commerce promotes civilisation, and at the same time "the martial spirit" (Hume [1742]1987: II, ii, 11). Moreover, speaking of Sparta:

> But though the want of trade and manufactures, among a free and very martial people, may *sometimes* have no other effect than to render the public more powerful it is certain, that, in the common course of human affairs, it will have a quite contrary tendency. Now, according to the most natural course of things, industry and arts and trade increase the power of the sovereign as well as the happiness of the subjects.
>
> ([1742] 1987: II, i, 9)

The final edition of the *Essays* added "Of the Jealousy of Trade". This text, which denounces the use of trade policy as a weapon of war, is inserted prior to the essay "Of the Balance of Power" – with no obvious economic content – and "Of Taxes" and "Of Public Credit" that concern the financing of public expenditure. These are Hume's economic publications in the strictest sense (they were completed with the essays "Of Some Remarkable Customs", "Of the Populousness of Ancient Nations" and "Idea of a Perfect Commonwealth"). As the reader can see, the essays appear disparate in their themes and subjects. In the first two essays, "Of Commerce" and "Of Refinement in the Arts", Hume takes a stand in the debate concerning the relationship between increasing wealth and virtue. We are in the core of a standard debate of morals and political philosophy. Then

Hume seems to change the topics and the following three essays – "Of Money", "Of Interest", "Of the Balance of Trade" – express the core of his economic analysis. The first two texts affirm the neutrality of money.

So, the topics of the *Essays* appear to be very heterogeneous. It is nonetheless easy to find some coherence in the essays published in 1752.

The essay "Of Money" opens with the famous proposition:

> Money is . . . none of the wheels of trade: It is the oil which renders the motion of the wheels more smooth and easy. If we consider any one kingdom by itself, it is evident, that the greater or less plenty of money is of no consequence; since the prices of commodities are always proportioned to the plenty of money.
>
> (Hume [1742] 1987: II, iii, 1)

An increase in the quantity of money within an isolated economy has no effect on wealth. That is why money is neutral. Consequently, money is not part of either the wealth of an individual or an economy.

The essay "Of Interest" extends this analysis by seeking to show that a variation in the quantity of money can only have a *transitory* effect on the interest rate, a transition due to the length of time necessary to modify the money's value, caused by the variation of its quantity. The final analysis shows that the effects on money prices concern both the numerator and the denominator of the interest rate, which, in the end, simply remains unchanged in the face of the variation of the quantity of money. It is therefore "real causes" that must explain variations of long-term interest rates.

Finally, the most famous essay, "Of the Balance of Trade", is often credited with anticipating the monetary approach to balance of payments: the argument supposes that any international commercial advantage (disadvantage) can be explained by internal prices lower (higher) than the external prices. This implies an inflow (outflow) of money causing a movement of prices that eliminates this initial advantage (disadvantage) without affecting international prices. Hence the quantity of money cannot endlessly accumulate within (leave) the economy in question. There is an automatic mechanism that – when international prices are unchanged – sets the balance in the quantity of money. The real effects of a variation in the quantity of money are thus transitory.

Hume's economic discourse has a coherence that clearly emerges if we read the essay "Of the Balance of Power", omitted from the *Economic Writings* published in 1955 by Rotwein, and that is no longer present in the book *David Hume's Political Economy* edited by Schabas and Wennerlind (2008). Reading this essay, as Hume had intended, after "Of the Balance of Commerce", one switches from the balance of foreign trade to the balance of power in Europe; and this is no coincidence.

After having attempted to show that the politics of the balance of powers between cities was practised in ancient Greece, Hume is surprised by the fact that this maxim had been omitted by both Rome (which enabled it to build its empire) and by its adversaries (which had therefore allowed the construction of the Roman Empire that provoked the fall of its adversaries). Yet the situation of Great Britain is comparable to that of Rome. The "excess" committed by Great Britain in its struggle against France (initiated in the days following the 1688 Revolution) led to an imminent catastrophe. Under the pretext of implementing the maxim of the balance of powers in Europe, the British, animated by a "jealous emulation" (Hume [1742] 1987: II, vii, 15), undertook an entirely different policy, characterised by "our own imprudent vehemence" (ibid.) that aimed not to preserve the balance of powers in Europe, but to establish British domination on the continent. From then on, the maxim of the balance of power became a maxim of imperial expansion. "Enormous monarchies are, probably, destructive to human nature; in their progress, in their continuance, and even in their downfall, which never can be very distant from their establishment" (Hume [1742] 1987: II, vii, 19). This essay echoes the proposition in "Of Refinement on Arts" that imputes the decadence of Rome not to an increase in wealth but to the extension of the empire (Hume [1742] 1987: II, II, 13).

These considerations regarding British foreign policy give meaning to the other economic essays. This imperial policy cannot be financed by taxes, and Hume showed that it cannot be financed by the external trade surplus since this is inevitably ephemeral. The external trade surplus cannot therefore constitute the "English Treasure" evoked by Thomas Mun, for instance. The wars could thus only be financed by public credit, Hume tells us in "Of Public Credit" that concludes the series of *Political Discourses*, the content of which is essentially economic: "It must, indeed, be one of these two events; either the nation must destroy public credit, or public credit will destroy the nation" (Hume [1742] 1987: II, ix, 28).

According to Hume, the growth of the public debt threatened Great Britain's constitutional order in three ways. First, in order to reimburse its debt, the government was able to exact a toll to replace the tax that the taxpayers' representatives did not want to or were unable to vote. Consequently, the government had to collect a tribute from the citizens. This measure brought Great Britain's situation back to one of "Oriental despotism". This issue signified the *violent* death of public credit and of the Constitution. A second issue is public bankruptcy, a measure used by continental absolute monarchies and that signified the *natural* death of public credit and, once again, of the Constitution (the "lesser evil" solution that Hume therefore favoured). Third and otherwise, it seems probable that Great Britain – since it could no longer lead this policy of balance of powers in Europe due to lack of resources – would became the victim of the invasion of a dominant continental power. The latter outcome would signify the end of the nation, destroyed by public credit.

The monetary discourse in the *Essays* thus falls within the framework of a coherent *political* position. The increase in the wealth of nations not only does not corrupt their military virtues, but may also, through public credit, stimulate their nationalism and give rise to the constitution of new empires financed by the growth of the public debt. The real danger of an increase in wealth therefore does not reside in an excess of moral refinement, but in the exacerbation of national passions financed by public credit.

The affirmation of the neutrality of money thus serves above all to criticise the mercantilist theories (as Mirabeau and Smith will call) whereby commercial surplus would allow building up a war treasure. It is not a part of a theory of money. We must therefore not misjudge the essentially political dimension of the *Essays*. Yet, naturally, the neutrality of money affirmed in the *Political Discourses* had to be argued on economic grounds, as Tucker or Oswald asked for soon after the publication of the book (cf. Rotwein 1955: 190, 197, 202). For instance, they posed the question of knowing by which process an increase in the quantity of money would be able to leave real economic variables unchanged. This argument is strong, as Hume himself used the fact that an economy without money remains backward and poor. Here, we find the expression of the central tension above mentioned: how can we accept the idea of the neutrality of money if we accept that a non-monetary economy is necessarily poorer than a monetary economy?

I can therefore conclude this section dedicated to Hume. The wars were provoked, in the final analysis, by the aggressive passions dominating over the reasonable policy of the balance of powers. Prudence required the complete mastery of these passions. However, the possibilities of financing offered by public credit authorised, on the contrary, that they be unleashed. Finally wars threaten the British constitution.

# II

### *An empire as glorious as it was costly. Adam Smith and his enemy: the wars are the result of the mercantile system*

It is striking to note that the question of the war and its financing was broached in very different terms by Smith and by Hume. As we know, the final chapter of *The Wealth of Nations* is titled "Of Public Debts". The origin of the public debt is, however, the same: the financing of the war through borrowing. However, the intellectual and political landscape that Smith belongs to is very different. I will first describe the intellectual innovations that characterise this point in *The Wealth of Nations*.

Among the contributions Smith enjoyed from his encounter with the Physiocrats in Paris, there is one that has not attracted much attention, to my knowledge. He nonetheless most likely inherited from Mirabeau and Quesnay the term "mercantile system".[4] This is what enables him to refer to the enemy against which he wrote *The Wealth of Nations* and that Hume himself targeted *subconsciously* in his *Essays*, by targeting the theses of T. Mun. But in *The Wealth of Nations* we find "The title of Mun's book, *England's Treasure in Foreign Trade*, became a fundamental maxim in the political economy, not of England only, but of all other commercial countries" (Smith A. 1776–1976: 434). However, the main thing to note here is that the mercantile system is not only characterised by this maxim. The mercantile system affirms that what is good for the merchants is good for the Empire. The "main target" [of *The Wealth of Nations*] "lay in the use made of such doctrines by mercantile pressure groups attempting to pass off what was their collective interest as being the interest of the nation at large" (Winch 1993: 93). It is this confusion between the interests of one class – that of the merchants and industrialists – and the interests of the Nation or the Empire that defined the *partiality* that characterises the mercantile system.

By thus referring to the adversary – whom Hume fought in the dark, so to speak – Smith shifts the playing field. While Hume was attacking blindly, Smith changes the problem's terms. The adversary is not only a passion; it is a passion which uses the knowledge of economic reasoning to defend its own interests. The mercantile system thus referred not only to an erroneous intellectual system, but also to a political – and historical – reality that had to be transformed. Here, we are no longer dealing with national passions that it are futile to seek to control. Instead, we are dealing with interests that are certainly powerful, but which the science of the legislator ought to be able to master. It is not a matter of simply showing that the arguments of the partisans of the mercantile system are specious; we must also demonstrate how the mercantile system can be transformed into a system of natural liberty. In a nutshell: the mercantile system was not the fruit of ignorance, it was the product of the entire history of Europe since the fall of the Roman Empire. Smith dedicated Book III of *The Wealth of Nations* to establishing this thesis.

To be convinced of the divergent paths taken by Hume and Smith, we can compare their conclusions. While Hume resolved to deem absolute monarchy the least damaging solution for British freedom, Smith proposes (prudently, of course) a constitutional reform of the Empire, which in certain aspects anticipates the French Revolution.

There was therefore not only an intellectual necessity, but also a political emergency to come.

This is what I would like to show now, by focusing on the core of the mercantile system according to Smith: the colonial monopoly.

According to Smith, the mercantile system was rendered dangerous in Great Britain by the illusion that it engendered. It seems to me that the most impressive effect of colonial monopoly (and therefore the mercantile system as a whole) was to promote the belief that the exceptional rate of profit that it engendered was the *natural* rate.[5] This illusion is laden with consequences, which I shall attempt to show, with reference to the text of *The Wealth of Nations*:

> The monopoly of the colony trade besides, by forcing towards it a much greater proportion of the capital of Great Britain than what would naturally have gone to it, seems to have broken altogether that natural balance which would otherwise have taken place among all the different branches of British industry. The industry of Great Britain, instead of being accommodated to a great number of small markets, has been principally suited to one great market. Her commerce, instead of running in a great number of small channels, has been taught to run principally in one great channel. But the whole

system of her industry and commerce has thereby been rendered less secure, the whole state of her body politic less healthful than it otherwise would have been.

(Smith 1776–1904: II, 118)

Colonial monopoly disrupts the balance of the economy by concentrating the risks on a single sector of activity. The text continues, now developing a medical metaphor, as follows:

In her present condition, Great Britain resembles one of those unwholesome bodies in which some of the vital parts are overgrown, and which, upon that account, are liable to many dangerous disorders scarce incident to those in which all the parts are more properly proportioned. A small stop in that great blood-vessel, which has been artificially swelled beyond its natural dimensions, and through which an unnatural proportion of the industry and commerce of the country has been forced to circulate, is very likely to bring on the most dangerous disorders upon the whole body politic.

(Smith 1776–1904: II, 118)

However, it is not the diagnostic of this disease that is important here, but rather its political extensions. Smith immediately continues:

The expectation of a rupture with the colonies, accordingly, has struck the people of Great Britain with more terror than they ever felt for a Spanish armada, or a French invasion. [i.e. the "death of the Nation"] It was this terror, whether well or ill grounded, which rendered the repeal of the Stamp Act, among the merchants at least, a popular measure. In the total exclusion from the colony market, was it to last only for a few years, the greater part of our merchants used to fancy that they foresaw an entire stop to their trade; the greater part of our master manufacturers, the entire ruin of their business; and the greater part of our workmen, an end of their employment. A rupture with any of our neighbours upon the continent, though likely, too, to occasion some stop or interruption in the employments of some of all these different orders of people, is foreseen, however, without any such general emotion. The blood, of which the circulation is stopped in some of the smaller vessels, easily disgorges itself into the greater without occasioning any dangerous disorder; but, when it is stopped in any of the greater vessels, convulsions, *apoplexy*, or death, are the immediate and unavoidable consequences. If but one of those overgrown manufactures, which, by means either of bounties or of the monopoly of the home and colony markets, have been artificially raised up to an unnatural height, finds some small stop or interruption in its employment, it frequently occasions a mutiny and disorder alarming to government, and embarrassing even to the deliberations of the legislature. How great, therefore, would be the disorder and confusion, it was thought, which must necessarily be occasioned by a sudden and entire stop in the employment of so great a proportion of our principal manufacturers.[6]

This passage is important for the development of my argument, as it allows us to understand that it is not only the loss of the colonial markets, but, above all, the political amplification that results from the anticipation of this loss, that provokes the "apoplexy". So, what does the latter consist of? What are the "disorders", the "mutinies", provoked in Great Britain by the question of American independence, which Smith only alludes to (the "repeal of the Stamp Act") and which nonetheless require the (progressive) establishment of the system of natural freedom?

In order to answer these questions it is important to examine some elements of the political context at the start of writing of *The Wealth of Nations* (the late 1760s).

Historians (John Brewer [1976], Nancy Koehn [1994] and Grayson Ditchfield [2002]) have underlined the fact that the political scene changed considerably in the early 1760s. It is striking how they illustrate perfectly some part of Hume's analysis.

This factor of change is the end of the Seven Years' War, three years after the accession of George III, under Bute's ministry, which negotiated the Treaty of Paris in 1763. The choice of Bute (a Scotsman) to replace the Old Corps of Whigs (William Pitt, the Duke of Newcastle) was also perceived to be the choice of a *compromising* peace with France, to the detriment of the prolongation of the victorious war, right through to France's definitive collapse. Great Britain came away from the Seven Years' Wars largely victorious. However, this peace seemed far too generous for France in the eyes of a considerable portion of English public opinion.

The government's main concern was how *to manage the public debt*, which as we know had considerably increased during the Seven Years' War.[7] Increasing the direct tax was deemed impossible and Bute's attempts to raise the indirect taxes was met with fierce opposition; there was nothing left to do but tax the colonial settlers, if only to finance the maintenance of a garrison designed to protect them from the natives. Grenville thus passed the Stamp Act[8] in March 1765. Agitation against this tax developed in the colonies of North America. From the start of autumn in 1765, the news concerning the American riots against the Stamp Act reached Great Britain. The settlers were becoming organised and threatening to boycott English products.[9] At the same time, the Marquis of Rockingham (powerfully aided by his secretary Burke) led a campaign that aimed to organise London's merchants so that they and their colleagues across the British territory could put pressure on their representatives to abolish the Stamp Act by emphasising the losses the American boycott threatened to make them suffer. The Stamp Act was thus repealed, after a stormy debate at the House of Commons that began in January 1766.

This is precisely the episode that Smith was alluding to, as we saw, when he evoked the "terror" provoked by the threat of a rupture with the colonies, that is, a rupture of colonial monopoly. It is this "terror" that the repeal of the Stamp Act provoked.

It is an open question as to how this new "party" was going to conduct itself with the extra-parliamentary groups with which it had to collaborate in opposition. The Rockingham Whigs supported a highly aristocratic conception of politics. According to them, only those who had "a natural and fixed influence"[10] on society were capable of preserving the peace in society and the government. Preserving this aristocratic privilege was the *raison d'être* of this opposition party. The agitation, the riots caused by shortages (in 1766[11] and 1769, then at the start of the 1770s), the first waves of violence associated with industrialisation, and the consequences that disturbed the peace in 1763 were solely attributed to the disastrous influence of the courtiers' cabal (Bute and his supporters) who had sought to destroy the "connexion" required for the equilibrium of the political body. This denunciation of Bute's politics could only be effective by basing itself on public opinion and therefore on extra-parliamentary interests: those of merchants and manufacturers.

Curiously, the governmental instability that had characterised Great Britain since George III's accession ended at that time and, against all odds, Lord North stayed in power from 1770 until the Battle of Yorktown in 1782. This can be at least partly explained by the fact that economic instability, then the war, forced the opposition to compromise with the government. The tension connected with the management of the colonial empire was coupled with an economic crisis in 1772 (Sheridan 1960). This "sacred union" led to an affirmation of the identity of the merchants' interests with those of the Empire. There was evidently no proclamation of the fusion of these interests (we have already noted the elitism of the Rockingham Whigs, and this was shared by all of the British political factions), but they tended to band closer together.[12]

### Was what was good for the East India Company good for the empire?

The economic growth in Great Britain in the 1760s was impressive. The East India Company participated even more strongly in this growth through the fact that, since 1765, it was the de facto ruler of Bengal, Bihar and Orissa, from which it directly took an estimated income of between £2 and £4 million per year,[13] since it had acquired the *diwani*, that is, the right to deduct land, seigniorial and fiscal revenues. Certain "well-informed" contemporaries even imagine that these revenues taken from Bengal could pay for all of the Company's expenditures both in India and in China. Considerable speculation on the Company's shares seems to have developed, with their dividend growing by 10 per cent in 1766 and by 12.5 per cent in 1767.

But it seems that these forecasts were disappointed, since, according to Bowen (1989), the agents of the Company had to draw on the Company in London (from £210,000 in 1768–1769 to almost £1,600,000 in 1771–1772). This perhaps indicates that these loans directly or indirectly supported the Company's share prices and undoubtedly that the net gains made from the *diwani* were largely overestimated; in fact, the Company had to enter into a costly conflict with the Raja of Mysore, Hyder Ali, which at least partially accounts for this brutal reversal of its financial situation. Finally, the terrible famine that ravaged Bengal, causing the deaths of possibly a third of the population (apparently this represented 10,000,000 fatalities), definitely weakened the Company. It is still under debate as to whether, as Smith affirms (1776–1904: II, 33), the Company's commercial and fiscal policy caused this catastrophe. What is certain is that it at least aggravated the situation (Rajat Kanta Ray 1998).

Thus two essential questions posed by the political organisation of the British Empire intersect (Marshall 1998):

1    On the one hand, the question posed by this surprising event of a private company having conquered a vast territory (Bengal, Bihar and Orissa): how are the relations between the East India Company and the government of Great Britain to be envisaged?[14] Smith, as we saw, highlights the fact that the Company was in a state of distress, in the early 1770s, when it requested a loan from the government. Between 1769 and 1771, the Company borrowed £2,000,000 from the Bank of England and again £1,500,000 during the 1772 crisis (Bowen [1989: 537]).

2    On the other hand, and almost symmetrically, how was the empire to be financed without (literally) tyrannising the British subjects settled on the other side of the Atlantic? This was to incite the first radicals to pose the broader question of fairness in representation for all British citizens, and, broader still, the question of the relations between voters and Parliament.

Finally, these two colonial questions were to coincide by way of a seemingly anodyne measure taken by Lord North's government. In order to allow the East India Company to repay its loan as quickly as possible, the latter passed the Tea Act[15] in 1773.

### Adam Smith's politics (continued)

We now understand to which events Smith is referring when he describes the "apoplexy" of the British political body provoked by the mercantile system. As we have seen in the long reference cited earlier, he was explicitly referring to the campaign against the Stamp Act led by the Rockingham Whigs by relying on the merchants and manufacturers that feared the loss of the markets through the American boycott, just as he refers almost as openly to popular emotions such as those of Spitalfield, or those of the Scottish linen weavers. More profoundly, it is easy to show that the supporters of the repression with regard to the colonies (from Lord Bute to Lord North), just as those who, on the contrary, support a conciliatory policy with regard to the settlers (like the Rockingham Whigs) *all* share the conviction that the commercial interests of the merchants and manufacturers *are* those of Great Britain and its empire. To convince oneself of this, it suffices to compare Smith's position here with that of Burke. In 1775, very shortly before the publication of *The Wealth of Nations*, the latter had presented this idea in his "Speech on Moving His Resolutions for Conciliation with the Colonies":

> But, it will be said, is not this American trade an unnatural protuberance, that has drawn the juices from the rest of the body? The reverse. It is the very food that has nourished every other part into its present magnitude.
>
> (Burke 1775: 126)

It is striking to note that the qualification of "unnatural protuberance" that here refers to the effect of colonial monopoly is almost the same metaphor as the one that would be used by Smith, which suggests that either it is already well known, or that Smith responded to Burke, since Burke draws a conclusion from this that is the opposite to that of Smith. Far from being a threat that renders the British economy more fragile, colonial commerce has stimulated it considerably. The merchants' interests thus appear to be perfectly aligned with the general interest. Burke, a defender of the established order, naturally defends the colonial monopoly that is Smith's target. Readers of Hayek will appreciate the irony of the situation.

The thesis whereby England's interests (or those of Great Britain) were identical to those of the merchants is obviously not a new one. This was affirmed by all supporters of the mercantile system since Thomas Mun, at least. However, the novelty of the 1760s resides in the fact that this common position was no longer restricted to the merchants' writings, but was resolutely affirmed by British *political* leaders, that is, by the British aristocracy. It was affirmed by both the opposition and its spokesperson, Burke, and by Thomas Whately, Secretary of the Treasury in Grenville's government, then Under-Secretary of State of Lord North's government, and a firm supporter of the repression in the colonies of North America, or by Lord North himself (see Koehn 1994).

Therefore, I shall risk the following hypothesis: the constitution of a real opposition party by Rockingham and Burke led them, as we have seen, to seek out an alliance with the business community. Consequently, they opened up a process of one-upmanship between them and the government, which led them to pose the colonial question on the grounds of the identification of the merchants' and manufacturers' interests with the interests of the empire. This is why Grenville himself declared that his government's priorities were the commercial interests of Great Britain (Koehn 1994: 123) The colonial question obviously brings the defence of the mercantile system to the fore, and each of its positions is justified in the name of the same defence of the interests of the merchants' and manufacturers' *class*.[16] The merchants' interests demand privileges (pricing protection, export subsidies), and the core of this arsenal is colonial monopoly. To call, as Smith did, for the abolition of these privileges, while conserving the colonies, thus meant requesting and supporting free circulation within the Empire. Such measures could only be expected from *impartial* legislators, and not from Lord

North or his opposition, who confused the interests of the merchants' class with that of the Empire. It was this growing proximity between the capitalists on the one hand, and the legislators, that is, the British aristocracy, on the other, that deeply concerned Smith.

David Hume thought that the increase in the public debt, a consequence of the warlike politics of Great Britain, would lead to the destruction of its constitution.[17] Smith, for his part, feared that the trading company spirit would threaten the constitution of the British Empire, and that the expansion of the latter risked propelling it towards tyranny, just as the Rome's expansion had led to the destruction of the republic. Is it necessary to recall that Gibbon published the first volume of *The History of the Decline and Fall of the Roman Empire* in 1776 with the same publisher who published *The Wealth of Nations* several weeks later?

Is it also necessary to recall the conclusion of Book I of *The Wealth of Nations?* After having affirmed that the landowners' interests and those of the workers always conform to the general interest, Smith concludes with a few more hometruths:

> The proposal of any new law or regulation of commerce which comes from this order [of the merchants and manufacturers] ought always to be listened to with great precaution, and ought never to be adopted till after having been long and carefully examined, not only with the most scrupulous, but with the most suspicious attention. It comes from an order of men whose interest is never exactly the same with that of the public, who have generally an interest to deceive and even to oppress the public, and who accordingly have, upon many occasions, both deceived and oppressed it.
>
> (Smith 1776–1904: 278)

While Book I of *The Wealth of Nations* ends with this firm warning, the whole book itself concludes with a project for reform of the Empire in which the General States would draw together the representatives of all the components. The colonies, Smith tells us, would be the "impartial spectators" (Smith 1776–1904: II, 484) and thus allow the merchants to be kept at the *right distance* from the legislators. The reformed *British Empire would prevent Great Britain from falling into the tyranny of capitalists' domination*, which was still capable of seducing the legislators.

I have shown elsewhere[18] how Smith explained very clearly, in *The Theory of Moral Sentiments*, the deeply rooted connivance, founded on a shared love of systems, which united great men of state and entrepreneurs. As we can see, the mercantile system (the British capitalism of the 18th century) does not threaten British society by its inefficiency, which was dramatic in Bengal, but less so in the United Kingdom. The threat that colonial expansion brought to bear on its republican constitution was far worse. It was freedom that was at stake, and the mercantile system could transform this into tyranny, just as the extension of the Roman Empire had destroyed the Republic and placed monarchs in power who were constantly at risk of becoming tyrants.

The danger threatening Great Britain was therefore no longer the violent (Oriental despotism) or natural death (the absolute monarchy) of public credit, or the death of the nation, but despotism of an entirely new variety: the despotism of the merchants and manufacturers. As Smith wrote, to characterise the mercantile system:

> To found a great empire for the sole purpose of raising up a people of customers may at first sight appear a project fit only for a nation of shopkeepers. It is, however, a project altogether unfit for a nation of shopkeepers; but extremely fit for a nation whose government is influenced by shopkeepers. Such statesmen, and such statesmen only, are capable of fancying that they will find some advantage in employing the blood and treasure of their fellow-citizens to found and maintain such an empire.
>
> (Smith A. [1776–1904]: II, 129)

How could the nation be rid of this influence? This was the final problem posed by *The Wealth of Nations*.

Hume and Smith were very close. Both wanted to found the science of politics, or the science of legislator. However, on war, such an important matter, they differ profoundly. The causes of the war are different: national passions for the first, colonial interest for the second. Naturally the consequences differ also: for Hume, absolutism (the bankruptcy) was the least bad option; for Smith, a profound reform of the British Empire was necessary to avoid the partiality of the mercantile system.

## Notes

1 A part of this chapter was published in the Edward Elgar *Handbook of the History of Economic Analysis*. I warmly thank the editor for permission.
2 This proximity was expressed, for instance, through the fact that Hume had made Smith his "literary executor" (Ross 1995: 289).
3 See also Diatkine (2016).
4 "Inconséquences absurdes du système mercantile" (Mirabeau 1763: 329).
5 We know that in *The Wealth of Nations*, the natural rate of profit is given (along with the natural rates of wage). This point, which was to be perceived by Ricardo as an inadmissible contradiction, is accepted here. We can therefore deduce, I believe, that the natural profit rate is a conventional phenomenon, from which all capitalists (on the same market place) seek to escape, but which competition tends to impose.
6 Ibid. My emphasis.
7 It almost doubled, passing from nearly £70,000,000 to £130,000,000.
8 The Stamp Act cited by Smith, cf. supra, p. 10.
9 On this see Robert Middlekauff (1982).
10 Burke, in Brewer (1976: 195).
11 I evoked those of Spitalfield earlier.
12 The British situation described here is very close to Schumpeter's analysis (1954: 394) when he underlined the fact that in the "great nations", the bourgeoisie "did not rule politically" in the beginning of the 19th century (except in the

United States and Louis Philippe's France) and however "in all countries the governments, however unbourgeois in origin and structure [. . .] backed the economic interest of the business class almost without question and *did their best to protect them*" (italics are mine). This seems a very good description of the British situation criticized by Smith in *The Wealth of Nations*. However, quite paradoxically, Schumpeter added "Still more important, they did so in a spirit of laissez-faire [. . .] That is what will be meant in this book by Economic Liberalism".

13  "Letter from Lord Clive to the Directors", 30 Sept. 1765, Fort William – India House Correspondence, iv, pp. 337–8, cited by H. V. Bowen (1989: 189). Indeed, this sum can be aligned with the value of importations from the East Indies: £1,101,000 in commodities were imported to England and Wales from 1750 to 1751. This amount doubled in 1772–1773, if we take into account the importation to Scotland.

14  In 1757 the opinion voiced by Charles Patt and Charles Yorke limited the prerogatives of the crown on the lands that the East India Company (or other colonisers) had acquired by treaty, grant or conquest. These lands were the full properties of the Company, which instigated a rupture with the (Norman) feudal tradition whereby the sovereign was the eminent owner of the land.

15  The Tea Act authorised the Company to access the North American market, by directly delivering and selling tea, without paying any customs duties other than those provided under Townshend's legislation. This law was thus combined with the latter to affirm the pre-eminence of the London parliament. Furthermore (and especially?), this law seriously harmed the interests of the smugglers who were active in the port of Boston. The rejection of this law led to the famous Tea Party of Boston.

16  A point that is often forgotten today: Smith, like most of his compatriots of the 18th century, reasons spontaneously in terms of social classes. These are not only characterized by their type of revenues, or by collusive behavior on the market (which Smith evokes, naturally), but above all, by shared views. They are therefore truly political categories.

17  Hume (1777–1889); Essay IX: "Of Public Credit".

18  See Diatkine (2010).

# References

Bowen, H. V. (1989). "Investment and Empire," in P. J. Marshall (Ed.), *The Oxford History of the British Empire, the Eighteenth Century*, Oxford, Oxford University Press, 1998.

Brewer, J. (1976). *English Politics in the First Decade of George III's Reign*, Cambridge, Cambridge University Press.

Burke, E. (1775). "Thoughts on the Cause of the Present Discontents and the Two Speeches on America, 1.1. 25," Econlib.org.

Clower, R. W. (1969). "Introduction," in R. W. Clower (dir), *Monetary Theory*, Harmondsworth: Penguin Books, 17–18.

Diatkine, D. (2010). "Vanity and the Love of System in Theory of Moral Sentiments," *The European Journal of the History of Economic Thought*, 17, September: 3.

Diatkine, D. (2016). "Hume," in *Handbook on the History of Economic Analysis*, London: E. Elgar.

Ditchfield, G. (2002) *George III, an Essay in Monarchy*, Palgrave.

Hume, D. ([1739–1740] 1983). *A Treatise of Human Nature*, L. A. Selby-Bigge (Ed.), Oxford: Oxford University Press.

Hume, D. ([1742] 1987). *Essays Moral, Political and Literary*, E. Miller (Ed.), Indianapolis: Liberty Fund.

Koehn, N. (1994). *The Power of the Commerce*, Ithaca, NY, Cornell University Press.

Lucas, R. E., Jr. (1996). "Nobel Lecture: Monetary Neutrality," *Journal of Political Economy*, 104(4), August, 661–682.

Marshall, P. J. (1998). "The British in Asia: Trade to Dominion, 1700–1765," in P. J. Marshall (Ed.), *The Oxford History of British Empire*, vol. III, Oxford, Oxford University Press.

Middlekauff, R. (1982). *The Glorious Cause: The American Revolution, 1763–178*, Oxford University Press.

Mirabeau, V. R. (1763). *Philosophie rurale ou économie générale et politique de l'agriculture*, Amsterdam: Les libraires associés.

Ray, R. K. (1998). "Indian Society and the Establishment of British Supremacy, 1765–1819," in P. J. Marshall (Ed.), *The Oxford History of the British Empire, the Eighteenth Century*, Oxford: Oxford University Press.

Ross, I. S. (1995). *The Life of Adam Smith*, Oxford: Oxford University Press.

Rotwein, E. (1955). *David Hume: Writings on Economics*, Madison, WI: University of Wisconsin Press.

Schabas, M. (1994). "Market Contract in the Age of Hume," *History of Political Economy*, 26(supplement): 117–134.

Schabas, M., and Wennerlind, C. (Eds.). (2008). *David Hume's Political Economy*, Abingdon: Routledge.

Schumpeter, J. A. (1954). *History of Economic Analysis*, London: George Allen and Unwin.

Sheridan, R. B. (1960). "The British Credit Crisis of 1772 and the American Revolution," *The Journal of Economic History*, 20, June: 2.

Smith, A. (1776–1904). *An Inquiry into the Nature and Causes of the Wealth of Nations*, E. Cannan (Ed). London: Methuen.

Wennerlind, C. (2001). "The Link Between David Hume's *Treatise of Human Nature* and His Fiduciary Theory of Money," *History of Political Economy*, 33(1), 139–160.

Wennerlind, C. (2005). "David Hume's Monetary Theory Revisited: Was He Really a Quantity Theorist and an Inflationist?" *Journal of Political Economy*, 113(1), 223–237.

Wennerlind, C. (2008). "An Artificial Virtue and the Oil of Commerce: A Synthetic View of Hume's Theory of Money," in C Wennerlind and M. Schabas (Eds.), *David Hume's Political Economy*, Abingdon: Routledge, 105–126.

Winch, D. (1993). "Moral Philosopher as Political Economist," in H. Mizuta and C. Sugiyama (Eds.), *Adam Smith International Perspectives*, Houndmills and London: Macmillan, 85–112.

# 3 Hume and Smith on morality and war

*Shinji Nohara*

## 1 Introduction

Adam Smith did not write on the specific subject of war, but it was central to his views on society, and gave him occasion to reflect on the partiality of sympathy; that is, in many cases, sympathy is not extended to all human beings with the same intensity, and thus is not sufficient to prevent wars.

Even though Smith never discussed war *per se*, his views on the subject have been extensively studied. Smith is affiliated with the liberal school, which holds that harmony of interests leads to peace (Carr 1946; Waltz 1959; Howard 1978). However, as A. Wyatt-Walter argued, although Smith believed in the effect of commerce on peace, he was sceptical about the harmony of interests, and blamed war on wealth, which created the means to prepare for war and the motivation for a poorer country to attack (Wyatt-Walter 1996). L. Hill rightly regarded Smith not as an anti-war liberal, but as one who understood both anti-war ideals and the social reality where states almost necessarily waged war (Hill 2009). Furthermore, P. Minowitz (1989) argued that Smith saw mercantile policy as the cause of war in the modern age, and relegated the seizure of wealth to the historical past. Finally, F. Coulomb has argued that, for Smith, the first duty of the sovereign was defence, rather than economic prosperity (Coulomb 1998).

In spite of this attention to Smith's political and economic perspectives, I contend that there is a need for more consideration of Smith's thoughts on the relationship between morality and war. I wish to argue that Smith considered war in regard to sympathy (see Section 5). Whereas sympathy is usually directed towards particular individuals, it also influences popular sentiment towards one's own and other nations. Because we tend to sympathize with people whom we know, this knowledge can inspire a sense of solidarity. When there is a conflict between communities, there is usually an absence of familiarity, which might exacerbate antipathy. As I shall argue in this chapter, Smith regarded the partiality of sympathy as a potential source of support for waging war, since in international relations, sympathy heightened the citizens' love of their country at the cost of due respect for other nations. The partiality of sympathy was therefore connected to the problem of war.

In Thomas Hobbes's theory of the social contract, the dichotomy between the state of nature and that of war ended with the establishment of government. Both Hume and Smith rejected Hobbes's social contract theory, as well as his notion that the state of nature was a state of war. As a result, comparison between Smith and Hume is helpful in clarifying the intellectual implications of Smith's stance on war in relation to morality and justice. Hume inspired Smith's thinking in his considerations on human nature, but they differed on the origins of war.

The relationship between morality and war as discussed in the works of Hume and Smith was influenced by the Seven Years' War (1756–1763), which gave them occasion to contemplate the partiality of morality. Smith also considered the Seven Years' War from a historical perspective.

Therefore, this chapter explains Hume's and Smith's views on war, both textually and contextually. It describes their ideas on the partiality of sympathy and the associated problems in regard to war. Section 2 of the chapter argues that Hume's and Smith's ideas about war were influenced by the Seven Years' War. Based on this background, Smith situated war within his developmental theory of society (Section 3). The difficulty posed by the problem of war was linked with its relationship to morality. In this regard, Smith criticized Hume's explanation of common interest and justice (Section 4). Smith considered the merits and deficiencies of the partiality of sympathy, both of which were linked with the problem of war (Section 5). Beyond the domestic framework, the partiality of sympathy was also relevant to international relations (Section 6).

## 2  The Seven Years' War and Smith

In this section, I focus on Smith's criticism of the mercantile system in Book IV of *The Wealth of Nations*.

Hume and Smith were influenced by the Seven Years' War, during which the British and French fought in Europe, North America and India. The conflict was hugely expensive. One reason for the war was a rivalry between the two countries over colonial trade and the acquisition of colonies.

Hume wrote 'The Jealousy of Trade' in 1759 (on this dating, see Jessop 1938). He wrote,

> nothing is more usual, among states which have made some advances in commerce, than to look on the progress of their neighbours with a suspicious eye, to consider all trading states as their rivals, and to suppose that it is impossible for any of them to flourish, but at their expence.
>
> (Hume 1985b: 327–328)

Hume recognized the potential danger of this jealousy. War is an opportunity to gain economic benefits and colonies at the expense of other states. 'Jealousy of Trade' is related not only to political economy but also to political hostility and war (see Hont 2005). In addition, 'jealousy of trade' is 'more usual, among states which have made some advances in commerce', that is, 'commercial states' in his term (Hume 1985b: 330). As a result, 'jealousy of trade' and its consequences, such as war, are peculiar to the modern 'commercial state'.

However, Hume also admitted the merit of 'jealousy of trade'. He said, 'the emulation among rival nations serves rather to keep industry alive in all of them' (Hume 1985b: 330). Jealousy of trade is a source of both prosperity and hatred; it results in international competition of trade, which results in prosperous, competitive economies, as well as economic rivalry and conflict.

Smith also saw trade as the source of both economic prosperity and conflict. When he denounced the 'mercantile system' in Book IV of *The Wealth of Nations*, he was referring to the links between the danger of waging war and a theory that sees the surplus of foreign trade as the cause of wealth. He wrote:

> the more, that most insignificant object of modern policy, the balance of trade, appears to be in our favour with some particular countries, the more it must necessarily appear to be against us with many others. It was upon this silly notion, however, that England could not subsist without the Portugal trade, that, towards the end of the late war, France and Spain, without pretending either offence or provocation, required the king of Portugal to exclude all British ships from his ports, and for the security of this exclusion, to receive into them France or Spanish garrisons. Had the king of Portugal submitted to those ignominious terms which his brother-in-law the king of Spain proposed to him, Britain would have been freed from a much greater inconveniency than the loss of the Portugal trade, the burden of supporting a very weak ally.
>
> (Smith 1981: IV. vi. 13–14)

Here, Smith mentioned France's and Spain's ultimatum to Portugal to prohibit British trade during the Seven Years' War. In the latter half of the war, the French foreign minister, Choiseul, wanted to exclude British ships from Portugal to block trade between Britain and Portugal; he wanted French merchants to monopolize the trade with Portugal. At the same time, Charles III, the Spanish king, wanted to develop manufacturing and industry in Spain, rather than rely on British imports. Furthermore, he noticed that British smugglers were depriving Spain of revenue. As a result, France and Spain formed an alliance, and in 1761 demanded that Portugal stop trading with Britain. They wanted to exclude British goods from France, Spain, Naples, and the Netherlands, as well as Portugal (Christelow 1946).

Although this demand was rejected (because Portugal was invaded), this scheme suggests that in addition to Britain, other European nations wanted to adopt a mercantile policy that would enable a surplus in their balance of trade. This policy forced Britain to protect its own industries through customs, navigation law, and so on. In the 17th century, Britain had already taken political steps to develop and protect its manufactures. What France and Spain merely wanted to emulate was British policy. In reality, the adoption of the mercantile policy resulted in war, along with trade rivalry between Britain and Portugal. To Smith, the Seven Years' War showed the dangers of the mercantile policy.

In the Seven Years' War, mercantile policy was linked with colonial trade. By monopolizing colonial trade, merchants gained huge profits at the cost of the 'natural balance which would otherwise have taken place among all the different branches of British industry' (Smith 1981: IV. vii. c. 43). As a result, 'the maintenance of this monopoly has hitherto been the principal, or more properly perhaps the sole end and purpose of the dominion which Great Britain assumes over her colonies' (Smith 1981: IV. vii. c. 64). Therefore, the protection of the monopoly on colonial trade was a major cause of the consolidation of the British Empire.

Smith recommended the abandonment of this policy. At the end of *The Wealth of Nations*, he says,

> it is surely time that Great Britain should free herself from the expense of defending those provinces in time of war, and of supporting any part of their civil or military establishments in time of peace, and endeavour to accommodate her future views and designs to the real mediocrity of her circumstances.
>
> (Smith 1981: V. iii. 92)

As the Seven Years' War has shown, mercantile policy led to war. Smith noted that had Britain and other European states abandoned their mercantile policies, there would have been fewer conflicts.

After Britain gained French territories in North America after the war, it had to spend more on defence. As the author of *The Present State of the Nation* argued, the cost of this war was without parallel. Victory led to credit, and credit to debt, whereas in France, defeat prevented it from obtaining any loans (Knox 1768: 5–14). Like other thinkers, Smith also warned of the increase of national debt due to war, although national debt was helpful for paying off the cost of war. Smith wrote,

> Were the expence of war to be defrayed always by a revenue raised within the year, the taxes . . . would last no longer than the war. The ability of private person to accumulate, though less during the war, would have been greater during the peace than under the system of funding. War would not necessarily have occasioned the destruction of any old capitals, and peace would have occasioned the accumulation of many more new.
>
> (Smith 1981: V. iii. 50)

Although national debt supported British victories in war, it was harmful to peace, which could lead to prosperity through the accumulation of capital.

Nonetheless, Britain became a commercial empire, without abandoning war as a tool of foreign policy. Smith proposed,

> France and England may each of them have some reason to dread the increase of the naval and military power of the other; but for either of them

to envy the internal happiness and prosperity of the other, the cultivation of its lands . . . is surely beneath the dignity of two such great nations.

(Smith 1982a: VI. ii. 2. 3)

The English and French held antipathy to each other due to their sympathetic preference for their own nation and its interests. An impartial spectator, however, knows the reciprocity of foreign trade.

The 'mercantile system', as one type of political economy, could lead to war. To avoid it, Smith initially criticized the mercantile system. He then denounced the imperial project. Instead, he presented his own principles of political economy to show that a country's wealth and prosperity are not incompatible with that of any other. Like Hume, for Smith, economy was a source of both prosperity and war. However, unlike Hume, whose political economy requires the maintenance of a 'jealousy of trade', Smith recognized that 'jealousy of trade' was based on antipathy between states. This antipathy was based on each nation's self-interest: the partiality of sympathy. In this manner, Smith linked war with morality.

## 3 War and the historical progress of society

The Seven Years' War made Smith reconsider his four stages theory with respect to morality.

Before mentioning this point, I would like to explain Smith's four-stages theory. This theory sees society as experiencing the four stages of development; that is hunting, pastoral, agricultural and commercial (see Meek 1976). The means of subsistence and property is related to war in all four stages.

In a hunters' society, the most primitive people rely on wild animals and plants for survival.

> Every man is a warrior as well as a hunter . . . His society, for in this state of things there is properly neither sovereign nor commonwealth, is at no sort of expence, either to prepare him for the field, or to maintain him while he is in it.
>
> (Smith 1981: V. i. q. 2)

Smith does not depict this stage as a state of war, as Hobbes did. However, unlike Jean-Jacques Rousseau, Smith does not regard the lack of property ownership as leading to peace. In this stage, there is no standing army, but people nonetheless waged war.

In a pastoral society, people learn to keep domestic animals as property. In this state, people take their livestock with them when they move. In this state, the rise of property leads to the establishment of government. Pastoral people have certain advantages over societies of hunters. Smith said,

> An army of hunters can seldom exceed two or three hundred men. The precarious subsistence which the chance affords could seldom allow a greater

number to keep together for any considerable time. An army of shepherds, on the contrary, may sometimes amount to two, or three hundred thousand. As long as nothing stops their progress . . . there seems to be scarce any limit to the number who can march on together . . . Nothing . . . can be more dreadful than a Tartar invasion has frequently been in Asia.

(Smith 1981: V. i. a. 5)

Wandering people can move easily, and, accustomed to riding horses, they can be stronger warriors than the more advanced people, as in the case of the German invasion of Rome (Smith 1981: III. ii. 1–3). For Smith, barbarism is linked with military strength.

However, unlike many contemporaries who worried about the decline of Western Europe, Smith thought that the military revolution introduced expensive weapons, which poor countries cannot afford (Smith 1981: V. i. a. 43; for the military revolution, see Brewer 1988).

In an agricultural society, there is almost no division of labour, and people are self-sufficient. Husbandmen, unlike shepherds, need settlements, and so it might be more difficult to go to war. However, in the off-season, husbandmen could go to war. In these three stages, militias did the fighting.

The final stage is a commercial society, in which the expansion of the market brought about the division of labour. People practice a trade and purchase the necessities they do not produce. In this stage, war interrupts business. A standing army, not a militia, wages war in a commercial society (Smith 1981: V. i. a. 8–12).

The four-stages theory was linked with the problem of who could be soldiers. In commercial society, a standing army is necessary. Although Smith belonged to the Poker Club, whose objective was to raise a militia in Scotland (Ross 2010: 142), he knew the limits of militia in a commercial society. Although Smith was criticized for his defence of a standing army (Ross 2010: 365; see also Robertson 1985), he admitted the role of 'military exercises' to preserve 'the martial spirit of the great body of people'. However, he argued, 'martial spirit alone, and unsupported by a well-disciplined standing army, would not, perhaps, be sufficient for the defence and security of any society' (Smith 1981: V. i. f. 59). In this way, he historicized military virtue, saying that it was effective mainly in the earlier stage of development (on this point, see Pocock 2003: Chap. XIV).

Smith had recognized a similar historical change in the standing army in *Lectures on Jurisprudence* (1762–63; Smith 1982b, LJ(A), iv. 76–87): 'in a state where arts, manufactures, and handicrafts are brought to perfection . . . they therefore will not go out to the wars' (Smith 1982b, LJ(A), iv. 79). Thus, military virtue based on a militia could not be maintained in a commercial society. By historicizing military virtue, Smith situated morality in the social structure.

However, there was one exception. In *The Wealth of Nations*, Smith described the strengths of militias. In considering the Seven Years' War, he said,

Should the war in America drag out through another campaign, the American militia may become in every respect a match for that standing army, of which the valour appeared, in the last war, at least not inferior to that of the hardiest veterans of France and Spain.

(Smith 1981: V. i. a. 27)

A courageous militia could defeat standing armies who had endured several campaigns. Thus, the Seven Years' War made Smith reconsider the possibility of militia, which was maintained by military virtue; and, because military virtue was linked with the four-stages theory, here Smith reconsidered his four stages theory with respect to morality.

Although Pocock saw a change in Smith's social ideals from civic humanism to commercial prosperity (Pocock 2003: Chap. XIV), Smith remained a civic humanist, because he saw a role for military virtue even in commercial society. It is true enough that Smith paid attention to the strength of a standing army in comparison with militia in commercial society (Smith 1981: V. i. a. 44). However, commercial prosperity might result in decreasing military virtue, which might, in turn, result in military weakness, even in commercial society. In this explanation, Smith linked society and history to civic virtue, which still matters in commercial society.

## 4 Hume's considerations on common interest and justice and Smith's criticism

Hume thought that war could be caused by conflict over property (Hume 2007: 3. 2. 3. 2), unlike Hobbes, who blamed discord on differences of opinion. Hume considered the cause of human conflict in general through considering civil war.

One might occasionally covet others' property. Thus, to keep justice at all times, one should reflect *a posteriori* the public interest of the universal observation of justice to protect others' property. If one behaves only from instinct, one might violate justice. Natural morality, like sympathy, is not sufficient for the attainment of social order. According to Hume, although human beings have natural sociability, people can show sympathy only to their families and relatives. This partiality of passion could mean that one might behave morally towards one's family, but not towards strangers. This difference was the obstacle to social order (Hume 2007: 3. 2. 2).

Unlike Hobbes, Hume saw sociability as natural. One can distinguish between moral good and evil through feelings (Hume 2007: 3. 1. 2. 11). When one feels pleasure by observing some action, it is called morally good; similarly, when one feels pain, it is called morally evil. Therefore, morality is derived, not from reason, but from passion. Hume said, 'all the affections readily pass from one person to another, and beget correspondent movements in every human creature' (Hume 2007: 3. 3. 1. 7).

Nevertheless, Hume does not think that natural sympathy produces justice. Humans pursue three kinds of happiness or good; 'internal satisfaction of our mind, the external advantages of our body, and the enjoyment of such possessions as we have acquir'd by our industry and good fortune'. Whereas the former two could not be transferred, possessions were 'expos'd to the violence of others' (Hume 2007: 3. 2. 2. 7). The only way to attain the security of property would be

> by a convention enter'd into by all the members of the society to bestow stability on the possession of those external goods, and leave every one in the peaceable enjoyment of what he may acquire by his fortune and industry.
>
> (Hume 2007: 3. 2. 2. 9)

This convention is

> only a general sense of common interest; which sense all the members of the society express to one another, and which induces them to regulate their conduct by certain rules. I observe, that it will be for my interest to leave another in the possession of his goods, *provided* he will act in the same manner with regard to me.
>
> (Hume 2007: 3. 2. 2. 10)

In this process, although 'self-interest is the original motive to the *establishment* of justice', that is, the basis of the sense of justice, sympathy towards public interest supports the moral approbation of keeping justice (Hume 2007: 3. 2. 2. 24).

Hume's position on common interest was criticized by Smith, who said,

> That it is not a regard to the preservation of society, which originally interests us in the punishment of crimes committed against individuals, may be demonstrated by many obvious considerations . . . The concern which we take in the fortune and happiness of individuals does not, in common cases, arise from that which we take in the fortune and happiness of society. We are no more concerned for the destruction or loss of a single man, because this man is a member or part of society . . . we demand the punishment of the wrong that has been done to him, not so much from a concern for the general interest of society as from a concern for that very individual who has been injured . . . The concern which is requisite for this, is no more than the general fellow-feeling which we have with every man merely because he is our fellow-creature.
>
> (Smith 1982a: II. ii. 3. 10)

Here, Smith criticized Hume's view of the formation of justice by the shared understanding of the common interest. Smith regarded as unnatural Hume's view of people's direct understanding of the general rule of justice. To Hume, the shared sense of justice can be attained by people's agreement about 'common interest' in the protection of justice. For Smith, common interest is too abstract, and what people are really concerned about are particular incidents. For Hume, justice should be artificial, because natural sympathy could be partial. Whereas, for Hume, the formation of morality and justice presupposes the universality of justice, Smith's idea of justice depends on each individual's interactions, through which morality and justice are formed spontaneously. This spontaneous morality and justice provide people with the cause of preventing conflict, unlike Hume.

Hume thought that justice by natural sympathy could result in conflict. Due to the discrepancy of passions, people's natural sympathy is irregular; the gradual, individualistic formation of natural sympathy could be partial and precarious, hence easily violated. Thus, Hume thought justice was artificial; natural morality was not sufficient for the establishment of social order, and might result in conflict. For Hume, ensuring a secure government always involved tackling the potential danger of conflict. This is why Hume emphasized the role of government in maintaining internal security. In contrast, Smith showed how morality could lead to justice, and not necessarily to conflict.

## 5  Morality, justice, and war in *The Theory of Moral Sentiments*

Unlike Hume, Smith saw justice as natural, the basis of which is sympathy. This section examines Smith's consideration of morality and justice and their connection to war.

Smith bases morality on natural human sentiments, such as sympathy. He wrote,

> How selfish soever man may be supposed, there are evidently some principles in his nature, which interest him in the fortune of others, and render their happiness necessary to him, though he derives nothing from it except the pleasure of seeing it.
>
> (Smith 1982a: I. i. 1. 1)

Smith bases the origins of morality not on self-interested consideration, but on natural morality. As a spectator, one sees an action by others, and judges it to be morally good or not. Conversely, everybody knows that others also judge everyone's behaviour. Since one naturally wants to gain sympathy from others, one tries to adapt one's behaviour in order to be approved by others.

As this society enlarges, the shared standard of moral approbation extends from small to large societies; in reality, he said, 'our regard for the multitude is compounded and made up of the particular regards which we feel for the different individuals of which it is composed' (Smith 1982a: II. ii. 3. 10). Thus, the shared sense of morality could be achieved.

Specifically, regarding justice, when one sees some violence being committed by a particular person, one pities the injured and resents the perpetrator. As Smith said,

> resentment seems to have been given us by nature for defence, and for defence only. It is the safeguard of justice and the security of innocence. It prompts us to beat off the mischief which is attempted to be done to us, and to retaliate that which is already done.
>
> (Smith 1982a: II. ii. 1. 4)

Smith saw justice as based on human natural sentiments, such as resentment. Here, Smith criticized Hume's idea of justice based on self-interested consideration of the general benefit in society. Justice for Hume is artificial, because natural morality is not sufficient for justice, which needs people's intentional agreement on the rules of justice. For Smith, it is uncertain how people directly conceive the general interest of justice.

Here, one can wonder how Smith solved Hume's problem with the partiality of natural sentiments of justice. Smith argued,

> the violation of justice is injury: it does real and positive hurt to some particular persons, from motives which are naturally disapproved of. It is, therefore, the proper object of resentment, and of punishment, which is the natural consequence of resentment. As mankind go along with, and approve of the violence employed to avenge the hurt which is done by injustice, so they much more go along with, and approve of, that which is employed to prevent and beat off the injury, and to restrain the offender from hurting his neighbours.
>
> (Smith 1982a: II. ii. 1. 5)

Although the sole agent of enforcing justice is government, Smith is not connecting justice with government. Although Smith admitted the necessity of government, his basis of universal obedience of the rule of justice is different from Hume's convention of justice fortified by a state. Hume based justice on the self-interested calculation of the benefit of obedience to the general rule of justice, and which therefore extended to universal justice, whereas Smith's individualistic approach to morality and justice lacks universal rules of justice. In spite of that, Smith thought that people could share an implicit sense of justice.

Smith faced another problem in the sixth edition of *The Theory of Moral Sentiments*. Although Smith regards sympathy as a fellow-feeling, and the 'fellow' could be any 'fellow-creature', and therefore universal, sympathy has limits. He said,

> every individual is naturally more attached to his own particular order or society, than to any other. His own interest, his own vanity, the interest and vanity of many of his friends and companions, are commonly a good deal connected with it
>
> (Smith 1982a: VI. ii. 2. 9)

Thus, people are more attached to their own, or to what is familiar, and do not love everyone equally.

Hume saw this partiality of sympathy as the reason why natural sympathy was not fit for the maintenance of justice, but Smith saw some merit in it. A nation is 'the greatest society upon whose happiness or misery, our good or bad conduct can have much influence. It is accordingly, by nature, most strongly recommended to us' (Smith 1982a: VI. ii. 2. 2). Smith praised 'the patriot who lays down his life for the safety, or even for the vain-glory of this society as appearing to act with the most exact propriety' (Smith 1982a: VI. ii. 2. 2). Smith approved of devotion to one's nation.

Patriotism is linked with war. Smith argued,

> foreign war and civil faction are the two situations which afford the most splendid opportunities for the display of public spirit. The hero who serves his country successfully in foreign war gratifies the wishes of the whole nation, and is, upon that account, the object of universal gratitude and admiration.
>
> (Smith 1982a: VI. ii. 2. 13)

Sympathy can lead to the moral approbation of patriotic behaviour, such as waging war courageously. Sympathy as fellow-feeling is the basis of public virtue. Here, one can see the influence of civic humanism, as argued by Pocock (2003). In this respect, Smith affirmed sympathy as patriotic fellow-feeling.

By contrast, Hume thought that moral virtues such as courage were evaluated by the public utility, not sympathy itself. He said, 'we may observe, that whatever we call *heroic virtue* . . . is either nothing but a steady and well-establish'd pride and self-esteem, or partakes largely of that passion'. This self-esteem is not denied morally, but evaluated according to its

> utility. [ . . .] Heroism, or military glory, is much admir'd by the generality of mankind. They consider it as the most sublime kind of merit. Men of cool reflection are not so sanguine in their praise of it. The infinite confusions and disorder, which it has caus'd in the world, diminish much of its merit in their eyes.
>
> (Hume 2007: 3. 2. 2. 13–15)

He makes the point that natural civic virtue is different from the defence of public benefit.

Whereas Smith saw civic virtue as morally good, Hume did not equate it with public utility. Both recognized that sympathy could be partial. However, unlike Hume, Smith regarded this partial sympathy as leading to justice and public spirit.

However, in a civil war, this partiality could exacerbate social disorder. He said, 'the leaders of the discontented party seldom fail to hold out some plausible plan of reformation', and 'often propose, upon this account, to new-model the constitution, and to alter' the established system of government. As a result, he argues,

> Those leaders themselves, though they originally may have meant nothing but their own aggrandisement, become many of them in time the dupes of their own sophistry, and are as eager for this great reformation as the weakest and foolishest of their followers. Even though the leaders should have preserved their own heads, as indeed they commonly do . . . yet they dare not always disappoint the expectation of their followers; but are often obliged,

though contrary to their principles and their conscience, to act as if they were under the common delusion.

(Smith 1982a: VI. ii. 2. 15)

Because people and their leaders wanted the sympathy of their own group, they tended to behave partially. Thus, sympathy could lead to a civil war.

Overall, Smith considered both the advantages and disadvantages of the partiality of sympathy. This partiality could be the cause of civil war, as well as that of courage in waging war. Thus, the partiality of sympathy was intimately linked with war in Smith's philosophy.

In international relations, Smith saw the limits of courage in waging war. The partiality of sympathy could not resolve international conflicts.

## 6 Hume and Smith on international relations

This section explains how Hume and Smith connected the partiality of sympathy with war in international relations.

Hume thought that justice in international relations could be easily violated (Hume 2007: 3. 2. 11). In international relations, where there is no supreme judge, each state could prefer its own interests rather than the interests of international justice. Although Hume advocated international peace based on the balance of power, he knew that it could be abused. In 'Of the Balance of Power' (1752), Hume, citing the War of the Austrian Succession, wrote, 'we seem to have been more possessed with the ancient GREEK spirit of jealous emulation, than actuated by the prudent views of modern politics' (Hume 1985a: 339). In ancient Greece, every member of the *polis* made efforts to keep the balance of power from the 'jealousy of the conquerors' (Hume 1985a: 333). Jealousy derives from one's feeling of others' superiority (Hume 2007: 2. 2. 8). Although jealousy can be harmful, in international politics, jealousy leads to suppressing others' superiority by keeping any state from becoming too strong, so it is helpful for preserving the balance of power. Hume regards human passion, not reason, as the force behind the balance of power.

However, what he emphasized here are the drawbacks caused by the abuse of the desire for preserving the balance of power. From Hume's historical perspective, after the Glorious Revolution (1688–1689) Britain fought a series of large and expensive wars with France. After the peace under Walpole, the War of the Austrian Succession raged from 1740 to 1748, which revived the hostility between Britain and France. Thus, Hume feared the abuse of the balance of power. Jealousy is both the foundation of the balance of power and the cause of war.

Smith wrote,

> The most extensive public benevolence which can commonly be exerted with any considerable effect, is that of the statesmen who project . . . for the

preservation either of . . . the balance of power. The statesmen, however . . . have seldom any thing in view, but the interest of their respective countries.
(Smith 1982a: VI. ii. 2. 6)

The balance of power was meant to preserve international harmony, but, in reality it was a pretext for military intervention.

Although sympathy could become the impartial spectator, by which people could sympathize and judge others equally and universally, one does not easily sympathize with people of other countries. About the limits of sympathy in international relations, Smith argued,

The love of our own nation often disposes us to view, with the most malignant jealousy and envy, the prosperity and aggrandisement of any other neighbouring nation. Independent and neighbouring nations, having no common superior to decide their disputes, all live in continual dread and suspicion of one another. Each sovereign, expecting little justice from his neighbours, is disposed to treat them with as little as he expects from them. The regard for the laws of nations, or for those rules which independent states profess or pretend to think themselves bound to observe in their dealings with one another, is often very little more than mere pretence and profession.
(Smith 1982a: VI. ii. 2. 3)

Although the partiality of sympathy such as patriotic fellow-feeling might increase courage in the defence of a country, in international relations, by patriotic sympathy, people increase jealousy and antipathy against their other nations, which could intensify conflict.

Smith proposed,

The man of real constancy and firmness, the wise and just man who has been thoroughly bred in the great school of self-command, in the bustle and business of the world, exposed, perhaps . . . to the hardships and hazards of war, maintains this control of his passive feelings upon all occasion.
(Smith 1982a: III. 3. 25)

However, in civilized society, unlike in barbarous society, humanity rather than self-control is 'more cultivated' (Smith 1982a: V. 2. 8). Here, a man of self-discipline provides the meta-ethics over the conventional rule of justice and morality. In other words, 'the love of mankind' is different from the narrow interest only in one's own nation.

However, in war, when neither side considers the sentiments of the other, the rules of justice, treaties, and commerce are ignored. Innocent citizens lose their homes, and are sometimes killed. Rulers can do this, even under international law. Smith said, 'of the conduct of one independent nation towards another, neutral nations are the only indifferent and impartial spectators. But they are placed at so great a distance that they are almost quite out of sight' (Smith 1982a: III. 3. 42).

Although individuals, not nations themselves, have sympathy, when considering international relations, by the partiality of sympathy, people sympathize with their own nation rather than others, which can exacerbate antipathy. The antipathy could result in war. War presents an opportunity to think about the limits of morality based on sympathy.

## 7 Conclusion

The Seven Years' War made a deep impression on Hume's and Smith's thought. It inspired them to consider war.

War gave Smith occasion to consider the limit of sympathy. Smith wrote,

> The love of our nation often disposes us to view, with the most malignant jealousy and envy, the prosperity and aggrandisement of any other neighbouring nation . . . From the smallest interest, upon the slightest provocation, we see those rules [the law of nations] every day, either evaded or directly violated without shame or remorse. Each nation foresees, or imagines it foresees, its own subjugation in the increasing power and aggrandisement of any of its neighbours.
>
> (Smith 1982a: VI. ii. 2. 3)

Sympathy might not exist between peoples who did not know each other. This could lead to war. To prevent war, Hume advocated the balance of power as keeping each state from becoming too strong, not as preventing it from waging war.

For Smith, in a given society, the partiality of sympathy could be the cause of civil war as well as a source of courage in waging war. Thus, the partiality of sympathy was connected with war. In international relations, Smith saw the limits of courage in waging war. The partiality of sympathy could not resolve international conflicts.

To consider this problem, Smith connected the partiality of sympathy with economic consideration. Whereas the modern economic system can lead to prosperity, it produces the peculiar cause of war. In every stage of society, waging war is linked with property. Unlike in the past, in commercial society commercial interests were another cause of war, which could result from the jealousy of trade, which, in Smith, was linked with the mercantile policy. The jealousy was based on the partiality of sympathy. Thus, morality, political economy, and war were interconnected.

## References

Brewer, J. (1988). *The Sinews of Power: War, Money, and the English State, 1688–1783*, Cambridge, MA: Harvard University Press.

Carr, E. H. (1946). *The Twenty Years' Crisis 1919–1939*, London: Macmillan.

Christelow, A. (1946). 'Economic Background of the Anglo-Dutch War of 1762', *The Journal of Modern History*, 18(1): 22–36.

Coulomb, F. (1998). "Adam Smith: A Defence Economist," *Defence and Peace Economics*, 9(3): 299–316.

Hill, L. (2009). "Adam Smith on War (and on Peace)," in I. Hall et al. (Eds.), *British International Thinkers From Hobbes to Namier*, New York: Palgrave Macmillan, Chap. V.

Hont, I. (2005). Jealousy of Trade: International Competition and the Nation-State in Historical Perspective, Cambridge: Belknap Press of Harvard University Press.

Howard, M. (1978). *War and the Liberal Conscience*, London: Temple Smith.

Hume, D. (1985a). "Of the Balance of Power," In *ditto, Essays moral, Political, and Literary*, E. F. Millar (Ed.), Indianapolis: Liberty Fund, pp. 332–341.

Hume, D. (1985b). "Of the Jealousy of Trade," In *ditto, Essays moral, political, and literary*, edited by E. F. Millar, Indianapolis: Liberty Fund, pp. 327–331.

Hume, D. (2007). *A Treatise of Human Nature: A Critical Edition*, D.F. Norton and M.J. Norton (Eds.), Oxford: Clarendon Press.

Jessop, T.E. (1938). A Bibliography of David Hume of Scottish Philosophy, London: A Brown & Sons.

Knox, W. (1768). *The Present State of the Nation*, London: J. Almon.

Meek, R.L. (1976). *Social Science and the Ignoble Savage*, Cambridge: Cambridge University Press.

Minowitz, P. (1989). 'Invisible Hand, Invisible Death; Adam Smith on War and Socio-Economic Development', *Journal of Political and Military Sociology*, 17, Winter: 305–315.

Pocock, J.G.A. (2003). The Machiavellian Moment: Florence Political Thought and the Atlantic Republican Tradition, Princeton: Princeton University Press.

Robertson, J. (1985). The Scottish Enlightenment and the Militia Issue, Edinburgh: J. Donald.

Ross, I.S. (2010). *The Life of Adam Smith*, second edition, Oxford: Oxford University Press.

Smith, A. (1981). *An Inquiry Into the Nature and Causes of the Wealth of Nations*, R.H. Campbell, A.S. Skinner, and W.B. Todd (Eds.), Indianapolis: Liberty Fund.

Smith, A. (1982a). *The Theory of Moral Sentiments*, D.D. Raphael and A.L. Macfie (Eds.), Indianapolis: Liberty Fund.

Smith, A. (1982b). *Lectures on Jurisprudence*, R.L. Meek, D.D. Raphael, and P.G. Stein (Eds.), Indianapolis: Liberty Fund.

Waltz, K.N. (1959). *Man, the State and War: A Theoretical Analysis*. New York: Columbia University Press.

Wyatt-Walter, A. (1996). "Adam Smith and the Liberal Tradition in International Relations," *Review of International Studies*, 22(1): 5–28.

# 4    Industrialism and war in the French social sciences in the early 19th century

*Philippe Steiner*

In early 19th century France war was not an issue that could be overlooked. The French Republic had been successfully defended against European monarchies; Bonaparte then prolonged the state of war. Taking up Montesquieu's ideas about "*doux commerce*" and the antinomy of commerce and war, a political economist (Jean-Baptiste Say), a political theoretician (Benjamin Constant), and a sociologist (Auguste Comte) reflected on the new connections between economy and warfare. These three leading publicists – to use the vocabulary of the time – developed what may be called the "peaceful industrial society thesis", that social relations in an industrial society will lead citizens to cherish peace, creating a nation oriented towards the production and exchange of a growing mass of wealth. To emphasize the paradoxical nature of this thesis on the relation between industry and warfare at a time when the latter reached a new climax, the chapter will first of all review Carl von Clausewitz's view on modern war. According to this great master of military strategy, and in contrast to industrialist thinkers, Bonaparte's military strategies had opened the way to war as an *absolute form* of violence, probability, and politics. For Clausewitz the nation remained central, but a nation made up of people capable of being moved by a political passion for the greatness of their nation, a passion that would give the art of war a new and terrible direction.

Following on from this introduction, the chapter will consider the works of Jean-Baptiste Say, the leading French economist of that time. Say developed an articulated view of the connection between the new industrial world and the waning of war – a real *tour de force* when one bears in mind the fact that the first edition of his *Traité d'économie politique* was published in 1803, one year after the unsatisfactory declaration of peace in May 1802 at Amiens, and two years before the beginning of the long series of Napoleonic wars. The fall of the French emperor and the ensuing peace leading to the reestablishment of the monarchy in 1814, and then again in 1815 led Say to develop his views further. Say was not the alone in making such arguments. Benjamin Constant, a leading contemporary political thinker, took up some of these ideas in several books published towards the end of the Empire, connecting the economic and political dimensions of the liberal worldview. Industrialism thus became an explicit political philosophy. Finally, Auguste Comte's positive philosophy introduced the thesis of

industrial peace to a broad audience, explaining why warfare would fade away in
the course of human history.

## Introduction: Clausewitz and the new art of war

To understand the changes introduced by the French Revolution and the Empire
we can begin by considering the way in which Carl von Clausewitz, the greatest
military thinker of the period, understood the situation in terms of the art of war
that emerged from these political changes.

   The first chapter of his book *On War*, beyond defining war in terms of a duel
and a form of logic of "going to extremes" (Clausewitz 1832–4: 52–53), organ-
izes a conception of war organized around three elements: violence, the laws
of probability and warfare's "subordination as a means to the political goal"
(Clausewitz 1832–4: 69; see also 703–710).[1] This is also the central topic of
Book VIII, chapter 3, which is devoted to the goal of war and the amount of effort
required (Clausewitz 1832–4: 678–690).

   According to Clausewitz, the close connection existing between the goal of
a war and the means to be deployed in its successful prosecution is mediated
by political considerations. What does Clausewitz mean by "political considerations"? The initial answer is a conjectural history distinguishing the various forms
of war, from the Tartars to the 19th century. However, the most important point
here is the distinction that Clausewitz draws between the 17th and 18th centuries, and what happened subsequent to the French Revolution. In the former
period, wars were embedded in the "European balance of power" and were conducted according to what he called a "Cabinet approach", where battles were
comparable to diplomatic dispatches (Clausewitz 1832–4: 683). In this form of
warfare economic resources were fairly well known, since they were based upon
the size of the population and the amount of taxes that a king could levy on
subjects considered to be his personal property. Everything changed with the
Revolution: "War was thus becoming an affair of the people', and a people of
30 million who conceived themselves to be citizen of the nation" (Clausewitz
1832–4: 687). Primitive violence was unleashed because the energy and enthusiasm of the government and the population blurred the limits of what could be
mobilized for military effort. Clausewitz summarized his thinking by this apho-
ristic sentence: "If war is part of politics, the former will naturally endorse the
nature of the latter. If politics is grandiose and powerful, war will be the same,
and it could even achieve its *absolute form*" (Clausewitz 1832–4: 704). Nationalism seemed to him the new element in an era of the birth of nation-states: rein-
troducing the people modified the whole conception of war, with the emergence
of mass armies (France), the *Landsturm* (Prussia), and partisan warfare (Spain).
The nation could therefore be associated with the mobilization of nationalistic
passions that lent the art of war its absolute form of violence.

   What of the economy? What of the link between the subordination of war to politics and the economy of the nation? This is a blind spot in Clausewitz's thinking.
This does not mean that he thought that war and the economy are in opposition,

in the way that a cooperative approach to the making of the social order could be opposed to a non-cooperative one;[2] it is well-known that Clausewitz drew signifi-cant parallels between both domains, notably when he said that battles were to war what money payments were to financial transactions (Clausewitz 1832–4: 79). However, beyond these general comments, Clausewitz disregarded economic con-siderations;[3] and this is also true of the historical essays that he wrote at the time, exemplified by his study of the military disaster that had befallen his own country (Clausewitz 1825–8: chap. I). The crux of the matter was the general connection between army and administration on the one hand, and army and a "general spirit of the people" on the other (Clausewitz 1825–8: 15). Both were conceived as the basis for the political dimension of military affairs and of the goal of warfare. He did not consider Industrialism to be the key change, but instead the new role for people and nation, culminating in the unleashed violence of modern war, some-thing that found confirmation in the course of the following century.

## 1 Say, industry, and the cost of war

It needs to be pointed out that Say was himself directly involved in the war of the first Republic: volunteering as a soldier, he served in the "*Section des arts*" in 1791, and took part in the fighting between the European monarchical coalition against the French Republic.[4] If his anti-war views were important for the con-struction of a vision of a peaceful industrial society, this is no indicator of some inner cowardice, or reluctance to commit himself to the defense of his mother country when he thought that right and reason were on his side.

Say's originality is already evident in this first edition of 1803, where he laid the basis of what would be later called "industrial society": if, according to Adam Smith's well-known statement, a commercial society is one in which individuals sell their goods in a market, an industrial society is one in which individuals are more the producers of goods and services than merchants sell-ing their goods in a market (Steiner 2003b). The core component of the first type of society is the market, together with the rule according to which mar-ket exchanges occur; the core component of an industrial society is the rule according to which goods and services are produced with machinery, with the energy and resources provided by nature, and with the intensive use of scien-tific knowledge. The production of utility comes first, as the structure of Say's books makes clear.

### 1.1 The first edition of the Traité d'économie politique

Say's views on war were presented in the 10 pages devoted to the necessary expenditure on an army, a section that can be found in the chapter on public expenditure. He approached the issue with a brief historical sketch, going from the hunter-gatherers of the past to the present civilized industrial society, agricul-tural societies being the intermediate form of society. He analyzed how war was related to the functioning of the economy in these three different social states.

Those making their living from hunting and pastoral activities enjoyed a great deal of time additional to that necessary for the production of food and the few necessities of life. Consequently, men were easily transformed into warriors at very little cost; this was the case with the Eastern "Barbarians" and with Arabic tribes in the time of Mahomet. And this was still true of agricultural societies, at least when there was no overlap between harvest and war; this economy-and-war system thus existed for a long time in Europe, from the Ancient Greeks to the European societies in the Middle Ages (Say 1803: II: 420).

Everything changes "when manufactures, commerce and arts are diffused in a nation" (Say 1803: II: 421). The first explanation of this change is nothing less than the Smithian principle of the division of labor: in an industrial society, farmers cultivate land not only for their own needs, but also to provide food to other members of society. They cannot abandon their work without jeopardizing the subsistence of many citizens. This is even more important for manufacturing workers. What of landowners? They have a great deal of free time and can go to war at their own expense, as previously happened with the nobility during the monarchical period. However, according to Say, landowners are increasingly inclined to sacrifice a part of their income rather than personally risk their life in a war. The same is true for the capitalists, who "have the same taste, needs and opinion as the landowners" (Say 1803: II: 422). Accordingly, war is now one profession among others in the social division of labor; an increasing amount of specialized education and training is required, together with increasing resources for the artillery and the navy. The social relation between the economy and war thus boils down to an issue of costs. War is increasingly costly because of new weapons, and because of the need for specialized personnel; the odds in warfare are increasingly moving in favor of the wealthiest societies; but wars are costly, even for the victor. In brief: according to Say, the opportunity cost of war is high.

The other side of Say's economic understanding of war relates to these costs. Current taxes usually being as high as is possible, they cannot be increased in the event of a war; a loan must be raised in order to pay for the war:

> In the position of modern states, with the huge cost entailed by war, no nation could pay for a war with the current resources obtained from the population [. . .] If the choice is to double the spending, or die, then nations have no other choice than a loan [. . .] How could the English nation have paid, during the nine years of the last war, that £146 million that the war cost her beyond her current spending, when she struggles to pay her current expenditure and the interest on her borrowings? Loans are thus a mean of defending a nation, and also, unfortunately, a means to attack others. This is a new weapon, more formidable than gunpowder, with which any nation that does not want to be in a inferior position must deal as soon as one nation has succeeded in employing it.
>
> (Say 1803: II: 519–520)

Beyond these economic considerations, Say has a negative moral evaluation of warfare: when not dictated by pressing necessity, war must be considered to be "the most execrable crime" (Say 1803: II: 427). These moral dimensions were however left out of this edition, and developed either in his booklet on morality (Say 1817), or in the unfinished manuscript of his *Politique pratique* (Say 2003).[5]

This first edition of the *Traité* contains two significant departures from Smith's approach to the subject. The first is a minor change in the economic classification of soldiers, who Smith sorted assigned to the unproductive class. They are more than unproductive, wrote Say: they are "destructive workers" since

> not only do they not enrich society with any new product, not only do they consume the products necessary to their activity, but they are often led to destroy, without any personal benefit, the hard-won products resulting from the labor of others.
>
> (Say 1803: II: 427)

More importantly, while Say admitted (following Smith) that standing armies are superior to militias, he did not endorse the Smithian idea that there could be a benefit from the feeling of security enjoyed by the king thanks to his army, a sense of security that was extended to the people. For Say, the principal danger comes from the immense cost of the standing army. Say changed his mind on this issue later on.

## 1.2 Say's views of the peaceful industrial order

In subsequent editions Say modified substantially the content of his *Traité*, the issues of war and the financing of war being no exception – I will deal with the first of these in this section. Some of these changes were certainly due to the political situation, since the second edition of the *Traité* was published after the fall of the first Napoleonic Empire (April 1814), an Empire that Say deeply despised;[6] but they were also explained by Say's thinking on this complex topic, going far beyond the changing military fortune of the French emperor.

First, Say removed his historical treatment of societal stages, and the possibility of turning different economic agents into warriors. He relied more on his own principles and ideas, and less on those of Smith; he was no longer so eager to use the kind of conjectural history that his "master" had employed in *The Wealth of Nations*. The first chapter went straight to the present situation, explaining why industrious men no longer had the possibility of becoming warriors, given their strong involvement in the division of labor.

Second, from the fourth edition of his *Traité* Say modified the end of the chapter, emphasizing the role of an enlightened public in the withering away of war. Instead of relying on moral arguments concerning the cruelty of war and the vanity of politicians, he invoked the "slow but infallible progress of enlightenment" (Say 2006: 951). An enlightened public will understand that war is costly, even for a victorious nation. It will understand even more readily that taxes have never fallen after military success. With the progress of enlightenment and the greater hold of reason on public affairs, the domination of foreign countries will no longer be a legitimate goal for modern political leaders.

The key point in Say's thoughts about war is therefore a connection between an economically enlightened public and the management of public affairs. This *political* perspective in his *political economy* rests on two principles. The first states that a government that provokes war declares war upon its own citizens:

> The sole interest of subjects (*administrés*) is free communication among themselves, and so to be at peace. All nations are naturally friendly towards each other, and two governments who make war on each other are no less at war with their own subjects than they are with their adversaries.
>
> (Say 2006: 951)

The second is about the cost of the war, and the need for the public's agreement to pay for it:

> But since public opinion has made progress, it will continue to do so. Precisely because war has become costlier than ever, it is impossible for the governments to enter into a war without the explicit or implicit agreement of the public. Such agreement will become harder and harder to obtain, to the extent that the public becomes more enlightened.
>
> (Say 2006: 953)

Hence, Say endorsed the view that a militia, with some help from some cavalry and artillery, would suffice in the event of war. In his chapter advocating militias, Say notes that some military thinkers – Machiavelli, Guibert, and General Tarayre[7] – were also in favor of this kind of defensive organization. Writing when he did, he could not refer to Carl von Clausewitz's book, but that would also express a positive view on these matters. Clausewitz's views on military affairs after the dramatic changes introduced by the French Revolution and Bonaparte are of relevance here. Hence, according to Say, the inner strength of a nation is to be found in sound institutions and the profound sentiments that connect citizens to the nation by virtue of these sound institutions. As in the previous editions of his *Traité*, the reader has to turn to the chapter devoted to public credit to find the other side of Say's views on war. Generally, he expressed the same idea, with the important addition that the financing of war must be given especial consideration.

Finally, Volume 5 of Say's *Cours complet d'économie politique pratique* contained a series of four chapters devoted to war and the appropriate organisation of defense policy.[8] As explained elsewhere (Steiner 1998), Say here reprised topics already discussed in the first edition of the *Traité*; there are many passages dealing with the issue of morality, and notably the malevolent role that Say attributed to vanity – or "sinister interest", in the Benthamite terminology that he used from time to time – and unsound interest (Say 1828–30: V: 177, 178, 188, 193). However, these moral considerations were now directly connected to political factors, and particularly to the positive role that Say attributed to the enlightened public opinion that was his personal goal as a political economist,[9] supported by a representative political system: "The progress of enlightenment will move opinion towards peace, and the progress of the representative system will strengthen the power of this opinion" (Say 1828–30: V: 181).

Importantly, Say here developed at length his views on the defensive role of military forces and connected that idea to the effectiveness of militias. Say contrasted industrial behavior (individual effort, respect for the legal system, critical thinking) with military behavior (idleness, passive obedience, cruelty, lack of critical spirit), emphasizing that the latter was not appropriate for useful industrial citizens (Say 1828–30: V: 196). He then stressed that the economic and political dimensions of the issue belonged together, for in a social state in which men are turned into slaves and exploited to the profit of their master they would do nothing for the defense of the nation; the defensive system that he endorsed therefore required political support: "At this point I believe that the political constitution of the government must assist the defensive system so that it may be rendered efficient" (Say 1828–30: V: 189).

He then laid emphasis upon the advantages of using militias in a defensive system. First, there is great economic benefit, since militias are far less costly than a standing army; second, they are politically much less dangerous, since it is imprudent to place large armies in the hands of a malevolent ruler – here it is clear that Say has in mind Bonaparte's political and military strategy (Say 1828–30: V: 201–202). In a footnote, Say added a technical comment concerning the relative strength of defensive and aggressive strategies. Here he refers to the first application of a new source of energy to military weapons, with the first attempts to build steam-powered artillery:

> Scientific progress seems to advance in favor of the defensive system. If, for example, it is possible to use steam-powered artillery, thanks to which guns can fire hundreds of projectiles in a few minutes, then this will be introduced in fortresses rather than in mobile armies.
>
> (Say 1828–30: V: 203n2)[10]

Say lastly considered the navy. He largely associated navies with the colonial policy of European nations, a policy that he vigorously condemned as a valueless inheritance of the "jealousy of trade" that had been nurtured by the mercantile system (Steiner 1996). In his view, there was no need to keep West Indian colonies under the rule of metropolitan countries since, once again, the costs of such a policy exceeds the gains. Moreover, Say did not consider it to be the duty of a government to protect merchants wherever they might choose to develop commercial enterprise; merchants should be sufficiently prudent to assess the risk they were willing to take, and accept it if they thought it profitable to do so (Say 1828–30: V: 209–201).

## 2 *Constant, peace, and the liberty of the Moderns*

Benjamin Constant also devoted attention to the issue of war within modern society. The shadow of Bonaparte looms over his considerations on war and what a policy of aggression in 19th-century Europe might bring. Say was in personal contact with members of the Coppet group (Steiner 2003), notably Jean-Charles-Léonard Simonde de Sismondi and Constant himself. When in 1819 Constant delivered his famous lecture they both were lecturing at the Athénée Royal in Paris. It is likely that, beyond important differences in their views regarding the role of passions, religion, and politics (Faccarello and Steiner 2008), there was some mutual influence regarding their understanding of the complex nexus between war, economy, and politics in an industrial society. There are many parallel statements in their writings during this period. Both agreed that the development of market exchange and industry had brought about important changes; both claimed that war was unsuited to the behavior, way of life and expectations of individuals living in an industrial society.

There are two sides to Constant's writings: on economic matters he follows Say, while on politics he differs significantly, the second part of his pamphlet on conquest and usurpation examining the form of tyranny that a military ruler would produce (Holmes 1984: chap. 8). These two aspects of his thinking on war and the social-economic conditions of industrialism are closely connected, thanks to a bold claim that industry and war are broadly similar: "War and commerce are nothing but two different means of achieving the same goal, possessing what one's wishes" (Constant 1814: 993).

Constant had read Say's *Traité*, and quoted him on several occasions. Even if he was still thinking in terms of a Smithian commercial society, he based a significant part of his argument in favor of a peaceful industrial order on the idea that the cost of a war exceeded the benefits that a victorious nation could gain (Constant 1814: 994, 1005). Equally important was the fact that he accepted the idea that warfare was no longer suited to normal life in an industrial society, where people expect to be able enjoy the benefits of leisure, affluence and industry (Constant 1814: 994).

Constant added the consequences of war and the impact of a standing army on the morality of a nation to his considerations. He believed that the search for glory was at odds with the quiet passions of an industrial society, in which self-interest was the common motivation for action; he also argued that morality would be jeopardized, since, in an industrial society, men would not go to war unless they were misled by government (Constant 1814: 1004). However, Constant parted from Say in claiming that beyond a rational behavior oriented to the production of goods and utilities, passions are a necessary part of social life, including the social life of an industrial society. A passion for military glory may exist and be cultivated, as happened with Bonaparte, even if such passion is contrary to the normal functioning of industrial society. He also parted from Say on the question of a standing army: he regarded a standing army as necessary for the defense of the nation, whatever the dangers that it may represent for the liberty of the citizen (Constant 1814: 1001–1003). Consequently, national debt is a necessary evil (Constant 1815: 1204ff).

On the political front, the most important element is the distinction between ancient and modern forms of liberty, civil liberty or *independence* (Constant 1814:

1044; 1819: 495, 506). Independence is the natural corollary of the formation of a commercial-industrial society – Constant's famous lecture was organized around this thesis. This entails the creation of representative government, providing a form of political liberty that can be reduced to the ability to vote when called upon to do so. However, while the issue of independence is connected to commerce and war, it is also important to see its strong connection with the growth of a market society, something that Say had well understood from his reading of Smith's *Wealth of Nations.* In the first edition of his *Traité,* after a series of chapters on the distribution of wealth, Say had added a chapter of three pages under the title "Concerning the independence that industrial incomes provide for modern people" (Say 1803: II: 262–264). In these few pages he made clear that present society was founded upon market independence in the sense that any industrial man, even if deprived of landed property or capital, enjoyed an independence originating in an absence of dependence upon a few wealthy customers; instead he sold the produce of his industry to a large number of small customers. While some of these small customers might individually cease buying his goods and services, they were not in a position to control his industrial decisions. Furthermore, according to Say, this independence was beyond the reach of government; this was demonstrated by the example of a conqueror who might be able to change a government and require the payment of tribute, but who could not change the way in which an industrial-cum-market exchange economy functioned.

Constant suggested that the extra free time enjoyed by Moderns, given their limited personal commitment to their political liberty, was the necessary basis of their industrial activity. However, Constant was afraid that individuals content with their independence could easily lose their political liberty, relying on the despot leaving their civil liberty untouched: "The danger with the liberty of the Moderns is that we relinquish too easily our right to participate in political power, once enjoying the benefits of our civil independence, and pursuing our personal interest" (Constant 1819: 512–513).

Constant thus suggested that it was necessary to connect civil with political liberty, the latter being necessary for the full development of the former because it was the source of morality: "our destiny is not only happiness, but improvement; and political liberty is the most powerful, the most energetic engine for improvement that Heaven gave us" (Constant 1819: 513). Furthermore, political liberty was also important, since through voting and a minimal commitment to political affairs citizens could express their views on political decision-making voting for their representatives when the government budget was at issue. The cost of war had become so large that government must necessarily rely on public loans, and thus a commercial society "not only enfranchises individuals, but with the creation of credit makes the government dependent" (Constant 1819: 511).

Constant and Say were pointing to changes that provided citizens with the prospect of controlling government through economic functions; hence issues such as taxes, public loans, public credit, and public debt became central to the development of civil liberty and its connection with political liberty. This was a crucial condition for avoiding the perils of war. But, contrary to their expectations, the development of capital markets and related financial institutions significantly changed the rules of the game and the possibility of controlling government through voting on the budget.

## 3 Government spending, parliaments, and international finance

Say would have concurred with Constant on the dangers associated with a lack of interest in public affairs justified in terms of the pursuit of individual interests.[11] He was also convinced that citizens could control government through voting on the budget. Initially, the chief purpose was to explain that public credit meant trust—trust that the government would repay money borrowed from lenders willing to subscribe to bonds (public debt). In these circumstances, trust was founded upon the close interest that capitalists took in government economic policy, notably with regard to taxes; how reliable might the government's machinery of taxation be in raising sufficient funds. Hence the issue of trust boiled down to the level of political trust between citizens and government, and this was crucial in getting the budget accepted by parliament. Say was adamant on this point, which was directly connected to his claim concerning the growth of an enlightened public thanks to the diffusion of political economy:

> What has above all contributed to the progress of political economy during the last twenty-five years is the grave circumstances that enveloped the civilized world. Government spending increased to a scandalous level [. . .]. Enormous taxes, levied upon nations under more or less specious pretexts, being insufficient, a resort to credit became necessary; to raise credit it became necessary to reveal resources and needs; and the public revelation of the state's accounts, the need to justify in the eyes of the public the workings of the administration, have induced a moral revolution in politics whose course cannot be checked.
>
> (Say 2006: 44–46)

This key link between politics and economy was added in the third edition of the *Traité* – it is likely that Say, always cautious in this domain, would have been reluctant to make such a claim before the definitive dismissal of Bonaparte, a ruler whom he despised – and the addition was retained until the final edition. However, the study of political economy led him to the discovery of a new and powerful source of difficulty in making government dependent on its citizens. Up until the fourth edition in 1819 the chapter devoted to public credit mentioned the utility of financial markets and financial techniques for dealing with the enormous costs of war (Say 2006: 1048). In 1825, in the last edition of his *Traité*, Say extensively rewrote the chapter devoted to public credit, and added some new points regarding the danger that the development of international finance represented.

The development of modern financial techniques radically altered the relationship between government, public credit, and the funding of additional public expenditure.[12] From the end of the Napoleonic wars government finance no longer relied on the usual techniques, where a loan was publicly offered and capitalists either bought bonds or ignored the offering, depending on the degree of trust between public and government. Instead governments offered the loan to a company of financiers who then sold by piece what they had bought in bulk (Say 2006: 1058). Say had no objection to this development of the market system; as long as the capital needed was really useful to the nation such a financial system was sound enough, since active competition between capitalists could reduce the cost of the loan. However, this way of raising loans might prove costly for a government, and consequently for citizens, because a lack of trust could be balanced by a significant discount offered to financiers – paying only a given percentage of the bond's face value – when it was thought that selling public bonds on an open market would be too difficult. The most important point here is political, since the intermediation of a company of financiers weakens the connection between government and citizens: the bonds were sold on various European financial markets without there being any need to obtain political approval from citizens. Foreign capitalists did not care about the well-being of the borrowing nation; they did not inquire about who was right and who was wrong in a military dispute; they just considered their profit[13]:

> In the quarrels between nations, justice is often in a weak position. Anybody who is not the strongest party must have reason on his side. This is not the point that matters for the people moved by their pecuniary interest; they follow the party that pays the most [. . .] They do not examine whether the government respects the right of the nations or not, whether it acts against the established state of enlightened thinking, if it seek to plunge the nation back into ignorance, superstition and disorders that characterized without exception previous centuries; but they examine whether the government has obliging legislators able to endorse the taxes, and well-disciplined soldiers able to make the people pay those taxes.
>
> (Say 2006: 1060)

With the development of the financial European markets, Say discovered that governments can evade the political constraints associated with need for national representatives to vote on the budget. And this could in turn provide them with the resources needed to stimulate the more nationalistic tendencies of an industrial society.

The last volume of Say's *Cours complet* followed on with two chapters on the issue of public loans, and one on the manner in which this new financial technique had harmful political consequences, by providing financial resources to bad governments.[14] Say added a new chapter arguing against speculation on futures markets, stating that such speculation amounted to no more than placing bets, producing nothing of use for the nation. Hence the connection between war, politics, and political economy became much more complicated, the development of a market structure in industrial society undermining the peaceful but frail political basis of the social state.

## 4 Comte: the "Military Spirit" vs. the "Commercial Spirit"

During the 1830s and 1840s the peaceful industrial thesis was reassessed by Auguste Comte, who further elaborated an idea that he had initially put forward in the late 1810s during his early intellectual association with Henri Saint-Simon, and when he was personally connected with the liberal thinkers, notably Say.[15]

In his long lecture on the revolutionary crisis and the decline of the "military regime and spirit", together with the "theological system" (Comte 1830–42: II: 614ff), Comte emphasized the peaceful credo at the heart of his philosophy of history. After the 16th century, when "war was unswervingly considered the main aim of governments" (Comte 1830–42: II: 517), the colonial expansion of European countries – something that Comte denounced on account of the associated institution of slavery – produced a long series of war. Wars became commercial wars, an endpoint in the transformation of military spirit since "the bellicose spirit, in order to provide itself with permanent activity, subordinates itself to the industrial spirit" (Comte 1830–42: II: 523), offering the prospect of new world of use to the development of industry. In its final phase the withering away of war was owed to three causes: first, the irrevocable disrepute into which the military caste fell following the *levée en masse* (mass army) of the French Revolution, where it had become apparent that, after a short period of training, civilians could outdo professionals when the defense of the nation was at stake; second, the end of the commercial wars; and finally, the way of life of industrial populations (Comte 1830–42: II: 614–616). A standing army is increasingly limited to the maintenance of public order in a period disturbed by the last sparks of the revolutionary spirit which prevented European societies finding their social equilibrium.

This way of thinking matches that of Say and Constant in the 1810s and 1820s, with one important caveat, since Comte believed that industrial society was not the end of history. There was, according to his philosophy, an impending future in positive society. In his next important work – *Système de politique positive* (Comte 1851–4) – he sought to outline this social state by invoking an economy of altruism contrasted with that of market transactions. In line with Constant's argument about the common properties of war and commerce, Comte explained that there were four different ways of gaining access to resources: through war, gift-giving, market exchange, and inheritance. He presented these as four different forms of resource transfer, as summarized in Table 4.1.

He argued that fully peaceful economic activity should function in such a way that market exchange would have little impact on the functioning of positive society. Here Comte came back to his positive remarks on the division of labor, identified in the *Cours* as the great discovery of modern economists. He explained that voluntary transmission was instrumental in the accumulation of

*Table 4.1* Resource transfer according to Comte (1851–4, II: 155)

| Forms of transfer | Disinterested | Interested |
|---|---|---|
| Violent | **Inheritance** | **War** |
| Voluntary | **Gift-Giving** | **Exchange** |

capital, and therefore important to the division of labor which made "each active citizen to work for others" (Comte 1851–4: II: 159). This collective dimension of economic activity, exemplified by the division of labor, became the central tenet of Comte's approach to altruism in industrial society. He suggested that the division of labor be considered at both a given point in time, and as something that occurred through the succession of generations (Comte 1851–4: II: 405). Hence the importance attributed to the law governing bequests as a gratuitous form of transmission that was as important as gift-giving in realizing the idea of altruism. Comte asked why, if such solidarity objectively existed, present citizens were unable to understand what they actually did, and why they conceived their exchanges and the division of labor in terms of self-interest. This discrepancy arose from "modern anarchy" – a general term pointing to the lack of any regulatory apparatus in the economic domain, and the spread of an individualistic way of thinking. The issue of altruism was thus bound up with the critique of the importance given to market exchanges. Nevertheless, in the *Système* Comte sought to explain how disinterested behavior was at work within industrial society, even in its present unsatisfactory and incomplete form.[16]

Hence by the middle of the 19th century, the initial ideas developed by the industrialists were significantly modified; a peaceful social state was no longer based on commerce and the spread of market exchange, but on the purposeful limitation of the impact of the latter on the former. To be really peaceful, the industrial social state should severely restrict market exchange, and open the door to a new motivation for action, altruism.

## Conclusion

Say, Constant, and Comte elaborated responses to debate that had continued throughout the 17th and 18th centuries over the relationship between commerce and politics (Hont 2005), going beyond the benefit the government of a nation might obtain from the development of a market system (Foucault 1978): Does commerce, and more generally economic activity, bring peace, because market exchanges are based on reciprocity? Or does it bring "jealousy of trade", according to the well-known essay from David Hume? Does international commerce between nations bring general peace and prosperity, or does it represent a new form of imperialism – so-called free trade imperialism – to the benefit of the leading economic nation (England at that time)? Does it imply the subordination of other nations, those who try to follow the path of the leader, compelling them to prohibit free trade in order to build their own industries and foster their competitive strength? This issue is a complex one, as Istvan Hont has superbly demonstrated; but it is all the more complex because it is intertwined with the dramatic changes in the European and international politics associated with the American and then the French Revolutions, followed by the European wars between 1791 and 1815.

According to the theoreticians of the industrial social order, peace is the natural outcome of the new economic life, provided that the political constitution of the nation gives to an enlightened public the possibility of regulating the activity of government through voting on taxes and the management of public credit. Industrial activity directed towards the maximization of the utility produced, together with welfare as a generalized social goal, would induce enlightened citizens to rein in the jealousy of trade that politicians and inconsistent entrepreneurs were inclined to promote as a form of national economic policy. Hence peace should be considered to be the future of industrial society. There were still important differences between the industrialist thinkers: should market forces be the backbone of economic cooperation and reciprocity, or should it be the "noble art" of gift-giving, as Comte suggested? But, for now, peace seemed to be within reach.

There is therefore a striking contrast between the views of the theoretician of military strategy and the industrialist thinkers. If they both understood that dramatic changes had occurred in the relation of politics and war, they differed on the nature of these changes. Industrialists stressed the peaceful elements of economic activity, where individuals are both consumers and producers looking for cheap products and efficient systems for mass production, and also enlightened citizens eager to regulate their governments by parliamentary decision on the budget and the amount of public loans. Clausewitz on the other hand stressed the new role given to people ready to fight for their mother country, for the nation, opening the road to a new period of large-scale wars. For the industrialists, the decades to come would convey all the advantage attached to interested behavior – or non-interested in the case of Comte – oriented towards the pleasures of a comfortable life; for the theoretician of war, the time was ripe for the politics of the nation, with its new form of "jealousy", in which people would enthusiastically abandon their industrial and commercial activity and lend war its absolute form of violence.

## Notes

1  Raymond Aron's interpretation of Clausewitz's work has emphasized the importance of this distinction (Aron 1976).
2  On the general connection between war and economy, see Christian Schmidt's book (Schmidt 1991). Nevertheless, his approach is still somewhat economistic, in the sense that he limits himself to a game theoretic approach – cooperative *and* non-cooperative games – to politics.
3  This was one of the criticisms raised by Eric Ludendorff, the former German chief of the general staff, in his book on total war (Ludendorff 1935: Introduction and chap. 3).

4 Say mentioned the episode in some papers written when he was one of the editors of the *Décade philosophique et littéraire* – see notably *La Decade*, "Histoire: compte rendu Campagne du duc de Brunschwick", 10 Prairial an III, n°40: 410, and Germinal an IV, n°20: 93.

5 In these writings Say identified "vanity" as the motivation to action by warmongers. According to him, self-interested behavior is prosocial in the sense that the interest of both parties can be satisfied through pacific exchange, whereas vanity implies that one's interest is satisfied because others are deprived of their due.

6 Say was so relieved by the fall of Bonaparte that he wrote an unusual eulogy to the Russian emperor Alexander I on the opening pages of the second edition (Say 2006: I: xcv).

7 Jean-Joseph Tarayre was a Republican who volunteered during the Revolutionary wars and then participated to the Napoleonic wars, ending up as a low-ranking general (*général de brigade*). After the re-establishment of the French monarchy he became a liberal member of Parliament. Jacques Antoine-Hyppolite, comte de Guibert, was a major French military thinker in the later 18th century who wrote *Essai général de tactique*, London, 1772 – on Guibert, see Edward Mead Earle (1944: chap. 3), Raymond Aron (1976: note xii); and also Christian Schmidt (1990) on his economic thinking.

8 Chapter 18: "State expenditure for its defense"; chap. 19: "On the aggressive and the defensive system"; chap. 20 "On the defense of a state by a militia"; chap. 21: "Expenditure on the navy". These chapters belong to the part devoted to consumption, as was already the case in the *Traité*.

9 "A nation must stake the triumph of its vanity in the well-being that it enjoys, and not in the humiliation of rival vanities. And, step by step, the progress of political economy will mitigate the influence of national rivalries and those mistakes into which one may fall when national interests are at stake" (Say 1828–30: V: 178). "When nations become more enlightened a court arises for judging the weak and the strong, nobody being able to ignore its judgment. It is public opinion" (Say 1828–30: V: 179).

10 This footnote is certainly written with recent advances in steam-powered weaponry in mind. In 1814 François de Chasseloup-Laubat, a French officer, experimented with a device in which six guns could fire 900 rounds in a few minutes; 10 years later, Jacob Perkins, an American engineer, built a weapon firing 800 hundred rounds per minute that was publicly exhibited at Greenwich. Contemporary armies did not adopt them; however, by the end of the 19th century machine guns (and barbed wire) would strongly advantage the defense, as was demonstrated in the lethal battles of WWI, notably in 1914 and 1915.

11 In the manuscript of his *Politique pratique*, Say wrote a couple of passages under the following heading: "How the neglect of public affairs would affect individuals" (Say 2003: 648–649).

12 Say quoted Dufrêne de Saint Léon's recent book on public finance, *Etudes du credit public et des dettes publiques*, Paris, 1824.

13 In this case, Say did not understand that self-interested financial capitalists could regulate governments' war policies in providing or not providing the funds necessary to their bellicose views. Later on, Karl Polanyi suggested that, from 1815 to 1914, the long peace that European countries enjoyed was, in the beginning, due to the "Holly alliance" and, then, after the revolutionary period of the 1840s, due to the financial community that did not want to see its money interests jeopardized by a general European war (Polanyi 1944: chap. 1). Henceforth, until the formation of two opposite sets of alliance (England, France and Russia, on the one hand, Germany, the Austrian empire and Italy on the other) there were only limited wars in Europe from 1815 to WWI. In the middle of the 19th century,

Pierre-Joseph Proudhon was aware of the strength of the financial interest, as shown in his essay on the Parisian Stock Exchange (Proudhon 1857: 25, 163–164, 460ff), but the goal of the book was to critique this situation and not to understand its peaceful effects.

14  "These kinds of loans are disastrous for the interests of nations, since governments that are not led by a high morality are rendered indifferent to the price paid for the capital they need to advance their intentions" (Say, 1828–30: VI: 162).

15  Saint-Simon was personally connected with Say and Constant (Gouhier 1964: II: 32), and so was his secretaries (Augustin Thierry and then Comte) as testified by Comte in two letters to John Stuart Mill (Levy Bruhl 1899: 338, 382). However, these industrialist thinkers split in the 1820s.

16  While a follower of some of his main ideas, Herbert Spencer retained the liberal view of the opposition between the "military" and the "industrial" systems. This is particularly obvious in volume III of his *Principles of Sociology* (Spencer 1896). Furthermore, he rejected Comte's interpretation of altruism in his *Data of Ethics*.

# References

Aron, R. (1976). *Penser la guerre, Clausewitz. L'âge européen*, Paris: Gallimard.

Clausewitz, C. von (1825–8) [1976]. *Note sur la Prusse dans sa grande catastrophe de 1806*, French translation, Paris: Champ Libre.

Clausewitz, C. von (1832–4) [1955]. *De la guerre*, French translation, Paris: Minuit.

Comte, A. 1837–1842 [1975]. *Cours de philosophie positive*, Paris: Herman.

Comte, A. 1851–1854 [1890]. *Système de politique positive, ou Traité de sociologie instituant la religion de l'Humanité*, Paris: Larousse.

Constant, B. 1814 [1957]. "De l'esprit de conquête et de l'usurpation dans leurs rapports avec la civilisation européenne," in B. Constant (Ed.), *Œuvres*, Paris: Gallimard.

Constant, B. 1815 [1957]. "Principes de politique," in B. Constant (Ed.), *Œuvres*, Paris: Gallimard.

Constant, B. 1819 [1980]. "De la liberté des Anciens comparée à celle des Modernes," in B. Constant (Ed.), *De la liberté chez les Modernes*, Paris: Hachette, 491–515.

Dufresne de Saint Léon, Louis-César-Alexandre (1824). *Etudes du crédit public et des dettes publiques*, Paris: Bossange.

Earle, E. M. (1944). *Makers of Modern Strategy: Military Thought From Machiavelli to Hitler*, Princeton: Princeton University Press.

Faccarello, G. and Steiner, P. (2008). "Religion and Political Economy in Early 19th Century France," *History of Political Economy*, 40(Annual Supplement): 27–61.

Foucault, M. (1978 [2004]). *Sécurité, territoire, population: cours au Collège de France*, Paris: Gallimard-Seuil.

Gouhier, H. (1964). *La jeunesse d'Auguste Comte et la formation du positivisme*, second edition, Paris: Vrin.

Holmes, S. 1984 [1994]. *Benjamin Constant et la genèse du libéralisme moderne*, French translation, Paris: Presses universitaires de France.

Hont, I. (2005). *Jealousy of Trade: International Competition and the Nation-State in Historical Perspective*, Cambridge, MA: Harvard University Press.

Levy-Bruhl, L. (Ed.) (1899). *Lettres inédites de John Stuart Mill à Auguste Comte publiées avec les réponses de Comte*, Paris: Félix Alcan.

Ludendorff, E. (1935 [1936]). *La guerre totale*, French translation, Paris: Flammarion.

Polanyi, K. (1944 [2002]). *The Great Transformation. The Political and Economic Origins of Our Time*, Boston, MA: The Beacon Press.

Proudhon, P-J. (1857). *Manuel du spéculateur à la Bourse*, fourth edition, Paris: Garnier frères.

Say, J-B. (1803). *Traité d'économie politique ou simple exposition de la manière dont se forment, se distribuent, et se consomment les richesses*, first edition, Paris: Déterville.

Say, J-B. (1817). *Petit volume contenant quelques aperçus des hommes et de la société*, Paris: Déterville.

Say, J-B. (1828–1830). *Cours complet d'économie politique pratique*, Paris: Rapilly.

Say, J-B. (2003). "De la politique pratique," in J.-B. Say (Ed.), *Œuvres morales et politiques, Œuvres complètes de Jean-Baptiste Say*, vol. V, Paris: Economica.

Say, J-B. (2006). *Traité d'économie politique ou simple exposition de la manière dont se forment, se distribuent, et se consomment les richesses, variorum edition, Œuvres complètes de Jean-Baptiste Say*, vol. I, Paris: Economica.

Schmidt, C. (1990). "L'économie de la force publique selon Guibert", in G. Faccarello and P. Steiner (Eds.), *La pensée économique pendant la Révolution française*, Grenoble: Presses universitaires de Grenoble, 323–335

Schmidt, C. (1991). *Penser la guerre, penser l'économie*, Paris: Odile Jacob.

Spencer, H. (1896). *The Principles of Sociology*, vol. III, London: William and Norgate.

Steiner, P. (1996). "Jean-Baptiste Say et les colonies ou comment se débarrasser d'un héritage intempestif?" *Cahiers d'économie politique*, 27–28: 153–173.

Steiner, P. (1998). "The Structure of Say's Economic Writings," *European Journal of the History of Economic Thought*, 5(2): 227–249.

Steiner, P. (2003a). "Say, les Idéologues et le Groupe de Coppet: la société industrielle comme système politique," *Revue Française d'Histoire des Idées Politiques*, 18(2): 331–361.

Steiner, P. (2003b) "La théorie de la production de Say," in A. Tiran and J.-P. Potier (Eds.), *Jean-Baptiste Say: nouveaux regards sur son œuvre*, Paris: Economica, 325–360.

# 5 Studying economics as war effort

## The first economic treatise in the Ottoman Empire and its militaristic motivations[1]

*Deniz T. Kılınçoğlu*

## 1 Introduction

The introduction of economics as a post-Smithian discipline into the Middle East in the early 19th century was primarily militaristically motivated. The first known treatise of economics in the Ottoman Empire is a manuscript, titled "Risâle-i Tedbîr-i ʿUmrân-ı Mülkî" ("A Treatise on the Administration of the Prosperity of the Country/State"), and it was written exclusively for the Ottoman political-military elite in the mid-1830s. The anonymous author of this 84-page manuscript begins the text with the argument that military technologies and the organization of warfare became more sophisticated and centrally administered in the modern age, and this loaded a heavy burden on state finances. He maintains that the European statesmen and thinkers searched for finding effective methods for administering state finances under these political-military circumstances, and these efforts paved the way for a new scientific discipline called economics. The main objective of the author in his treatise is to introduce this new "science" to the Ottoman political-military elite as an instrument for the administration of an effective war economy, as well as a guide to bring prosperity to the country. The knowledge of economics, the author believes, is essential for any statesman who would like his country to survive and prosper in the economy-centered modern age.

Focusing on the militaristic objectives and content of the first-known example of Ottoman-Turkish economic literature, this article examines the relationship between economics and war in the early 19th-century Ottoman Empire. It also sheds light on the linguistic and cultural dynamics of the transmission of economic ideas into the Ottoman Empire through an investigation of the author's style of translation and adaptation of ideas and concepts from his main European source, namely Jean-Baptiste Say's *Cours complet* (1828–29).

Joseph Spengler, in his classic work on "the international transmission of economic ideas," emphasized "the social processes underlying the transmission of ideas from culture to culture and from nation to nation" (Spengler 1970: 133). This Ottoman manuscript provides us with an excellent case to observe the dynamics of the intercultural transmission of economic ideas, shaped primarily by the relationship between "the content transmitted" and "the milieu of potential receivers," in Spengler's terms (Spengler 1970: 143–149). The author of the manuscript suggests openly that economics should be translated selectively based on the conditions and needs of one's country. He benefits from Jean-Baptiste Say's work in this fashion. Moreover, in addition to localizing the examples that he copies from Say, he gives Islamic touches to certain concepts and arguments. By picking a rather secondary issue in his European source(s) – economics and war – and placing it at the core of his own narrative, he reflects the main concerns of his social milieu and audience, namely the political-military elite of the Ottoman Empire. In dealing with the relationship between economics and war, he even proposes an original thesis suggesting that economics is a product of the military revolution in early-modern Europe. All in all, this early 19th-century Ottoman manuscript is an important text in which we observe the dynamics of innovation as well as adaptation in the process of intercultural transmission of economic ideas.[1]

This study begins with a brief discussion about some basic facts and observations about the manuscript itself. Then it provides a textual analysis to reveal its main arguments and theses, especially regarding the connection between economics and war. The final part before the conclusion places the manuscript in its historical and intellectual context with regard to the military, political, and economic conditions of the Ottoman Empire in the early 19th century, and through comparisons with the main source of the text, Jean-Baptiste Say's *Cours complet*.

## 2 The introduction of economics in the Ottoman Empire and "Tedbîr-i ʿUmrân-ı Mülkî"

In the first half of the 19th century, economic theories and ideas from Europe were transmitted to the Ottoman Empire in a rather unsystematic way, mostly through occasional newspaper articles on the economic conditions and policies of the empire (Kılınçoğlu 2015: 23–25). An economic literature in Ottoman-Turkish began to emerge in the early 1850s with the adaptations of Pellegrino Rossi's (1787–1848) *Cours d'économie politique* (1840), and Jean-Baptiste Say's (1767–1832) *Catéchisme d'économie politique* (1815).[2] The only exception to this is an anonymous and unpublished 84-page manuscript located in the National Library of Austria, titled "Risâle-i Tedbîr-i ʿUmrân-ı Mülkî" ("A Treatise on the Administration of the Prosperity of the Country/State," henceforth *TUM*). It is the earliest known Ottoman study on economics with content and style resembling European examples. It is also, to our best knowledge, the first treatise on this subject penned in the entire Middle East. The manuscript is a clean copy with a vignette and text borders painted in gold on the first two pages, and all main titles written in red ink. All these indicate that it was presented to an Ottoman dignitary or was commissioned by the state. However, neither the records of the Ottoman state archives nor Ottoman economic literature of the following decades mentions this manuscript. Therefore, we do not have any information about the specific readership and the intellectual impact of this work.

As for the audience, the author states the main objective of the work as introducing economics to the Ottoman political-military elite as a useful tool for state administration. As will be discussed in more detail in this chapter, the author explains the importance of this discipline with a discussion on the recent game-changing military technologies and institutions that gave the Europeans an upper hand, and the emergence of this new discipline as a result of European efforts to develop effective methods for financing the new and more costly military system (*TUM*: 1–6). In this respect, this first Ottoman treatise on economics constitutes an illuminating example that reflects the initial motivation for the Ottomans to study economics as a science of state administration, especially in military context.

The title of the manuscript itself provides us with valuable clues about the Ottoman understanding of economics at the time. First, this "distinct science, . . . which is generally named as *économie politique* in European languages," in the author's words (*TUM*: 32v), is rendered into Turkish as a science of "administration." Borrowing the term from the German case, we can see an obvious cameralist *Staatswissenschaft* understanding of the discipline in its early period in the Ottoman Empire. Second, instead of a more literal translation provided earlier, "Tedbîr-i Umrân-ı Mülkî" can also be translated loosely as "the administration of the wealth of (a) nation" with reference to the (symbolically) founding text of the discipline, Adam Smith's *The Wealth of Nations* (1776). Since the word "nation," in modern political sense, had not yet been used in the Ottoman-Turkish language then, the author prefers to use the word "*mülk*" (meaning estate, property, state, country, and so on depending on the context), as an equivalent to both state and country, the latter being an amalgamation of state and society.[3] This usage seems congruent to what Adam Smith also meant by "nation" in *The Wealth of Nations*. A third point about the title is that it reflects an attempt to adapt this new knowledge coming from Europe into the domestic cultural and intellectual setting with the help of traditional Islamic intellectual vocabulary. As will be seen later, the author refers to the ideas of the prominent medieval Muslim philosopher, Ibn Khaldun (1332–1406), in various parts of the text. "Ibn Khaldun uses the terms '*umran*' [prosperity] and '*imar*' [development] to express economic activities and the level of economic development" (Kozak 1999: 1). The author of *TUM* not only employs the former term to render the name of the discipline of economics into Turkish, but he also uses both terms as a pair ("*umran`ü `imaret*" – prosperity and development) to denote economic development in the modern sense (*TUM*: 31–31v). In this respect, he brings Adam Smith and Ibn Khaldun together and produces a preliminary version of "Islamic" economics.

The manuscript is undated. However, there are several indicators showing that it was written in the mid-1830s. First, the author refers to an article from an Ottoman newspaper (*Takvîm-i Vekâyi*) published in February 1833[4] (*TUM*: 31). In reference to Malthus's *An Essay on the Principle of Population*, whose first edition was published in 1798 and its more influential revised second edition in 1803, the author notes that it was published "thirty years ago." Considering that the author mentions a "3-volume" edition of Malthus' work (*TUM*: 31), it is likely that he refers to the 1809 edition in French (Malthus 1809). Finally, the author discusses the necessity of establishing a council of commerce (*"meclis-i ticâret"*) in the Ottoman Empire (*TUM*: 40), which was later put into practice in c. 1839 (Çakır 2000: 368). Therefore, we know that the text belongs to the period of 1833–1839.

The outline of the study hints at an influence of Jean-Baptiste Say's tripartite/ quadripartite structure (namely, separate parts on the production, circulation, distribution, and consumption of wealth), which he developed in the second edition of *Traité d'économie politique* (1814), and then (with some modifications) in the *Cours complet d'économie politique pratique* (1828–29).[5] A close examination of the text reveals that the author benefited from Say's *Cours complet*. For instance, the following passage from *TUM*, along with other examples mentioned later in this article, is an evidence to support this thesis:

> [T]he sand exits naturally and lays under our feet without much value and use. Yet, the manufacturer of glass and bottles takes this abundant sand from its place, mixes it with other materials into a paste, and [eventually] produces the transparent thing called glass, which keeps cold and rain outside and allows sunlight into houses, and other similar valuable objects, with the help of fire and various production processes.[6]
>
> (*TUM*: 6–6v)

In Say's earlier works, such as *Traité d'économie politique* (1803: 1: 10–11), there are in-passing references to turning sand into glass as an example for manufacturing processes. Yet, the idea of turning a "worthless material" like sand into a useful therefore valuable commodity like glass with an explanation of its manufacturing process only exists in *Cours complet* with an obvious resemblance in details to the previous quote:

> Le sable est une matière dépourvue de presque toute valeur. Un verrier en prend, y mêle de la soude, expose ce mélange à un feu violent qui en combine les parties, et en fait une matière homogène, pâteuse, qu'à l'aide de tubes de fer, on souffle en larges bulles. On fend ces bulles, on les étend; on les laisse refroidir graduellement; on les coupe ensuite dans différentes dimensions, et il en résulte ce produit transparent, étendu, qui, sans empêcher la lumière du jour de pénétrer dans nos maisons, ferme l'accès au froid et à la pluie.
>
> (Say 1828: 1: 171–172)

After the sand-glass example, Say refers to the production of straw hat and wool cloth (in different stages from the farmer to the dyer) in the same context (Say 1828: vol. 1: 173–174). We read the same examples in *TUM* following the sand-glass example (*TUM*: 7–7v). The only differences between the two texts are in the specifics. For example, the dyestuff (indigo) in the last stage comes from the East and West Indies in *Cours complet*, whereas in the Ottoman manuscript it is from Edirne and Bursa (two major Ottoman cities) in addition to the Indies.

In the light of this information about the main source of the manuscript, the outline of the *TUM* with corresponding sections (roughly) in *Cours complet* can be presented as in Table 5.1.

As can be seen in the following comparison chart, *TUM* is not a translation (nor a proper adaptation) of *Cours complet* in its entirety. The author benefits from Say's work for the general outline, definitions of basic economic concepts and principles, and certain specific examples. A close reading of the text demonstrates that *TUM* is a noticeably original work (in textual rather than theoretical sense), especially compared to many subsequent examples in Ottoman economic literature.[12] First, the author, throughout the text, chooses his examples for professions, industries, and commodities from the Ottoman economy and everyday life. For instance, in the part on the international circulation of commodities, he gives an example about a ship leaving the harbor of Izmir (Smyrna) full of cotton and silk – two major export items of the Ottoman Empire at the time – for the British market (*TUM*: 22). Besides, he provides economic comparisons of various Ottoman provinces (*TUM*: 33v–34). Second, the author refers to Islamic law (p. 42), and mentions and quotes earlier prominent Muslim scholars, especially Ibn Khaldun (pp. 34v–35, 43). The chapters with most original content, in this respect, are the introduction and the fifth chapter, which include many domestic references and examples. The text also includes comparative arguments regarding the Ottoman economic and political system vis-à-vis European cases with an obvious "we, the Ottomans" tone.

*Table 5.1* The outline of the TUM with corresponding sections in *Cours complet*

| TUM | Cours complet |
| --- | --- |
| 1. Preface | |
| 2. Introduction | |
| 3. Chapter 1: On the definition of wealth and the ways and means of its production[7] | *Première division – De la nature des richesses; Deuxième division – Chap. IV. De ce qu'il faut entendre par la Production des richesses.* (Vol. 1) |
| 4. Chapter 2: On the classification of industries that produce wealth[8] | *Deuxième division – Des opérations productives – Chap. VII – Classification des industries* (Vol. 1) |
| 5. Chapter 3: On various instruments and tools that humans use to produce wealth[9] | *Deuxième division – Chap. VIII – Des instruments généraux de l'industrie et des fonds productifs* (Vol. 1) |
| 6. Chapter 4: On the nature of capital, its use to produce wealth, and its accumulation[10] | *Deuxième division – Chap. X – De la nature et de l'emploi des capitaux; Chap. XIII – De la formation des capitaux* (Vol. 1) |
| 7. Chapter 5: On the meaning of prosperity and development, and the ways and means to achieve them[11] | (Partly) *Sixième partie. Du nombre et de la condition des hommes* (Vol. 4); *Histoire abrégée des progrès de l'économie politique* (Vol. 6) |
| 8. Conclusion | |

Although the author copies examples and arguments from Say, he does not cite his source. Considering the translation culture of the age, this is not surprising. As Evelyn Forget notes in the case of translations of economic texts between English and French in the 18th and 19th centuries, it was an age without "well-specified intellectual property rights" which provided translators with a wide "creative freedom." Dissemination of ideas, rather than remaining loyal to the original source, was the principal concern for translators. (Forget 2010: 655). We observe a similar situation in the case of *TUM*. It is worth noting that conveying and popularizing "useful" ideas, rather than producing loyal translations or making original contributions to economics, was to remain as the primary objective in Ottoman economic literature of the subsequent decades. In *TUM*, and in some later examples,[13] the process of tailoring European texts into the Ottoman socio-cultural and intellectual context blurred the divisive line between original work and translation/adaptation.[14]

## 3  War, state, and economics in *TUM*

*TUM* opens with a rather unusual introductory statement for an economic text:

> After the discovery of gunpowder in recent times and the consequent invention of firearms – which had been unknown in the old days and during the times of old states – and [especially when] their use in wars became common, military methods and the grounds of military victory have changed. [These changes] forced modern states and nations to reshape their domestic policies. This short treatise is about [these changes and especially about] how principles and policies regarding the prosperity of a country have turned into a specific and codified science [as a result].
>
> (*TUM*: 1v)

After this short preface about the importance of economics and the main objective of the text comes the author's introduction, in which he explains these military and consequent political changes at length (*TUM*: 1v–4). Explaining how the invention of firearms altered military organization, techniques, and conscription methods, he concludes that the modern age requires a systematically and continuously drilled standing army equipped with latest-technology arms. In the old military formation, the author maintains, the army was formed by the occasional mobilization of the subjects of the state, whose courage, determination, and muscle power determined the result of wars. Besides, subjects/soldiers joined campaigns with their own weapons when called for, and travelled with their own means. Moreover, during peace times, the state was not responsible for the provisioning of the subjects/soldiers. The modern military system however, the author continues, requires considerable financial resources for continuous provisioning and training of the soldiers during both peace and war times, as well as equipping them with new-technology weaponry and related supplies (such as rifles and cannons and their ammunition, etc.). Besides, producing this new weaponry and their supplies necessitates the establishment of new industries, which also require considerable financial means (*TUM*: 2v–3v).

After four chapters on the main principles and concepts of economics, in which the author does not touch upon military issues, he returns to the issue of the establishment of standing armies in the modern age and how it paved the way for the emergence of the discipline of economics. First, he argues that the prosperity of a country builds on population increase, accompanied by increasing national wealth and production (*TUM*: 27v–32v). In this part, he copies examples from *Cours complet*, such as on the population of France, and comparisons between Holland and Poland in this context (Say 1828: 4: 310–312, 322). Then, he connects this discussion to how the discipline of economics emerged in Europe as a result of inquiries about increasing public prosperity and wealth:

> [I]n recent times, European countries [developed] principles and methods to achieve this goal into an independent science, like other modern sciences. It is called *économie politique* in European languages. It can be translated into Turkish as "administration of civil wealth" [*tedbîr-i mâl-ı medenî*] or "administration of public prosperity" [*tedbîr-i 'umrân-ı mülkî*].
>
> (*TUM*: 32v)

The author continues with a detailed discussion on this matter under a separate section, titled "A Digression":

> That the principles and methods regarding the development of state and country reached into an independent science and a codified art is among the new European developments and methods. It is clear that the states of the bygone era did not know it. Because, during the times of previous states, the use of firearms and the organization of a well-trained standing army did not exist. All subjects of the state, whose age and body were fit for war, constituted the army. In times of both war and peace, the expenditures [by the state] on soldiers and on their equipment did not amount to significant amounts. Therefore, the [central] administration of the prosperity of the state and country focused on the protection of the subjects, borders, and justice in the country. The production of wealth, on the other hand, was left to the care of the citizens themselves.
>
> (*TUM*: 33v–34)

The author goes on to restate that the establishment of a standing army, with its continuously drilled soldiers equipped with sophisticated weaponry, loaded a heavy burden on the treasuries of modern European states. This led Europeans to ponder the methods of increasing state revenues through increasing the production of national wealth. Europeans' studies and discussions on this subject paved the way for new and systematic methods, which proved to be effective in bringing development and prosperity. As a result, the author observes, "the Western states and others that imitate [the former]" gained an apparent superiority vis-à-vis the earlier states in terms of both wealth and military strength (*TUM*: 34v).

In old times, the author argues, the wealth of a state depended primarily on continuous pillage and plunder that came as a result of military conquests and victories. Since the "scientific" principles of modern economics about creating wealth and welfare did not exist then, many states failed to turn military booty into permanent wealth-creating mechanisms. In the new age, he maintains, the power of a state rests on public prosperity and economic development (*TUM*: 34v). Beyond being a historical argument, these words sound like a serious warning to the Ottoman policy-makers of the time. Referring to the organic view of the state, he reminds his readers that "scholars of the past" divided the life cycle of states into three stages: birth and growth, stagnation, and decline (*TUM*: 34v–35). Here, the author seems to be referring primarily to Ibn Khaldun and his well-known theory of history:[15]

> When the time is up, (the end of the dynasty) cannot be put off for a single hour, nor can it be advanced.
>
> In this way, the life span of a dynasty corresponds to the life span of an individual; it grows up and passes into an age of stagnation and thence into regression.
>
> (Ibn Khaldûn 2005: 138)

The author of *TUM* observes that states that relied only on militaristic sources of wealth could not avoid this well-known law of history and eventually decayed. Yet, economics, he claims, provides modern statesmen with practical guidance to circumvent this previously unavoidable law of history by taking measures for long-term development and prosperity. This makes economics an essential topic of study for all statesmen who wish their country and state survive and prosper in the modern age, instead of falling and decaying like earlier examples[16] (*TUM*: 35). In this respect, the author regards modern economics and its systematic application by statesmen as a specific criterion to separate modern states from pre-modern ones. To emphasize the importance of this thesis for his own age, the author suggests a comparison of the "East and West" in this context:

> A short glance at the conditions of the Western and Eastern nations and states provides us with a solid evidence for the strength of this claim. In the old ages, many conquerors, and powerful and legendary rulers appeared from time to time in the Eastern countries like India, Persia, and Bukhara. They conquered and ruled far-away regions and numerous countries. However, in our age, the source of power and greatness of the rulers of the Eastern countries is tied to the condition of their observance of the principles and methods of [economic] development and of increasing the population of the country. [Yet] it is obvious that their lack of efforts [in this direction] and ignorance of this knowledge lead to the decline of their power and

prominence. On the other hand, it is equally clear that Western states and others that follow [the West] obey this rule of the age and already enjoy the fruits of applying the methods and principles of development.

(*TUM*: 35v)

Then the author turns to the history of economics to explain how it was born as a result of the collective effort of European statesmen, intellectuals, and businessmen in the previous century. The European statesmen, he contends, have been looking for new methods to increase national wealth and public prosperity for more than a century. In these explorations, they benefited especially from the "guidance of merchants" who are the most experienced and knowledgeable about the everyday working of the economy.

Finally, eighty years ago, two excellent philosophers, namely Quesnay in France and, his contemporary, British Hume, gathered the theoretical aspects of the principles of the administration of public prosperity, connected [these principles] to the aforementioned science [economics], and organized its methods in specialized volumes.[17] Later, philosophers of rational sciences and theoretical knowledge in France, England, and Italy, followed these studies and devoted their knowledge and investigations to examine the theoretical aspects of the administration of public prosperity, and they dedicated all their time and effort to explain all its principles and branches. . . . The well-known name given to these [people] in all European languages is *économiste*.

(*TUM*: 36–36v)

In this part, the author benefits from the chapters on the history of economics in Volume 6 of *Cours complet*. Jean-Baptiste Say states here that after earlier and rather unsystematic efforts to explain economic phenomena, economics as a discipline began to take shape around the mid-18th century. Say mentions the works of Quesnay, Hume, and Smith as the landmarks of this progress; and especially the work of Quesnay, he notes, proclaimed the birth of this new "order of ideas" (Say 1828: 6: 380–381). As was seen earlier, the author of *TUM* follows suit and refers to the works of Quesnay and Hume as the founding texts of the discipline. Interestingly enough, however, he does not mention Smith at all, neither in this part nor in the rest of the text. It is also worth noting that the author never mentions Say's name either. Instead, he refers to Say by noting, "one of the famous French writers states" when he uses an example from *Cours complet* (*TUM*: 8). It is a mystery why the author never cites Smith and Say openly, whereas he mentions the names of Quesnay, Hume, and Malthus in relevant parts.

As for the development of economic literature, the author continues,

In [these] eighty years, and especially in the last forty-fifty years when this science reached maturity, countless books and treatises were written and published in the languages of England, France, and Italy. In fact, a recent publication from 1829 [or 1830][18] registers 2376 volumes, only in French, published between 1815 and 1824, on the theory and practice of this science and its branches such as [works on] agriculture and industry.[19]

(*TUM*: 36v)

The author does not cite his source for this specific information. The source he mentions seems to be published around the same years as *Cours complet*, but it does not include such an account of books on economics. Therefore, for this specific information, he might have benefited from a catalogue of books published in France or another work on economics and economic literature.

Having emphasized the extent of economic literature in European languages, the author goes on to compare it with the situation in classical languages, and he finishes the chapter with a note on his own contribution in this regard:

> In short, methods and principles of [economic] development emerged from the law of [our] age . . . There is no trace of [this science] in prominent ancient languages like Arabic, Persian, Greek, and Latin, which were . . . rich in knowledge in terms of various arts and sciences. [Economic knowledge] exists only in European languages in this age, and the objective of this short treatise is to explain this science to the honorable gentlemen [i.e. the Ottoman military-political elite] who are not familiar with any of these languages.
>
> (*TUM*: 37)

The author acknowledges that his short manuscript can only serve as a brief introduction to the "ocean of knowledge" provided by this discipline (*TUM*: 37).

In his conclusion, he puts forward his practical suggestions on how to bring the knowledge of economics into the Ottoman Empire through translations and especially through original treatises in Turkish, written according to the specific conditions of the empire.

> One way to do this is translating and studying the best examples of this science . . . and putting its applied principles into action. Yet, the difficulties and handicaps of achieving the goal through this way are obvious.
>
> (*TUM*: 38)

First of all, the author suggests, European economists built their ideas on the economic conditions of their own countries. Therefore, a great portion of their ideas and explanations are irrelevant to the level of economic development in the Ottoman Empire, thereby practically useless for the Ottomans (*TUM*: 38v). Second, the author continues, translation of this science into Turkish cannot be done properly only with some knowledge of European languages. It requires "translators who have spent a long time studying the books on this science." However, he notes, such translators do not yet exist in the empire (*TUM*: 38v–39). His solution builds on his observations on the emergence of economics in European countries. He suggests that the best way to achieve useful economic knowledge for the Ottoman Empire is to establish a "council of commerce" that would coordinate the efforts of statesmen and merchants towards this goal. Merchants, according to the author, are experienced and knowledgeable not only in the trade of commodities, but also in the production processes of the goods that they deal with. He believes that especially the merchants of Istanbul, the capital and the commercial hub of the empire, are always up to date about the economic conditions in many parts of the empire thanks to their agents and partners in other commercial centers and ports (*TUM*: 40v). Therefore, they have the practical knowledge of how the Ottoman economy works and how it can be developed through certain measures in commerce, agriculture, and industry.

In addition to the merchants, the author suggests, the council should include people who have studied European economic literature and the methods and practices that European governments have put into action to bring about economic development in their countries. These people should only be the most knowledgeable ones on these matters, regardless of their religious and even citizenship affiliations (*TUM*: 42v). The author, thereby, offers a pragmatic and meritocratic approach to choosing members of such a council, implying that non-Muslim subjects of the empire and even Europeans should be welcome to serve the Ottoman Empire in this matter, provided that they are the most qualified people for this task.

The author is confident that if such a council is established, the Ottoman Empire, "within twenty years," can reach the level of economic prosperity and welfare of the European nations that they have achieved in two hundred years (*TUM*: 42v–43). As noted earlier, a council of commerce was established in the empire in 1839. However, it did not live up to his expectations regarding the development of economic knowledge in the Ottoman Empire. Moreover, the next "twenty years" after the establishment of this council did not bring about the economic development in the Ottoman Empire as he wished for.

## 4   *TUM* in historical and intellectual context

The main objective of *TUM* and its arguments regarding the establishment of a modern standing army resonate with the political-military historical context in which it was penned. The late 1820s and especially the 1830s were the heyday of Ottoman military reform. The reform process in the Ottoman army started in the early 1790s, during the reign of the reformist sultan, Selim III (r. 1789–1807), as part of his French Revolution-inspired comprehensive reform program in the empire, known as the *Nizam-ı Cedid* (the New Order). The sultan and his retinue were aware that the Ottoman army had long lost its military strength vis-à-vis its European rivals, which had brought a series of humiliating defeats with their fiscal and political consequences. Especially the Russo-Ottoman wars of 1768–92 revealed the ineffectiveness of the Ottoman military system. As a result, establishing a modern army trained by European experts and equipped with the latest European technologies constituted the backbone of this project.[20] At the core of the military reform was to replace the traditional central infantry units, the Janissaries, with well-trained, well-equipped, and disciplined units. Realizing this existential threat, the Janissaries resisted the change with their considerable military and political power. The Janissary resistance culminated in a rebellion in 1807 which cost the sultan not only his throne, but his life.

The resistance from the Janissaries decelerated the military reform in the empire and preserved their political-military power until 1826. The idea of replacing the Janissaries with modern units, however, remained vital in the minds of Ottoman reformers of the age. Also a reform-minded ruler, Sultan Mahmud II (r. 1808–1839), who followed Selim III's footsteps, decided to solve the problem once and for all, and at all costs. The so-called Auspicious Incident of 15 June 1826 wiped off the ages-old institution with a merciless massacre of the Janissaries through artillery fire as well as individual executions. The downfall of the Janissaries reinvigorated the military reform project in the empire. Mahmud II reinstituted the project of building a modern standing army with its educational and industrial branches. His reform project was a comprehensive one similar to Selim III's *Nizam-ı Cedid*, yet the military reform was at its core. The new army grew from 12,000 troops to 160,000 between 1827 and 1837 (Yıldız 2009: 475). In addition to its various costs from the ordnance to the new barracks, "Salaries for the officer corps and related staffs grew tremendously in an era of great fiscal crisis" (Aksan 2013: 376). All in all, "Ottoman military reforms of [the late eighteenth and early nineteenth period] are invariably accompanied by treasury reform and an acute shortage of cash" (Aksan 2013: 72). The author of *TUM* penned his treatise under these military-political and fiscal conditions, not only to provide intellectual support and legitimacy to the ongoing military reform, but also to present economics as a scientific guide to deal with the fiscal difficulties of the process.

It should be noted that military-related fiscal difficulties of the Ottoman central government did not start at the dawn of the 19th century. On the contrary, the sophistication of military technologies and strategies, especially after the integration of firearms, placed considerable burden on the Ottoman fiscal system starting as early as the late 15th century. In this respect, the author's narrative is open to misinterpretation as it implies all these changes in military technologies with their financial dimensions occurred in Western Europe, leaving non-Europeans (including the Ottomans) behind with their obsolete military methods and technologies. For example, regarding the author's argument that courage and muscle power alone determined the results of wars in the past, we must note that this does not apply to most of Ottoman military history. As early as the mid-15th century, the Ottomans had a well-equipped and salaried standing army, which preceded many of its European counterparts, with thousands of soldiers equipped with the latest-technology firearms.

The Ottomans adopted hand firearms in the late 14th century, and their use increased gradually in the following decades. According to a contemporaneous German source, during the Ottoman campaign to conquer Vienna in 1532, "of 10,000 Janissaries present in the campaign some 9,000 were equipped with handguns, whereas the remaining 1,000 had only pole-arms" (Ágoston 2004: 24).

During the same time period, the artillery corps and gun carriage units became integral parts of the standing army, the costs of which were covered by the central state. As a well-known evidence for the effectiveness of these units, heavy and light artillery units played the decisive role in the Ottoman conquest of Istanbul in 1453 (Ágoston 2004: 1). According to the estimates of Gábor Ágoston, the artillery corps and supporting units (such as artillery carriers) employed 1,171 soldiers in 1514, and the number reached as high as 15,307 by the end of the next century (Ágoston 2004: 30). Until the 18th century, the Ottoman artillery remained superior to or on par with that of many of its major rivals like Austria and Russia.

The growth of such a technologically well-equipped and regularly drilled military force added a growing burden on the Ottoman fiscal system. As the Ottoman army and its weapons developed, its costs led to chronic budget deficits. The state had to have recourse to popularly unfavorable domestic fiscal measures such as debasement and increased taxation, in addition to the growing scope of tax-farming practices. While such measures paved the way for various social and political upheavals starting from the 16th century, they did not solve military-related fiscal deficits permanently. In the meantime, the Ottoman army began to lose its edge to its European rivals, which became obvious especially in the 18th century. Despite the significant expansion of the number (and thereby the fiscal burden) of the Janissaries, the effectiveness of the Ottoman army went down gradually due to the declining level of training and discipline. Moreover, as the wars got longer and ended in more defeats than victories, the military-induced fiscal crisis turned into a vicious circle. Longer and unsuccessful campaigns drained fiscal resources, and the fiscal weakness undermined the military power (Genç 2000: 27–28; Cezar 1986: 71–73). As a result, in the 17th and especially 18th centuries, growing fiscal problems of the central government became a major concern for the Ottoman statesmen (Aksan 2013: 72–75, 184–185).

A radical and comprehensive military reform and its fiscal prerequisites occupied a central place in Ottoman political literature of the late 18th and early 19th centuries (Aksan 1993). The misleading narrative of the "old ages" in *TUM* reflects the discourse of the reformist literature of the era that treats the traditional Ottoman army and especially the Janissaries as a primitive and obsolete formation.[21] In short, *TUM* reflects the main objectives, concerns, and discourse of the Ottoman political-military elite of the age regarding the question of military reform with its fiscal and economic dimensions.

Beyond the military-political and fiscal context which shaped the text, there is an obvious economic textual context that inspired the author in developing his theses. His words about standing army as a distinguishing mark of modern states remind us of Adam Smith's ideas about the subject matter in *The Wealth of Nations*. Smith compares two alternative forms of military organization, namely "militia" and "standing army," which mainly belong to the pre-modern and modern ages, respectively:

> The practice of military exercises is the sole or principal occupation of the
> soldiers of a standing army, and the maintenance or pay which the state

affords them is the principal and ordinary fund of their subsistence. The practice of military exercises is only the occasional occupation of the soldiers of a militia, and they derive the principal and ordinary fund of their subsistence from some other occupation. In a militia, the character of the labourer, artificer, or tradesman, predominates over that of the soldier; in a standing army, that of the soldier predominates over every other character; and in this distinction seems to consist the essential difference between those two different species of military force.

(Smith 1843: 292)

Smith then explains how the invention of the firearms changed the nature of wars and the main factor that determined their result:

Before the invention of fire-arms, that army was superior in which the soldiers had, each individually, the greatest skill and dexterity in the use of their arms. Strength and agility of body were of the highest consequence, and commonly determined the fate of battles. [. . .] Since the invention of fire arms, strength and agility of body, or even extraordinary dexterity and skill in the use of arms, though they are far from being of no consequence, are, however, of less consequence.

. . .

Regularity, order, and prompt obedience to command, are qualities which, in modern armies, are of more importance towards determining the fate of battles, than the dexterity and skill of the soldiers in the use of their arms.

(Smith 1843: 292–293)

The great change introduced into the art of war by the invention of fire-arms has enhanced still further both the expense of exercising and disciplining any particular number of soldiers in time of peace, and that of employing them in time of war. Both their arms and their ammunition are become more expensive. A musket is a more expensive machine than a javelin or a bow and arrows; a cannon or a mortar than a balista or a catapulta. [. . .] The cannon and the mortar are not only much dearer, but much heavier machines than the balista or catapulta, and require a greater expense, not only to prepare them for the field, but to carry them to it.

. . .

In modern war the great expense of fire-arms gives an evident advantage to the nation which can best afford that expense, and consequently to an opulent and civilized over a poor and barbarous nation.

(Smith 1843: 296)

The similarity between these words and the ideas presented in *TUM* may bring to mind that the author of *TUM* might have referred to Smith's magnum opus. This, at first sight, seems rather unlikely. Because, to our best knowledge, Ottoman intellectuals did not use Smith's massive work to study economics. They instead referred to shorter and more practical catechisms like those of Say (Kılınçogʻlu 2015: 22). Besides, there is no strong evidence (similar to the sandglass example mentioned earlier) that testifies to a direct link between these two texts. However, if the author benefited from *The Wealth of Nations*, this would lead us to a more surprising and important finding, which increases the historical importance of the manuscript. If this is the case, we can conclude that *TUM* is the first work which directly introduced Adam Smith's own ideas and words to the Ottoman intellectual sphere. Yet, we are still far from having enough evidence to claim that the author borrowed these ideas directly from Adam Smith.[22]

Since we already know that the author's main source was Say's *Cours complet*, we can also assume that the parallels between *The Wealth of Nations* and *TUM* may owe their existence to a transmission through Say's work. Say also regarded standing army as a distinctive institution of modern nation-states and pointed out to the extra fiscal burden it created for governments. In *Traité d'économie politique*, for example, he states:

> [The] extensive application of science, and adaptation of fresh means and more ample resources to military purposes, have made war far more expensive now than in former times. It is necessary nowadays, to provide an army beforehand, with supplies of arms, ammunition, magazines of provision, ordnance, &c, equal to the consumption of one campaign at the least. The invention of gunpowder has introduced the use of weapons more complex and expensive, and very chargeable in the transport, especially the field and battering trains.[23]
>
> (Say 1821, 2: 306–307)

Later in *Cours Complet*, he put forward similar ideas:

> L'art de la guerre est devenu plus compliqué au sein d'une civilisation plus avancée. Plusieurs parties de cet art exigent maintenant des connaissances, des talents, une longue pratique, qui ne peuvent se rencontrer dans les milices nationales composées d'hommes qui tous exercent ou sont appelés à exercer d'autres professions. L'artillerie, le génie, la cavalerie, veulent des hommes instruits de longue main et qui consacrent leur vie entière à la profession des armes. Sans cela, on aurait trop d'infériorité en combattant un ennemi armé des progrès de cet art. Il faut donc avoir, en permanence, de ces corps instruits que l'on ne peut pas former au moment du besoin.
>
> (Say 1828, 5: 202)

These words demonstrate that the arguments in *TUM* about the essential connection between modernization and establishing a well-equipped and well-trained standing army were probably inspired by Jean-Baptiste Say's (and indirectly by Adam Smith's) ideas, as well as the Ottoman political-military reality of the age. The author of *TUM*, however, takes these ideas to another level by suggesting that economics itself was a result of the modernization of military technologies and its financial requirements in (Western) Europe.

Finally, a short comparative analysis of the state-centered approach to economics in *TUM* is necessary to understand the manuscript in its intellectual-historical context and also to see the change in Ottoman economic thinking in the 19th century. Regarding the importance of economics, the author argues that although economic knowledge is useful for everybody, "studying this knowledge is definitely more important and necessary for statesmen, who are the men of decision making and administration" (*TUM*: 39v). Whereas his main source, Jean-Baptiste Say, attributed a completely different importance to economics and economic education. As Philippe Steiner puts it:

> From the outset, Say aimed at the intellectual formation of the citizen of an industrial society. This was because he thought social life to be no longer dominated by politics and religion but by industry, everyday activity related to the production, distribution and consumption of wealth. Political economy meant more than the conceptual tools related to a given area: it was a broad political worldview, what we have called a *philosophie économique*. This underpins his political view of the teaching of political economy; and this view was not conservative, as became the case among French economists after the 1840s – Say was a republican eager to promote a more egalitarian society, a society in which everyone would benefit from economic progress and would enjoy the comforts of life.
>
> (Steiner 2012: 77)

Therefore, even if the author of *TUM* shares Say's dream about everybody benefiting from economic progress, the approach and the ultimate goal in *TUM* could not be more different than the egalitarian and republican nature of Say's thinking. The Ottoman author also wished public prosperity and wealth, yet this was not an end in itself. The ultimate objective of achieving a wealthy society was to provide the state with military and political might vis-à-vis its enemies.

The author's state/military-centered approach to economics and especially his presenting economics as a science of state administration reflect the implicit cameralist approach to economics in Ottoman economic thinking in the first half of the 19th century. There is no reference to any works or figures of German-Austrian cameralism in the text. However, we can think of a possible indirect influence of cameralism on the author's economic and political thinking. In the early 1790s, an Ottoman intellectual and statesman, Ebubekir Râtib Efendi (1750–1799), served as the Ottoman ambassador to Austria. During and after his service, he penned two highly influential treatises on the Austrian social, political, and economic system. In these works, he introduced a new approach, inspired by the Austrian model, to the relationship between the state and economy in Ottoman economic and political thought. He suggested that the strength of a state depended on a strong army, which should be supported by a strong economy. And a strong economy can be built only through active state policies aiming at having a big, healthy, and productive population living in peace and prosperity. At the center of Ebubekir Râtib Efendi's economic model, therefore, was

94 *Deniz T. Kılınçoğlu*

the indispensable active role of the state to produce wealth and welfare in the country, which in turn provide the state with necessary means to build a strong political and military power (Yeşil 2010: 226–235, 333–365). Ebubekir Râtib Efendi's works were among the most influential reform treatises of the early 19th century (Şakul 2005: 123–124). After him, other Ottoman reformists entertained similar ideas in their works.[24] Therefore, although we do not come across any direct references to German-Austrian cameralist literature in *TUM*, it is likely that its central idea, which emphasizes the connection between the state/army and the economy, was shaped by earlier Ottoman interpretations of cameralism.

Later, in the second half of the century, and especially in the 1870s and 1880s, the Sayan understanding of economics came to dominate Ottoman economic literature with a society-centered approach and an overt criticism of the bureaucratic-militaristic nature of traditional Ottoman economic mentality. Prominent intellectuals who wrote on economics in this era, like Münif Pasha (1828–1910) and Ahmed Midhat Efendi (1844–1912), emphasized that economic knowledge should be studied not only by the elites, but by the entire population. Both of these influential intellectuals, among others, contributed to the popularization of economics in Ottoman society through their books and articles published in popular periodicals. The main objective of the popularization efforts was the intellectual (re)formation of Ottoman citizens with this new *philosophie économique*, in Sayan sense, as a first step towards building an industrial society in the Ottoman Empire.[25]

Also in the 1870s and 1880s, the idea that economic development of the country, rather than the military and fiscal strength of the central state, should have a priority in government policies came to dominate Ottoman economic literature. Reminding of the thesis presented in *TUM*, we come across arguments in Ottoman economic literature of this era comparing "the old times" when military power determined the economic power of the empire, and "modern times" when the relationship was reversed. For example, the most prominent and influential intellectual of the era, Ahmed Midhat Efendi makes the distinction between the "old wealth" and "new wealth," which are the results mainly of militaristic and capitalistic means, respectively. According to him, the "old wealth" in the Ottoman Empire has long vanished because military conquests came to a halt, and the Ottomans could not have yet built "new wealth" through a capitalist-industrial development process. Similar to the author of *TUM*, Ahmed Midhat Efendi argues that modern economics teaches us that the wealth built by military means is fragile and temporary, since it is always under the threat of a more powerful enemy. The wealth of "artisan and merchant nations," on the other hand, are more likely to endure in the long run (Ahmed Midhat 1879: 113–114).

Similarities between *TUM* and later Ottoman works on economics do not necessarily entail a direct influence of the former on the latter. However, such similarities and deviations between these texts provide us insights in the evolution of Ottoman economic thinking and especially the impact of modern economics in Ottoman social, political, and intellectual change in the age of reform.

## Conclusion

An unpublished and anonymous manuscript, titled "Risâle-i Tedbîr-i ʿUmrân-ı Mülkî," is the first treatise of modern economics in the Ottoman Empire, and to our best knowledge, also the first one in the entire Middle East. It was penned in the mid-1830s, when the Ottoman Empire was going through a comprehensive and mostly strenuous institutional rebuilding process in the military and fiscal spheres. The author of *TUM*, by writing this treatise, aims at introducing economics to the Ottoman political-military elite as a scientific guide for the effective fiscal and economic administration of the empire. This, he believes, is essential to establish and maintain a strong and technologically-advanced army, thereby a powerful state.

The author benefits mainly from Jean-Baptiste Say's *Cours complet* for both outline and content. Yet, the manuscript in its entirety is not a translation of Say's work. He instead adapts Sayan economics into the Muslim-Ottoman cultural and intellectual context with the help of notions and examples taken from Islamic and Ottoman sources, from the work of Ibn Khaldun to the Ottoman economy and everyday life. Moreover, acknowledging his work only as a first step, he calls for a prospective collective effort of Ottoman statesmen, merchants, and intellectuals to produce a genuinely "Ottoman" synthesis of economics to produce a more tailor-made version of the discipline that addresses the specific economic conditions and problems of the empire.

Although the author of *TUM* puts the military reform at the center of his arguments, he realizes that the modern age is the age of economy and economic development, not military conquest and booty. He suggests that the long-term survival of a state depends primarily on the prosperity of the country. This, the author maintains, can only come as a result of careful practical application of modern economic knowledge by statesmen. Economics and its political usage, therefore, separates the modern states from the pre-modern states, and powerful states from those in decline. Accordingly, the knowledge and practice of economics determines the ultimate fate, as well as the wealth, of a nation in the modern age, according to the author. These arguments are clear warnings to the Ottoman statesmen about the urgency of adopting this new discipline as a guide for state administration. In all these respects, *TUM* is an important historical document illustrating the intellectual impact of modern economics on Ottoman political and economic thinking in the age of reform.

## Notes

1 I thank the participants of the 4th JSHET-ESHET Conference (2015) and HES Annual Conference 2016, especially Akihito Matsumoto, Philippe Steiner, and Andrea Maneschi for valuable comments and suggestions on an early draft of the manuscript. I also thank the anonymous reviewer for his insightful comments and suggestions.
This research was supported by Middle East Technical University-Northern Cyprus Campus, Research Projects Fund (project code: SOSY-15-D-3).
2 For a review of the literature on this issue, see Cardoso (2003).

3 For more information on these works, see Özgür and Genç (2011) and Kılınçoğlu (2015: 26–27).

4 The contemporary equivalent for "nation" in Turkish is "millet." Although the same word existed in Ottoman-Turkish before the second half of the 19th century, it mostly referred to a specific religious community, like Jews or Orthodox Christians, not to the entire society living under the administration of the same "nation"-state.

5 As İlber Ortaylı indicated earlier, the article that the author refers to was published in issues 54 and 55 of *Takvîm-i Vekâyi*, not in 56 as the author mistakenly states (Ortaylı 2000: 457). It appeared in the section of "Foreign Affairs" (*Umûr-ı Hâriciyye*). The long introductory title of the article announces that "This is a translation of an article on economics [*tedbîr-i 'umrân-ı mülkî*] which was published in a British journal. It is about the effective reasons in the increase of the number of human population in Europe" ("Tedbîr-i 'Umrân-ı Mülkî'ye Dâir İngiliz Gazetelerinden Birinde Münderic Bir Maddenin Tercümesidir" 1833). According to Ortaylı, the article was translated by the author of the manuscript (Ortaylı 2000: 457). Ortaylı provides no reasons for what made him reach this conclusion, but his claim is supported by the fact that the translator/author of the article uses the term "tedbîr-i 'umrân-ı mülkî" for economics. This usage was not common at the time.

6 For a comparison of *Traité d'économie politique* and *Cours complet*, and Say's objective to produce a more popular and practical manual of economics in the latter, see Steiner (1998: 235–239).

7 All translations from Ottoman-Turkish are mine. I provide literal translations as much as possible to convey the sense of the text itself, which at times comes with stylistic compromises in English.

8 "Ta'arîf-i mâl ve ânın hudûs ü husûlünde cârî olan a'mâl ü ef'âl beyânındadır[.]"

9 "Husûl-i mâlın mevkûf-ı 'aleyh olduğu 'amelin 'alâ-hidetin ta'rîf ve aksâm-ı mu'teberesine tenvî' ü taksîmi beyânındadır[.]"

10 "Tâife-i insânın ihdâs-ı mâl emrinde isti'mâl iylediği âlât ü edevât ve sâir esbâb-ı müstahsile-i emvâl beyânındadır[.]"

11 "Kıymet-i mâl-ı sermâyenin hakîkat-i zât ü mâhiyyeti ve ânın husûl-i mâl emrinde tarîk-i isti'mâli ve efrâd-ı nâsın mülk ü tasarruflarında sûret-i teksîr ü terâkümü beyânındadır[.]"

12 "'Umrân ü 'imâretin hakîkat-i ma'nâsı ve husûlü mevkûf-ı 'aleyh olduğu mebâdî' ü esbâbın mebnâsı beyânındadır[.]"

13 For a review of Ottoman economic literature in the 19th century see Kılınçoğlu (2015: 21–73).

14 Most notably in Ahmed Midhat Efendi's *Ekonomi Politik* (1879).

15 Forget suggests that this was consciously used especially by women translators "to offer their own scientific insights" in the male-dominated intellectual world of 18th- and 19th-century France and Britain. (Forget 2010: 675)

16 Ibn Khaldun's ideas and especially his organic view of the state were very influential in Ottoman political thought of the era. In the late 17th and early 18th centuries, prominent Ottoman intellectuals such as Kâtip Çelebi (1609–1657), Na'îmâ (1655–1716), and İbrahim Müteferrika (1674–1745) introduced Ibn Khaldun's ideas into the Ottoman intellectual climate. Especially with the first (unfinished yet frequently copied) translation of *The Muqaddimah* into Turkish in 1720s, the influence of his theory on the life cycle of the states grew among Ottoman intellectuals and statesmen especially in the context of the question of "Ottoman decline." (For the development and later impact of the question of Ottoman decline, see Kafadar [1997].) In the early 19th century, Ottoman reformists were well-acquainted with his ideas thanks to this translation and also various Ottoman interpretations of his work, such as those of Kâtip Çelebi and Na'îmâ. (For the

impact of Ibn Khaldun on Ottoman political thought, see Fleischer [1984], Aksan [1993], and Lewis [1993].)

17 As another evidence indicating that the author is referring to Ibn Khaldun's views here, the author, in the previous page, defines "civilization" in the Ibn Khaldunian sense, as "the opposite of nomadic condition [*zıdd-ı bedâvet*]" ("Tedbîr-i 'Umrân-ı Mülkî," n.d.: 34). The social, economic, and cultural conflict between nomadic and urban (sedentary) cultures and communities, and the idea of nomadism as the direct opposite of the higher civilizational form of urban culture constitutes the heart of Ibn Khaldun's social theory.

18 Quesnay's *Tableau économique* was published in 1758, and Jean-Baptiste Say in *Cours complet* – the main source of *TUM* – refers to "*les Essais de Hume*" which was published in 1752 (Say 1828: vol. 6: 397). Considering that "Tedbîr-i 'Umrân-ı Mülkî" belongs to the 1830s, these works had really been published "eighty years" before this manuscript.

19 The author gives the year 1245 in Hijri calendar, which corresponds to 1829 or 1830 depending on the exact date.

20 The years 1230–39 in the Hijri calendar.

21 For the impact of the waning of Ottoman military power on Ottoman political thought in this period, see Aksan (1993).

22 For important examples and an analysis of this literature, see Aksan (1993).

23 Giving a satisfactory answer to whether the author benefited directly from *The Wealth of Nations* requires a more detailed intertextual analysis, which goes beyond the scope of the present study. I hope to answer this question through an ongoing research project on the intellectual sources (both Ottoman and European) and historical conditions that shaped the content and style of the manuscript.

24 Cf. the French original:

> lorsque le mouvement imprimé aux esprits par la révolution française a perfectionné dans les armées de la république, l'application des sciences aux opérations militaires, les ennemis des Français se sont vus dans la nécessité de s'approprier les mêmes avantages. Tous ces progrès, ce déploiement de moyens, cette consommation de ressources, ont rendu la guerre bien plus dispendieuse qu'elle ne l'était autrefois. Il a fallu pourvoir d'avance les armées de tout ce qui leur était nécessaire pendant le cours au moins d'une campagne: armes, munitions de guerre et de bouche, attirails de toute espèce. L'invention de la poudre à canon a rendu les armes bien plus compliquées et plus coûteuses, et leur transport, surtout celui des canons et des mortiers, plus difficile.
>
> (Say 1803: 2: 424)

25 See for example, Behic Efendi's similar arguments in his work "Sevanihü'l-Levayih" (1803; (Beydilli 1999: 49–53). Behic Efendi notes that he built his arguments on previous Ottoman reform treatises and consular reports without naming any specific source (Çınar 1992: xxxvii–xxxviii). Since Ebubekir Râtib Efendi's works were well-known and well-respected in these genres, it is likely that these works influenced Behic Efendi's own treatise on reform.

26 For a more in-depth analysis of the connection between economics and social reform in the late Ottoman Empire, also see Chapter 3 of Kılınçoğlu (2015).

## References

Ágoston, G. (2004). *Guns for the Sultan: Military Power and the Weapons Industry in the Ottoman Empire*. New York: Cambridge University Press.

Ahmed, M. (1879). *Ekonomi Politik*. İstanbul: Kırkanbar Matbaası.

Aksan, V. H. (1993). "Ottoman Political Writing, 1768–1808," *International Journal of Middle East Studies*, 25(1): 53–69.

Aksan, V. H. (2013). *Ottoman Wars, 1700–1870: An Empire Besieged*. Oxon: Routledge.

Beydilli, K. (1999). "Küçük Kaynarca'dan Tanzimât'a Islâhât Düşünceleri," *İlmî Araştırmalar: Dil, Edebiyat, Tarih İncelemeleri*, 8: 25–64.

Çakır, C. (2000). "Tanzimat Dönemi'nde Ticaret Alanında Yapılan Kurumsal Düzenlemeler: Meclisler," *Sosyal Siyaset Konferansları Dergisi*, 43–44: 363–379.

Cardoso, J. L. (2003). "The International Diffusion of Economic Thought." In W. J. Samuels, J. E. Biddle, and J. B. Davis (Eds.), *A Companion to the History of Economic Thought*, Malden, MA: Blackwell, 622–633.

Cezar, Y. (1986). *Osmanlı Maliyesinde Bunalım ve Değişim Dönemi: XVIII. Yy.'dan Tanzimat'a Mali Tarih*, Istanbul: Alan Yayıncılık.

Çınar, A. O. (1992). "Es-Seyyid Mehmed Emin Behic'in Sevanihü'l-Levayih'i ve Değerlendirilmesi." Unpublished M.A. Thesis, İstanbul: Marmara University.

Efendi, B. (1803). "Sevanihü'l-Levayih". Hazine nr. 370. Topkapı Palace Library.

Fleischer, C. (1984). "Royal Authority, Dynastic Cyclism, and 'Ibn Khaldûnism' in Sixteenth-Century Ottoman Letters," In B. B. Lawrence (Ed.), *Ibn Khaldun and Islamic Ideology*. Leiden: E. J. Brill, 46–68.

Forget, E. L. (2010). "'At Best an Echo': Eighteenth- and Nineteenth-Century Translation Strategies in the History of Economics," *History of Political Economy*, 42(4): 653–677.

Genç, M. (2000). *Osmanlı İmparatorluğu'nda Devlet ve Ekonomi*, İstanbul: Ötüken Neşriyat.

Ibn Khaldûn. (2005). *The Muqaddimah: An Introduction to History*, N. J. Dawood (Ed.). F. Rosenthal (Trans.), Abridged edition. Princeton, NJ: Princeton University Press.

Kafadar, C. (1997). "The Question of Ottoman Decline," *Harvard Middle East and Islamic Review*, 4(1–2): 30–75.

Kılınçoğlu, D. T. (2015). *Economics and Capitalism in the Ottoman Empire*, London: Routledge.

Kozak, İ. E. (1999). "İbn Haldun: Ekonomi ve Toplum İlişkisi." *T.D.V. İslam Ansiklopedisi*. İstanbul: Türkiye Diyanet Vakfı.

Lewis, B. (1993). "İbn Khaldūn in Turkey." In *Islam in History: Ideas, People, and Events in the Middle East*, New Edition, Revised and Expanded. Chicago: Open Court, 233–236.

Malthus, T. R. (1809). *Essai sur le principe de population, ou, Exposé des effets passés et présens de l'action de cette cause sur le bonheur du genre humain . . .* 3 vols. Paris: J. J. Paschoud.

Ortaylı, İ. (2000). "Osmanlılarda İlk Telif İktisat Elyazması." In *Osmanlı İmparatorluğu'nda İktisadî ve Sosyal Değişim: Makaleler 1*. Ankara: Turhan Kitabevi, 455–461.

Özgür, M. E., and Genç, H. (2011). "An Ottoman Classical Political Economist: Sarantis Archigenes and His Tasarrufat-ı Mülkiye," *Middle Eastern Studies*, 47(2): 329–342.

"Risâle-i Tedbîr-i 'Umrân-ı Mülkî." n.d. Mxt. 1169. Österreichischen Nationalbibliothek.

Rossi, P. (1840). *Cours d'économie politique*, Bruxelles: Société Typographique Belge.

Şakul, K. (2005). "Nizam-ı Cedid Düşüncesinde Batılılaşma ve İslami Modernleşme," *Dîvân İlmî Araştırmalar*, 19: 117–150.

Say, J-B. (1803). *Traité d'économie politique, ou, simple exposition de la manière dont se forment, se distribuent et se consomment les richesses*. 2 vols, Paris: Chez Deterville.

Say, J.-B. (1814). *Traité d'économie politique, ou, Simple exposition de la manière dont se forment, se distribuent et se consomment les richesses*, Seconde édition. 2 vols, Paris: Chez Antoine-Augustine Renouard.

Say, J.-B. (1815). *Catéchisme d'économie politique, ou Instruction familière qui montre de quelle façon les richesses sont produites, distrubuées et consommées dans la société, etc.*, Paris: Impr. de Crapelet.

Say, J.-B. (1821). *A Treatise on Political Economy; or, the Production, Distribution, and Consumption of Wealth.* Translated by C.R. Prinsep. 2 vols. London: Printed for Longman, Hurst, Rees, Orme, and Brown.

Say, J.-B. (1828). *Cours complet d'économie politique pratique : ouvrage destiné à mettre sous les yeux des hommes d'état, des propriétaires fonciers et des capitalistes, des savants, des agriculteurs, des manufacturiers, des négociants et en général de tous les citoyens, l'économie des sociétés.* 6 vols. Paris: Chez Rapilly.

Smith, A. (1843). *An Inquiry Into the Nature and Causes of the Wealth of Nations.* Edinburgh: Thomas Nelson.

Spengler, J.J. (1970). "Notes on the International Transmission of Economic Ideas," *History of Political Economy*, 2(1): 133–151.

Steiner, P. (1998). "The Structure of Say's Economic Writings," *The European Journal of the History of Economic Thought*, 5(2): 227–249.

Steiner, P. (2012). "Cours, Leçons, Manuels, Précis and Traités: Teaching Political Economy in Nineteenth-Century France," in M.M. Augello and M.E.L. Guidi (Eds.), *The Economic Reader: Textbooks, Manuals and the Dissemination of the Economic Sciences during the 19th and Early 20th Centuries.* Abingdon, Oxon: Routledge, 76–95.

"Tedbîr-i 'Umrân-ı Mülkî'ye Dâir İngiliz Gazetelerinden Birinde Münderic Bir Maddenin Tercümesidir." 1833. *Takvîm-i Vekâyiʿ*, 54, 3–4.

Yeşil, F. (2010). *Ebubekir Râtib Efendi (1750–1799): Aydınlanma Çağında Bir Osmanlı Kâtibi*, İstanbul: Tarih Vakfı Yurt Yayınları.

Yıldız, G. (2009). *Neferin Adı Yok: Zorunlu Askerliğe Geçiş Sürecinde Osmanlı Devleti'nde Siyaset, Ordu ve Toplum (1826–1839)*, İstanbul: Kitabevi.

# 6 Economic non-intervention and military non-intervention in John Stuart Mill's thought

*Philippe Gillig*

## Introduction

John Stuart Mill wrote numerous texts on war, and particularly about military intervention in foreign civil wars. His position seems *prima facie* to be a critique of the right of interference, as suggested by his famous article "A Few Words on Non-Intervention" (1859), a text regarded by Martin Walzer in *Just and Unjust Wars* as opening a non-interventionist tradition in political philosophy (Walzer 1977: 87–96). The concept of intervention plays a fundamental role in the history of liberalism under any meaning of the term. Mill, undeniably one of the figureheads of liberalism in the 19th century, advocates non-interference not only in military affairs but also in civil and economic matters. Indeed, in *On Liberty* (1859), as an enthusiastic reader of W. von Humboldt, he defends State non-interference in individual choices, as long as these choices cause no harm to others (the so-called harm principle). By the same token, in his *Principles of Political Economy* (1848) he supports State non-intervention in economic matters as the general rule (*Principles*, V, xi, 7). Although these viewpoints have been widely discussed in the literature, especially in the theory of international relations, they have mainly been treated separately. The purpose of this chapter is precisely to bring together his defence of economic and military non-intervention and assess their coherence, a point that to our knowledge has not yet been examined.

We will first highlight that Mill is a consistent defender of the non-intervention principle, in economic as well as in military affairs. Still, in neither case does he consider that this principle should be applied strictly, and he dwells at length on the many exceptions to such a general rule. This chapter aims to show that these exceptions share a common characteristic: the immaturity of the person or people concerned. In fact, according to Mill, *laissez-faire* no longer applies when one is dealing with children and minors *lato sensu* (*Principles*, V, xi, 8–9), while military non-intervention no longer applies in the case of "barbarian" peoples, that is to say infant-peoples (part I).

However, in a second part we will shed new light onto a well-known paradox that has troubled many commentators at least since Harris (1964) and up to present times:[1] How can we reconcile his qualified anti-interventionist stance with the fact that he was employed for more than half his life in the East India

Company, a militarized private enterprise based on the principle of commercial monopoly, or in other words a *kat'exochen* symbol of mercantilism? Can we resolve Mill's non-interventionist liberal thinking with an apparent active participation on his part in British economic and military imperialism? This chapter shows to what extent one may answer the question positively, arguing that the very status and prerogatives of the East India Company, at the time Mill was in office, have often been wrongly interpreted, more or less consciously, as an economic imperialist structure.

# 1  J. S. Mill, partisan of non-intervention conceived only as a general rule

In his *Principles of Political Economy*, Mill asserts unambiguously that trade has irenic virtues: "It is commerce which is rapidly rendering war obsolete, by strengthening and multiplying the personal interests which are in natural opposition to it" (Mill 1848: 594). Mill even contends that the development of international trade is the leading cause in eradicating war, and *ipso facto* for the progress of civilization in the world:

> And it may be said without exaggeration that the great extent and rapid increase of international trade, in being the principal guarantee of the peace of the world, is the great permanent security for the uninterrupted progress of the ideas, the institutions, and the character of the human race.
>
> (Mill 1848: 594)

Before presenting the arguments underpinning Mill's defence of "*doux commerce*", let us make two clarifying remarks. When one wonders whether trade is a source of peace, it is imperative to clarify what is meant by "trade". For if Mill is in favour of the thesis of "doux commerce", "commerce" must be understood as free trade between nations, and not as the other great type of trade in the history of economic ideas, namely mercantilism, which to the contrary rests on an interventionist policy that promotes a trade surplus by any means. Second, it should be clear from the outset that when Mill defines himself as "liberal" or promotes "liberalism" it is almost always in the political sense of the term, in accordance with the usage in the 19th century (see for instance Mill 1839). Indeed, before the last quarter of that century, when English-speaking authors discussed liberalism in the economic sense of the term, they resorted mainly to the term "free trade" or "*laisser-faire*". Therefore, if the use of the epithet "liberal" is strictly speaking anachronistic to characterize Mill's economic ideology, it is nonetheless relevant.

## *Moral benefits of international trade*

In his demonstration of the virtues of free trade, Mill asserts that the indirect intellectual and moral benefits of trade far exceed their direct economic benefits.

And the foremost of these benefits is world peace. Indeed, the moral benefit here consists basically of the intercourse of peoples: trade leads to the development of communications, but also to the discovery of other people's traditions, which ultimately is conducive to human progress. Mill believes that not only does every nation borrow its arts and its customs from its neighbours, but also that every nation needs to compare its own standards and values with those of other countries – this is, to put it in Hegelian style, the confrontation with alterity. No human beings can develop their own qualities without perpetually opening themselves to different people. Therefore, Mill asserts the civilizing mission of the merchants: "Commercial adventurers from more advanced countries have generally been the first civilizers of barbarians" (Mill 1848: 594).

It is interesting to notice that Mill – here as on many occasions – presents a puzzling proximity with Marx (and Engels), who also sees market globalization as a phenomenon that enables man to leave his existential particularity (*Besonderheit*) and to open to the world and thus access universality (*Allgemeinheit*), despite the fact that the fulfilment of this historic task entails a parallel and temporarily increasing exploitation of workers.[2] Others of Mill's texts such as *On Liberty* suggest even more clearly this (implicit) Hegelian background (see Knüfer 2011).

Anticipating Herbert Spencer's evolutionism (*Principles of Sociology*, 5th part), Mill considers that the history of mankind is that of a transition from societies based on war to societies focused on trade and industry: "the industrial career, which is the principal occupation of the modern, as war was that of the ancient and mediaeval world" (Mill 1848: 890). Thus the nations that entered modernity are precisely those which moved from the "struggle of war" to the "struggle for riches", that is to say the market competition for the appropriation of wealth which is, in Mill's eyes, a state of things that has the virtue to stimulate societies to develop their arts and thus prevent them from stagnating (Mill 1848: 754).

In so arguing, does Mill advocate replacing one war with another, substituting the military war for the economic? A careful reading of his texts actually reveals that the development of market rivalry is, to him, a mere fact, and is no ideal. Mill thinks and hopes that the reign of competition in his time is but a transitory state "until the better minds succeed in educating the others into better things" such as to "cultivate freely the graces of life" (Mill 1848: 755). And when defending competition, Mill does not plead for a system of perpetual struggle for existence and selection of the fittest, but rather in favour of a regulated emulation between individuals, something he also names "friendly rivalry" (Mill 1848: 792):

> the best state for human nature is that in which, while no one is poor, no one desires to be richer, nor has any reason to fear being thrust back, by the efforts of others to push themselves forward.
>
> (Mill 1848: 754)

### Economic advantages of free trade: a general rule with exceptions

A second argument is more implicit and provides the foundation for Mill's support of "doux commerce": this is the theory of "comparative advantages", stated by a number of writers in the early 19th century, and whose most famous version is that of Ricardo in his *Principles of Political Economy and Taxation*. Mill himself endorses the Ricardian approach and even supplements it in chapters XVII and XVIII of his *Principles*. This theory, in direct opposition to the mercantilist approach prevailing since the Renaissance, is based on the idea that free trade, far from being a *"guerre d'argent"* (war for money) as Colbert believed or as Montchrestien did before him, is a positive-sum game. It cannot be emphasized too strongly that such an analysis invalidates the whole concept of a trade war, since it rests on the idea that all nations without exception (that is to say, even those which are less productive in all sectors than any other nations) always have an interest in specializing in one or more sectors of production and thus to exchange their surplus abroad.[3] At worst, a country cannot increase its overall production compared to the autarkic situation; but it can never in any way experience a decrease in national income due to foreign competition. In short, there are no losers in this very general theory of international trade.

In fact, there are of course many circumstances that limit the degree of validity of this abstract model. And Mill is aware of this, or at least in part, since he is one of the few classical economists (along with C. F. Bastable[4]) to uphold the theory of "educational protectionism" (Mill 1848: 918–920) – while making no reference to Friedrich List.[5] This very idea of a State protection of "infant industries" as a transitional policy on a road which will lead eventually to free trade is typical of the way Mill justifies State intervention in general. Immaturity is definitely at stake. As far as economics is concerned, the general principle of non-intervention meets an exception in the case of immature persons or agencies. Mill contends in the *Principles* that *"laisser-faire"* is the "general rule", and that the burden of proof lies with those who wish to intervene (Mill 1848: 944). But Mill also denounces the failure of the theories that advocate minimal State intervention in domestic affairs. In the last chapter of the *Principles*, titled "Of the Grounds and Limits of the Laisser-faire or Non-interference Principle", he defines the *laisser-faire* principle as meaning that "the business of life is better performed when those who have an immediate interest in it are left to take their own course" (Mill 1848: 946). If this maxim appears largely true in the field of production, in as much as the producers know best what is to their advantage to produce, the consumers however are not always the best judge of what they want to consume. Mill thus shows, in §8 of the chapter, that the lack of education is a case which induces market failure ("the uncultivated cannot be competent judges of cultivation", Mill 1848: 947), and legitimizes free public elementary instruction. On this very issue, Mill opposes the idea of the liberal French economist Dunoyer, according to whom instruction should be provided by pecuniary enterprises because they would ensure that people's wants are suited. Mill retorts that "between what [people] spontaneously choose, and what they will refuse to accept when offered, there is a breadth of interval proportioned to their deference for the recommender" (Mill 1848: 948). Besides, in the following section of the same chapter (§9), Mill puts forward that market negotiations with children is a further instance where *laisser-faire* is inadequate: "Freedom of contract, in the case of children, is but another word for freedom of coercion" (Mill 1848: 952). So, the issue of immaturity is a central – though not unique – argument in favour of a limitation on the non-intervention principle in economics. This very argument is also at the root of his theory of military intervention.

### The exception to the principle of military non-intervention

In "A Few Words on Non-Intervention", Mill asserts that intervention in civilized countries plagued by civil war is not legitimate because it hinders the effort that peoples must make *by themselves* to acquire their freedom. However, in the case of "barbarous" peoples, an intervention may be legitimate and even morally required:

> To suppose that the same international customs, and the same rules of international morality, can obtain between one civilized nation and another, and between civilized nations and barbarians, is a grave error [. . .]. In the first place, the rules of ordinary international morality imply reciprocity. But barbarians will not reciprocate. They cannot be depended on for observing any rules. Their minds are not capable of so great an effort, nor their will sufficiently under the influence of distant motives.
>
> (Mill 1859a: 118)

His famous essay *On Liberty*, published the same year, provides a similar explanation: the fundamental principle of civil liberty, which is based on the idea that each individual is sovereign over himself, his body and his mind, does not concern immature people or children. "Despotism is a legitimate mode of government in dealing with barbarians, provided the end be their improvement" (Mill 1859b: 224). The concept of *immaturity* must be understood here in close meaning to that used by Kant in "Was ist Aufklärung?" as an incapacity to make use of one's own reason, since Mill defines "barbaric" humanity as men not "capable of being improved by free and equal discussion" (Mill 1859b: 224).

Accordingly, in his article on the American Civil War, Mill uses the "infant" argument to support military intervention against the Confederates. Mill rejects the idea put forward by some southerners that the Civil War was due to higher tariffs on exports of raw materials (cotton in particular) decided by the northern States, which were less concerned than their southern counterparts with this business. To Mill, it was not the suppression of free trade that was the true cause of the Confederates' decision to secede but the abolition of slavery, the only institution which requires "that human beings should be burnt alive" (Mill 1862: 136). Confederate States are thus "barbarians" who deserve a "crusade of civilized Europe" (Mill 1862: 141), which should be regarded as "a war to protect other human beings against tyrannical injustice" (Mill 1862: 142).

In doing so, Mill defends intervention only because a second prerequisite is fulfilled: a civilized nation is endangered. *A contrario*, in "A Few Words on Non-Intervention", Mill rejects military intervention with barbarian peoples if they are not dangerous. If a civilized government can and must sometimes intervene militarily speaking in the territories of a barbarous people, it is only when this people is a "neighbour" one and when this neighbor is the cause of insecurity:

> A civilized government cannot help having barbarous neighbours: when it has, it cannot always content itself with a defensive position, one of mere resistance to aggression. After a longer or shorter interval of forbearance, it either finds itself obliged to conquer them, or to assert so much authority over them, and so break their spirit, that they gradually sink into a state of dependence upon itself.
>
> (Mill 1859a: 119)

Mill's legitimation of intervention is then only in pursuit of the security of civilized nations. Conversely, in "A Few Words on Non-Intervention" Mill rejects military intervention against barbarians, to the extent that they are sufficiently far away not to represent any danger. Thus Mill does consider that there is no reason for civilized nations to intervene against polygamy among Mormons, in spite of the "barbarian" aspect of such a practice, and all the more so as the victims (the fairer sex) do not call for help. Therefore, persons unrelated to the Mormons may not legitimately intervene, since a community cannot force another to be civilized: "I am not aware that any community has a right to force another to be civilised" (Mill 1859b: 291). Only "fair means" are appropriate to make them change (such as sending missionaries).

Overall, Mill appears to be consistent when defending exceptions to the non-intervention principle in various matters. He therefore belongs fully to the "*doux commerce*" tradition initiated by Savary and Montesquieu,[6] and continued in France by Léon Walras (who expected to get the Nobel Peace Prize for his general equilibrium model developed in his *Éléments d'économie politique pure*!) or in Britain by Richard Cobden (the leader and co-founder of the Anti-Corn Law League). All these authors felt that free trade is cardinal for humanity, and more for its moral virtues than its economic ones. What should we think, therefore, of Mill's active participation in the highly interventionist East India Company, this private association of merchants benefiting from a monopoly on commercial and maritime relations between Asia and Great Britain and, having additionally received a delegation of sovereignty, was allowed to pass treaties with local rulers, to mint coins, to administer justice, and to maintain armies?

## 2 J. S. Mill, unwitting defender of British imperialism?

As noted by Sullivan (1983), Mill inherited an anti-imperialist liberal tradition to whom colonies generally do not represent any economic benefit or political advantage. Smith, Bentham and James Mill considered that Britain maintained its colonies to satisfy the interests of the minority in power at the expense of the majority. Bentham, however, and especially Mill's father, had a different perspective on India (and Ireland). While Smith considered these territories to be backward nations from a merely economic perspective, James Mill regarded them also as less civilized nations, whose state of barbarism makes its inhabitants unable to govern themselves; consequently, British intervention might provide for better government than the Indians themselves were capable of.

Contrary to his predecessors, Mill argues that colonization presents an economic interest because it could absorb the excess of capital of the mother country (in the case of settler colonies). Nevertheless, he takes the argument of a civilizing mission for Britain (in the case of dependencies without settlers) and, indeed, gives it even greater strength, while adopting a less patronizing tone than his father. Actually, Mill distinguishes two categories of dependencies ruled by a sovereign power: settler colonies which are "composed of people of similar civilization to the ruling country; capable of, and ripe for, representative government" – European settler colonies – and native uncivilized colonies (Mill 1861: 562). India belongs to the latter kind, along with Africa and also Ireland. To the extent that these are "barbarian" areas, they have an interest in Britain bringing its light, carrying a benevolent despotism, and hence engaging in military intervention.

We will show that in both cases Mill's stance is globally consistent with his commitment towards liberalism.

### The empire[7] as a catalyst for free trade and peace

Concerning white settler colonies, Mill appears to be in line with his defence of liberal ideas. On the moral and political side, the empire does not in Mill's eyes constitute an end in itself, but rather is a "step [. . .] towards universal peace, and general friendly co-operation among nations" (Mill 1861: 565). Great Britain does not need its settlements; colonization is actually a gift she makes to create world peace. In the last chapter of the *Considerations on Representative Government* Mill gives four arguments to substantiate this thesis:

1   The empire renders war impossible between the many communities possessed, which would otherwise be independent;
2   The empire prevents these communities from being absorbed by a despotic or belligerent State, or at least a State that does not have the pacifist ambitions of Britain;
3   Britain guarantees the opening of the markets between member countries of the Empire, and therefore avoids hostile tariffs and mutual exclusion;
4   The British Empire has a positive moral influence, because Britain is the country that "best understands liberty" (Mill 1861: 565) and has reached the highest degree of morality in its foreign relations.

Interestingly, the third argument shows that in Mill's mind, the empire is not the antithesis of free trade. So, on the economic side Mill stays loyal to free trade and explicitly discards mercantilism as a "vicious theory" (Mill 1861: 562). Further, the empire promotes "doux commerce" because it ensures peace precisely to the extent that it guarantees free trade in an increasingly protectionist world.

This ode to Britain's foreign policy may be linked with the one found at the beginning of "A few Words on Non-Intervention": "There is a country in Europe [. . .] whose foreign policy is [. . .] to arrest obstinate civil wars, to reconcile belligerents" (Mill 1859a: 111). Yet public opinion on the Continent accuses this policy of being selfish and driven by secret interests, especially the acquisition of new markets. For Mill, this is the consequence of prejudices and of profound misunderstanding. He regards the case of the Suez Canal (built between 1859 and 1869) as symptomatic: France considers that it was the English influence in Constantinople which was the main obstacle to its realization. But on this matter Britain, being the first commercial nation, has the most to gain from the Canal, Mill replies. On top of that, such a project would facilitate trade between all countries and thus would stimulate production, relationships, and civilization as well. Since the improvement of material living conditions is a precondition of moral progress, it is therefore a way out of barbarism and war:

> An easy access of commerce is the main source of that material civilization, which, in the more backward regions of the earth, is the necessary condition and indispensable machinery of the moral.
>
> (Mill 1859a: 116)

Therefore, for a State to declare itself to be against so many obvious benefits to mankind as a whole is "to declare that [. . .] it is the enemy of the human race" (Mill 1859a: 117). Mill here reverses the traditional logic between trade and peace (according to which the former induces the latter), saying in substance that the country which refuses trade rejects world peace and deserves to be attacked. Such a nation would put its interests above those of humanity, which is a principle contrary to morality:

> So wicked a principle, avowed and acted on by a nation, would entitle the rest of the world to unite in a league against it, and never to make peace until they had, if not reduced it to insignificance, at least sufficiently broken its power to disable it from ever again placing its own self-interest before the general prosperity of mankind.
>
> (Mill 1859a: 117)[8]

In other words, against such a non-cooperative nation, it is necessary to wage war.

Using a utilitarian rationale, Mill also justifies State intervention in the economic matters of white settler colonies. Indeed, according to him the colonial lands should not be freely acquired and disposed of by settlers. Mill emphasizes the risk in terms of overall benefit to the colony and for humanity in general, due to the probable existence of strategic behaviour on the part of newly arrived settlers: if one allows individuals to appropriate free pieces of land, each will want to own the largest possible area, while their capital will be insufficient to fully exploit it, which is sub-optimal in terms of the global productivity of the colony:

> However beneficial it might be to the colony in the aggregate, and to each individual composing it, that no one should occupy more land than he can properly cultivate, nor become a proprietor until there are other labourers ready to take his place in working for hire; it can never be the interest of an individual to exercise this forbearance, unless he is assured that others will do so too. [. . .] It is the interest of each to do what is good for all, but only if others will do likewise.
>
> (Mill 1848: 959)

This constitutes one of the exceptions to the "*laisser-faire*" principle, being a "case [. . .] in which public intervention may be necessary to give effect to the wishes of the persons interested" (Mill 1848: 956).

The solution, says Mill, when individuals respecting their own interests are "unable to give effect to it except by concert" (Mill 1848: 956), is the intervention of public authorities through the law. Furthermore, along with some of his radical Benthamite friends who constituted the "Colonial Reformers", Mill was an enthusiastic advocate of the "Wakefield scheme" of colonization, which advocated British State intervention to prevent settlers from acquiring virgin lands gratuitously and to financially support colonization in Australia and New Zealand.

Mill is then also interventionist when "civilized" colonies are concerned. And the argument is of a utilitarian kind: it is in order to maximize the interests of Britain and humanity in general that colonies should be organized on a planned rational basis.

### *The empire as a means to national independence and individual freedom for backward colonies: a liberal apology for the East India Company*

Mill joined the East India Company (EIC) in 1823, at the age of 17, and served therein until its dissolution by the British Parliament in 1858, after more than 35 years of loyal service.[9] He was employed at the Examiner of Indian Correspondence, whose role was to prepare reports to be sent to the central government in India. Writing more than 1,700 reports during his career, he would like his father end up occupying the highest office of this service, that of chief examiner, in 1856.[10] J.S. Mill's Indian experience has been carefully connected with his overall intellectual development by Zastoupil (1994), and Varouxakis has recently provided a comprehensive discussion in the field of international political thought of the meaning of this experience within Mill's liberalism (Varouxakis 2013). However, the connection has not yet been made with Mill's economic liberalism. And one has to make clear that the Company had, at the time, nothing to do with the mercantilist organization it was in its origins.

First, the trade monopoly in India was repealed in 1813 (and the monopoly on China and on tea deleted in 1833), so that by being in its service the young Mill did not put himself at odds with his own principles of free trade. Moreover, since the *Regulating Act* of 1773 and especially since the *India Act* of 1784, the EIC had no longer been a simple association of private merchants unashamedly mingling trade, military conquest and political administration of a territory: its political function became totally subordinated to the British government, and was clearly separated from its commercial activity (which remained the prerogative of the merchants). Wars of conquest were then declared "Measures repugnant to the Wish, the Honour, and Policy of the Nation" (Mukherji 1915: 22). So, when Mill joined the East India Company, it had very little to do with its original version, and had grown from a commercial company paying for the services of military officers and mercenaries to an increasingly centralized and bureaucratized political administration that officially managed the foreign affairs of British power in India – the originality lying in the fact that a State should delegate the task of implementing its political decisions to a private company:[11] the company "is in fact the government agent for the administration of India" (Haudrère 2006: 223, translation mine). All these changes in the history of the Company occurred before Mill joined.

Thus presented, we should understand that Britain's foreign policy pursued through the East India Company did not contradict free trade nor thwart the liberal idea of emancipation of the Indian people. Mill never called for Britain (nor the EIC) to launch new conquests of uncivilized countries. He rather sought to legitimize the existing conquest and create the conditions for self-empowerment of the Indian people. In Mill's view, his office in India had nothing to do with serving merchants' interests:

> all experience testifies, it is that when a country holds another in subjection, the individuals of the ruling people who resort to the foreign country to make their fortunes, are of all others those who most need to be held under powerful restraint. They are always one of the chief difficulties of the government. Armed with the *prestige* and filled with the scornful overbearingness of the conquering nation, they have the feelings inspired by absolute power, without its sense of responsibility. Among a people like that of India, the utmost efforts of the public authorities are not enough for the effectual protection of the weak against the strong: and of all the strong, the European settlers are the strongest.
>
> (*Mill 1861: 571;*)

As early as 1838, in a letter to William Napier, he expresses his belief that the EIC is

> the government which of all others (except perhaps the U.S. of America) wishes to do, & does, most for the people under its sway, & the *protector* of the natives of India against the avarice & domineering spirit of rapacious European adventurers.
>
> (*Mill 1972: 1983;*)

One also realizes why in 1852 Mill vigorously testified before the House of Lords in favour of the East India Company and against the plans to place the administration of India under the supervision of a minister. Such a measure, he deems, "would be the most complete despotism that could possibly exist" (Mill 1852: 50), because even if the minister were under the control of Parliament, he would base his decisions on a very imperfect knowledge of India, of its traditions and of its people. Mill also recommends that the administration of "barbarous" dependencies be entrusted to independent expert bodies, precisely such as the East India Company, because they have unparalleled proximity to native people and are not subject to pressure from public opinion. When, in February 1858, Prime Minister Palmerston introduced a bill for the transfer of control of the Government of India from the EIC to the Crown, bringing about the end of "Company rule" in India, Mill saw fit to issue four different pamphlets advocating against the change, which took up the same arguments in favour of a council of experts who knew India from within and were independent of party politics. In 1861, in his *Considerations on Representative Government*, Mill reiterated his statement.[12]

On the other hand, Mill stated that the principles of justice and morality led to defending decolonization, if the colonies aspired to it. It was also necessary that native people be morally ready, for the very desire for national independence exists only among civilized peoples. But in the middle of the 19th century India did not fulfil this prerequisite, he believed (Mill 1852: 51). As Harris rightly points out, "the hard and unpalatable fact that Mill courageously faced was that cultural and political backwardness made despotism, alien or home-grown, inevitable" (Harris 1964: 201). Accordingly, temporary despotism led by civilized Europeans of the type conducted by the EIC was deemed preferable.

Moreover, Mill welcomed that British policy had set as a priority objective to defend the interests and promote the welfare of the Indian peasants (the *ryots*). Finally, he always recognized and condemned the violence and contempt with which the British treated the natives (both in India and in settler colonies), and rejected calls for revenge following the Indian soldiers' (the Sepoys) mutiny in 1857.

We may conclude then, with Tunick, that "the imperialism Mill defends is not self-interested but beneficent, not selfaggrandizing but reluctant. Intervention in the affairs of others is done not for commercial advantage but for moral purposes" (Tunick 2006: 591–592).

## Conclusion

Overall, Mill offers a fairly consistent and extensive defence of liberalism in economic and international affairs, which is at the same time non-dogmatic, insofar as he doesn't reduce it to simplistic tenets that would apply in all circumstances. Mill starts from a general rule which is eventually open to many exceptions, intervention being justified first and foremost in the case of immature people. Mill's liberalism appears particularly interesting, especially for current highly specialised

economists: since it highlights the acute civilizational effects of economic freedom and of trade between nations, his economic liberalism is deeply embedded
in political and moral considerations. On the other hand, Mill conceives of the
East India Company, as it functioned in the 19th century, quite paradoxically as
the best means to put an end to mercantilists and imperialist interests in India and
to create independence for this country.

Mill's argument nevertheless faces a problem, aptly raised by Knüfer: we have
already seen (at the end of our first part) that in "A Few Words . . ." Mill justifies military intervention against threatening barbarous neighbours. But, when
Mill comes to illustrate the barbarians on whom a civilized nation could legitimately intervene, he gives the example of Indian "neighbours" who threaten
the Crown's security. Now Mill remains silent on the question as to how these
barbarians have become British "neighbours". In other words, "he neglects or
denies the issue of the origin. It is as if the origin of the presence in India did not
have to be questioned and as if the conquest could be the legitimate basis of a
government" (Knüfer 2011, translation mine). Perhaps this is where some elements of imperialism do indeed lurk in Mill's liberal thought.

## Notes

1 A few years ago, Uday Singh Mehta raised the specific question of whether Mill's
defense of intervention allows one to describe him as "imperialist" (Mehta 1999).
Recently, some commentators, such as B. Jahn (2005) or A. I. Applbaum (2007),
have followed Mehta in answering in the positive, pointing to a fundamental contradiction between Mill's commitment to freedom in general and his refusal to
consider uncivilized peoples as worthy of being free. It is not the object of this
chapter to answer this question, but we think that a recent article by Aurélie
Knüfer seems to have resolved the paradox, arguing that Mill has a conception of
freedom as a "temporal praxis" (Knüfer 2012). This paper focuses much more on
the alleged *economic* imperialism entailed in Mill's participation in the East India
Company.

2 See Marx, *German Ideology*:

> this development of productive forces (which itself implies the actual empiri-
> cal existence of men in their world-historical, instead of local, being) is an
> absolutely necessary practical premise because without it want is merely made
> general, and with destitution the struggle for necessities and all the old filthy
> business would necessarily be reproduced; and furthermore, because only
> with this universal development of productive forces is a universal intercourse
> between men established, which produces in all nations simultaneously the
> phenomenon of the 'propertyless' mass (universal competition), makes each
> nation dependent on the revolutions of the others, and finally has put world-
> historical, empirically universal individuals in place of local ones.
>
> (Marx and Engels 1846, pt. I, author's translation)

See also Marx 1853, "The British Rule in India":

> [Oriental villages,] these small stereotype forms of social organism have been
> to the greater part dissolved, and are disappearing, not so much through the
> brutal interference of the British tax-gatherer and the British soldier, as to the
> working of English steam and English free trade. [. . .] English interference

> [. . .] dissolved these small semi-barbarian, semi-civilized communities, by blowing up their economical basis, and thus produced the greatest, and to speak the truth, the only social revolution ever heard of in Asia.
>
> (Marx 1853)

3 For the demonstration of this fundamental point we refer directly to Chapter VII of Ricardo's *Principles of Political Economy* or to Book III, chap. xvii of Mill's *Principles*.
4 See Baldwin (1969, 295, note 1).
5 However, Mill refers (critically) to the protectionist economist Henry Charles Carey (see *Principles*, V, x, 1).
6 The comparison of trade to a "soft" activity dates back, according to Hirschman, to Jacques Savary's work *Le Parfaict Négociant* published in 1675 (see Hirschman 2001: 58–59). This theme is also to be found in Montesquieu's *L'Esprit des lois*, especially in chapters 1 and 2 of book XX. Gournay and Turgot, meanwhile, speak of the "doux principes du commerce" (see Larrère 1992: 137–138).
7 The "empire" Mill experienced during his life corresponds to what historians call the "second empire", which extends from the 1780s to the 1870s (see for example Winks 1999). This "empire" – as it was progressively named at the time – has the following characteristics: the development of settlements (in Canada, Australia, New Zealand) which gradually became dominions, the formation of the Indian empire (whereas the "first empire" was mainly Atlantic based), but also the deepening of an informal empire based on economic and sometimes military domination (in Latin America, the Islamic world or China).
8 Mills grounds his argument here on the utilitarian arch-principle, namely that of the greatest happiness.
9 The EIC was definitively dissolved in 1874.
10 For further information about his service in the East India Company see Harris (1964).
11 The balance between the two powers (that of the Crown and that of the Company) is then considered to conform to the British constitution. This is in any case the argument developed by James Mill in his *History of British India* (1806).
12 For a complete view of the various texts written by Mill against the abolition of the East India Company see his autobiography (Mill 1873, 249 footnotes).

# References

Applbaum, A. I. (2007). "Forcing a People to Be Free," *Philosophy and Public Affairs*, 35(4): 359–400.
Baldwin, R. E. (1969). "The Case Against Infant-Industry Tariff Protection," *Journal of Political Economy*, 77(3): 295–305.
Harris, A. L. (1964). "John Stuart Mill: Servant of the East India Company," *Canadian Journal of Economics and Political Science/Revue Canadienne d'Economique et de Science Politique*, 30(2): 185–202.
Haudrère, P. (2006). *Les Compagnies des Indes orientales: trois siècles de rencontre entre Orientaux et Occidentaux, 1600–1858*, Paris: Desjonquères.
Hirschman, A. O. (2001). *Les passions et les intérêts: justifications politiques du capitalisme avant son apogée*. Translated by Pierre Andler. Paris: Presses Universitaires de France.
Jahn, B. (2005). "Barbarian Thoughts: Imperialism in the Philosophy of John Stuart Mill," *Review of International Studies*, 31(3): 599–618.

Knüfer, A. (2011). "Civilisade" et Intervention Chez Les Peuples Barbares Selon John Stuart Mill | Implications Philosophiques." Available at www.implications-philosophiques.org/ethique-et-politique/philosophie-politique/%C2%AB-civili sade-%C2%BB-et-intervention-chez-les-peuples-barbares-selon-john-stuart-mill/.

Knüfer, A. (2012). "Temps de la guerre civile, temps de l'intervention, selon John Stuart Mill," *Philonsorbonne*, 6: 23–39.

Larrère, C. (1992). *L'invention de l'économie au XVIIIe siècle: du droit naturel à la physiocratie*, Paris: Presses universitaires de France.

Marx, K. (1853). "The British Rule in India," in *Marx and Engels Collected Works (MECW)*, 12: 125–133. London: Lawrence and Wishart, 1979.

Marx, K., and Engels, F. (1846). *Die Deutsche Ideologie*. Marx Engels Gesamtausgabe (MEGA), I/5. Moskau: Marx-Engels-Lenin-Institut, 1932.

Mehta, U.S. (1999). *Liberalism and Empire: A Study in Nineteenth-Century Liberal Thought*, Chicago: University of Chicago Press.

Mill, J.S. (1839). "Reorganization of the Reform Party," In J.M. Robson (Ed.), *Essays on England, Ireland, and the Empire*. The Collected Works of John Stuart Mill, VI, Toronto: University of Toronto Press, 1982.

Mill, J.S. (1848). *The Principles of Political Economy With Some of Their Applications to Social Philosophy (Books III-V and Appendices)*. Edited by John Mercel Robson. The Collected Works of John Stuart Mill, III. Toronto: University of Toronto Press, 1965.

Mill, J.S. (1852). "The East India Company's Charter." in J.M. Robson (Ed.), *Writings on India*. The Collected Works of John Stuart Mill, XXX. Toronto: University of Toronto Press, 1990.

Mill, J.S. (1859a). "A Few Words on Non-Intervention," in J.M. Robson (Ed.), *Essays on Equality, Law, and Education*. The Collected Works of John Stuart Mill, XXI, Toronto: University of Toronto Press, 1984.

Mill, J.S. (1859b). *On Liberty*. Edited by John Mercel Robson and Jack Stillinger. The Collected Works of John Stuart Mill, XVIII. Toronto: University of Toronto Press, 1977.

Mill, J.S. (1861). *Considerations on Representative Government*. Edited by John Mercel Robson and Jack Stillinger. The Collected Works of John Stuart Mill, XIX, Toronto: University of Toronto Press, 1977.

Mill, J.S. (1862). "The Contest in America," in J.M. Robson (Ed.), *Essays on Equality, Law, and Education*. The Collected Works of John Stuart Mill, XXI, Toronto: University of Toronto Press, 1984.

Mill, J.S. (1873). *Autobiography*. Edited by John Mercel Robson. The Collected Works of John Stuart Mill, I, Toronto: University of Toronto Press, 1981.

Mill, J.S. (1972). *The Later Letters of John Stuart Mill 1849–1873 Part IV* (F.E. Mineka and Dwight N. Lindley, Eds.). The Collected Works of John Stuart Mill, XVII, Toronto: University of Toronto Press.

Mukherji, P. (Ed.). (1915). *Indian Constitutional Documents, 1773–1915*, Calcutta: Spink.

Sullivan, E.P. (1983). "Liberalism and Imperialism: J.S. Mill's Defense of the British Empire," *Journal of the History of Ideas*, 44(4): 599–617.

Tunick, M. (2006). "Tolerant Imperialism: John Stuart Mill's Defense of British Rule in India," *Review of Politics*, 68(4): 586–611.

Varouxakis, G. (2013). *Liberty Abroad: J.S. Mill on International Relations*, Cambridge: Cambridge University Press.

Walzer, M. (1977). *Just and Unjust Wars: A Moral Argument With Historical Illustrations*, fourth edition. New York: Basic Books, 2006.

Winks, R. (Ed.). (1999). *The Oxford History of the British Empire: Volume V: Historiography*, Oxford: Oxford University Press.

Zastoupil, L. (1994). *John Stuart Mill and India*, Stanford, CA: Stanford University Press.

# Part II
# Japan and World War II

# 7 New liberalism in interwar Japan

## A study of the magazine *The New Liberalism*

*Shimpei Yamamoto*

## 1 Introduction

In this chapter, I examine new liberalism in interwar Japan through a magazine, *The New Liberalism* (*Shin Jiyushugi*), published by the Association for New Liberalism (*Shin Jiyushugi Kyokai*). The idea of new liberalism in Japan arose in the late 1920s, influenced by Britain's new liberalism, which integrated social policy with classical liberalism. By analyzing the magazine, this chapter attempts to reveal the distinctive features of new liberalism in Japan, its aims, and the limitations of the movement. A variety of writers, such as Tsurumi Yusuke, Nitobe Inazo, Sawada Ken, Ishii Mitsuru, and Kiyosawa Kiyoshi, have contributed to this magazine.[1] These articles and records reveal how new liberals accepted Britain's new liberalism and how they reacted to Japanese politics and historical events, such as the Manchurian Incident.

Although many scholars at home and abroad have conducted research on liberalism in prewar Japan,[2] very few studies have examined "new" liberalism in Japan. In his study on democracy during the Taisho period,[3] Mitani (1995: 30) pointed out that centrist party movements arose in late 1920s Japan. He mentioned that there had been three different types of movements. The first movement was Tsurumi Yusuke's New Liberalism. He organized the Association for New Liberalism. The second was the foundation of the New Japan Alliance (*Shin Nihon Domei*) in 1925.[4] The last one was the new liberalism advocated by Ueda Teijiro, a professor of economics at Tokyo Commercial University (currently Hitotsubashi University). In this research, I focus on the first movement, the new liberalism led by Tsurumi Yusuke and the magazine published by his association. However, it is important to note that we need further research on the other movements as well. Besides Mitani's research, Ikeo (2014: 190–210) has traced the evolution of the way Japanese intellectuals accepted Keynesian economics, which accepted a role for the government in economics, just as new liberalism did. Tanaka (2000: 140–150) insisted that Hasegawa Nyozekan, a liberal journalist, also had an idea related to social liberalism.[5]

Little is known about Tsurumi Yusuke's works and the magazine *The New Liberalism*, even in the field of Japanese economic and political history. A rare exception is Ueshina Kazuma's recent study on Tsurumi. Ueshina (2011: 138–146) mentioned that three intellectuals, John Maynard Keynes, John Stuart Mill, and Leonard Trelawny Hobhouse, had influenced Tsurumi's new liberalism.[6] Some articles and biographical writings on Nitobe Inazo, the president of the Association for New Liberalism, have also pointed out his new liberalism.[7] Although these studies tell us about many aspects of their liberalism, they did not examine the magazine itself and the association's new liberalism as a movement. This chapter, therefore, focuses on the characteristics of the magazine published by their association and attempts to capture what they tried to achieve.

First, I will provide some basic information about the Association for New Liberalism and *The New Liberalism*. Second, I will highlight some important characteristics of the magazine. Third, I will examine how members of the association reacted to the Manchurian Incident. Finally, I will point out four reasons why new liberalism faded out in the mid-1930s.

## 2 The Association for New Liberalism and the magazine

### 2.1 New liberalism in Japan

*The New Liberalism* was first published in July 1928 by the Association for New Liberalism and was published monthly until 1935. A politician named Tsurumi Yusuke organized the association and asked Nitobe Inazo to be its president.

This new liberalism movement was influenced by Britain's new liberalism. New liberalism in Britain originated with J.S. Mill. Intellectuals such as T.H. Green, L.T. Hobhouse, and John Atkinson Hobson developed the idea. One aspect of new liberalism that differentiates it from classical liberalism is the concept of the development of personality. Hobhouse, one of the most eminent figures of new liberalism, remarked, "Liberalism is the belief that society can safely be founded on this self-directing power of personality, that it is only on this foundation that a true community can be built" (Hobhouse 1911: 59). At the same time, "such a fulfilment or full development of personality is practically possible not for one man only but for all members of a community" (Hobhouse 1911: 61–62).[8] This is another important characteristic of new liberalism. New liberalism gave a society, including the state, a more positive role in promoting the development of one's personality, whereas classical liberalism focused on eliminating state intervention from individuals' private sphere. In real politics, it became the basic idea for the liberal reforms adopted by the British Liberal Party in the early 20th century. Tsurumi explained the rise of new liberalism in Britain as follows:

> These people [J.S. Mill and T.H. Green] broke themselves of old Bentham's utilitarianism and gave liberalism an explanation of new idealism. That is to say, they said that the purpose of liberalism is to establish a social organization that aims to fulfill one's personality.
>
> Then, because the purpose is to fulfill one's personality, it means that we can remove things that prevent one's personality from full development by

state laws. Therefore, new liberalism came to abandon anti-statism, or *laissez-faire*, and accept regulations of state authority if necessary

(Tsurumi 1929: 17).

J.S. Mill was an intellectual who reached a new level of liberalism, introducing the concept of individuality. Freeden (1978: 23) stated, "Mill developed the qualitative aspects of character and personality into a supreme value." New liberals in Japan believed that T.H. Green completed this development of liberalism. Idealism became a ground of liberalism in Green's theory. Green's idealism saw the social institution as a necessary condition to develop personality. Society and institutions were just means to attain the ultimate end, the fulfillment of personality (Suzuki et al. 1932: 10). Green chose liberalism, as it was the best way to achieve this end. This is why they call his theory new idealism. Along with this development of liberalism in Britain, Tsurumi founded the Association for New Liberalism. It aimed to establish the concepts of liberty and personality among the Japanese people. The regulations of the society declared:

> This society advocates the concepts of personality and liberty, and spreads the spirit of tolerance and a strong sense of morality based on moderation. By doing so, we attempt to reconcile Japanese traditional idealism with foreign cultures and complete an education in sound constitutionalism throughout the nation.

The word "personality" and its concept were imported to Japan in the early Meiji Period. Inoue Tetsujiro, the first professor of philosophy at Tokyo Imperial University, and Nakajima Rikuzo, a professor of ethics at Tokyo Imperial University who introduced T.H. Green's theory, started to use the original Japanese word, *jinkaku*, as the equivalent for personality in the early 1890s.[9] It consists of *jin* (person) and *kaku* (status, rank or capacity). Scholars and educators influenced by Western ideas widely advocated the concept of *jinkaku* throughout the Meiji and Taisho periods in order to abolish old Confucian morals and establish Western-like individualism. One of the leading figures of this Personalism, *Jinkakushugi* (*shugi* means -ism), was Nitobe Inazo, the president of the Association for New Liberalism. As a student of Nitobe, Tsurumi, I assume, developed his idea of personality based on Nitobe's ideas.[10] Nitobe took the concept of personality from Christianity. Sako (1995) tells us, in the fields of ethics and philosophy, T.H. Green and Immanuel Kant had had great influence on the development of the concepts of person and personality in Japan. Overall, new liberals took their theoretical framework from new liberalism in Britain. What differentiated new liberals in Japan from those in Britain was that they had to deal with Japan's specific political and economic problems.

## 2.2 Liberalism, socialism, and militarism in Japan

In addition to the fulfillment of personality and liberty, the association spread the ideas of tolerance and moderation. When Tsurumi founded the association, he thought that Japan faced two ideologies, "the feudalistic idea of the ruling class in Japan's existing political parties and the communist idea, which is a leading principle of Japan's proletarian movement." Compared to these rising ideologies, "there are few voices that advocate for a gradual liberalism between the two extreme ideas" (Tsurumi 1927: 28).

The first Japanese socialist party was organized in 1906 and then forced to disband in a year. The Japanese Communist movement was revitalized after the Russian Revolution in 1917. The first Japanese Communist Party was established in 1922. The Communist movement, however, declined after 1925 when the government passed the Maintenance of Public Order Act. On the other hand, socialists and trade union members organized several proletarian parties around 1926, preparing for the first universal suffrage in 1928.

Nationalism had been a main driving force of Japan's modernization since the Meiji Restoration. However, once the rise of the military became serious in the late 1920s, it led the state in a wrong direction. One undeniable fact when we evaluate liberalism in prewar Japan is that it was overwhelmed by militarism and lost its power, which resulted in the devastating war in East Asia. Prewar Japan, especially after the Great Depression, suffered huge social disparities. The gap between a small number of rich capitalists, such as *zaibatsu*, financial combines, and the large numbers of poor laborers and peasants became wider.[11] Politicians were reluctant to undertake radical reforms to relieve the inequality. This absolute poverty is why Marxism, which people believed would unravel the fundamental contradiction of capitalism scientifically, was highly attractive to Japanese intellectuals and students. The military, too, appealed to the inability of party politics to deal with the economic depression and urged radical changes to how the government was organized. In particular, young military officers were aware of poverty in rural villages since many recruits were from there. As I will mention at the end of this chapter, many Japanese supported the military because they believed the military represented their only hope of relieving the depression.

This is very different from what we see when we look at prewar British history, in which the Labor Party, in a coalition with the Liberal Party, played an important role in instituting social reforms as a counterpart to the Conservative Party. Liberals in Japan tried to learn from Britain's experience to solve social problems in Japan. This is why the association adopted the policies of moderation and tolerance *vis-à-vis* the prevailing ideologies of Marxism and nationalism from the late 1920s to the early 1930s. If their movement had become large enough and enacted the social reforms that the Japanese desired, it would have prevented the rise of the military in the 1930s and the subsequent wars.

Of course, there are many different factors that distinguish Britain and Japan. Britain had a long tradition of constitutional monarchy and democracy established under a balance of powers. It had created a large empire led by deep-rooted colonialism by the time the Great Depression took place. Japan did not have a long history of democracy and large colonies. Its constitution allowed the military to exercise a relatively large amount of power. Those problems came to the fore during the Manchurian Incident in September 1931, which I will discuss later.

## 2.3 The time frame of this research

Although new liberalism is an important ideology that gave rise to the welfare states in the post-war period, the characteristics of the new liberalism movement in interwar Japan are not clear. Few copies of *The New Liberalism* exist today, and studies of the publication have not yet been conducted. The magazine was distributed to members of the association. In an essay on George Bernard Shaw in August 1928, the author Sawada Ken stated that the membership of the association was in the thousands (Sawada 1928: 24). Therefore, I estimate that the number of issues in circulation at that time was in the thousands. This is a small circulation compared to popular magazines such as *Chuo Koron* and *Kaizo*. Most of the issues that I obtained were from microfilms, kept in Tsurumi Yusuke Papers (*Tsurumi Yusuke Monjo*) in the Collection of Modern Japanese Political History Materials (*Kensei Shiryo*) at the National Diet Library. However, some issues are still missing from the collection. Even with the issues that I found personally, my collection is incomplete. I am missing almost all the issues from September 1928 to May 1930. Therefore, my research covers a few issues from 1928 and from 1930 to 1934. This chapter mainly focuses on issues published around 1931 and 1932, because these two years witnessed significant events, such as the Manchurian Incident, which brought Japan into World War II.

## 2.4 Tsurumi Yusuke, Nitobe Inazo, and other contributors

Tsurumi Yusuke was born in Gunma prefecture in 1885. He studied at the First High School (*Daiichi Koto Gakko*) and at Tokyo Imperial University. After working as a government bureaucrat in the Ministry of Railways from 1910 to 1924, he ran for a seat in the House of Representatives in 1928. He organized a small party, *Meiseikai*, and later joined *Rikken Minseito*. He was also a core member of the Institute of Pacific Relations (IPR) in Japan and known for writing novels and biographies. Tsurumi first met Nitobe at the First High School when Nitobe was the principal of the school. He became an important student and partner of Nitobe.

Nitobe Inazo was born in Iwate prefecture in 1862, during the late Edo period. He enrolled in Sapporo Agricultural School in Hokkaido in 1877 and became a Christian. He studied at Tokyo University and universities in the United States and Germany, and obtained a PhD in Agricultural Economics from the University of Halle in 1890. He worked in a variety of capacities, such as Technical Adviser to the Colonial Government in Taiwan, principal of the First High School, and professor of colonial studies at Tokyo Imperial University. From 1920 to 1926, he served as Under-Secretary General of the League of Nations. He was appointed a Member of the House of Peers in 1927 and worked as a representative of IPR during his last years.

Nitobe was a mentor to Tsurumi when Tsurumi was a university student. Nitobe also helped Tsurumi to find a job and arranged his marriage. Tsurumi accompanied Nitobe to America when Nitobe was appointed the first Japan-U.S.

exchange professor in 1911. This close personal relationship led Tsurumi to ask Nitobe to serve as president of the Association for New Liberalism in 1928.

There were some important contributors to *The New Liberalism*, other than Tsurumi and Nitobe. Ishii Mitsuru and Sawada Ken were directors of the Association. Ishii was a bureaucrat and a writer. Sawada was known as a biographer. Both writers published various articles or short biographies in almost every issue. Another interesting member was Kiyosawa Kiyoshi, who was well known as a liberal journalist. He often wrote essays about his trips to America and Europe.

## 3 Characteristics of The New Liberalism

The contents of the magazine consisted of a variety of themes and formats, such as articles on liberalism and parliamentary government as well as biographies, records of discussions, and examinations of Western countries. Most issues began with Tsurumi's essays about Japanese politics or a commentary on current events, followed by other writers' articles on politics, economics, or current events, and biographical essays. The end of each issue also served as a forum for readers to voice their opinions. In Table 7.1 I have listed the topics of the articles[12] and counted the total number of papers contained in the issues in 1931 and 1932 as an example.

Table 7.1 shows that the topics of the magazine were mainly related politics and foreign affairs rather that economics. However, articles on politics usually concerned economic issues too. It also shows that essays on women's suffrage and education, with examinations of Western countries and biographies, declined in 1932, while those on politics and foreign affairs and round-table talks increased. The main reason for this change was the Manchurian Incident in September 1931. I point out some important characteristics of the magazine in the following sections.

*Table 7.1* Contents of *The New Liberalism*

|  | *1931* | *1932* |
|---|---|---|
| Articles on Politics and Foreign Affairs | 13 | 21 |
| Articles on Economics | 0 | 2 |
| Examinations of Western Countries | 11 | 6 |
| Biography, Autobiography | 21 | 9 |
| Essays on Education | 2 | 1 |
| Essays on Women's Suffrage and Education | 4 | 0 |
| Other Essays | 9 | 13 |
| Book Reviews | 3 | 3 |
| Round-Table Talks and Discussions | 0 | 5 |
| Short Papers[1] | 0 | 5 |
| Free Short Essays[2] | 61 | 41 |
| Reader's Voices | 49 | 2 |

[1] Short papers were written by The Study Group for New Liberalism.
[2] Each issue contains around six free essays written by members that are shorter than one page.

## 3.1 A magazine for political movement and enlightenment

One important characteristic of this magazine is that it was neither an economic journal nor an academic journal seeking to introduce intellectuals to new theories or ideas. Instead, it was a magazine for political mobilization and education. When Tsurumi created the association, he also organized *Meiseikai*, a small party that claimed the mantle of new liberalism (*Meiseikai* broke up when Tsurumi lost an election in 1930). He tried to spread his new liberalism policy through the association and the magazine. The association thus kept a distance from the two largest parties, *Rikken Seiyukai* and *Rikken Minseito*.

*Rikken Seiyukai* and *Rikken Minseito* were two major political parties from the late 1920s and early 1930s. *Rikken Seiyukai*, or *Seiyukai*, was organized by Ito Hirobumi, the first prime minister in Meiji Japan, in 1900. A politician belonging to *Seiyukai*, Hara Takashi, formed a party cabinet in 1918 for the first time in Japanese political history. *Rikken Minseito*, or *Minseito*, was established by Hamaguchi Osachi in 1927. It showed its presence after the first universal suffrage in 1928, winning 216 of 466 seats (*Seiyukai* won 217 seats), realizing a two-party system in Japan. This political situation increased the role of small parties such as *Meiseikai* (Tsutsui 2012: 120).

As set out by the regulations of the society, the purpose of the magazine was to advocate the concepts of personality (*jinkaku*) and liberty, and educate the Japanese in sound constitutionalism. Therefore, it is hard to find academic discussions or systematic economic theories in the magazine. In "Lecture on Political Science," published in the magazine's first issue in July 1928, Tsurumi chose Walter Bagehot's *The English Constitution* as his favorite book. Tsurumi commented that Bagehot had been a banker and a chief editor of a magazine, so the society he had observed was a living society. Tsurumi remarked that his book was what a political science book should be (Turumi 1928a: 10–11). Therefore, it is possible that Tsurumi was not initially interested in establishing an economic theory or school, like Marxism. The magazine tried to educate the Japanese people through a variety of ways that they could easily understand. The association solicited not only intellectuals and politicians, but also workers, students and women. Members of the association organized public meetings in many cities and rural areas to spread their ideas.

## 3.2 Women's suffrage and education

Another important purpose of the magazine was to realize women's suffrage. In order to achieve this goal, the magazine strongly advocated education for women. For example, in "Towards Women" in July 1928, Tsurumi emphasized that the most urgent contemporary issue for women was to catch up with men in terms of intellect and discipline (Tsurumi 1928b: 24). In this essay, Tsurumi mentioned that women's suffrage would become a reality soon. The Japanese Diet passed the General Election Law in 1925, which gave the franchise to all males aged 25 and over. The first general election occurred in 1928. Movements for women's suffrage had permeated since the Taisho period. After the first general election for males, a bill for women's suffrage was submitted to the Diet in 1931. *The New Liberalism* supported this campaign.

Sawada Ken discussed the history of women's suffrage in the United States with a series of essays in the magazine, including "About Women's Suffrage" (June 1930) and "A Short History of Women's Suffrage in America" (July 1930). Ishii Mitsuru published a series of essays titled "A Story of Women's Civil Rights" (February– April 1931). The magazine also promoted female members to the association.

However, the campaign for women's suffrage lost steam after the House of Peers rejected the bill for women's suffrage in March 1931 and the Manchurian Incident took place in September 1931. As Table 7.1 indicates, essays on women's suffrage were not published in 1932, while a number of essays on politics and foreign affairs—many of them concerning the Manchurian Incident— increased. Women's suffrage in Japan was achieved after World War II.

### 3.3 Economic reforms

Although the magazine seemed to concentrate on politics and education, economic problems were also a very important subject. It is hard to separate economics from politics. Since there was a serious depression in Japan after 1929, economic recovery was an urgent issue. The most important policy that *The New Liberalism* proposed that would help Japan recover from the depression and protect liberalism was to help middle-class workers and farmers. Tsurumi remarked:

> As the pressure from large capitalists located on the right and skilled labor unions located on the left has intensified, liberals – the middle class and farmers[13] – located in the middle have been squeezed. As a result, the liberal ideas possessed by the middle class and the farmers who lost their economic basis have fallen, and extreme nationalism or conservatism in right wing and what Europeans call communism in left wing labor unions rise.
>
> (Nishio et al. 1932: 7)

Tsurumi saw that the main supporters of liberalism were middle-class workers and farmers, which meant that if these classes suffered a loss in status, new liberalism would lose support. The question was, then, how new liberalism could solve this problem.

There were some articles, such as "Political Essay" by Yamaji-sei or "Rakurinso Miscellaneous Notes" by Ishii Mitsuru, which discussed ongoing debates in the Japanese Diet. For example, "Political Essay" in February 1931 explained that, in 1931, the Japanese Diet had finally shifted its focus from abstract legal principles[14] to economic problems, such as how to recover from the depression and pass a law approving labor unions. He was especially concerned about whether the Labor Union Law would pass the Diet that year. However, these articles tended to merely describe or criticize current situations and problems, and did not present a counterproposal from the standpoint of new liberalism. For example, I could not find articles that strongly demanded enacting a labor union law. Several bills were submitted to the Diet in prewar Japan but all were rejected, and the first Labor

Union Law was enacted after World War II. This was similar to other issues. If new liberalism accepted government intervention, then how could it distribute income to the poor? How much should the minimum wage be? How could it realize its policies through the real political process? These topics cannot be found in the magazine and it is difficult to understand new liberalism's solution to economic problems. This is my impression of the issues published around 1931.

### 3.4 The Study Group for New Liberalism

This changed when some young members, including university students, organized The Study Group for New Liberalism (*Shin Jiyushugi Kenkyukai*) within the association in June 1932. Suzuki Shuji, a member of the study group, explained the purpose of the group. "This group," he said, "studies the essence of new liberalism and other political, economic, and diplomatic issues academically and practically, and the group should lay the groundwork for creating the association's platform or policy" (Ishii et al. 1932: 7). Thus, the group was organized to overcome the weakness that new liberalism had not proposed a clear policy to the public. Suzuki implied Tsurumi Yusuke was responsible for this weakness. "I think Mr. Tsurumi did not do a good job showing what new liberalism is. So if he does not have an idea, we should come up with one. This is the reason why the group was organized" (Ishii et al. 1932: 7). For those reasons, in the first meeting, they discussed that they needed to announce a concrete policy or party platform for the Association for New Liberalism. Some claimed that they had to conduct more research on the theoretical basis of liberalism, such as how new liberalism was to be defined, by studying J.S. Mill or T.H. Green. Others insisted that they should focus on practical problems, such as economic reforms in Japan. Therefore, they split the members into two groups, one for studying the ideas of liberalism and the other for researching practical issues. The agenda of the second meeting, held in July 1932, is as shown in Table 7.2.

*Table 7.2* Agenda of the second meeting of the Study Group for New Liberalism (*The New Liberalism*, September 1932: 4)

Introduction:
1. The Necessity of Studying the Nature of New Liberalism
2. The Origin of Liberalism
3. The Historical Development of Liberalism

Theoretical Issues:
1. The Difference between Liberalism and New Liberalism
    A. T.H. Green/B. Tsurumi Yusuke/C. Ueda Teijiro
2. Relationship between Liberalism and Philosophy
3. Relationship between Liberalism and Socialism
    A. Marxism/B. British Socialism/C. State Socialism

Conclusion:
The True Nature of Our New Liberalism and Its Necessity for Present Japan
Policy Agenda: [*no detail for this section*]

Extracts of the meetings were published in *The New Liberalism* in August and September of 1932. I summarize some important arguments from the second meeting below, since they provide us with a good example of how they understood new liberalism and other ideologies in this period.

During the section on the "Necessity of Studying the Nature of New Liberalism," they argued that socialism and nationalism had criticized liberalism in recent Japanese history and that there was a lack of research on liberalism. A member then reported that it had been said that the origin of liberalism was to be found in Greece and England. He emphasized that liberalism was not solely a child of modern capitalism, but that we could also find the origin of liberalism in ancient Greece.

During the section on the history of liberalism, another member traced the theories of four intellectuals. The first was Adam Smith. He established economics based not on the state but on the lives of people and insisted that the self-interest of each person was the driving force of the economic development. The state, therefore, should not intervene in economics and leave it in charge of one's free will. Jeremy Bentham, second, theorized Smith's liberal economics in the field of ethics. Based on his utilitarianism, expressed by the "greatest happiness of the greatest number," human beings will evade pain by themselves, making state protection unnecessary. However, when the harmful effects of the industrial revolution, such as labor problems, emerged in mid-19th century Britain, people developed a growing doubt about this type of liberalism, a concern that the conventional individualism would not work well. This caused the rise of Chartism, Fabian Society, trade unions, and socialism. J.S. Mill, the third intellectual, brought about a major breakthrough in liberalism. He insisted that the purpose of liberalism was to develop human potential as much as possible. Therefore, he allowed state intervention in order to cultivate human potential. Finally, T.H. Green accomplished what Mill was trying to do.

Discussing the difference between Liberalism and New Liberalism, another member of the study group examined Tsurumi and Ueda's new liberalism. He reported that the core of Tsurumi's new liberalism could be summarized as Personalism (*jinkakushugi*) and that his Personalism was very close to Green's. On the other hand, Ueda's new liberalism focused more on economics. He emphasized the self-coordination of free competition. The Japanese government had protected domestic industries for the purposes of encouraging rapid industrialization in the early Meiji period. The protection still existed in the 1920s and capitalists used it for their privileges, oppressing small enterprises and laborers. If the government stops protecting capitalists, oppressive rule over them will end. Ueda insisted that we needed to break the monopoly of capitalists and to promote free trade. At the same time, he opposed socialism, insisting that it inhibits the spirit of entrepreneurship. In contrast with old liberalism, he did not simply claim that personal liberty should be free from state intervention, but he insisted that liberty should develop the natural talent of each person well. Comparing these different types of liberalism, a member remarked:

> I think we have a certain spirit of new liberalism, although we have different interpretations. We should avoid sectionalism and formed a united front

of liberals, hoping for development of liberalism. In this sense, when we are ready, we want to organize a large lecture meeting or demonstration with large Japanese figures such as Ueda Teijiro, Kawai Eijiro, and Shidachi Tetsujiro.

(Suzuki et al. 1932: 9)

This shows the possibility of more charitable debates on liberalism if it was realized. Although I cannot find evidence that they had lecture meetings with other profound liberals in Japan, there were some round-table talks organized by a liberal journalist, Ishibashi Tanzan, for the magazine *Toyo Keizai Shimpo*. For example, in June 1933 Tsurumi Yusuke and Kiyosawa Kiyoshi joined a round-table talk with Ishibashi Tanzan, Ueda Teijiro, Hasegawa Nyozekan, Ashida Hitoshi, and other intellectuals (Ishibashi et al. 1933: 24–36). The theme of this meeting was not liberalism but U.S.-Japan relations. Nevertheless, it shows that liberals had developed a certain network to discuss and share ideas and opinions. We need further research on the relations and alliances of Japanese liberals during the interwar period. It is also important to compare *The New Liberalism* with other magazines, such as *Toyo Keizai Shimpo*, in order to evaluate the power and influence of liberalism in prewar Japan.

Finally, the discussion inside the study group moved on to the relationships between liberalism and Marxism, British socialism, and state socialism. First, Marxism was considered the fastest way to achieve the ideal society in Japan, where the proletariat constituted most of the population. A member pointed out that once the ideal society became a reality, the society might be similar to what liberals imagined to a certain extent. Second, British socialism means the socialism adopted by the British Labor Party. It is possible to regard it as an advanced version of new liberalism. A member pointed out that we could find resemblances between new liberalism and British socialism, whereas classical liberalism had little resemblance to it. British socialism is similar to new liberalism because it rejects violent revolution, accepts reforms through parliament, and respects freedom of speech. Third, state socialism means fascism, which covers Italian fascism, the Nazis, and Japanese nationalism. A member introduced Tsuchida Kyoson's critical study of fascism. Tsuchida, a scholar of Japanese classical literature, emphasized society, individualism, utilitarianism, and egalitarianism as characters of modernism. Fascism was a movement that emphasized its antithesis, namely community against society, collectivism against individualism, activism against utilitarianism, and anti-egalitarianism. According to Tsuchida, this dichotomy would be lifted up, as Hegel's dialectic approach, to a comprehensive truth and it would include the perfection of human beings.[15] The member concluded that this perfection of human beings was also a goal of new liberalism.[16] It seems that they had planned to discuss practical issues after they talked about theoretical issues (we can see the item "Policy Agenda" at the end of the schedule). However, they closed their discussion here and there was no record of any discussions concerning practical issues.

As far as I know, this was the most organized discussion of new liberalism in the magazine. Of course, it may not be a profound argument. Members of the group were not experts on the topics that they presented and some of them were even university students. Many of them seemed to have learnt about liberalism from studies published by Japanese scholars such as Kawai Eijiro, who is famous for introducing T. H. Green's philosophy to Japan. Nevertheless, their sketch of liberalism tells us about some important characteristics of the association. First, they thought that their ideas were closest to those of the British labor party or British socialism. Second, they had different views on their definition of new liberalism. For example, a member introduced T. H. Green's idealism, explaining that society and institutions were merely means to achieve the fulfillment of personality as the ultimate end. Another member raised an objection to Green's theory and stated that it was unrealistic to expect the fulfillment of personality in the labor class. He insisted that Mill's modest idea was more useful to the new liberalism. It seems that they could not solve the disagreement.

After these meetings, members published short papers on their research in subsequent issues. These papers included "On Liberty" (October and November 1932), "Notable Dutch East India" and "Community and Society" (December 1932), "Population Flow as a Social Problem" and "New Liberalism and Community" (January 1933). For example, "Population Flow as a Social Problem" investigated population growth in Japan and the gap between urban and rural areas, pointing out that rural villages were suffering from the out-migration of the young (Takizawa 1933: 9–10). However, it did not propose a clear solution to the population problem. "New Liberalism and Community" posed a question: How do we control this individualistic economy characterized by *laissez-faire*? Furthermore, what freedom should we protect against the control? (Sawada 1933: 10–11) Although these are very essential questions, the author did not provide his own ideas on how to control the economy and what to protect from that control.

In conclusion, it seems that they could not complete their mission to articulate the general principles of new liberalism. I could neither find minutes of the third meeting nor a final report in the magazine. Though the short papers showed some useful economic and philosophical discussions, they did not provide clear answers to the ongoing problems. Their research remained independent dots and it was difficult to draw a line connecting these dots. In spite of these weaknesses of the study group, it still reveals many of their ideas on new liberalism.

Furthermore, in a short essay titled "From New Liberalism to the Establishment of a New Liberal Party" in January 1933, a member strongly requested that the association take more practical action. He stated, "I have great doubts about the current new liberalism movement. To be honest, I demand concrete and practical methods for current new liberalism movement." He continued as follows:

> Show us the concrete and substantial purpose of new liberalism. Then move on to the establishment of a New Liberal Party.

Make new liberalism a practical movement like in 19th century Britain. . . .
Policies can be carried out only when a political party is organized. Therefore, the urgent need is to establish a New Liberal Party.

(Takahashi 1933: 11)

Although no political party was founded, we can see here more and more
members of the association starting to feel that they had to expand their movement to the next level.

# 4 The Manchurian Incident and New Liberalism

## 4.1 Supporting the Manchurian Incident

In September 1931, the Kwantung Army, a Japanese army group that was
defending Kwantung and the South Manchurian Railway in northeast China,
destroyed the South Manchurian Railway and went on to occupy Manchuria over
the following months. The Manchurian Incident opened the way for the Japanese
military to take control of Japanese policymaking and indeed the government
itself. It also aroused suspicion in international circles, including the League of
Nations and the United States. At this point the Japanese army announced that
the Chinese army had destroyed the Manchurian railway, only a very few people
being aware that it had been plotted by the Japanese army in an effort to acquire
Manchuria. Taking this into consideration, the majority of public opinion and
newspapers, including *Asahi* and *Mainichi*, took a favorable view of the incident
and subsequent invasion of China (Tsutsui 2012: 216–220), apart from some
intellectuals, like Yoshino Sakuzo.[17] Responsibility for Japanese policy after the
Manchurian Incident rests not only with the army and politicians but also with
these sides.

How did the members of the Association for New Liberalism react to and
interpret the incident? After the Manchurian Incident, essays and arguments
regarding the incident loomed large in *The New Liberalism*. Most essays and
discussions in the magazine showed approval of the incident. For example, Ishii
Mitsuru dealt with the Manchurian Incident in October 1931. In his essay, he
first criticized America for interfering with Japan's action over Manchuria. He
reminded readers of the Triple Intervention, the diplomatic interference from
France, Germany, and Russia, who demanded Japan return Liaodong Peninsula
to China, and called on them to raise their voices in anger.

He pointed to the hundreds of incidents that had taken place between China
and Japan in recent years, and finally the explosion of the railway planned by
the Chinese army as the cause of the incident. Japan had only 14,000 troops in
Manchuria and they had to protect Kwantung, the South Manchurian Railway,
together with a million Japanese residents and Koreans. On the other hand,
it was said that Zhang Xueliang, a military leader who ruled Manchuria, had

330,000 troops and that 200,000 of them were stationed in Manchuria. Ishii stated:

> If so, this [small] number of [Japanese] army [soldiers] reacted against the Chinese army in self-defense. There is no reason for Western nations to see it as a problem, and no reason for America, which lies so far away from us, to pay attention. Even people like us, whose principle is peace in normal situations, wish to express wholehearted gratitude for the actions undertaken by the Japanese army today.
>
> (Ishii 1931: 4)

This distrust of China, the League of Nations and America is one of the typical reactions that appeared in the magazine immediately after the Manchurian Incident.

### 4.2 Positive and negative views

Of course, we can find both approval and criticism of the incident in the magazine. During a round-table talk organized by the association in December 1931, Tsurumi Yusuke mentioned the occupation of Manchuria. Although the Japanese army orchestrated the incident, he believed that it should be interpreted as an expression of the will of the Japanese middle class and farmers to expand economic opportunities and resources. This view derived from a strong notion shared by many Japanese that Japan did not have enough land to maintain its increasing population and to provide jobs for everyone. On the contrary, Western nations had large colonies and had introduced protective trade policies, excluding Japanese export products. America, too, had vast amounts of land, and had prohibited Japanese immigration to America with the Immigration Act of 1924. Another speaker, Ichikawa Hikotaro, agreed with Tsurumi's views and remarked that the acquisition of Manchuria—its land and resources—would relieve the difficulties of the middle class and farmers, and result in a society that was more individualistic and liberal. He concluded that it would bring about a bright future for liberalism in Japan.

However, Tsurumi questioned the manner (*saho*) in which the Japanese army occupied Manchuria. It seems that he expected Japan to advance to Manchuria on economic lines, using private companies. He pointed out that it was very important for the Japanese people to think that what Japan was doing was proper. The League of Nations and the United States criticized Japan because they thought that what Japan was doing was basically wrong. Tsurumi also emphasized the absence of a long-standing tradition of liberalism and individualism in Japan thus:

> For three thousand years, we have not been trained in the kind of individualism that forms an independent spirit. As a result, the deeply rooted idea of personal liberty against collectivism did not take root in this country by tradition. . . . Therefore, once we are in a state of emergency and have to deal

with a difficult situation, Japanese liberal thought vanishes away as if heavy seas had swept over it.

(Nishio et al. 1932: 7)

In "Collective Crisis and Personal Liberty" in January 1932, he remarked in similar terms that this absence meant that personal liberty was suppressed once Japan faced a national crisis such as the Manchurian Incident. He stated:

It is very disappointing from the standpoint of liberalism that there was no clear opposition from the Japanese people at the time of the Manchurian Incident. . . .

We must not overlook that Japanese society is too intolerant of different opinions concerning the so-called national crisis. It will be a huge obstacle to becoming a great nation.

(Tsurumi 1932: 2)

He criticized the Japanese people for intolerance of contrasting opinions when they faced a national crisis.

Though we can find negative views on the Manchurian Incident, such as Tsurumi's criticism, most members seemed to view the incident with keen enthusiasm. As I pointed out in the previous section, the association was looking for solutions to help the middle class in order to strengthen the new movement favoring liberalism. However, they were unable to find, let alone offer, practical solutions to restore the economy. Therefore, they were tempted to believe and hope that the Manchurian Incident could solve their difficult problems. However, the power of the military was strengthened after the incident to the extent that liberalism would no longer be an acceptable option.

## 5 The fall of new liberalism and the rise of militarism

### 5.1 The four reasons why new liberalism declined

The new liberalism movement could not become a mainstream ideology in 1930s Japan. I would like to point out four reasons that the movement ceased in the late 1930s. The first reason was Nitobe Inazo's death in October 1933. Although he did not publish many articles in the magazine, he was a symbol of the association from the beginning. The second reason was the rise of militarism in Japan after the Manchurian Incident and Japan's withdrawal from the League of Nations. The pressure on liberalism, including the censorship of publications, increased from day to day. *The New Liberalism* became a quarterly magazine after December 1933. Tsurumi pointed out that Nitobe's death and the pressure on liberalism were the reasons for the change of course (Tsurumi 1933: 8). However, these were only external reasons. The third and more substantial reason that the movement could not gain power was that new liberalism in Japan did not establish a political party or economic school. As Matsui (1998: 57–62) pointed out, liberal economist Kawai Eijiro, discussing Tsurumi's new liberalism, remarked:

> In the end of the Taisho period, new liberalism was advanced by Teijiro Ueda and Yusuke Tsurumi. However . . . though Tsurumi slightly perceives idealistic philosophy, he does not extend his idea to liberalism as social thought. His policy toward social life is ambiguous and difficult to understand.
>
> (Kawai 1934: 422)

It is quite natural that Kawai, who dedicated his life to establishing a systematic theory of social thought, criticized Tsurumi's new liberalism as unsystematic. He was half-right, because as we saw, most articles in *The New Liberalism* were not systematic papers, but represented, rather, a variety of essays, biographies, and discussion notes. However, this style was deliberate. In the first issue of the magazine, Tsurumi mentioned Walter Bagehot and called on his writers to observe "a living society" in order to study political science. This practical style of the magazine was intended to be a valuable way to change society, as Walter Bagehot's *Economist* had. Moreover, their purpose was to educate common people by introducing the concepts of liberty and individualism and constitutionalism through words familiar to their readers. However, this practical character had a weakness. They were unable to propose clear ideas as new liberals and practical policies to attract people and mobilize them for a political campaign. This weakness should be attributed not only to the format and content of the magazine but also to the way in which the organization was set up. If the association had formed a large political party, they might have rejected the pressure on liberalism and pursued their goals even after Nitobe's death.

There was also a fourth reason underneath these three: the lack of a long-standing tradition of liberalism in Japan. The new liberalism movement was introduced to Japan from Britain. However, the Japanese people or society could not establish the concepts of liberty and individualism in the way the British people had done. This is one of the main reasons that prevented Japan from establishing a large political party that stood for liberalism. Once Japan faced a national crisis, personal liberty that opposed the dominant idea was easily suppressed.

For these reasons, *The New Liberalism* went out of existence in 1935. As Japanese politics failed to solve the economic problems, the presence of the military increased.

### 5.2 Rise of militarism and the end of the two-party system

In "On Liberty" in June 1933, Nitobe described a story, which he had heard from an acquaintance, about how peasants felt during the ongoing depression:

> in rural areas, peasants often say we cannot hope for the political parties to save us. Politicians will not understand our economic situation and sentiment. So it is better that the army takes care of us. Eighty percent of soldiers

in the army come from rural areas. So the someone who knows our situation best is the army. We want to rely on the army, which knows us well, because we feel much safer than asking politicians who have no sympathy for us and just eat and drink every day. We therefore want politics by the military even if it is called fascism.

(Nitobe 1933: 5)

Nitobe warned of the current situation, implying that if peasants suffered poverty and politics achieved nothing, then militarists would become their only hope. The two-party system in Japanese politics collapsed after Prime Minister Inukai Tsuyoshi, who was reluctant to accept the founding of Manchukuo, was assassinated on 15 May 1932 when young navy and army officers and activists tried to take over the government. After the assassination, Saionji Kinmochi, the last elder statesman, assigned Saito Makoto to organize the National Cabinet by imperial order. Banno (2008: 120–121) pointed out that Japanese democracy in the prewar period had achieved a party cabinet, universal suffrage, and a two-party system. However, it could not have a major political party that stood for social democracy in the end. Those who wanted social reforms needed to entrust their hope to Marxism first and then the military. The May 15 incident and other acts of terrorism were called the Showa Restoration, which would restore the corrupted government. A wide swath of the population sympathized with the young officers who committed the acts.

## 6 Conclusion

The Association for New Liberalism was organized by the politician Tsurumi Yusuke in 1928. The association published a monthly magazine, *The New Liberalism*, from July 1928 to 1935. The magazine contained a variety of articles, essays, biographies, and records of discussions. The purpose of the magazine was to establish the concepts of personality and liberty and spread sound constitutionalism to the Japanese. Against both Nationalism and Marxism, they called for a policy of tolerance and moderation, aiming at gradual social reforms. The magazine also promoted women's education and helped to bring about women's suffrage.

Economic problems were one of the important issues covered in the magazine, especially after the Great Depression in 1929. New liberals regarded the middle-class workers as supporters of liberalism. They tried to relieve the unemployment among workers and poverty in rural areas. However, it was difficult for them to propose concrete policies to save them. The members organized The Study Group for New Liberalism in June 1932 within the association to provide a clear definition of their new liberalism and a party platform to solve practical issues. Although the research and discussions conducted by the group reveal how they understood new liberalism and other ideologies, they could not reach a consensus and did not publish a party platform or a final report.

After the Manchurian Incident, *The New Liberalism* had two reactions. The first and major reaction was to support the Japanese army's action to occupy

Manchuria. Some members thought that acquisition of Manchuria could save middle-class workers by offering them jobs and producing natural recourses. On the other hand, some members such as Tsurumi questioned how the Japanese army took Manchuria. Tsurumi also cited the weakness of liberalism and individualism in Japanese society. This weakness was especially obvious after the Manchurian Incident. Japanese society did not accept opposition to the incident.

In the last section, I pointed out four reasons why the new liberalism movement could not grow powerful enough to change society. Nitobe's death and the rise of militarism affected the decline of the magazine. They could neither establish a political party, nor an economic school, nor propose concrete policy as an association. The last reason is the lack of a long-standing tradition of liberalism and individualism in Japan.

New liberalism in interwar Japan was not powerful enough to become a mainstream ideology. Had it done so, it could possibly have helped prevent the subsequent wars. As I said in section 2, there was a huge disparity of wealth and social inequality in prewar Japan, which Marxism and the military promised to reduce. This is one of the reasons why intellectuals and students were attracted to Marxism and why the Japanese people at large started to support the military in the 1930s, as Nitobe had warned. New liberalism also sought to reduce social inequality by saving the middle class and farmers. If the ideology had been strong enough to change Japanese society, it could have been a counterpart to Marxism and the military, perhaps preventing the military's dominance and the ensuing wars.

## Acknowledgement

This work was supported by JSPS KAKENHI Grant Number JP16K17096.

## Notes

1 For Japanese names, the convention is that the family name comes first.
2 Nolte (1987), for instance, focused on one of the most influential liberals, Ishibashi Tanzan, and his contributions to Japanese liberalism.
3 Taisho is a Japanese regnal year that covers 1912 to 1916. The Meiji period covers 1868 to 1912, and the Showa period covers 1916 to 1989.
4 The New Japan Alliance was a political group organized in 1925 by politicians such as Goto Humio, Maruyama Tsurukichi, Tazawa Yoshiharu, and Konoe Humimaro. Maruyama and Tazawa later joined Tsurumi's new liberalism movement (Ito 1969: 48 and 59–60).
5 Tanaka calls Hasegawa's idea "social democracy."
6 From Keynes, Ueshima pointed out, Tsurumi learned about a way to control capitalism while avoiding *laissez-faire* and socialism. His view on the development of one's personality and the role of the state or society in helping achieve that development derived from Hobhouse's new liberalism. Finally, Mill's rejection of radical reforms brought Tsurumi the idea that we can only accomplish political reforms through a gradual and eclectic approach between radicalism and conservatism.
7 For Nitobe's liberalism, see Yamamoto (2015b).

8 An anonymous author, X.Y.Z., posted a memorial written for Hobhouse in September 1929. The author praised his contribution to the British intellectual world that was about to move from an ideal liberalism to social democracy. Hobhouse did not believe that individuals should be assimilated to the absolute State as the Bosanquet School insisted. The author also noted that his ideas were a remote cause of the great victory of the British Labor Party. (X.Y.Z., 1929: 29)

9 For the development of the concept of personality in Japan, see Sako (1995).

10 He explained, "because Trinity became a main Christian doctrine, those who believed in Christianity needed to have substantial knowledge of the person. . . . In the West, people believe 'God is a person and man is a person too.' . . . and they always compare their imperfect person with the perfect God, trying to improve themselves" (Nitobe, 1934: 564). For Nitobe's Personalism, see Yamamoto (2012: 92–94) and Yamamoto (2015a: 52–53).

11 Minami (1996: 108) showed that the Gini coefficient in 1920s and 1930s Japan exceeded 0.5, while in postwar Japan it hovered around 0.3.

12 When papers contained several topics, I categorized those papers based on the main issue.

13 He used the word *nomin*. In Japanese, *nomin* means both farmers and peasants. He mentioned independent farmers in America as supporters of liberalism just before this quote. Therefore, it is reasonable to assume that he counted relatively rich farmers among the supporters of new liberalism. However, it does not mean that they did not care about poor peasants in rural areas. Many essays in the magazine were concerned with poverty in rural villages and discussed how to eliminate it.

14 In 1930, the Japanese right wing and politicians of *Seiyukai* criticized Hamaguchi's cabinet for signing the London Naval Treaty without the agreement of the Naval General Staff Office, because they thought it violated the supreme command authority of the emperor.

15 Tsuchida (1934: 471) explained his idea of the perfection of human beings in terms of freedom and control. Individuals must be free in the first place. However, this does not means that one can do whatever one wants. A person's desires must be totally unified with one's higher personality and be controlled and modified by it. A person is truly free only when he/she achieves the purpose of the higher personality.

16 This does not mean that new liberals accepted fascism. Essays from 1932 and 1933 showed that they rejected fascism. For example, in the seventh round-table talk in February 1933, Tsurumi insisted that Japan would not produce persons like Mussolini and Hitler, because people are well educated and the country is industrialized. He concluded that the only and best way Japan should proceed was to improve constitutional politics (Tsurumi et al. 1933: 8).

17 Yoshino, a professor of politics at Tokyo Imperial University who advocated democracy in the Taisho period, questioned the incident embarked upon by the military forces, saying, "We were told not to drink from 'Robber's Spring' even if thirsty" (Yoshino 1932: 32).

## References

*For *The New Liberalism*, all issues except April 1929 were found in Tsurumi Yusuke Papers (*Tsurumi Yusuke Monjo*) in the Collection of Modern Japanese Political History Materials (*Kensei Shiryo*) at the National Diet Library, Document Number 3304 and 3943–3946.

Banno, J. (2008). *Nihon Kenseishi* [A History of Japanese Constitutional Politics], Tokyo: Tokyo Daigaku Shuppankai.

Freeden, M. (1978). *The New Liberalism: An Ideology of Social Reform*, Oxford: Oxford University Press.

Hobhouse, L.T. (1911). "Liberalism," in J. Meadowcroft (Ed.), *Liberalism and Other Writings* (Cambridge Texts in the History of Political Thought), Cambridge: Cambridge University Press, 1994, 1–120.

Ikeo, A. (2014). *A History of Economic Science in Japan: The Internationalization of Economics in the Twentieth Century*, Oxon: Routledge.

Ishibashi, T. et al. (1933). "Nichibei Shinzen Mondai Zadankai [Round-Table Talk for Japan-U.S. Friendship]," *Toyo Keizai Shimpo*, June: 24–36.

Ishii, M. (1931). "Shin ni Kore Kokuji Tatan no Aki [This Autumn Is Truly Eventful]," *Shin Jiyushugi* [*The New Liberalism*], October: 4–5.

Ishii, M. et al. (1932). "Dai 1 Kai Shin Jiyushugi Kenkyukai Shoroku [An Abstract of the First Meeting of the Study Group for New Liberalism]," *Shin Jiyushugi* [*The New Liberalism*], August: 7–10.

Ito, T. (1969). *Showa Shoki Seijishi Kenkyu* [*A Study on Political History in Early Showa Period*], Tokyo: Tokyo Daigaku Shuppankai.

Kawai, E. (1934). 'Jiyushugi no Saikento [Rethinking Liberalism],", in *Fasshizumu Hihan* [*A Criticism of Fascism*], Tokyo: Nippon Hyoron Sha, 388–436.

Matsui, S. (1998). "Tsurumi Yusuke to Kawai Eijiro: Koyu 33 Nen [Tsurumi Yusuke and Kawai Eijiro: 33 Years of Friendship]," *Waseda Daigaku Daigakuin Bungaku Kenkyuka Kiyo* [*The Bulletin of the Graduate School of Literature at Waseda Gakuin University*], 4(44): 53–64.

Minami, R. (1996). *Nihon no Keizai Hatten to Shotoku Bumpu* [*Economic Development and Income Distribution in Japan*], Tokyo: Iwanami Shoten.

Mitani, T., 1995, *Shimpan Taisho Demokurashi: Yoshino Sakuzo no Jidai* [*Taisho Democracy: the Era of Yoshino Sakuzo, New Edition*], Tokyo, Tokyo Daigaku Shuppankai.

Nishio, K. et al. (1932). "Dai 5 Kai Hombu Zadankai [The Fifth Round-Table Talk]," *Shin Jiyushugi* [*The New Liberalism*], February: 2–12.

Nitobe, I. (1933). "Jiyushugi ni tsuite [On Liberalism]," *Shin Jiyushugi* [*The New Liberalism*], June: 2–5.

Nitobe, I. (1934). *Seiyo no Jijyo to Shiso* [*Affairs and Ideas in the West*], in Vol. 6 of *Nitobe Inazo Zenshu* [*Complete Works of Nitobe Inazo*], Tokyo: Kyobunkan, 1969, 469–646.

Nolte, S.H. (1987). *Liberalism in Modern Japan: Ishibashi Tanzan and His Teachers, 1905–1960*, California: University of California Press.

Sako, J. (1995). *Kindai Nihon Shisoshi niokeru Jinkaku Kannen no Seiritsu* [*The Establishment of Concepts of Personality in the History of Modern Japanese Thought*], Tokyo: Shinchosha.

Sawada, K. (1928). "Febian Shou [Fabian's Shaw]," *Shin Jiyushugi* [*The New Liberalism*], August: 20–24.

Sawada, S. (1933). "Shin Jiyushugi to Kyodo Shakai [New Liberalism and Community]," *Shin Jiyushugi* [*The New Liberalism*], January: 10–11.

Suzuki, S. et al. (1932). "Dai 2 Kai Shin Jiyushugi Kenkyukai Shoroku [An Abstract of The Second Meeting of The Study Group for New Liberalism]," *Shin Jiyushugi* [*The New Liberalism*], September: 4–14.

Takahashi, E. (1933). "Shin Jiyushugi-ron yori Shin Jiyushugi Seito Jyuritsu ni Oyobu [From New Liberalism to the Establishment of a New Liberal Party]," *Shin Jiyushugi* [*The New Liberalism*], January: 11–12.

New liberalism in interwar Japan 137

Takizawa, T. (1933). "Shakai Mondai toshite Mitaru Jinko Kozui [Population Flow as a Social Problem]," *Shin Jiyushugi* [*The New Liberalism*], January: 9–10.

Tanaka, H. (2000). *Nihon Liberarizumu no Keifu: Hukuzawa Yukichi, Hasegawa Nyozekan, Maruyama Masao* [*A Genealogy of Japanese Liberalism: Hukuzawa Yukichi, Hasegawa Nyozekan, and Maruyama Masao*] (Asahi Sensho), Tokyo: Asahi Shimbun Shuppan.

Tsuchida, K. (1934). "Kokka Shakaishugi Hihan [A Criticism on State Socialism]," in Vol. 3 of *Tsuchida Kyoson Zenshu* [*Complete Works of Tsuchida Kyoshon*], Tokyo: Daiichi Shobo, 1935, 463–481.

Tsurumi, Y. (1927). *Chudo wo Ayumu Kokoro* [*A Mind to Choose a Moderate Course*], Tokyo: Dainihon Yubenkai Kodansha.

Tsurumi, Y. (1928a). 'Seijigaku Koza [Lecture on Political Science]', *Shin Jiyushugi* [*The New Liberalism*], July: 8–12.

Tsurumi, Y. (1928b). "Fujingata ni Mukatte [Towards Women]." *Shin Jiyushugi* [*The New Liberalism*], July: 24–25.

Tsurumi, Y. (1929). "Jiyushugi to Shin Jiyushugi [Liberalism and New Liberalism]" *Shin Jiyushugi* [*The New Liberalism*], April, Special Edition, 13–18.

Tsurumi, Y. (1932). "Shudan teki Kiki to Kojin Jiyu [Collective Crisis and Personal Liberty]" *Shin Jiyushugi* [*The New Liberalism*], January: 2.

Tsurumi, Y. (1933). "Zasshi Henko no Jijyo wo Chinshite Kaiin Shokun ni Uttau [A Sincere Apology to Our Subscribers Regarding the Publication Frequency and an Appeal to Them]," *Shin Jiyushugi* [*The New Liberalism*], December: 8.

Tsurumi, Y. et al. (1933). "Dai 7 Kai Hombu Zadankai Shoroku [An Abstract of the Seventh Round-Table Talk]," *Shin Jiyushugi* [*The New Liberalism*], April: 3–14.

Tsutsui, K. (2012). *Showa Senzenki no Seito Seiji: Nidai Seitosei wa Naze Zasetsu Shitaka* [*Party Politics in Prewar Showa Period: Why Two-Party System Failed?*] (Chikuma Shinsho), Tokyo: Chikuma Shobo.

Ueshina, K. (2011). *Koho Gaiko no Senkusha Tsurumi Yusuke 1885–1973* [*A Pioneer of Public Diplomacy, Tsurumi Yusuke 1885–1973*], Tokyo: Fujiwara Shoten.

X.Y.Z. (1929). "The Death of Hobhouse," *Shin Jiyushugi* [*The New Liberalism*], September: 29.

Yamamoto, S. (2012). "Taishoki niokeru Nitobe Inazo no Demokurashi Ron [Nitobe Inazo and Democracy in Taisho Period]," *Keizaigaku Zasshi* [*Journal of Economics*], Osaka Shiritsu Daigaku Keizai Gakkai [The Economic Society of Osaka City University], 113(2): 85–103.

Yamamoto, S. (2015a). 'Kyusei Daiichi Koto Gakko niokeru Nitobe Inazo no Shidosha Kyoiku Ron: *Koyukai Zasshi* wo Chushin nishite [Nitobe Inazo's Idea on Education at the First High School: Focusing on His Speeches in the *Alumni Magazine*]," *Keizaigaku Zasshi* [*Journal of Economics*], Osaka Shiritsu Daigaku Keizai Gakkai [The Economic Society of Osaka City University], 115(4): 47–68.

Yamamoto, S. (2015b). "Nitobe Inazo: Senzenki Hoshuteki Jiyushugi no Ichidanmen [Nitobe Inazo: A Cross Section of Conservative Liberalism in Prewar Japan]", in H. Sato and N. Nakazawa (Eds.), *Hoshuteki Jiyushugi no Kanosei* [*The Possibility of Conservative Liberalism*], Kyoto: Nakanishiya Shuppan, Chap. 6.

Yoshino, S. (1932). "Minzoku to Kaikyu to Senso [Race, Class, and War]," *Chuo Koron*, January: 27–38.

# 8 Economic research in national higher commercial schools in wartime Japan

*Tadashi Ohtsuki*

## 1 Introduction

In 1949, when the new system of higher education in Japan came under way, the educational system for economics was based on the economics departments. In many cases, these institutions had been higher commercial schools or economics departments in imperial universities under the former educational system. When surveying the effects of the wars on Japanese economists and their research, it is essential to study the economists in relation to their wartime activities. Such studies, however, are still limited despite the nearly 70 years that have gone by since the war.[1] There are various reasons for this, and in the first place the fact that the historical materials are lacking because they were burned during or after the war. If any are left, they are not always easy to access. However, an increasing quantity of material is becoming available thanks to the recent and rapid construction of the online system by the National Diet Library and libraries attached to the universities that were formerly higher commercial schools. Second, with some exceptions such as Akamatsu Kaname, most economists who actually experienced or directly participated in the war have not willingly commented on this topic. This has caused a discontinuity in the history of Japanese economic thought before and after the war. This study will focus on research by the economists who belonged to the national higher commercial schools, in the hope that it may help correct this situation.

## 2 Higher commercial schools in Japan: an overview

### 2.1 Establishment

After the isolationist period, the new Meiji government soon imported academic subjects from 'Western' countries, including economics and commercial studies. In this period, these subjects were not regarded as part of higher education in Japan. It was in the late 1870s and 1880s that they became part of higher education. Throughout the development of economics and commercial studies in Japan, two higher educational institutions played important roles: imperial universities and national higher commercial schools.

In 1878, Imperial University – later renamed Tokyo Imperial University and now known as the University of Tokyo – began to offer lectures on economics before the establishment of a higher commercial school in 1884. But these lectures were only a part of a course in literature. The first lecture was delivered by E. F. Fenollosa (1853–1908), who majored in philosophy. He taught the economics of J. S. Mill, W. S. Jevons, J. E. Cairnes, and so on until 1884. From 1881 to around 1889, the first Japanese lecturer, Tajiri Inajiro (1850–1924), who had studied at Yale University, also lectured on economics. After Tajiri, Wadagaki Kenzou (1860–1919) became the second lecturer. He taught both classical economics and the German historical school after returning from his studies at London University, King's College, and Berlin from 1880–1884. After Fenollosa, Udo Eggert (1848–93) came to the Imperial University to teach finance, and then Karl Rathgen (1855–1921) arrived from Germany to teach statistics.[2]

Kyoto Imperial University, established in 1897, started to offer lectures on economics in 1899. This was part of a course taught by the faculty of law. As at Tokyo Imperial University, the economics mainly taught in Kyoto was that of the German Historical School. The first lecturer was Tajima Kinji, who studied under Wadagaki and Kanai Noburu of Tokyo Imperial University, and then under A. Wagner and G. von Schmoller at Berlin University. The second was Toda Kai-ichi, who was known for his theories of industrial policy.[3] In this period, as Yagi (1999: 17) points out, "economics in Imperial University was assimilated into the framework of the German style economics, and could not be free from it easily." In 1919, these two imperial universities formed their departments of economics. In the 1920s, the other imperial universities also established economics courses attached to the departments of law and literature – Tohoku Imperial University in 1922 and Kyusyu Imperial University in 1924. Economics as taught there was similar to that at Tokyo and Kyoto Imperial Universities.

The case of higher commercial schools was quite different. In 1884, the first government-run higher commercial school in Japan was attached to the 'Tokyo School of Foreign Languages' (*Tokyo Gaikokugo Gakko*, presently known as Tokyo Gaikokugo Daigaku or Tokyo University of Foreign Studies). It was named the '*Tokyo Gaikokugo Gakko shozoku Koto Syogyo Gakko*', being modeled on the 'Institut Supérieur de Commerce d'Anvers' founded in 1852 in Antwerp, Belgium, then one of the pioneers of business education in Europe.[4]

In the following year, this commercial school was merged with the '*Tokyo Shogyo Gakko*' (Tokyo School of Commerce), which was originally established by Mori Arinori (1847–1889), who later became Minister of Education, in 1875 as a private school called '*Shoho Koshujo*' (Commercial Training School). In this merger, the higher commercial school was reduced in status. In 1887, however, it was raised to a higher status again as the '*Koto Shogyo Gakko*' (Higher Commercial School), in 1902 being renamed the '*Tokyo Koto Shogyo Gakko*' or the 'Tokyo Higher Commercial School'. Now it is known as Hitotsubashi University.[5] From the early 1900s to the 1920s, the number of higher commercial schools modelled on the Tokyo Higher Commercial School grew.

With the return of tariff autonomy, the abolishment of extraterritorial rights in 1899 and the increased demand for business students to be trained in commerce and foreign languages, the Japanese government established the second higher commercial school in Kobe in 1902. Osaka, the next most commercially prosperous city after Tokyo, was not chosen, but instead established the municipal 'Osaka Higher Commercial School' in 1901. The three higher commercial schools developed into Universities of Commerce in the 1920s: Tokyo Higher Commercial School reorganized as 'Tokyo University of Commerce' in 1920, Kobe Higher Commercial School as 'Kobe University of Commerce' in 1929, and 'Osaka City Commercial College' as 'Osaka University of Commerce' in 1928. Later they came to be called the 'Big Three Commercial Universities'.

Following Kobe, three more higher commercial schools were established: Nagasaki and Yamaguchi in 1905, and Otaru in 1910. From the geographical point of view, their location was significant: the former two were located near what was then the continental part of Japan, and the latter had easy access to Russia.

The 1910s again saw prosperity caused by WWI. This enabled Prime Minister Hara Takashi (1856–1921) to implement the 'positive policy', which included the enhancement of national defense, the expansion of higher education, the promotion of industry, and the development of transportation. Additional graduates from higher commercial education were required. This led to the foundation of other eight higher commercial schools in the first half of the 1920s. They included Nagoya in 1920, Fukushima and Oita in 1921, Hikone and Wakayama in 1922, Yokohama and Takamatsu in 1923, and Takaoka in 1924.[6] Map 8.1 shows their locations.

## 2.2 Education

In contrast to education in imperial universities, education in higher commercial schools had distinctive features: practical education, economics, foreign languages, and finally foreign trade education. These subjects were introduced because of influences of the 'Institut Supérieur de Commerce d'Anvers'.

The curricula of the higher commercial schools included both classroom and practical learning. The first and second grade students acquired expert knowledge of commerce in the classroom, and then the third grade students put it into practice through simulation classes. A few higher commercial schools, such as Otaru and Nagoya, provided more practical education.[7] The principal of Otaru Higher Commercial School, Watanabe Ryusei,[8] emphasizing pragmatism as advocated by John Dewey, constructed a special room for 'practical commerce', where simulation-classes of commercial systems, banks, warehouses, insurance, and transportation were undertaken. He also built a soap factory for further practical business education based on F.W. Taylor's management theories (Otaru Syouka Daigaku 1961: 30–31).

The textbooks used to teach economics in the case of Tokyo Commercial School in 1886, for example, were *Political Economy for Beginners* by M.G. Fawcett (1870), *Money and the Mechanism of Exchange* by W.S. Jevons (1875), *The*

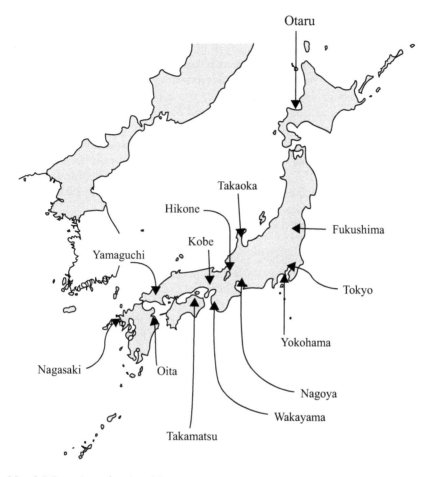

*Map 8.1* Location of national higher commercial schools and commercial universities in mainland Japan (1924), the map of Japan based on: http://www.sekaichizu.jp/

*History, Principles, and Practice of Banking* by J.W. Gilbart (1882), *Principles of Political Economy* by J.S. Mill (1848), *Free Trade and Protection* by H. Fawcett (1878), *The Theory of Foreign Exchange* by G.J. Goschen (1861), *Traité de la science des finances* by P.L. Beaulieu (1877), and *The Principles of Political Economy* by H. Sidgwick (1883).[9] As from the end of the 1880s, economics taught at imperial universities began to be influenced by the German Historical School. However, Fawcett's book (1870) was selected also at Kobe Higher Commercial School in 1928, (Kobe Koto Shogyou Gakko Gakuyukai-nai Toudai-shi Hensyukai Ed. 1928: 16). In 1908, Kyoto Imperial University had added a course on Marxian economics by Kawakami Hajime. The higher commercial schools, however, did not offer it.

In the commercial schools, the most important foreign language was English for convenience in international business world while in imperial universities German was preferred (Yagi 1999: 17). This was because imperial universities were required to develop human resources to fill the government posts necessary to the modernization of Japan whose models were in many cases German. In higher commercial schools, students were required to study another foreign language in addition to English. In most schools, they could choose from Chinese, French, or German. Some schools also offered classes in other languages. The choice of the foreign language was dependent on the geographical situation of each higher commercial school. For example, at Otaru located near China and Russia, students could choose from French, German, Chinese, Russian, or Spanish (Otaru Syouka Daigaku 1961: 40 and 77). The same options were available at Takaoka Higher Commercial School, which also had easy access to continental Asia (Takaoka Koto Shogyou Gakko Ed. 1926: 6), while Yamaguchi Higher Commercial School, near the Korean Peninsula, taught Korean and Chinese (Yamaguchi Koto Shogyou Gakko 1905: 24).

Almost all higher commercial schools offered special courses in foreign trade, which had close connections to the languages offered. After the outbreak of WWI in 1914, international trade rapidly increased. The next year, in order to adapt to this situation, Yamaguchi Higher Commercial School established the one-year 'China trade seminar course' for those who graduated from the three-year higher commercial school course. This was followed by the establishment of the 'international trade course' at Nagasaki Higher Commercial School in 1917. In this course, the following subjects were taught: international public and private law, colonial policy, international finance, and international trade. Students could also choose languages such as Dutch, Malay, and Portuguese (Nagasaki Koto Syougyou Gakko Ed. 1935: 111–113).

Besides these courses for graduates of the higher commercial schools, in March 1929, the Ministry of Education decided to attach a one-year course to the higher commercial schools for graduates of middle level education.[10] The course aimed to develop trade, especially in China, the South Sea area, and South America (Sakudo and Eto Ed. 1970: 81). In 1929, Yamaguchi, Nagasaki, and Yokohama higher commercial schools opened similar short-term courses.

With the establishment of such trade courses, lecturers inevitably began to pay attention to the economic affairs in the related areas. As will be mentioned in the next section, this educational peculiarity influenced the directionality of research by economists at higher commercial schools.

### 2.3 Research

Lecturers studied economic theories introduced from Western countries, and presented their papers in journals published by higher commercial schools. As the educational environment developed, the amount of research by lecturers gradually increased. Their research, however, was distinguished by its practical economic focus on local industries.

*Economic research in wartime Japan* 143

All the higher commercial schools organized a research group, department, section, or institute. In 1914, Kobe Higher Commercial School had a research section ('Cyousa-ka'), which developed into a research institute ('Shougyou Kenkyu-sho') in 1919. It mainly aimed to collect articles from newspapers, like similar institutes in Germany (Sakudo and Eto 1976: 258–259). Besides Kobe, this kind of group was opened in the Research Building ('Kenkyu-kan') of Nagasaki Higher Commercial School founded in 1919, and the industrial research bureau of Yamaguchi Higher Commercial School ('Shougyou Kenkyu-sho') in 1921.[11]

Moreover, some research groups or institutes engaged in studies specific to their local areas. For example, the research section attached to Wakayama Higher Commercial School began in 1925 to study the local agricultural industries including the production of mandarin oranges, rice, and pyrethrum. The research on mandarin oranges, then and now the principal product of Wakayama, was started by Moriya Mamoru and Mikami Risaburou.[12]

Takaoka Higher Commercial School started the research on the local patent medicine industry – in 1927. Shirohama Masaharu and Uehara Senroku took part in the research, and published the three volumes of *The Historical Collection of a Patent Medicine Industry in Toyama Prefecture* in 1935.[13]

One of the best known of such research projects was that on the woolen industry in the Bisai near Nagoya Higher Commercial School. In 1926 the 'Bureau of Business Research (Sangyou Chousa Shitsu)'[14] was established by the idea of Akamatsu Kaname (1896–1974), who had just come back from his studies in Germany and Harvard Business School from 1924–26.[15] In the bureau, empirical analysis of woolen industries modeled on that of Harvard was begun under his leadership.[16] Akamatsu also presented the 'Wild Geese-Flying Pattern Theory'[17] or '*Gankou Keitai Ron*' in his original Japanese expression in 1935. It explains the pattern of development of an industry imported from a developed country into a developing one.[18] This theory was published in English after WWII and is still applied to analyze the development of developing countries. In addition to the woolen industry other important local industries such as watchmaking and pottery were also researched.

Besides these higher commercial schools, Fukushima Higher Commercial School organized the 'Tohoku Keizai Kenkyu-sho' or 'Economic Research Institute of Tohoku Area' in 1921. In 1923, Hikone Higher Commercial School established the research department ('Cyousa-ka'), which was reorganized in 1926 as the research section ('Kenkyu-bu'). In 1928,[19] this section included the 'Omi Shonin Kenkyu-kai' (the research group of merchants in the Omi district).[20]

The commitment of these economists to the local industries was peculiar to higher commercial schools. In the 1930s, a new peculiarity also appeared there.

## 3 Higher commercial schools in wartime

The most seriously affected segment of education in wartime Japan was commercial education, including economics. In the early 1930s, 'new thoughts' like socialism or Marxism had already been banned because they were regarded as against government policy. Because of this regulation, books on 'new thoughts' or the left wing were removed from school libraries. Moreover, in 1932 the Ministry of Education began to take measures against left-wing thoughts (Sakudo and Eto Ed. 1976: 412–413). In fact, students who expressed these thoughts were arrested. At Nagoya Higher Commercial School in 1933, 15 students were rounded up (Hotta 2005: 44).

From 1936, students were given special lectures several times per year on Japanese culture, the Imperial Household and its significance, wars, and the wartime economy. After the Marco Polo Bridge Incident in July 1937, the contents and the system of education were also changed. Students were forced to give labor service outside schools. In comparison to middle-level commercial education, however, control over higher-level education was not so strict till the beginning of the 1940s. At least students could receive the commercial education for three years, which was the standard period required for graduation at that time (Hotta 2005: 44–47; Sakudo and Eto Ed. 1976: 440–451).

From around this period, higher commercial schools began to assume the role of educational institutes for studies on the colonial development of Japan. With the growth of Japanese territories through the wars in Asia, higher commercial schools provided businesspeople with higher commercial knowledge and foreign language skills, and also began to research customs and markets in the new colonial areas of Japan for further commercial and industrial development.

### 3.1 The increase in Asian studies: the interests of economists and their actual works

With the expansion of Japan's colonial territory, the significance of colonial studies increased rapidly. As mentioned above, most higher commercial schools opened special courses on foreign trade. In the latter half of the 1930s, these courses multiplied. In 1938 Otaru Higher Commercial School opened an East Asia course for the graduates of higher education. In 1939, Hikone Higher Commercial School also opened a China course, which was renamed 'East Asia course' in 1941. In 1940, both Oita and Takaoka higher commercial schools also established East Asia courses. Fukushima Higher Commercial School did the same in 1938. The normal three-year course also added subjects on colonial policy in the third year. In order to adapt to the social situation and satisfy educational demand, lecturers needed to acquire knowledge on Asian areas and to research colonial studies, in addition to their studies on local industries, regardless of their original academic specialty.

For example, Hikone Higher Commercial School, before the establishment of the course, had established the 'Ishokumin Kenkyu-shitsu' (research room on emigration and immigration) in 1930 and the 'Kaigai-jijyou Kenkyu-Kai' (research group on the foreign affairs) in 1931.[21] With Professor Abe Arata's trip to the Republic of China in 1931, more and more lecturers were ordered by the Ministry of Education to make an official overseas trip to continental Asia, among them Professor Tanaka Syusaku (geography) and Eguchi Yukio (currency) to

Manchuria and China in 1933, Professor Okazaki Ayanori (population) in 1936, Professor Iwama Iwao (management) in 1937, and Professor Hagaya Arimichi (economics) in 1938 (Ryosui-kai 1984: 81). The original fields of the lecturers were not always related to Asian studies, but some of them even presented papers on this topic.[22]

This was true of Yokohama Higher Commercial School. In 1924, it established a research institute ('Kenkyusho'). In 1936, part of it organized the 'Boueki Kenkyu-kai' (a research group on trade). In January 1941, the research institute was reorganized as the 'Taiheyou Boueki Kenkyu-syo', a research institute for trade in the Pacific Ocean (Yokohama Koto Shogyou Gakko 1943: 33, 180–181). The members of the institute included Tajiri Tsuneo (head), Tokumasu Eitaro, Morita Yuzo, Koshimura Shinzaburo, Ide Fumio, and Shimoda Reisa among others. From 1941 to 1943 it published the series of Japanese translations and original books titled *Taiheiyou Sangyou Kenkyu So-sho* (Series on the Industries in the Pacific Area). In this series, Ide presented translations regarding the economic affairs of East India (Indonesia) and Thailand, though his main research area was finance and had no direct connection to these areas. He also presented an original paper on the finance of East India, a topic more closely related to his original academic interest. Koshimura, whose academic background was interest in economic circulation, also applied his method to the analysis of economic circulation in East Asia.

This situation meant that first, the topics with which the lecturers engaged were not so closely connected to their original academic interests; second, they applied their original academic methods as best they could to the surveys of the colonial territory of Japan, in response to the demand of society then. Such a tendency was also found in other schools, such as Nagasaki and Yamaguchi.

### 3.2 Compulsory reorganization of higher commercial schools in 1943

In 1943, with the escalation of the war in Japan, national higher commercial schools were compulsorily changed into the three types of schools in Table 8.1, and the new educational system started in the spring of 1944.

This institutional change meant that the terms 'commerce' or 'commercial' were regarded as against national policy. From October 1943, along with this reorganization of commercial education, students who did not major in natural and applied sciences were forced to go to war under the student mobilization

*Table 8.1* Categories of reorganized higher commercial schools after 1943

| After reorganization | Previous higher commercial school |
| --- | --- |
| 1 Technical junior college | Hikone, Wakayama, Takaoka |
| 2 Industrial management junior college | Nagasaki, Nagoya, Yokohama |
| 3 Junior college of economics | Yamaguchi, Otaru, Fukushima, Oita, Takamatsu |

order. For example, in the case of Nagoya Higher Commercial School, 90 students were mobilized (Hotta 2005: 48).

In the technical junior colleges, economics was removed completely from the program of study. For example, it was difficult for Takaoka Higher Commercial School to oppose this institutional change, because it lacked engineers with higher-level knowledge or a background in the development of industries in the local area (Toyama Daigaku Keizaigaku-bu, Etsurei-kai 1978: 536). Almost all the teachers except for Sahara Takaomi (finance) moved to another school (five professors) or resigned (four lecturers). For instance, Nagao Yoshizou (economics) moved to Otaru Junior College of Economics (ibid.: 1025), and Jyuhou Masaji (commerce; the research manager) moved to Shanghai University in the spring of 1944 (ibid.: 600). Instead, only two lecturers, along with some lecturers from factories near the school, were available to teach industry. This shows the inadequate educational environment then (ibid.: 144).

The contents of the journal '*Kenkyu Ronsyu (Research Papers)*' published by the school also changed as the war advanced. In 1929, when the first volume was published, it included studies on economic theories from foreign countries (ibid.: 55). The 13th volume published in 1940, however, was devoted to the problems of East Asia and the war. The last volume published under the organization of the higher commercial school in June 1944 was a special edition on the economy of the Japan Sea area. The other publications by the research institute attached to the school also ceased to come out. After that, economic studies also stopped. This was true of Hikone (Ryosui-kai 1984: 98) and Wakayama higher commercial schools as well.

At some industrial management junior colleges, such as Yokohama Higher Commercial School, lectures on economics or commercial studies continued. But lecturers in English and other foreign languages stopped because of the significant decrease of classes in those subjects. Instead, lectures on applied sciences such as industrial management, electricity and engineering were added (Gojyunen-shi Hensyu Iinkai 1975: 253–255). The school stopped publishing its journal '*Shogaku*' (*Commercial Studies*) in 1942 and the aforementioned 'Taiheiyou Sangyou Kenkyu So-syo' (Series on the Industries in the Pacific Area) in 1943.

Nagoya and Nagasaki higher commercial schools also stopped publishing their journals in 1944 after becoming technical junior colleges. Nagoya Higher Commercial School published '*Shogyou Keizai Ronsou (Collection of Treatises on Commerce and Economy)*' till September, 1944; Nagasaki Higher Commercial School also continued its publication of '*Shogyou to Keizai (Commerce and Economy)*', which was finally renamed as '*Keiei to Keizai (Business Administration and Economy)*', until June 1944, avoiding the word 'commerce' in the title of the journal. These publications did not include studies on economics in Western countries.

Some differences can be found between the junior college of economics and the two schools above. At Otaru Higher Commercial School, for instance, in the spring vacation of 1944, the lectures on social policy given by Minami Ryozaburo still included the theories of A. Smith, R. Malthus and the theory of marginal utility (Otaru Syouka Daigaku Hyakunen-shi Hensan-shitsu Ed. 2011:

522–523), while Tezuka Jyurou,[23] who studied the mathematical economics of H. H. Gossen, had resigned from the school in 1942. The school was required to add a new lecture on factory management from the beginning of the 1944 fiscal year, but that was all (Otaru Kosho-shi Kenkyu-kai Ed. 2002: 61).[24] But in this period, Minami's lecture on economics changed rapidly to a nationalistic perspective. Students of this school began to study theoretical economics on their own, such as Marshall, Jevons, Ricardo, and the theory of marginal utility that had been taught by Minami before (ibid.: 239), and entered their papers in an essay contest organized by the school. Among the 1945 papers is a paper on the new mercantilism, which studied classical economics and the German Historical School (Ara 1945). This was written by Ara Kenjiro (1925–2002), who became professor of economics at Hitotsubashi University after WWII.

The Otaru school journal '*Shogaku Tokyu (Investigations on Commercial Studies)*' also continued to be published until 1945, although the number of copies printed decreased. In 1945, 500 were printed, down from 3,850 in 1937, and publication frequency also decreased, from three times to twice a year until 1944. Even in 1945, this journal was still published once, but in April 1944 the title was changed to '*Hoppo Keizai Kenkyu (Studies on the economy in the Northern area of Japan)*', removing the word 'commerce' from the title and adding the name of the region instead (ibid.: 71–5). The main topic of the journal was economic affairs in the northern territory and the local area. Such tendencies were also found at Takamatsu, Yamaguchi, and Oita higher commercial schools.[25]

Fukushima Higher Commercial School continued to publish the journal '*Shogaku Ronsyu (Journal of commerce, economics and economic history)*' until September 1944, without changing the name. Like Otaru Higher Commercial School, it mainly emphasized the study of economic affairs, or the economy of the local area. In the last volume, however, an article appeared on Keynes's theory of money and interest (Kumagai 1944). It was written by Kumagai Hisao (1914–1996), then professor at the higher commercial school, and played a significant role in the development of welfare economics in Japan after the war.

Near the end of WWII, most studies were on the economic affairs of local areas or colonial parts of Japan in order to meet the social demand. The number of theoretical studies was small. But such buds, which would flourish in post-war Japan, did not disappear completely.

### 3.3 The research institute of Tokyo University of Commerce[26]

In any study of economic research in wartime Japan, mention of research at the Tokyo University of Commerce cannot be avoided.[27] This is because the research institute attached to the university was nationalized in February 1942, and then became involved in the research activities of the military administration. This made a difference between the research carried out at this university and that of other national higher commercial schools.

Although Tokyo Higher Commercial School was the first national higher commercial school, and then in 1920 also became the first national commercial university when it was renamed 'Tokyo University of Commerce', it could not establish a research institute until 1940 because of the refusal of the Ministry of Education to approve a budget for it. It had only an economic research department in 1909, which concentrated on collecting materials and data published by banks, companies, exchanges, as other bureaus attached to higher commercial schools did (Maruyama 1989: 67). Ueda Teijiro (1879–1940), then president of the university, recognized the necessity of an institute: "It will be important to cultivate human resources to work in China. Tokyo University of Commerce also has to make a contribution. [. . .] We also need a research institute" (Ueda 1963: 315). A research tour in China and Manchuria for a month in 1939 gave him more definite ideas about the establishment of an institute.[28]

A donation by Kagami Kenkichi (1879–1940),[29] a graduate of Tokyo Higher Commercial School and then president of Tokyo-Kaijyou Fire Insurance Company,[30] enabled the establishment of the research institute in April 1940. It was named the '*Toua Keizai Kenkyusho*' ('Institute of East Asian Economic Research'), and was established in the library of Tokyo University of Commerce, with four departments: research, resources, statistics and general affairs. Akamatsu Kaname was director of the research department, Sugimoto Eiichi (1901–1952) was director of the statistics department, Odabashi Sadajyu (1904–1984) was director of the resources department, and the director of general affairs post was vacant. Akamatsu intended to run the institute on the model of Nagoya Higher Commercial School.[31]

In February 1942, the institute became government-run and began empirical studies on East Asia, including publications and overseas and domestic research. The first volume of the series *Touakeizai Kenkyusho Kenkyu Sousyo* (Research Series of the Institute) was *Toua Nougyo Seisan-shisu no Kenkyu* (Researches on the Index of Agricultural Products in East Asia) by Yamada Isamu (1909–86) in March 1942. But the series could not be continued because of the war.

In pursuit of their research aims, the lecturers actually went to continental China and published the reports *Toua Keizai Kenkyu Houkoku* (Reports on the Economy in East Asia).[32] In the area of domestic economic research, the institute established a committee on the measurement of the power of the defense economy ('Kokubo Keizai-ryoku Sokutei Iinkai'). The committee aimed to measure the economic power of wartime Japan using quantitative factor such as national income, financial planning, and economic cycles. It consisted of Nakayama Ichiro (head), Kito Nisaburo, Okawa Kazushi, Tsuru Shigeto, and others. The committee concluded that Japan could not sustain the war effort, but the detailed reports were burned.

At Tokyo University of Commerce, a research project in Southeast Asia was also carried out in cooperation with the Japanese military administration from the end of 1942. According to members of the institute at that time, after the attack on Pearl Harbor on December 8, 1941, they had a meeting and had the following discussion.

> We were to work for the military administration, but the purpose was thoroughly academic research in the Southeast [Asian] areas. So our position did

not change. That was very important . . . We went there and cooperated with the military administration, but in fact we did not really want to do so. We did want to go on with our academic researches.

(Tokyo-daigaku Kyouyou-gakubu Kokusai-kankeiron
Kenkyu-shitsu Ed. 1981: 121)

According to members, Itagaki Yoichi (1908–2003) and Yamada Hideo (1917–2002),

We were told that our status would be higher if we became military governors. But Professor Yamanaka [Tokutaro] and Professor Sugimoto did not want to accept this condition. Rather we would like [to go on with the research] as Professors of Tokyo University of Commerce . . . We, who are engaged in academics, did not attend the research as military governors.[33]

(Hitotsubashidaigaku Gakuenshi
Hensanjigyou Iinkai Ed. 1983: 45)

The members of Tokyo University of Commerce agreed among themselves that they would assist the military, while focusing mainly on academic researches and also retaining their status as professors (Fukami 1988: 120).

In September 1942, the then President Takase Sotaro (1892–1966) of Tokyo University of Commerce was asked by his younger brother Takase Keijiro (1905–1982), who was then Lieutenant Colonel of the Imperial Headquarters, to cooperate with the General Army in Southeast Asia through research activities. This was because the Japanese Army (the 25th Army) had no researchers and little reference materials or information on the occupied area at the beginning of Japan's military administration (Akashi 2006a: 8). He accepted the request (Akamatsu 1975: 44). According to Akamatsu's autobiography, however, when he learned of Takase's acceptance, Akamatsu said he "would like to dispatch as few members as possible because the institute was in its early stage" (ibid.). But Professor Sugimoto said that "we should cooperate with the army thoroughly", and also "asked Akamatsu to go to Southeast Asia as a leader"[34] (ibid.).

Finally on December 18, 1942, the research group commanded by Akamatsu left Kobe port for Singapore, where the headquarters of the Japanese military administration in Southeast Asia were[35] (Akamatsu 1975: 44; Fukami 1988: 122–123). At the beginning, the group comprised more than 40 people including 18 members from Tokyo University of Commerce. Among the members the following lecturers were included: in addition to Akamatsu, Sugimoto Eiichi, Yamanaka Tokutaro, Takahashi Taizou, Odabashi Sadajyu, Kawai Ryotaro, Ishida Ryujiro, Itagaki Yoichi, Uchida Naosaku, Yamada Hideo, Yamada Isamu, and others. Two members of the team came from Kobe University of Commerce (Yamashita Kakutaro and Nomura Torajiro) and Keio University (Harashima Susumu and Ogawa Takao), and one each from Takaoka Higher Commercial School (Mukai Umeji), the Ministry of Education (Watanabe Baiyu), and the 'Institute for Islamic Areas (Kaikyoken Kenkyu-jo)' (Suzuki Tomohide) (Akamatsu 1975: 44).[36]

At first, the army intended to assign the research on Malaya, Sumatra, and Burma to the research group from the South Manchuria Railway Company. The research on Java was to be assigned to the Toua Kenkyusho (the Research Institute on East Asia), on North Borneo to the Taiheiyo Kyoukai (the Research Association on the Pacific Ocean), and on the Philippines to the Mitsubishi Keizai Kenkyusho (the Mitsubishi Economic Research Institute). The research group of the Tokyo University of Commerce was required to oversee all the groups (Akamatsu 1975: 44). They had a meeting in Japan before the beginning of the research and another after arriving at the research site. But the research did not go as well as had been expected. They researched respectively as they liked. Moreover, the group from the university was not welcomed by the army. The Japanese military administration demanded not academic research but practical research for the development of natural resources because the war situation was already worsening for Japan. Thus, Akamatsu decided to change the research on his arrival in 1943. He added surveys on the minimum requirement of life such as clothing and food, [ways to] increase agricultural products, and supply and demand in the labor force to win the mind of the native people. Social affairs, such as land systems, religions, and industry were also included. The survey on the lives of the natives was done by Yamada Isamu, who had published researches on the Index of Agricultural Products in East Asia. Such research, however, did not improve the performance of the group.

In early 1944, academic research was not a matter of significance. By the middle of 1944, the research activities were completely stopped. Instead, Akamatsu and others, especially Itagaki Yoichi, made efforts to win over native people such as the overseas Chinese, Sultans, and Muslims in Malaya.[37] Akamatsu thought it important to permit Malaya to gain its independence from Britain because it would help Japan's army if the natives there resisted the British Armed Forces. But this idea was not permitted by the Imperial Conference. He then "decided to conduct a movement for the independence of Malaya by himself" and asked "the leaders of the natives there to take part in it", explaining that "Malaya would be governed by Britain again [after the end of WWII]". Shortly thereafter the movement was approved by the Japanese army, regardless of the Imperial Conference. Before the end of the war, through this movement Indonesia became decolonized from the Netherlands, while Malaysian independence was realized after the war (ibid.: 46–47).

Some of the economists at Tokyo University of Commerce advanced their studies, following their wartime experience. Yamada Isam studied statistics and the 'Input Output Table'. Okawa also studied quantitative analysis and is known for his work on the long-term statistics of the economic development of Japan. Itagaki presented his studies on nationalism in Asia beginning in the 1950s, and also engaged with the problems of its economic development.

## 4  Conclusions

The research carried out in higher commercial schools and commercial universities had close connections to both the industrial and colonial development of Japan during the war. Colonial development took on particular importance as from the 1930s. Most research on Asia or economic affairs was prompted by social demands and had no direct connection with the researcher's original academic interests. Some researchers made further progress after WWII, clearly as a result of their wartime experiences, though in some cases they did not refer to this point directly. The scope of research was not limited solely to economics, but also covered Asia studies: Yamada Hideo is known for his studies on British Malaysia, and Uchida for his studies on Overseas Chinese. Moreover, Itagaki worked on the creation of the 'Asia Keizai Kenkyu-sho' (Institute of Developing Economies), which was accomplished in 1958. The research institutes attached to the higher commercial schools or universities were also reopened or reorganized after 1949 under the new educational system, and have continued economic research to the present time. The Nagasaki institute is now called the 'Tounan Asia Kenkyu-sho' (The Research Institute of Southeast Asia); that of Yamaguchi University is the 'Toua Keizai Kenkyu-sho' (Institute of East Asian Economic Affairs). The other institutes, under new names, have also engaged in empirical analysis, extending the scope of research. They can unquestionably be said to have formed a significant part of the basis for the development of economics and economic research in Japan.

## Notes

1   Makino (2010), Karashima (2015), Ohtsuki (2010: chapter 9), Suehiro (2006a), Yagi (1999: chapter 8) and Yanagisawa (2008) are the recent studies.
2   For the details, see Mizuta and Suzuki (1988), Tamanoi (1971: 27–60), and Yagi (1999: 9–14).
3   For the details, see Kyoto Daigaku Keizaigaku Kenkyu-ka, Keizaigaku-bu-shi Hensan Iinkai (1999: 12–30).
4   Julian van Stappen (1852–1915), a graduate of the 'Institut Supérieur de Commerce d'Anvers', came to teach commercial studies (mainly accounting) in 1885 (National Archives of Japan 1885).
5   See Watanabe M. (1999).
6   Besides these schools in the mainland of Japan, four national higher commercial schools were established in what was then the colonial area of Japan: Taipei and Tainan in 1919, Pyongyang in 1922, and Dalian (Dairen) in 1936.
7   Regarding Nagoya Higher Commercial School, see Watanabe, S. ed. (1931: 47–50).
8   With regard to him, see Hotta (2005: chapter 3).
9   Tokyo Shougyou Gakko (1886: 17–18).
10  Middle level education consisted of five years' schooling for students aged 12–16.
11  Otaru Higher Commercial School also had the 'Sangyou Cyousa-kai' (research group on industry) since its establishment. It aimed to research the local industries, but it did not work well (Otaru Syouka Daigaku Hyakunen-shi Hensan-shitsu ed. 2011: 282).
12  Moriya (1934, 1937) and Moriya and Mikami (1934).
13  See Takaoka Koto Shogyou Gakko ed. (1935). Masuda Shiro, Uehara Eikichi and Muramatsu Yuji, who were all students at Tokyo University of Commerce then, also engaged in editing the book. Masuda and Muramatsu later became Professor of Tokyo University of Commerce, and Uehara became Professor of Matsusho Gakuen.
14  This translation can be found in Akamatsu (1975: 38). We can also find another translation "The Industrial Research Bureau" on the back cover of Sakai and Akamatsu (1935).

15 For the details, see Hirakawa (2013), Ikeo (2008), and Ohtsuki (2011: 293–296).
   Akamatsu called this bureau "The third window". According to Akamatsu, "universities should absorb the lights of academics through three windows" (Akamatsu 1975: 38). "The first window" is a library, in which accomplished studies are kept. 'The second window', mainly for natural science, is a laboratory or an astronomical observatory, in which intuitive facts are absorbed, and are composed into a conception. In "the third window" intuitive facts and the composed conceptions are analyzed based on the accomplished studies, which as a result newly generate a law or tendency. Such way of thinking of him was based on his synthetic dialectics.
16 E. F. Penrose also advanced his research on quantitative index of products with the help of Japanese lecturers and students during his stay at Nagoya from 1925–30. See Penrose (1975, 1987).
17 This English translation was given by Shinohara Miyohei.
18 This was presented in Akamatsu (1935) for the first time. For the details, see Ohtsuki (2010, 2011).
19 This information was cited from the appendix of Ryosui-kai (1984).
20 Omi is the former name of Shiga prefecture where Hikone Higher Commercial School was located, and is known for the Omi merchants in Japan.
21 This was attached to the research section of the school mentioned in the previous section.
22 One of the journals was "*Kaigai-jijyou Kenkyu*" (Studies on the Foreign Affairs) published by the research group of foreign affairs.
23 He is also known for his Japanese translation of "Éléments d'économie politique pure ou théorie de la richesse sociale" by L. Walras.
24 See also Otaru Syouka Daigaku Hyakunen-shi Hensan-shitsu ed. (2011: 562).
25 Takamatsu Higher Commercial School published the '*Shouko Keizai Kenkyu (Studies on Commerce and Economy)*' from 1925. It was renamed the '*Takamatsu Kosho Ronsou (Journal of Takamatsu Higher Commercial School)*' in 1941. This was continued till 1944, and in 1945 the title continued to be published under the name '*Takamatsu Keisen Ronso (Takamatsu Economic College Review)*'. Oita Higher Commercial School continued to publish the '*Syougyou Ronsyu (Journal of Commercial Studies, Oita)*' till 1944. But they did not change the name.
26 This is dependent on Ohtsuki (2010: chapter 9). See also Ikema et al. (2000: 128–130), Majima (2016), and Akashi and Yoshimura eds. (2008) available in English.
27 This university was also compelled to remove the word "Commerce" from its name, and renamed 'Tokyo University of Industry' ('Tokyo Sangyou Daigaku') in 1944.
28 For the details, see Akamatsu (1941) and Ueda (1939).
29 Regarding him, see Suzuki ed. (1949).
30 Present Tokio Marine & Nichido Fire Insurance Co., Ltd.
31 In April 1939, he moved from Nagoya Higher Commercial School to Tokyo University of Commerce.
32 Yamamoto (2011, chapter 9) examined the sixth report by Takahashi Taizou, published in 1945 (Takahashi 1945). This report was on an estimation of the national income in the economy of the South Sea Area.
33 This reference did not tell which of the three members made this statement.
34 Akamatsu was surprised at Sugimoto's change to right-wing thinking, because he studied Marx. According to Akamatsu, such a change was caused by his feeling a sense of Japan's crisis (Akamatsu 1975: 44).
35 Sugimoto, Yamanaka, Takahashi and Odabashi had started before the group (Maruyama 1989: 170).
36 Not all the members participated from the beginning. For the details, see also Akashi (2006a) and Ohtsuki (2010, chapter 9).
37 For the details, see also Itagaki (1988).

# References

Akamatsu, K. (1935). "Wagakuni Youmou Kougyouhin no Boueki Susei," *Syougyou Keizai Ronsou*, Nagoya: Nagoya Higher Commercial School, 13(1): 129–212 [Trend of the trade of woolen products of Japan].

Akamatsu, K. (1941). "Ueda-Sensei to Syou-dai Touakeizai Kenkyusho", *Hitotsubashi Ronsou*, Tokyo: Tokyo University of Commerce, 7(1): 112 [Professor Ueda and Institute of Economic Research of East Asia attached to Tokyo University of Commerce].

Akamatsu, K. (1975). "Gakumon Henro", In Kojima (Ed.) 1975: 9–68 [Autobiography].

Akashi, Y. (2006a). "Kaisetsu," in Akashi Youji ed. and annotation 2006b, vol. 1: 7–17 [Comments on Akashi ed. and annotation 2006b].

Akashi, Y. (Ed. and annotation) (2006b). *Nanpou Gunseki Kankei Shiryou 35* (22 vols.), Tokyo: Ryuukei-shosya [*Historical Materials of the Japanese Military Administration in Southeast Asia. Reprinted Edition*].

Akashi, Y. and Yoshimura, M. (Eds.). (2008). *New Perspectives on the Japanese Occupation in Malaya and Singapore, 1941–1945*, Singapore: NUS Press.

Ara, K. (1945). "Shin-Jyusyousyugi wo Ronzu", *Hoppo Keizai Geppo*, 192, Otaru: Otaru Keizai Senmon Gakko, Hoppo Kezai Kenkyu-sho [On New Mercantilism].

Fukami, S. (1988). "Tounan-Asia niokeru Nihon Gunsei no Cyousa," *Nampo Bunka*, Tenri Nampou Bunka Kyoukai, 15: 119–151 [Researches by the Japanese Military Administration in Southeast Asia].

Gojyunen-shi Hensyu Iinkai (1975). *Kagayaku Hakua*. Yokohama: Gojyunen-shi Hensyu Iinkai [*Fifty Years History of Faculty of Economics and Business Administration, Yokohama National University*].

Hirakawa, H. (2013). "Akamatsu Kaname to Nagoya Koto Syougyo Gakko," *Keizai Kagaku*, Nagoya: Nagoya University, 60(4): 13–64 [Akamatsu Kaname and Nagoya Higher Commercial School].

Hitotsubashi-daigaku Gakuenshi Hensanjigyou Iinkai (Ed.) (1983). *Dainiji-taisen to Hitotsubashi*, Tokyo: Hitotsubashidaigaku Gakuenshi Hensanjigyou Iinkai [*WWII and Hitotsubashi University*].

Hotta, S. (2005). *Nagoya Koutou Syogyo Gakko*, Nagoya: Nagoya Daigaku Daigaku Bunsyo Shiryou-shitsu [*History of Nagoya Higher Commercial School*].

Ikema, M., Inoue, Y., Nishizawa, T., and Yamauchi, S. (Eds.). (2000). *Hitotsubashi University, 1875–2000: A Hundred and Twenty-Five Years of Higher Education in Japan*, Basingstoke: Macmillan.

Ikeo, A. (2008). *Akamatsu Kaname*, Tokyo: Nihon Keizai Hyouron-Sya [*Biography of Akamatsu*].

Itagaki, Y. (1988). *Asia tono Taiwa*, new edition, Tokyo: Ronsou-sya [*Dialogues with Asia*].

Karashima, M. (2015). *Teikoku Nihon no Asia Kenkyu*, Tokyo: Akashi Shoten [*Asian Studies in the Japanese Empire*].

Kobe Koto Shogyou Gakko Gakuyukai-nai Toudai-shi Hensyukai (Ed.) (1928). *Toudai Nijyu-gonen-shi*, Kobe: Kobe Higher Commercial School, Toudai-shi Hensyukai [*Twenty Five Years History of Kobe Higher Commercial School*].

Kojima, K. (Ed.) (1975). *Gakumon Henro*, Tokyo: Sekai Keizai Kenkyukai [*Akamatsu: His Life and Works*].

Kumagai, H. (1944). "Kahei to Rishi," *Shogaku Ronsyu*, Fukushima: Fukushima Keizai Senmon Gakko, 16(1): 39–65 [Money and Interest].

Kyoto Daigaku Keizaigaku Kenkyu-ka, Keizaigaku-bu-shi Hensan Iinkai (1999). *Kyoto Daigaku Keizaigaku-bu Hachijyu-nen-shi*, Kyoto: Kyoto Daigaku Keizaigaku-bu Hachijyu-syunen Kinen Jigyou Jittuko Iinkai [*Eighty Years History of the Faculty of Economics, Kyoto University*].

Majima, S. (2016). "The Japanese Military Administration Department of Research Reports on Singapore's Wartime Economy," *Toyo Bunka Kenkyu* (*Journal of Asian cultures*), Tokyo: Research Institute for Oriental Cultures, Gakushuin University, 18: 459–510.

Makino, K. (2010). *Senjika no Keizaigakusya*, Tokyo: Cyuou Kouron-sya [*Economists in Wartime*].

Maruyama, Y. (1989). *Sensou-no Jidai to Hitotsubashi*, Tokyo: Jyosuikai [*Wartime and Hitotsubashi University*].

Mizuta, H., and Suzuki, M. (1988). "His Majesty's University: Tokyo Imperial University," in C. Sugiyama and H. Mizuta (Eds.), *Enlightenment and Beyond: Political Economy Come to Japan*, Tokyo: University of Tokyo Press, 97–120.

Moriya, M. (1934). *Kome no Cyousa* (*Sangyou Kenkyu* 2), Wakayama: Wakayama Higher Commercial School, Sangyou Kenkyu-bu [*Studies on Rice*].

Moriya, M. (1937). *Kisyu-san Jyocyu-giku* (*Sangyou Kenkyu* 3 and 4), Wakayama: Wakayama Higher Commercial School, Sangyou Kenkyu-bu [*Pyrethrum Produced in Wakayama Prefecture*].

Moriya, M. and Mikami, R. (1934). *Kisyu Mikan* (*Sangyou Kenkyu* 1), Wakayama: Wakayama Higher Commercial School, Sangyou Kenkyu-bu [*Mandarin Oranges in Wakayama Prefecture*].

Nagasaki Koto Shogyou Gakko (Ed.) (1935). *Nagasaki Koto Shogyou Gakko Sanjyunen-shi*, Nagasaki: Nagasaki Higher Commercial School [*Thirty Years History of Nagasaki Higher Commercial School*].

National Archives of Japan (1885). "Berugi-kokujin Stappen Yatoiire-no-ken", *Kobunroku, Meiji 18, 142*, Tokyo: National Archives of Japan, available by microfilm Reel No. 056300 [The Employment of Van Stappen].

Ohtsuki, T. (2010). "Akamatsu Kaname no Gankou-Keitai-Ron to Sono Tenkai," Ph. D Theses of Tokyo University of Foreign Studies [AKAMATSU Kaname's '*Gankou Keitai Ron*' and its Development – His Nagoya Period and The Perspectives of a Stage Theory of Economic Development].

Ohtsuki, T. (2011). 'The Background of K. AKAMATSU's '*Gankou Keitai Ron*' and Its Development: Early Empirical Analysis at Nagoya', in H. Kurz, T. Nishizawa and K. Tribe (Eds.), *The Dissemination of Economic Ideas*, Cheltenham: Edward Elgar, 292–314.

Otaru Kosho-shi Kenkyu-kai (Ed.) (2002). *Otaru Kosho no Hitobito*, Otaru: Otaru University of Commerce [*Peoples of Otaru Higher Commercial School*].

Otaru Syouka Daigaku (1961). *Ryotuu-kyu Gojyunen-shi*, Otaru: Otaru University of Commerce [*50 Years History of Otaru University of Commerce*].

Otaru Syouka Daigaku Hyakunen-shi Hensan-shitsu (Ed.). (2011). *Otaru Syouka Daigaku Hyakunen-shi: Tsu-shi Hen*, Otaru: Otaru University of Commerce Press [*A Hundred Years History of Otaru University of Commerce: Overview Volume*]. (Available on the website of the Library, Otaru University of Commerce: https://barrel.repo.nii.ac.jp. Accessed 29/09/2016)

Penrose, E.F. (1975). "My Nagoya Era and Professor Akamatsu", In Kojima (Ed.), 1975: 323–327.

Penrose, E. F. (1987). "Memoirs of Japan, 1925–1930," in R. Dore and R. Sinha (Eds.), *Japan and World Depression*, New York: St Martin's Press, 6–13.

Ryosui-kai (1984). *Ryosui Rokujyunen-shi*, Hikone: Shiga Daigaku Keizai-gakubu Ryosui-kai [*Sixty Years History of Faculty of Economics, Shiga University*].

Sakai, S., and Akamatsu, K. (1935). *Cyousa Houkoku 17th*, Nagoya: The Industrial Research Bureau [*Researches of Woolen Industries in Japan 3*].

Sakudo, Y., and Eto, T. (Eds.). (1970). *Hana Naki Yama no Yamakage no*, Tokyo: Zaikai Hyouron Shinsya [*Sixty Five Years History of the Faculty of Economics, Yamaguchi University*].

Sakudo, Y., and Eto, T. (1974a). *Oita Daigaku Keizai-gakubu Gojyunen-shi*, Tokyo: Zaikai Hyouron Shinsya [*Fifty Years History of the Faculty of Economics, Oita University*].

Sakudo, Y., and Eto, T. (1974b). *Fukushima Daigaku Keizai-gakubu Gojyunen-shi*, Tokyo: Zaikai Hyouron Shinsya [*Fifty Years History of the Faculty of Economics, Fukushima University*].

Sakudo, Y., and Eto, T. (1976). *Kobe Daigaku Ryousou Shichijyunen-shi*, Tokyo: Zaikai Hyouron Shinsya [*Seventy Years History of the Faculty of Economics, Kobe University*].

Suehiro, A. (2006a). *Ajia Cyousa no Keifu*. In Suehiro responsible (Ed.), 2006b: 21–66 [Genealogy of Researches in Asia].

Suehiro, A. (responsible Ed.). (2006b). *Teikoku Nihon no Gakuchi* vol. 6, Tokyo: Iwanami Shoten [*Knowledge of Imperial Japan. Asia as Area Studies*].

Suzuki, S. (Ed.) (1949). *Kagami Kenkichi Kun wo Shinobu*, Tokyo: Kagami Kinen Zaidan [*In Memory of Kagami Kenkichi*].

Takahashi, T. (1945). *Nanpo Keizai niokeru Kokumin Shotoku no Suisan nikansuru Ichi-shiryou*, Tokyo: Tokyo Sangyou Daigaku Toua Keizai Kenkyu-sho [*A Reference on an Estimation of the National Income in the Economy of the South Sea Area*].

Takaoka Koto Shogyou Gakko (Ed.) (1926). *Takaoka Koto Shogyou Gakko Ichiran Taisho 14–15*, Takaoka: Takaoka Higher Commercial School [*The Curriculum of Takaoka Higher Commercial School, 1924–5*].

Takaoka Koto Shogyou Gakko (Ed.).(1935). *Toyama Baiyakugyou-shi Shiryou-syu*, Takaoka: Takaoka Higher Commercial School [*The Historical Collection of a Patent Medicine Industry in Toyama Prefecture*].

Tamanoi, Y. (1971). *Nihon no Keizaigaku*, Tokyo: Cyuou kouron-sya [*Economics in Japan*].

Tokyo-daigaku Kyouyou-gakubu Kokusai-kankeiron Kenkyu-shitsu (Ed.) (1981). *Interview Kiroku D. Nihon no Gunsei* 6, Tokyo: Tokyo-daigaku Kyouyougakubu Kokusai-kankeiron Kenkyu-shitsu [*Records of Interview on Japanese Military Administrations* (1978. Mar~1979. Mar., by Akashi Youji)].

Tokyo Shougyou Gakko (1886). *Tokyo Shougyou Gakko Ichiran Meiji 19*, Tokyo: Tokyo Shougyou Gakko [*The Curriculum of the Tokyo School of Commerce, 1886*].

Toyama Daigaku Keizaigaku-bu, Etsurei-kai (1978). *Toyama Daigaku Keizaigaku-bu Gojyunen-shi*, Toyama: Toyama Daigaku Keizaigaku-bu, Etsurei-kai [*Fifty Years History of the Faculty of Economics, Toyama University*].

Ueda, T. (1939). "Mansyu, Hokushi, Cyushi no Kyukou Shisatsu," *Bungeishunjyu Genchi Houkoku Jikyoku Zoukan*, Tokyo: Bungeishunjyu-sha, 21: 170–173 [Hurried Inspections of Manchuria, North China and Central Part of China].

Ueda, T. (1963). *Ueda Teijiro Nittuki Bannen-hen*, Tokyo: Ueda Teijiro Nittuki Kankoukai [*Diary of Ueda Teijiro: In His Later Years*].

Watanabe, M. (1999). "Tokyo Gaikokugo Gakko no Kengaku kara Dokuritsu made", in Tokyo Gaikokugo Daigaku-shi Hensan Iinkai (Eds.), *Tokyo Gaikokugo Daigaku-shi*, Tokyo: Tokyo University of Foreign Studies: 43–78 [From the Establishment to the Independence of the 'Tokyo School of Foreign Language'].

Watanabe, S. (Ed.) (1931). *Kenryou Jyusyu-nen shi*, Nagoya: Kitan-kai, Nagoya Higher Commercial School [*Ten Years history of Nagoya Higher Commercial School*].

Yagi, K. (1999). *Kindai Nihon no Syakai Keizai-gaku*, Tokyo: Chikuma Syobou [*Social Economics in Modern Japan*].

Yamaguchi Koto Shogyou Gakko (1905). *Yamaguchi Koto Shougyou Gakko Ichiran Meiji 38–39*, Yamaguchi: Yamaguchi Higher Commercial School [*The Curriculum of Yamaguchi Higher Commercial School, 1905–6*].

Yamamoto, Y. (2011). *'Daitoa Kyoei-ken' Keizai-shi Kenkyu*, Nagoya: The University of Nagoya Press [*An Economic History of the "Greater East Asian Co-Prosperity Sphere"*].

Yanagisawa, O. (2008). *Senzen Senji Nihon no Keizai-shisou to Nazism*, Tokyo: Iwanami-Shoten [*Economic Thought and Nazism before and during the War*].

Yokohama Koto Shogyou Gakko (1943). *Yokohama Koto Shougyou Gakko Nijyunen-shi*, Yokohama: Yokohama Higher Commercial School [*Twenty Years History of Yokohama Higher Commercial School*].

# 9 Takata Yasuma's theory on power and his political stance on race

*Tsutomu Hashimoto*

## 1 Introduction

Takata Yasuma (1883–1972) was unarguably one of the greatest economic sociologists in 20th century Japan. He not only established his original theory of socio-economics but also wrote various political proposals for the unity of Asian races. However, there seems to be a serious paradox between his theoretical individualism and political collectivism.

In the beginning of his academic career, he was a radical individualist influenced by Georg Simmel's sociology. For Takata, the trend of individualization was not just a historical necessity but ultimately revealed a normative ideal of our modern society. In the future of modernization, the whole global society would be governed by ethnically hybrid citizens under an integrated world government. In such a regime, people could fully enjoy their individual lives.

From this perspective, however, Takata paradoxically considered that a construction of a political regime in the name of "extended racialism" was a necessary step toward an ideal individualistic society with a world government. Takata proposed that Japan or other strong nations should take responsibility to construct empires as "total societies" in order to enhance hybridization of blood and ethnicities. He conceived that world society would be brought through hybridization of blood in several empires but that empires among nations must be built through political struggles since certain ethnic groups had to surrender to other ethnic groups.

For Takata, individualistic society required a world empire rather than a nation. Thus, he was serious about the idea of imperial hegemony involving people in a relationship of mastery and obedience. He called his theoretical position "power-ism," which is contrasted with "egoism." Power-ism conceives of individuals as beings who satisfy their interest in power. Takata elaborated his concept of "power" and constructed a theory of historical stages of power relations. First, he explained a driving force of history in terms of group interests with which people dedicate themselves to the group beyond their individual interests. Second, he assumed that "power" is related to the human instinct that he called "self-sentiment of a sense of superiority." Although, led by this instinct, people would struggle with each other, they would stop struggling when such struggles properly revealed their real social status and they satisfied their sense of superiority.

From these two considerations, Takata approved of collective desires that produce political struggles among ethnic groups, while he envisaged an individualistic world society as a final result of these struggles. According to him, humans are neither autonomous beings who control their own desires nor persons who surrender themselves to their desires. Humans are led by, as it were, "the cunning of desire" which is a reformulation of G. W. Hegel's theory of the "cunning of reason" and develop an ideal individualistic society. In the beginning, desire tells us that race as a group identity is important. However, desire will finally tell us that race as a group identity is not important. Thus, the question is how to disentangle this paradox. This is also a central question for us when we evaluate Takata's theory of power and his recognition of social reality. In this chapter, I would like to examine the following two questions:

1   Why should we recognize that ethnic group is important, while our final ideal is a world society based on individualism?
2   How can the affirmation of racialism reach its negation, that is, an individualistic world society?

In the following section, I shall examine his theory on power and race. First, I examine his theoretical consistency in the light of its practical implications. Second, I examine the logical consistency between his understanding of race and his policy proposals. Third, I examine why and where his theory on race failed.

## 2  Race as a driving force: *Introduction to Sociology* and *A Theory of Power*

Takata's theory of sociology was systematically delivered in the following two books: *Introduction to Sociology* in 1922, and *A Theory of Power* in 1940. As stated earlier, he seems to be inconsistent when he praises racialism in politics because his theoretical concern is directed toward individualism. However, I first would like to show that his theory is highly consistent with his practical proposals.

### 2.1  "Desire as herd instinct" and "desire for power"

For Takata, the science of sociology is a science of law concerning people's interactions, which investigates social laws by extracting general elements from various social phenomena. In order to establish such a science of law, Takata first examined what kind of psychological tendencies can be the basis of the law in the light of "necessary and causal laws of a society." In accordance with G. Simmel and other sociologists, Takata assumes that our society is directed toward an ideal "*Gesellschaft*" in one united world. In order to make clear its causal process in history, he introduces his original two ideas called "desire as gregariousness or herd instinct" and "desire for power." He makes these two ideas his theoretical basis for explaining the law of society in his *Introduction to Sociology* published in 1922.

Takata conceives that both "desire as gregariousness or herd instinct" and "desire for power" are the basic causes of human behavior, although they are not teleological.[1] "Desire as gregariousness or herd instinct" is a basic desire to form our society or to make a "connection for connection," a connection through which we enjoy our coexistence regardless of our interests in the connection. This is a desire for our social affection or sociality, which is originally from a regional bond or blood relations.

According to Takata, there are two subcategories of this desire: the "desire for approaching" and the "desire for interaction (or traffic)." The "desire for approaching" is such a desire for "hanging around" a city and being absorbed in a crowd at night. The "desire for interaction," on the other hand, is such a desire people of the same status or in the same situation (although their temperaments and characters might be different) have for exchanging and transferring their spirit (Takata 1922: 46–47). Those desires do not presuppose any strong ties among people but just assume an individual tendency toward communication. For Takata, a desire for "corporation" among people toward common interest is accidental and non-permanent. It is not seen as a basis for the formation of our society. He notes that even the affective relationship between a mother and her child is not a basis on which to form our society.

In addition, Takata notes the following explanation in his theory: there are "desire for family-like intimacy" and "desire for imitation," both of which enhance the connection for connection and the formation of corporation. I would like to focus on the "desire for imitation" because this desire takes an important role in his theory, and its definition is unique. The desire for imitation is defined as the occurrence of the same emotional contents as the other person in one's own mind. The desire for imitation is also defined in terms of "sympathy" in which a person projects his/her emotion onto the other.[2] Moreover, "imitation" in Takata's theory is a foundation of altruistic tendency because people tend to have direct communications by imitating each other. It also makes people have affection for others through sympathy. According to Takata, "imitation" can help the function of herding, though it would not become a basic principle of our society (Takata 1922: 53–56).

On the other hand, the "desire for power" in Takata's theory is a principle of "differentiation" through which our society develops. For example, our desire to get profit or to show our own skills would enhance competition among people, and differentiate people in its recognition. However, it is interesting to see that Takata conceived that the desire for power includes "an instinct of struggle,"[3] which enhances homogenization and unification of a group, especially in a period of war. According to him, the "instinct of struggle" among nations would create empires and finally contribute to constructing a homogenous world society. Moreover, the instinct of struggle would ultimately transform itself into the "instinct of competition" in a world society. Thus, the "instinct of struggle" would bring about complete differentiation of individuals at the final stage of history. First, he conceived that the "desire for power" drives people to construct a "co-prosperity sphere" among several nations, and, subsequently, the same desire drives people to extend the sphere toward a world society.

In Takata's theory, we can admit two phases or characteristics of the basic two desires, namely, the "desire for gregariousness or herd instinct" and the "desire for power." These two desires have both functions of individualization (differentiation) and socialization (homogenization). "Desire as gregariousness or herd instinct" makes people form a *Gemeinschaft*, a corporate society, but it also keeps people separated in herding with other people. The "desire for power" makes people pursue group hegemony to which they belong, but this desire would finally transform itself into the desire for self-conservation at the final stage of history. According to Takata, an ideal *Gesellschaft* would be formed as an unintended consequence of human action through its cunning of reason led by those basic desires. To put it differently, we cannot make an ideal *Gesellschaft* through our conscious effort to bring it about.

It should be noted here that both the element of "imitation" in the "desire as herd instinct" and the element of "struggle" in the "desire for power" in his theory tend to affirm "collectivism." As we will see later, the function of "imitation," which starts from similarity of blood, enhances cultural connections of a race in its narrow sense and ethnic connections in its extended sense (for example, the Asian race). Racialism is not an ideal, but we are to pursue it led by our basic desire. Takata conceived that "desire as herd instinct" and "desire for power" are necessary components of the development of modern history toward an ideal individualism.[4]

## 2.2 Instinct of subordination and social fiction

Takata's magnum opus, *A Theory of Power*, gives several theoretical explanations for how people establish a racialist society driven by desire as herd instinct and the desire for power. Three things are to be pointed out.

First, he adds two theoretical devices in his theory of power: "instinct of subordination" and "social fiction (*Gitai*)." According to Takata, there is a desire for subordination as well as a desire for domination in our "desire for power." The desire for subordination comes not just from our economic consideration of its profitability but our self-humiliation as a negative sentiment. When we respect others and subordinate ourselves to them, we feel pleasure; we feel peaceful and empowered by them. This desire for subordination satisfies our desire to be a part of a "great entity" and contributes to making a stable foundation of our society (Takata 1940a: 30–31). When people share this desire for subordination and a few superior people rule them, the whole society is well ordered (Takata 1940a: 33–35). Here he assumes that many people do not have strong concern for ruling and leading others. If this is the case, a few superior people will successfully construct an "ethnic nation" as a great entity for the remaining people.

Nevertheless, many people might not want to have an ethnic nation as a great entity. Here, Takata introduces another theoretical device, "social fiction." When a small group of people tries to extend its power, the remaining people would take an attitude of non-resistance or disinterest against that group. They might take an attitude of passive support or tacit approval. Thus, the newly emerged power can establish itself as a dominant power. However, this dominance is just a "social fiction" since people merely show a passive recognition without having any firm will to resist. The new power would be able to extend its domination under such a condition (Takata 1940a: 121).

The real scope of this new power depends on its "internal power," namely its power to acquire people's spontaneous subordination. The internal power would be produced through the following three conditions: (1) social power that has already been established, (2) noble birth, and (3) personal talent. In contrast to this internal power, there is an external power that requires people to be subordinated by physical means. According to Takata, this external power is composed of (1) military power, (2) political power with legitimacy, (3) power of wealth, and (4) power of culture (Takata 1940a: 37–39, 42–53). Takata made a distinction between internal and external power and points out that there are two cases of acquiring domination: one is the case of acquiring external power, and the other is the case of acquiring internal power. The latter case includes "mixed marriage," "friendship," "acquisition of an honorable award," "acquisition of culture as a class status," and so forth. Takata analyzed the mechanism of how the internal power of superior people brings about their dominance and the ethnic entity as a group interest shared among people in the same region.

## 2.3 Wave-motion theory of power claim

So far, we have followed Takata's explanation of how people's subordination to a great entity is spontaneously produced. However, what kind of great entity or social institution is the most legitimate in attracting people's spontaneous subordination? We know various types of social institutions such as social democracy, communism, totalitarianism, conservatism, and so forth.[5] Racialism is just one of the aspects of the possible institutions. However, Takata conceived that racialism gives us a reasonable solution to the paradoxical courses of history.

In chapter 10 of *A Theory of Power*, Takata points out that the form of dominant organization swings between a type of central control and a type of dispersed power. He explains it by using a metaphor of "wave motion."

According to Takata, a transition or a development of a society happens linearly when the population increases. For example, a transition from blood relations to local relations or a transition from traditional society to a legal society happens spontaneously due to the increase in population. Of course, this conception is too abstract. In reality, there is a wave motion of ideas between control and freedom, solidarity and emancipation, individual and race, and so forth. A society would take a policy of collectivism when its relationship to the outside becomes antagonistic, whereas the same society would take a policy of emancipation when the situation is vice versa (Takata 1940a: 226). The wave motion between collectivization and individualization depends primarily on a change of the society's external conditions. However, it is fundamentally produced by internal causes, which are due to the excessive performance of one autonomous direction and more or less due to the "power claim" of its dominant players (Takata 1940a: 229).

> The shift between two types of dominant organizations [. . .] implies the shift between two types of mind as well. In a period of centralization, dominant people are those of high spirit, followers of traditional norms, and those who dedicate themselves to the transcendental order when it comes to a period of revolution. [. . .] On the other hand, in a period of decentralization, dominant people are those of sentimental, those of satisfying their freedom and desire, those of conquering their surroundings and in the end those of destructing all restrictions of their norms. [. . .] Such mind requires emancipation from control and increase of its own power.
>
> (Takata 1940a: 230)

Thus, Takata thought that our society swings between dictatorship and freedom due to the excessive claim of the dominant players. A claim of power by a superior person declines due to its excessiveness. Takata examined the wave process of the power shifts from his sociological perspective and asked how we can preserve and extend our long-term domination without any shift of power. This concern would give us a normative criterion for social policies. For Takata, one of the most important policy ideas was the austerity among the leading ethnic people that will bring them the final victory of global dominance.

Takata asked the following question: in the world where dominant people are cyclically changing, how can we become the last champion of history? According to Takata, the last champion would preserve its dominance in terms of its population at the last stage of history where all nations would merge into one *Gesellschaft*. Takata gave the following answer: we had better become a potential champion in the future rather than a real champion in the present. Thus, he suggested we empower our potentialities as a group by way of increasing population.

### 2.4 From merit to potentiality

As stated earlier, according to Takata, even though the dominant people cyclically change under the struggle among ethnic groups, the last champion would preserve its dominance in a world society. From this perspective, Takata asked how to become the last champion. To this end, he proposed the policy of austerity in order to increase the population and enhance potential dominance of future generations. The present generation of our ethnic group needs to content itself with a low standard of living. He raised this policy proposal based on Pareto's cycle theory of the elite in the following way.

Upper-class married couples tend to have fewer children because they have to spend a large amount of money to guarantee their children high status, a high level of education, and a stable life (Takata 1940a: 239–240). An elite couple tends to concentrate its energy on its work rather than on raising its children

(Takata 1940a: 241–242). In a modern meritocracy, talented people are selected from every stratum of society and asked to work in responsible positions. However, as a result of this merit selection, superior people tend not to leave many offspring, while they realize their merits and capabilities. In contrast, people who are not so talented tend to show their great reproductive power. This is paradoxical because the merit system or meritocracy brought a deterioration of the level of merit itself (Takata 1940a: 261).

In order to avoid the group's performance deteriorating, Takata proposed to restrict the work of the merit system. For example, we can partially adopt a semi-feudal status system as an alternative to meritocracy. In a semi-feudal system, talented people would not be able to obtain high status. They would not have enough opportunities to realize their capabilities. However, this restriction would encourage them to leave many offspring. As a result, those who are talented would increase in number but remain lower class. Under such a semi-feudal system of human resources, the number of superior people would increase. This would be a good resource for the nation to become a potential champion in the last stage of history. However, according to Takata, this was not an ideal system. The problem lay in the marriage among people of the same class. Based on this perception, he insisted that unconventional marriage among heterogeneous people in their vocation, birthplace, or class needed to be recommended because it worked for nurturing the superior nature of the group (Takata 1940a: 262).

As we will examine, while Takata affirmed a certain kind of elite status system, he proposed a project to go beyond our nation through hybridization among races and classes. For him, the most important issue was the number of potentially superior people who contributed to the dominance of the group in the future. For the sake of this vision, both conservative class society and progressive hybrid society were required in Takata's normative vision. The elite who was driven by a sense of prestige and the people who are in a position to dominate were not necessarily the proper type of people to contribute to making the *Gesellschaft* society. However, it is interesting to see that those people not adapting to a modern society can paradoxically become a driving force of history and bring about a world society of *Gesellschaft* as an unintended consequence.

Of course, when a nation exclusively seeks its potential power in the future, it will be defeated by other nations since the nation cannot show any dominant power in the present. Takata had a real eye for politics and perceived that we needed to conquer other nations in the situation of the "clash of the will to power" among ethnic groups. He stated that an individualistic global society would be brought about by a certain group that formed an "extended race" by assimilating other races and enhanced peaceful interactions among races (Takata 1940a: 289–305). In order to direct a will to power of an ethnic group effectively toward future domination, Takata proposed to nurture human resources as potential power. This view would give us a proper criterion to evaluate his idea of "Asian racialism." We shall examine it in the following two sections.

## 3 Formation of empire as a universal project

Takata paid attention to the process of modernization in Prussia or a unified Germany during the 18th and 19th centuries. The Kingdom of Prussia was a relatively underdeveloped country, and the subsequent German Empire hastened its modernization by mobilizing a "spirit of ethnicity" especially in an elite class and organized an authoritative system of bureaucracy. Takata's idea of an "ethnic nation-state" is basically based on Germany's case.

In addition, what he faced in real politics was that nonwhite races were discriminated against in the League of Nations or Treaty of Versailles in 1919. The Treaty of Versailles did not admit "equality among races" but only governance through "the self-determination of peoples."[6] In order to overcome the discriminatory treatment of nonwhite people, Takata conceived that it was important to increase the population of nonwhite races in a real world. Moreover, he thought that Japan should become politically dominant in universal values in place of Western countries and constitute an ideal of "equality of peoples" in the world. In order to achieve this ideal, he raised three tasks: (1) resolution of the differences among classes, (2) recognition of women's rights, and (3) abolition of racial discrimination (Takata 1935: 6).

Thus, Takata was a liberal egalitarian in economic policy, and he proposed to increase the wages of working-class people. According to him, if market competition of the survival of the fittest was approved, the Japanese people would fail to become the dominant ethnic group in the world. For example, by restricting market competition among big and small retail companies, the number of small retailers would increase and thereby contribute to enhancing potential human resources. Takata also remarked that the government should be responsible for the consequences of market competition. In order for people to coexist, it was necessary to improve the standard of living of proletarians, while protecting the status of middle-class people. For this purpose, the government needed to control the behavior of big capital and conglomerates (Takata 1940b: 291–292). Thus, Takata argued that egalitarian conditions were necessary for enhancing potential human resources in the light of political struggle among nations and empires.[7]

As for the issue of racial discrimination, Takata raised the following three proposals in order to improve the status of inferior groups: (1) to construct a power of self-defense in Japan in order not to be exploited by the world's great powers, (2) to give the same status as Japanese citizens to minority groups such as the Ainu or aborigines in Taiwan, and (3) to enhance hybridization of races (Takata 1935: 8). When nonwhite people are subordinated to the empires of white people, they cannot get equal rights among peoples or races. When nonwhite people build their own empires that discriminate against people under the system of feudalism or absolutism, they cannot realize the idea of equality. Thinking this way, Takata took a stance of cosmopolitanism rather than racialism and proposed to build a self-defending East Asian empire led by the Japanese race at the same time.[8] For him, self-defense by a race is a means to achieve the idea of equality of peoples and is a tactic that enhances a paradoxical development of history toward a world society.[9]

This stance was criticized not only by ultra-nationalism,[10] which tries to keep our race pure, but also by Miki Kiyoshi (1939), who proposed "(ethnic) fusion through common cultures." Takata's stance was unique. He had a pragmatic vision of political corporation among East Asian peoples in the light of the "self-defense of East Asia" (Takata 1939). He did not have any illusion on empire building since he noticed that there was an anti-Japanese trend in East Asian countries. What he could hope for in reality was just a coalition or solidarity among Asian nations. He rejected both ultra-nationalism and Asian communitarianism from a pragmatic point of view.

Nonetheless, he advocated a certain kind of racialism. In order to understand his racialism, let us examine his definition of the concept of "race."[11] According to him, race has its foundation in the self-integrity of a group and has its symbolic connotation in the image of extension toward the outside. Race means neither pure blood nor a fusion of cultures. In reality, race has the following three characteristics: (1) a certain degree of hybridization of blood, (2) commonality of traditional cultures, and (3) common fate due to the historical encounter of groups. Race is also defined as a product of solidarity based on our will to preserve and strengthen traditional cultures as a common project in various aspects of our life. According to Takata, the last definition of race is what builds the "spirit" of race.

In modern nation-states, race is a newly created product by the state (Takata 1935: 247).[12] In other words, a state can artificially produce a "race," and it can transform the composition of race through its extension of the territory toward an empire.

This conception of "race" gives us an answer to the second question listed at the beginning of this section: how can the affirmation of racialism reach its negation, that is, an individualistic global society? For Takata, the affirmation of "race" as an ethical entity was related to his policy proposal to establish an empire in which the government can artificially change the composition of race. Thus, for Takata, the idea of race or racialism has nothing to do with the idea of ultra-nationalism or Asian communitarianism. In his imagination, Asian peoples can merge, coexist, and be treated equally within such an extended empire constructed by Japan. From this perspective, Takata could expect an individualistic global society since the composition of the race can be extended unlimitedly to include all peoples in the world. The artificially constructed race can negate the unity of race in a traditional sense and finally enable a cosmopolitan individualistic society.

## 4 Where did he fail?

Takata's cosmopolitanism, however, revealed its political difficulties when he supported the 1937–1945 Sino-Japanese War. Here, we shall examine why and how he failed in his political proposals.

During the Sino-Japanese War, Takata's vision became very popular.[13] From the end of the Taisho era to the beginning of the Showa era, namely around the 1920s, Takata built his unique position that approved of nationalism or racialism against Marxism (Leninist communism) and Anglo-Saxon hedonistic individualism. Although all sides of society have denied his policy proposal (Takata 1942b: 12), it attracted people's sympathy in wartime.

Let us examine Takata's policy vision. According to him, many sociologists in the early 20th century dreamed that our world would finally be merged through hybridization of all kinds of blood (Takata 1942a: 210). However, in reality, almost all hybrid races are achieved through artificial unification of different races led by a dominant nation. In this sense, "nation is an inventor of new races in every case" (Takata 1942a: 214). Then the question would be how we can be responsible to make our world be composed of one race. According to him, under the condition of imperial struggle, the nation needs to extend its armament for the sake of its self-defense and to keep its population, body, and spirit in perfect strength (Takata 1942a: 23). The Japanese as a race can produce "solidarity" with other races and achieve "corporation among races" by hybridization of blood:

> Among the urgent items of business of our nation, which is composed of mixed races, is a corporation among them to secure its solid basis. How can this corporation be promoted? Domestically, there are two policies: one is a strong control by the nation. Reconciliation of races in past history has not been realized without strong force of a nation. This is not saying that we need to forcibly inject the culture of our race into the other. We just need to make our solidarity of fate through a nation . . . and to make peoples interact with each other in every aspect of living. The other is to secure all people's legitimate profits and to protect their lives in order not to injure their autonomy of reasoned behavior. These two policies are the way to make peoples confident in the power of the nation and therefore the way to be connected with each other through confidence in the nation.
>
> (Takata 1942a: 224–225)

"The prudence of the Japanese race" in East Asian peoples and all Japanese people is to treat our friendly East Asian peoples as brothers or "ours" and to protect their lives without depriving their profit in an oppressive way. This means that peoples in Japan are restricted from enjoying a rapid increase of their standard of living (Takata 1942b: 249).

With these concerns, Takata was pleased to see that the life of people in wartime was tightened.[14] To keep people in a low standard of living is not just to keep our race youthful[15] but also to enhance our power as domination. A low standard of living establishes friendship with other races (Takata 1942b: 27) and contributes to forming a new world order. Takata expected that the world would finally be composed of one race through the expansion of the order of nation-based empire. His confidence in this vision was reinforced by the negation of another cosmopolitan scenario that envisages the same world order through expansion of the *Gesellschaft* in commerce.

> When we make haste in constructing a *Gesellschaft*, we would be necessarily located in an inferior status [in the world]. . . . Each individual cannot help but feeling that it is difficult to contribute to the whole entity: the integrity of people would deteriorate and the population would not increase. . . . Consequently, we would be militarily defeated.
>
> (Takata 1942b: 160)

> Prosperity contains a germ of decline. What is able to be replaced in the decline is something socially delayed, which is found in communal society to some extent. . . . The retarded group in social progress would become a winner due to its delay. The advanced would decline and be replaced by the delayed.
>
> (Takata 1942b: 162)

Thus, according to Takata, in order to get a dominant global status in the world, the Japanese nation needed to be slow in making a *Gesellschaft* and to keep its national integrity. This argument was the logical extension of what he had already developed before the Sino-Japanese War.[16]

On the other hand, Takata advocated a new doctrine, which is called "East Asian Racialism" (Takata 1942b: 273), with the outbreak of the Sino-Japanese War. This doctrine might be justified in its abstract theoretical dimension, but I would like to point out that Takata might have made three erroneous judgments in real politics: (1) his support for the Sino-Japanese War, (2) his idea of instruction through "people descended from the gods," and (3) deeply embedded Japanese spirit.

## (1) Takata's support for the Sino-Japanese war

According to Takata, the political pressure of Western culture forced Japanese people to wake up and establish the Meiji Government in 1868 to emancipate themselves from Westerners by constructing a self-defense force. This project of emancipation produced the 1937–1945 Sino-Japanese War. While many Japanese intellectuals criticized it as a form of imperial colonization, Takata conceived of it as a settlement of the Manchurian Incident in 1931.

The Manchurian Incident was fabricated by the Japanese Army as an excuse for invading northern China, known as Manchuria. However, since it was led by the Japanese Army, big capitalists in Japan could not participate in constructing Manchukuo, a Japanese puppet state. This incident was not led by the power of capitalism. According to Takata, Japan could not help but fabricating the incident for its self-defense, because this country had run short of resources (Takata 1940b: 220–230). For the sake of its domination, Japan needed to be united with both Manchukuo and China. Since the peoples in these areas are physically and psychologically similar to the Japanese, we can have an image of "United East Asia" (Takata 1940b: 231–233). However, we need to direct our critical concern to the colonization of Manchukuo. Takata did not seem to take the problem of its colonizing procedure seriously.

### (2) Takata's idea of instruction through "people descended from the gods"

According to Takata, the organization of East Asian Racialism had to be stratified among peoples in order to construct a unified East Asia. It would be natural to assume that Japanese people take responsibility to lead other peoples (Takata 1940b: 237–238). Japanese people have enough power to obtain high status in East Asia to emancipate less-developed peoples against the dominance of Westerners (Takata 1940b: 248). Moreover, in his understanding, Japanese people are the descendants of the gods and have already mixed blood with three or four peoples. This people can mix more blood and construct a completely homogeneous race through a long period of hybridization (Takata 1942b: 240).

> Peoples in East Asia admit that their blood flows into our land and fuses with ours. Our homeland of Japanese peoples, in this sense, is the birthplace of people descended from the gods and it would exist in Mongolia or South Sea islands as well. We Japanese peoples not only take a central role in compiling blood and cultures among East Asian peoples but also have very intimate relations with all those peoples.
>
> (Takata 1942b: 241–242)

Thus, Takata admits that Japanese peoples play a special role in leading other peoples in constructing an empire in East Asia. The problem is his perception of Japanese peoples as the descendants of the gods. If this is the case, how can the Japanese peoples be very intimate with other peoples, while extending their homeland to Mongolia or the South Sea islands? He seems to be too optimistic on this point.

### (3) Deeply embedded Japanese spirit

In order to justify unequal treatment among peoples in what he call the "East Asian Racialism" regime, Takata describes his understanding of cultural stratification. According to him, culture in an ethnic group is multi-layered. In its surface layers are intellectual cultures such as industry, science, and technology. These are easily absorbed from other ethnic cultures. In its middle layers are the legal system (political organization) and mores (manners and customs), which change gradually with the influences of other cultures. In its basic layer, "the spirit which is inherent in this people waves continuously" (Takata 1943: 18). "When we focus on our spiritual culture which is latent in its base layer, there continues a time-honored old culture which is proper to the Japanese" (Takata 1943: 19).

From this understanding of layers of culture, Takata conceived that "all fundamental characteristics in Japanese culture came from its bottom, namely from its peculiar communal bond." He also remarked that a fundamental spirit of Japanese culture could be characterized as "self-devotion for the nation,"[17] or "naturalistic attitude which restricts material desires."[18] According to Takata, Japan as a nation must be composed of Japanese people in the first place. "When other peoples are incorporated formally in the line of its citizens, they constitute the nation as long as they are fused completely in this racial spirit" (Takata 1943: 55).

This understanding of nation in *Race and Economy II*, however, is completely different from what Takata said in his *Endurance of Race*, which was published a year earlier. In *Endurance of Race*, he criticized a naturalistic attitude, but in *Race and Economy II*, he saw it as important. As a cosmopolitan, Takata had emphasized the unnatural character of modern nations, which artificially enhances hybridization among peoples. However, he also justified a leading role for Japanese people because of their naturalistic attitude to preserve a basic layer of Japanese culture. This understanding would not be compatible with his vision of the artificial composition of the race in East Asian Racialism.

## 5 A theory of world society reexamined after World War II

We have examined three points that show his failure in practical judgment: (1) his support for the Sino-Japanese War, (2) his idea of instruction through "people descended from the gods," and (3) Japanese spirit in an old layer of our mind. Takata's theory of sociology might have had more persuasive implications and legitimacy as a normative vision when he did not develop these three value judgments.

However, the crucial issue in Takata's theory lies in another point: he did not describe an alternative scenario toward a world society when Japan lost the war. I think this was the limitation of his theory.[19] What kind of process toward a world society could have been led by the cunning of our desire for power when the Japanese empire was to fail?

After World War II, Takata published a book, *On World Society*, in 1947, and he showed a path toward a world society under the condition of a peaceful world regime. In this book, Takata reformulated his vision of history: the continuous increase of population and the voiceless progress of reason would tacitly and gradually promote the path toward a world society. However, he discarded the element of racialism or power-ism and just unfolded the one-sided logic of spontaneous tendency toward *Gesellschaft* in the world. Namely, he just pointed out that tendencies such as the expansion of basic society, extinction of races, dispersion of bonds, and development of interactions toward *Gesellschaft*, or intellectualization, would bring about a world society.[20]

However, he did not welcome the project of the United Nations, which supported the autonomy of each nation-state after the war. To the contrary, Takata envisaged a world society without appealing to the idea of unity of autonomous nations. He made a distinction between internationalism and cosmopolitanism. While internationalism approved the autonomy of each nation-state, cosmopolitanism sought to eliminate the functions of the nation-state as a middle group on behalf of a world society where each individual is treated as a final end. In the light of this distinction, Takata took the position of cosmopolitanism.

> A series of historical trends such as modernization, a series of trends of awakening and emancipation of individuals, or self-consciousness of individuals, showed that the primitive mentality [which gives a mysterious substance of nation or race and makes it anthropocentric] had been conquered. . . . When we keep our faith with this view of modernization, we cannot take the position of respecting a national personality, which regards respect of personality as secondary.
>
> (Takata 1947: 261–262)

> Thus, in a real world, there is no sufficient reason to see the conflict among nations as the ultimate fact and to see the project of the United Nations as the only way to perform a political procedure to make the world united.
>
> (Takata 1947: 262)

Here, Takata suggests a possible scenario toward a cosmopolitan society without any mediation of nations. This is a big transformation of his stance. In wartime, he conceived of a nation as a necessary medium to construct a world society. However, when it lost its ethical legitimacy after World War II, he envisaged a world society without any medium of nations. I admit that Takata's *On World Society* was a product of his deep apology for the war and shows his reconsideration of the role of nation.

He might have been able to develop his theoretical scenario by appealing to the other cunning of desire for a world society under the condition of a peaceful market economy after WWII. For example, he could have pointed out a dialectic between racialism and individualism in the following way: first, people are forced to devote themselves to increasing the population and to preserving economic nationalism in order to overcome their narrow egotistical concern. Second, however, neighboring peoples have gradually fused their blood and have tended to produce an extended race beyond each nation-state, and they would form a co-existing economic sphere. Then, finally, we would be able to envisage a world society by extending its scope.

Takata could have written this scenario. However, he did not describe any path toward a world society after the war. The question that we need to ask is exactly the same as Takata raised. How can we describe a path to making a world society beyond the nation-state regime? With Takata's theoretical contribution and insights such as "cunning of desire" and "power-ism," we can investigate further under the condition of peaceful relations among peoples.

# Notes

1  According to Takata, humans are not connected to each other due to their interest but are driven by their "desire for power" and make relations of domination and subordination among themselves. They are led to the *Gesellschaft* by its unintended consequences.

2  Precisely speaking, sympathy is not a desire. "The desire for imitation" here includes a non-desire element.

3  Takata included an instinct of struggle in war, which shows a principle of homogenization, into the desire for power as a principle of differentiation. He noted (Takata 1922: 67–68) in a footnote that he was conscious of this logical inconsistency. Takata argued that it would be less difficult to regard "instinct of struggle" and "instinct of competition" as one instinct because these two instincts have the same sociological significance in their function, although they are fundamentally different. This argument seems to show his theoretical dilemma.

4  Fujikawa (1993: 58–59) criticizes Takata's concept of the "desire as herd instinct" as follows. Takata first explains the existence of social groups by "desire as herd instinct." Then, Takata goes on to explain that the "desire for power" in individuals would enhance the construction of *Gesellschaft*, while restraining the group ego. In Takata's theory, "desire as herd instinct" is just used in the first stage of history. However, this understanding of Takata's theory is erroneous. Takata uses the concept of "desire as herd instinct" in his subsequent development of the theory of power.

5  In chapter 14 of *A Theory of Power*, Takata examines mutual relations between the ideas fabricated by power and the power fabricated by ideas. This connection holds to "the ideology as the super structure," which is formed by dominant people. According to Takata, ideas can help a rising power to emerge. However, ideas can only give a certain direction to our potential capabilities (Takata 1940a: 313).

6  Shinmei (1934) argues that Takata is an optimist like Don Quixote since he combines "reason for rational system," which leads us to the universal society with "irrational emotion," which leads us in turn to the ethnic society. Shinmei points out that Takata changed his stance from "universal humanism" to "racialism." Takata (1935) responded in detail to this criticism. Taido (1954) evaluates the consistency between Takata's theory and its ethnic orientation.

7

> With a voice in emergency, the Japanese spirit is uplifting and this is the most delightful thing as itself. There is no life in Japan without this spirit. However, we need to be cautious about its misuse such as to hinder the weak class of people from improving their status. It is true that in reality, things seem to go in this direction. To improve the status of proletariat and corporation is the primary purpose of the Japanese spirit.
>
> (Takata 1940b: 287–288)

8

> "I am a cosmopolitan. . . . A person cannot be a racialist and a cosmopolitan at the same time. . . . Since I am a cosmopolitan, I am not a racialist in its authentic sense" (Takata 1935: 5).

9

> An individual can reach his moral ideals step by step following imperatives of his practical reason. However, a group such as race is far more egotistical than individual. [. . .] We cannot expect any unity of races by way of improving the level of group morality. The course of history with combination of expansion

of each race, perfection of personality, and fusion among peoples, as shown by
G. Simmel's sociology, seems to bring about a world-nation.

(Takata 1935: 125)

10  Minoda Muneki (1894–1946) is one of the representatives of the Imperial Way of
Faction (*Koudouha*). However, Takata was critical of Shinto religion. An increase
in staff numbers at the National Research Institute of Ethnology, in which Takata
served as the head, was approved repeatedly during wartime from 1943 (when
it is founded) to 1945. Furuno Kiyoto (1899–1979), who was on the staff of
this institute and a successor of Takata's theory, has criticized an enforcement of
Shinto in constructing a Greater East Asian Co-prosperity Sphere. See Fukuma
(2008: 170–174).

11  Takata uses the word "race" or *"Minzoku"* in the sense of both "nation" and
"*Volk* (people)." He admits that there are common characteristics in these two
words. In this paper, I translated *Minzoku* into "race," "ethnicity," "nation," and
"people," case by case.

12

Starting from the stage of an ambiguous sentiment of belonging, it builds up
clear consciousness and finally a race as a group ego, which requires its expansion as itself. Then a race becomes a subject of collective will and seeks its
autonomy and development toward external spheres through its will. The aim
of this effort is to satisfy our will to power as a race.

(Takata 1935: 249)

13  Many criticisms pointed out Takata's transformation after the Sino-Japanese War.
For example, Kawamura writes, "Takata finally discarded his pacifism and cosmopolitanism because it became clear that his prospect has been damaged crucially
by the outbreak of the Sino-Japanese War" (Kawamura 1973: 260). He describes
how Takata transformed himself from a cosmopolitan in the Taisho era to a racialist in the Showa era. Yamamoto (1999: 59) also points out that he changed his
stance to East Asian Racialism, which tries to exclude Anglo-Saxons from dominance in Asia and finally the world. Utsu (1972) criticizes him because he followed an ideology of an absolute emperor system. Fujikawa (1993: 55, 59) writes
that it is unnatural to aim at ranking the life of the Japanese people in a high status
as itself, and he argues alternatively that communities could coexist under the
tendency toward *Gesellschaft* and intellectualization, if the satisfaction of "desire
for power" and the "development of society through division of labor" can compatibly proceed in order. On the other hand, Yoshino (2004) describes how his
vision on race is consistent since 1918, and it penetrates into his *On World Society*
in 1947. However, Kitajima (2002: 106–107) criticizes Takata for not examining
his wartime stance after the war.

14

Now the Greater East Asian War (the Pacific War 1941–1945) started with the
Manchukuo incident and the control over our life has started. . . . We would
come to feel gratitude to have a life of endurance, when we expect this restriction will be tightened and we regard it as our continuous public service to the
nation and as our eternal duty . . . to assist the nation, without regarding it as
temporary patience in wartime.

(Takata 1942b: 24–25)

15

> One of the methods to preserve the youth of the Japanese people is to over-come our desire for westernized life. In other words, it is to discard the idea, which aims at raising our living standard. . . . In order to preserve the eternal life of our race, individuals need to live a stoic life with self-training and self-discipline.
>
> (Takata 1942b: 262)

16 In addition, Takata was deliberate about the expansion of Japanese imperialism. Takata was opposed to the argument, which demanded an increase of population in order to send people to the south of the Japanese Empire (Takata 1942b: 220–221). Moreover, "[t]he transfer doctrine of peoples," which "plans to transfer approximately 10 thousand people in China to the south area including Australia, which enables Japanese people to move to mainland China" is by no means a national policy to adopt (Takata 1942b: 270).

17

> The primary ethics which we need to count is our self-devotion. Since each citizen is just a branch of the whole, which is called a nation, it is a natural duty for us to devote ourselves to the nation. However, the self-devotion reveals its peculiar form. The whole entity of the Japanese People is embodied in its emperor. Therefore, in people's consciousness, the devotion to this whole entity must appear as the devotion to the emperor. This loyalty constitutes a basis of national spirit. It also wears a kind of religious color.
>
> (Takata 1943: 19–20)

18

> The attitude of Japanese People to nature is not one which enhances their satisfaction of desire through its conquest. The attitude of Japanese People is to feel a sense of unity with nature without aiming at its conquest, as if they identify themselves with society.
>
> (Takata 1943: 26–27)

> The second characteristic of Japanese culture is, in all aspects of our life, a restriction on satisfying our material desire, adoption of natural appearance in itself to our life without molding nature artificially, simple life with these requirements in contrast to seeking the satisfaction of our desire, and active indifference about desire as its simple abandonment.
>
> (Takata 1943: 27)

19 Kiyono (1992) criticizes Takata's East Asian Racialism since it is the theory on race that supports the ideology of the Great East Asian Co-prosperity Sphere. This theory "enables us to excuse all Japanese imperialist invasions in the Fifteen Years' War (1931–1945 . . .) and to justify it as the self-defense of East Asian peoples" (Kiyono 1992: 51). I think that this evaluation is correct. On the other hand, Kiyono (1987: 120–121) points out that Takata's sociology collapsed by itself around 1934, when he discarded his vision of a world society that his systematic theory leads to and started to propose policy ideas without any responsibility, giving priority to the actual situation of society. This paper, however, shows that Takata proposed policy ideas on race from his theoretical perspective, and he was consistent until the end of World War II.

20 Takata notes that his basic framework on the idea of world society lies in his theory of minimizing developed in *A Study of Social Relations* (Takata 1925) and says
that the whole volume of *On World Society* is just a note on it (Takata 1947: 3).
This remark shows his elimination of the moment of racialism and group interest.

## References and further readings

Fujikawa, K. (1993). "On the Relationship Between Sociological Theory and Race in
Yasuma Takata," (Takata Yasuma ni-okeru Shakaigaku-riron to Minzoku-ron tono
Kanren) in *Japanese Sociological Review* (*Shakai-gaku Hyoron*), 43(4), pp. 421–435.

Fukuma, Y. (2003). "On Nationality of 'Sociology of Race': Yasuma Takata and Eizo
Koyama on Understanding of the Race," ('Minzoku-Shakaigaku' no Nationalism:
Takata Yasuma·Koyama Eizo no Minzoku-ninshiki wo tegakarinishite) in *Socioloji*,
47(3), pp. 19–36.

Fukuma, Y. (2008). "Institutionalization of Ethnological Study: Formation of the
Association of Ethnology in Japan and Its Transformation," (Minzoku-chi no
Seido-ka: Nihon Minzoku Gakkai no Seiritsu to Henyou), in I. Takenori (Ed.),
*Social Groups and Networks During the War in Japan* (*Senkan-ki Nihon no Shakai-
shudan to Network*), Tokyo: NTT Press.

Kawamura, N. (1973). *Studies on a History of Japanese Sociology* (*Nihon Shakaigakushi Kenkyu*), Vol. 1–2, Tokyo: Ningen-no-Kagaku Sha.

Kawamura, N. (1992) *Sociology of Yasuma Takata* (*Takata Yasuma no Shakaigaku*),
Tokyo: Inaho-Shobo.

Kitajima, S. (2002). *Yasuma Takata: Unmediated Unification between Theory and
Policy* (*Takata Yasuma: Riron to Seisaku no Mubaikai-teki-Gouitsu*), Tokyo:
Toushindo.

Kiyono, M. (1987). "On Yasuma Takata: An Essay on Sociological Approach to the
Issue of 'Race and Citizen'" (Takata Yasuma ron: 'minzoku to shimin' mondai
heno Shakaigakushi teki Approach no Kokoromi), *Ritsumeikan Review of Industrial Society*, 52, pp. 99–124.

Kiyono, M. (1992). "On Yasuma Takata's East Asian Racialism" (Takata Yasuma no
Toua-minzoku ron), in Senjika-Nihonshakai-Kenkyu (Ed.), *Japan During War:
Sociology of History in Early Showa Period* (*Senji-ka no Nihon: Showa-zenki no Reki-
shi Shakai-gaku*), Ohtsu: Kouji-sha.

Miki, K. (1939). *A New Principle of Thought in Japan* (*Shin Nihon no Shiso-Genri*),
Showa Research Meeting Office (Ed.), Tokyo: Showa Kenkyu-kai.

Shinmei, S. (1934). "Yasuma Takata·Shinzo Koizumi," (Takata Yasuma·Koizumi
Shinzo) in *Keizai-Ourai*, 9, (10) (pen name: XYZ), pp. 225–230

Taido, Y. (1954). *Takata's Sociology* (*Takata-Shakaigaku*), Tokyo: Yuhikaku.

Takata, Y. (1922). *Introduction to Sociology* (*Shakaigaku-gairon*), reprinted in 2003,
Kyoto: Minerva Shobo.

Takata, Y. (1925). *A Study on Social Relations* (*Shakai Kankei no Kenkyu*), Tokyo:
Iwanami Shoten.

Takata, Y. (1934). *Winning Strategy of the Poor* (*Hinja-Hisshou*), Tokyo: Chikura
Shobo, New Edition in 1940.

Takata, Y. (1935). *Issues on Race* (*Minzoku no Mondai*), Tokyo: Nihon Hyoron-sha.

Takata, Y. (1939). *On East Asian Race* (*Toua-Minzoku Ron*), Tokyo: Iwanami Shoten.

Takata, Y. (1940a) *A Theory of Power (Seiryoku-ron)*, reprinted in 2003, Kyoto: Minerva Shobo.

Takata, Y. (1940b) *Race and Economy I (Minzoku to Keizai I)*, Tokyo: Yuhikaku.

Takata, Y. (1942a) *On Races (Minzoku Ron)*, Tokyo: Iwanami Shoten.

Takata, Y. (1942b) *An Endurance of Race (Minzoku Taibou)*, Kyoto: Kouchou Shorin.

Takata, Y. (1943). *"Race and Economy II" (Minzoku to Keizai II)*, Tokyo: Yuhikaku.

Takata, Y. (1947). *On World Society (Sekai-Shakai Ron)*, Tokyo: Chugai-Shuppan.

Takata, Y. (1995). *Power Theory of Economics*, D. W. Anthony (Trans.), foreword by M. Morishima, Macmillan.

Utsu, E. (1972). "Some Issues on Takata's Theory of Sociology" (Takata Shakai-gaku Riron no Sho-mondai), in *Japanese Sociological Review (Shakaigaku-Hyoron)*, 23(2), pp. 47–64.

Yamamoto, S. (1999) "Academic and Ideological Connections Between Seido Shinmei and Yasuma Takata: On Sociological Theory and Race" (Shinmei Seido to Takata Yasuma no Gakumon-teki·Shiso-teki Koushou: Shakaigaku Riron to Minzoku Kenkyu wo Megutte), in *Studies on Sociology (Shakaigaku Kenkyu, Tohoku Shakaigaku Kenkyu-kai)*, special issue, in June, pp. 45–67.

Yoshino, K. (2004). "On the Image of Total Society which Yasuma Takata Describes: From on Race to on World Society" (Takata Yasuma no egaku "Zentai-Shakai" Zou: "Minzoku Ron kara Sekai-shakai Ron he), in *Hitotsubashi Ronsou*, 131(2).

Yoshino, K. (2005a). "On Poverty in an Affluent Society: Yasuma Takata and Kawakami Hajime" (Yutakana Shakai no Binbo Ron: Takata Yasuma to Kawakami Hajime), in *Hitotsubashi Kenkyu*, 30(3), pp. 35–52.

Yoshino, K. (2005b). "Yasuma Takata and the Power of Workers: What Lies Beyond Doctrines of Marx and Modern Economics" (Takata Yasuma to Roudou-sha no Seiryoku: Marx Gakusetsu to Kindai Keiai-gaku no Sakini-arumono), in *Hitotsubashi Ronsou*, 133(2), pp. 169–192.

Yoshino, K. (2006). "An Imagination of East Asian Community in early Showa Period: Takata Yasuma on Race in an Asymmetry" (Showa Shoki no Higashi Asia Kyoudoutai no Kousou: Takata Yasuma no Hitaishou-sei no Minzoku-ron), in *Socioloji*, 50(3), pp. 21–37.

# Part III
# Lessons from the 20th century world wars

This collaboration made it possible to assemble eminent scholars, including economists, in an institution called the Federal Union, the center of federalism movements. Robbins evolved economic aspects of federalism, whereas Beveridge had various roles such as organizing, conceptualizing, and publicizing. They had a great influence on federalism movements. It is also important to revalue their own economic thought as well as their impacts on others. Robbins attempted both to counter Keynes's 'insularity' and to apply his own methodology of economic theory into actual crises. Federalism was a natural result induced from his synthetic attitude as an economist. Beveridge, influenced by Robbins, Meade, and Keynes, became convinced that it would be indispensable to secure not only lasting peace but also maintaining full employment in the post-war era. He recognized the necessity of freedom from want, idleness, and war. The atomic bombing of Hiroshima and Nagasaki was a trigger to deepen his ideas on federalism.

# 10 How to avoid war

## Federalism in L. Robbins and W. H. Beveridge

*Atsushi Komine*

## 1 Introduction

### 1.1 Liberal federalists

As the rise of Nazism became increasingly evident in the 1930s, numerous intellectuals, starting slowly but later increasing, attempted to counter the mounting threat from militant nationalists. Among a variety of other alternatives on 'how to avoid wars', federalism was the most popular idea. In fact, plans for a federation appeared in a massive amount of literature and gained much popularity, particularly between September 1938, when the Munich Agreement was settled, and June 1940, when France surrendered to Nazi Germany.

Lionel Robbins (1898–1984) and William H. Beveridge (1879–1963) were at the centre of this federalism stream, not merely in Britain but in other European countries. They belonged to the same institutional idea: Federal Union. At first sight, their collaboration seems a little strange, because it is generally accepted that Robbins was closer to F. von Hayek, an uncompromising liberal or libertarian, whereas Beveridge was by far more similar to J. M. Keynes,[1] an interventional liberal or New Liberalist. As the four men proclaim themselves 'liberals', the contents of liberalism can be unveiled by examining their own words.

This chapter deals with an apparent riddle: why did the two eminent scholars (Robbins and Beveridge) as a team eagerly advocate federalism in the late 1930s and the first half of the 1940s? The answer shall be found by investigating both the motivation of their research and the relationship with their previous books, as well as briefly referring to the different position of Hayek's liberalism.

This chapter continues in the following manner: the rest of this section covers a short history of Federal Union. Sections 2 and 3 survey Robbins's and Beveridge's respective proposals for federalism. Section 4 examines Beveridge's background, methodology, and relationship with his previous works, all hidden in his proposals at first glance. Section 5 summarizes the arguments and leads to the concluding remarks.

### 1.2 A short history of federal union

Federal Union was not merely one of the nuclei in the federalism movement in Britain (and later in Europe), but also the core arena where eminent economists, as well as jurists and political scientists, played active and important roles. Its founding idea came from three young men in the autumn of 1938: C. Kimber, P. Ransome, and D. Rawnsley. Federal Union, established formally in November 1938, produced a provisional statement of aims "to form a nucleus of the future world federation" (Burgess 1995: 140) in the spring of 1939. By September 1939 a provisional council was appointed and the first edition of the weekly bulletin, *Federal Union News*,[2] was issued. The initial phase of the organization began with a fresh ideal for world union.

The second phase started with veteran experts. Beveridge led the creation of a research group around the summer of 1939, and later formally established the Federal Union Research Institute (FURI) in March 1940. The executive board of FURI consisted of 10 members, including L. Robbins, F. von Hayek, and B. Wootton. Beveridge was chairperson and Ransom was secretary. FURI had four active specialist committees, covering the economic, constitutional, psychological, and colonial aspects of federalism. Beveridge was chairperson of all of the committees barring the psychological one. The economists' committee had eight members whose beliefs ranged from socialism, new liberalism, to classical liberalism: they were E.F.M.D. Durbin, B. Wootton, H.D. Dickinson, J.M. Fleming, W.H. Beveridge, J.E. Meade, L. Robbins, and F. von Hayek. These eminent specialists, along with the other three committees, transformed earlier ideal but vague ideas into concrete or specific frameworks of federation. On 21–22 October 1939 (Howson 2011: 346), a conference of the Economists' Committee was held at the Master's Lodgings, University College, Oxford. Wootton prepared a report for this conference. At the beginning of 1940 a second conference was held, and this time Robbins drafted an agreed interim report.

Federal Union aroused enthusiastic and nationwide support right from the start and from people of almost all parties. In June 1940, there were 255 branches and more than 12,000 members (Burgess 1995: 141). However, due to difficulties dealing with this rapid enlargement and a subsequent financial crisis, the membership drastically decreased to 1,351 in March 1941. After getting on top of their debt problems, there was recovery in membership, to 4,727 in September 1944 (Burgess 1995: 142).

In 1946, Federal Union called the first international conference of federalists in Luxembourg. The debate focused on Europe versus the world. As the result of this conference, two organizations were set up: the World Movement for World Federal Government (WMWFG) and the European Union of Federalists. Federal Union became the British branch of both organizations, and still survives as an active organization today.

## 2 Robbins's federalism from an economic viewpoint

Bosco (1991) pointed out three outstanding exponents in the history of British federalism in the inter-war years: The first was Lord Lothian (Philip H. Kerr; 1882–1940), a private secretary to Lloyd George; the second Lionel G. Curtis

(1872–1955), writer and public servant; and the third Lionel Robbins. Robbins's writings on the economic causes of war "are today considered fundamental contributions to federalist theory" (Bosco 1991: 18). In fact, his two books, *Economic Planning and International Order* (Robbins 1937) and *The Economic Causes of War* (Robbins 1939), were pioneering works before FURI set up its economists' committee in order to consider the economic aspects of federalism. The two books also impacted Italian federalists. Luigi Einaudi sent them to Altiero Spinelli and Ernesto Rossi,[3] who, as anti-fascist activists at that time on the island of Ventotene, were impressed by Robbins's works (Pinder Ed. 1998: 2–4). In this section, I will reconstruct Robbins's ideas on federalism by focusing on his four writings: "Economic Factors and International Disunity" (Robbins 1940) and *Economic Aspects of Federation* (Robbins 1941), in addition to the above two books. His ideas are characterized into four headings: (1) a special meaning of 'planning'; (2) the shortcomings of nationalism; (3) the causes of war; and (4) an idea for federalism.

One of the most remarkable peculiarities in Robbins's ideas is a wider usage of the term 'planning'. Contrary to the expectation that he was on the side of Hayek and Mises in the controversy over the economic calculation problem, Robbins regards 'planning' as a concept embodied more in capitalism, and needless to say, also in socialism. Economic activity involves the disposal of scarce goods, which necessarily involves some kind of plan. Therefore, the "issue is not between *a* plan or *no* plan, it is between different kinds of plan" (Robbins 1937: 6, emphasis in original). When one plan and another plan use the same instruments, the one plan may, if there is no coordination or authority, be frustrated by the other. Conflicts may occur both between private sectors (consumers and producers) and between private agents and public sectors in national or international areas. "The result of our separate planning may be disorder and chaos" (Robbins 1937: 6). Which kinds of plan are worse? The answer lies in whether a coordinating system is available or not. In other words, a coordinating apparatus does not work well when used across different nation states.

Robbins points out three shortcomings of national planning, on the subjects of labour, goods, and money, respectively.

First, restrictions on migration are harmful. Generally and historically, it has been natural for workers to move from areas of lower productivity to areas of higher productivity. If this move is prohibited, the labour balance between supply and demand is not attainable. It is inefficient, as per Adam Smith's or Malthus's opposition to the Settlement and Removal Act (1662). In addition, Robbins notes that there is a serious dilemma between recent developments of social services (by a national plan) and worldwide welfare. If national planning raises the standard of living, the increase could be absorbed by immigration. Taxpayers in that country would not bear this situation. In the planned economy, the labour market is virtually protected. Robbins recognizes the new difficulties in migration after the era of the Liberal Reforms during the 1900s and 1910s. As I will mention later in Section 4.2, for Beveridge, this is the very reason that a federal power is necessary to resolve this dilemma.

Second, restrictions on trade are also hazardous. They produce potential demerits. If there are no restrictions on trade, imports would cost less in terms of possible equilibrium prices. Tariffs, quotas, and licence systems, irrespective of qualitative or quantitative regulations, "involve a diminution of international trade, a wasteful utilization of world resources. . . . [t]hey also involve a dislocation of the mechanism of international exchange" (Robbins 1937: 55). In this context, Robbins described Keynes, who might overlook potential sacrifices, as "disconcertingly insular" (Robbins 1937: 320).

Third, Robbins pays special attention to the recent monetary system since the abandonment of the gold standard in September 1931. He calls it "monetary nationalism . . . characterized by independent exchanges and divergent internal policies" (Robbins 1940: 33). For instance, the depreciation of one exchange has not been regarded by other countries as a balancing adjustment. Usually they subsequently take defensive action either of counter depreciation or of the imposition of obstacles to import exchange control (Robbins 1940: 35).

In each three cases, consciously or not, "national planning has a strong autarkistic bias" (Robbins 1937: 74). Although ordinary economists could also note these defects in separate national policies, one of other peculiarities in Robbins is that he connects them with the causes of war. His scope is beyond economic science, which he himself defined in his *Essay on the Nature and Significance of Economic Science* (Robbins 1932), and within applied economics or political economy. The causes of war are threefold: superficial phenomena (fear of other nations' restriction), the ultimate cause (independent national sovereignties), and an accelerating element (trade depression) (Robbins 1939: 88, 99, 89–90). The fear of other nation's restriction is, however, merely a superficial phenomenon, or an apparent characteristic. Unlike Hobbes's premise, Robbins does not regard the long-run interests of the human race as conflicting. It is not human instinct but the lack of the rule of law that is responsible for the outbreak of wars. Finally, the fear of war, caused by national sovereignties, could be accelerated during a time of depression.

In short, the ultimate cause of war comes from a non-economic element, the existence of independent national sovereignties. This nucleus emerges as the fear of losing opportunities in natural resources and colonial markets, economic elements, whereas the fear could be accelerated in slack trade, again an economic element.

Based on the foregoing diagnosis, Robbins advocates federalism as a highly possible solution: "a co-ordinating apparatus, a social order, a social plan is necessary" (Robbins 1937: 6, emphasis added).

The criterion does not lie in whether the social plan is executed by government or non-government, because "the utilitarian calculus weights governmental and non-governmental actions indifferently" (Robbins 1937: 227). Rather, it lies in whether the actions are egoistically national or discretionarily international. Moreover, the social plan involves the creation of a new institution or government on an international basis. He names his position "international liberalism", that is, "economic organization on an international scale" (Robbins 1937: 225).

Among numerous functions of government, "the first essential is security" (Robbins 1937: 238). If the citizens in any country are continually in danger of violence and war, it is impossible to build an orderly international division of labour, and a proper network of trade and financial relations.

Robbins concludes his arguments: "Without order, no economy: without peace, no welfare. . . . There is world economy. But there is no world polity" (Robbins 1937: 239). Robbins then considers the principal roles of a federal government. These roles relate to powers of the federal government to manage migration, trade, and monetary flow. They also associate with a division of labour between a national state and the federal government. The right policy is to secure, "*not that no regulation should be allowed, but that what regulation there is should be a federal and not a state function*" (Robbins 1941: 11, emphasis in original). Regarding tariffs, it is particularly important to avoid beggar-my-neighbour-policies, which would generate cumulative negative effects to each nation. Restriction or discrimination should be abandoned in a single state. Instead, "from the outset, any discrimination which is allowed must be a matter of federal control" (Robbins 1941: 16). Regarding the monetary system, it is difficult to settle a dispute about an optimal framework: a unity of currencies or exchangeable currencies. At this stage, Robbins postpones the final position, except one principle: "All that is necessary is that it should be agreed that the control of money and capital movements within the federation is essentially a federal function" (Robbins 1941: 22–23, emphasis in original).

The federal government has powers both to impose taxes on the member countries (or citizens) and to provide money for necessary agents. Furthermore, unlike his latest prescription in Robbins (1934), Robbins seems to drastically change his position over discretionary expenditure in bad trade, which means he was approaching the Keynesian position: during periods of depression it was, he said, desirable that "the federal authority should initiate special expenditure" (Robbins 1941: 25).

Robbins preferred a federation within advanced countries, that is, Europe excluding Russia, to that on a world scale.[4] For, in that area conflicts increased to a maximum point whereas their cultures and institutions were similar to one another, which led to a political and economic opportunity to integrate. Therefore, he concluded that "a strong Europe, in friendly relations with the United States, could maintain world order for generations" (Robbins 1940: 46).

In summary, Robbins' federalism goes beyond classical liberalism. When he claims that the "first need of the world is not economic but political revolution" (Robbins 1937: 245) by pointing out that the ultimate cause of wars lies in the political disorder (the conflicts between national sovereignties), he seems to adopt dichotomy between politics and economy, which means economy has spontaneous order whereas political elements destroy the order. Nevertheless, he puts stress on economic 'planning', in other words, certain type of constructivism or discretionary resolutions. His attitude becomes clearer when he shows his approval to 'special expenditure' during periods of economic depression. Economy needs a mediator, who is beyond the market mechanism *per se*.

This mediator is a federal government, especially in Europe. Although Robbins describes his position as 'international liberalism', it is possible to include it into the New Liberalism[5] (social liberalism).

## 3  Beveridge's federalism as a court of arbitration

It was before Robbins contacted the Federal Union movement[6] in May 1939 when Beveridge met one of its founders, Rawnsley, at Oxford in 1938. Yet, it was not until the autumn of 1939 when he was actively involved in the movement. As usual, he played significant roles in forming a philosophy, organizing proper institutions (including research groups), and publicizing its ideas. Although Beveridge and Robbins were not on especially friendly terms, as director and chair in economics at the London School of Economics and Political Sciences (LSE), they collaborated in many cases, such as industrial fluctuations research, free trade disputes, support for exiles from Nazism and so on. Ultimately, Beveridge was forced to resign the directorship of LSE in 1937, which he had held for more than 17 years, because of his reportedly dictatorial style. Hayek and Robbins were at the centre of the anti-Beveridge movement. Nevertheless, after 1937 there was another chance for Robbins and Hayek to collaborate with Beveridge in a specific arena: federalism. This fact itself reveals that a wider range of intellectuals could gather under the one philosophy.

Beveridge published three tiny books or pamphlets on federalism: *Peace by Federation?* (Beveridge 1940), the first volume of *Federal Tracts*, *Why I Am a Liberal* (Beveridge 1945a), an election pledge in his candidacy for Berwick-upon-Tweed for the House of Commons, and *The Price of Peace* (Beveridge 1945b), which he regarded as the final volume of his trilogy after one governmental report on social security (Beveridge 1942), and another non-governmental report on full employment[7] (Beveridge 1944). Around 1941, he ceased to participate in the Federalism movement because he became engaged in governmental war services more than ever, as did Robbins. Unlike Robbins however, Beveridge clearly returned to the movement after 1944 and led it until the last stage of his life.[8] It is vital to recognize that his 1945 works were envisioned just after the two volumes of his trilogy were published. Thus, it should be careful to note the similarities and differences between the 1940 work and the 1945 works.

Beveridge places the term 'security' at the centre of his arguments on how to avoid wars, along with the terms 'seed' and 'soil' of wars. Then he explains the merits of federalism by comparing national and international situations in the development of the civil society. He claims: "The purpose of federation is not the power of large nations but *security for citizens of all nations* and for their different cultures" (Beveridge 1940: 18, emphasis added).

The role of government should be to provide security in civil society. Yet, from an international viewpoint, the role had not been accomplished up to recent years. Beveridge explains this situation by adopting four historical stages of development. The first stage is self-defence, and the second the formation of a group to protect one another. Up to 1914, there had been only two ideas to resolve international conflicts, in response to the preceding two stages: military expansion (the right to individual self-defence) and alliance (the right to collective defence). In the civil society in a state, the third stage is 'hue and cry'. In English common law, which is traceable back to the 13th century, a private citizen (an able-bodied men), who witnessed a crime, should make hue and cry for the pursuit and capture of the criminal(s). The hue and cry must be kept up by a hundred of the inhabitants against the criminal(s) who may flee from town to town. In this way even bystanders are obliged to assist the arrest of the criminal(s).

After 1914, the third stage, corresponding to 'hue and cry', emerged even in the international sphere, that is to say, the idea and inauguration of the League of Nations. This international system was collective security based on members' individual armed forces. However it became to be fragile, as was the 'hue and cry' principle, as it depended on others' goodwill. Likewise, the League of Nations overestimated its ability of members' deterrence based on verbal persuasion. There were several reasons why the system failed: there had been no powers to execute justice; disarmament and collective security were incompatible; and national interests still conflicted with one another. These situations arose from the lack of an ultimate eminent federal authority to reconcile the conflicts on an international level.

At this third step, the danger of war increases under the soil of war based on the seeds of war. Beveridge enumerates six candidates as the seeds of war. (1) The natural pugnacity of mankind. In this viewpoint, human beings are greedy, selfish, and moved by irrational impulses. (2) The economic system or conditions, which are classified approximately by two groups: On the one hand, the blaming of capitalism or high finance system *per se* such as underconsumption or pressure of finance capital seeking outlets for investment. On the other, the blaming of economic inequality: an attempt by the 'have-nots' to enrich themselves by attacking the 'haves'. Beveridge, in support of Robbins (1939: 54), claims that these economic conditions should not be regarded "as direct or primary causes of war" (Beveridge 1945b: 34). (3) The special wickedness of Germans. Beveridge opposed the opinions that Nazi Germany and the totalitarian Japanese are special. He illustrates by examples of pacifistic ideas such as "Kant with his *Plan for Perpetual Peace*, cosmopolitan Goethe and his companion poet Schiller" (Beveridge 1945b: 35). He also pays attention to the British alliance with Germany (in 1898 and 1901) and Japan (in 1902). Specific nations or nationalities are not the ultimate causes of war. (4) The ambition of rulers. Beveridge admits that this can be one of the reasonable causes of war. It was true of Germany (Kaiser William II) and Japan. Japanese aggression cannot be attributed to poverty, because her standard of living was higher (Beveridge 1945b: 38). (5) Revenge. This factor could be true. A defeated nation is more prone to think of opportunities for revenge. "Thus war trends to breed war in endless chain, unless the chain is broken by a just peace" (Beveridge 1945b: 38).

Beyond the five possible causes of war, "the most potent in modern conditions is fear", fear of aggression from neighbouring countries, or fear of the loss of economic opportunities. The fear can easily rise under the soil of international anarchy. At the same time, this fear is itself the product of international anarchy. If there is no international order, "mutual fears drive nations headlong unwillingly over the edge of war" when war has once begun to seem possible.

In order to stop international anarchy, the fourth and final stage is necessary: the establishment of a federal union.[9] It corresponds to that of a police structure in civil society. Just as citizens enjoy their liberty under a legal and constitutional structure, nations could enjoy their liberty under the international rule of law. It is due to the existence of a police structure that conflicts between citizens do not usually give rise to brutal murders. "The rule of law between nations means that nations behave as if they were respectable private citizens" (Beveridge 1945b: 12).

Beveridge pointed out three sides of the division of labour between independent nations and the federal government. The first points are defence and foreign affairs: the two must hand over the reins to the federal government. The armed forces in each country should be abolished, gathered into one unit, and belong only to the federal government. This side had the largest merit. The second point was the handling of colonies (dependencies). As colonies are symbols of past conflicts between nations, they should be brought together to some extent, though it was not practical to realize a perfect transfer immediately to the federal government. The third point was on economic problems. This point is very complicated. It is difficult for the federal government to control all the aspects of economic affairs, but it is a first step in creating a court of arbitration to resolve numerous economic issues. For instance, it is useful to establish a clearing union and an international investment board, as Keynes advocated on occasion. At the same time, an advice institution, such as the International Labour Organization (ILO), is necessary. The economy is necessarily international, and business cycles almost simultaneously have a huge effect on each nation. Yet up to now, it was burdensome for the federal government to manage migration, trade, and currency on a large scale.

The most important condition of being members of the federal government is "a democracy, with effective provision for peaceful change of governments and policies and for free discussion and association in parties" (Beveridge 1945b: 19). The principal organizations resemble the system in a democratic nation: the mutual supervision system of judicial, legislative, and administrative branches of government. In addition, a bicameral system is desirable: assembly members in one house are elected from citizens directly, in proportion to population or constituency; whereas members in another are the representatives of each nation. Federalism is a partnership between nations. Its analogy is not a cooperative store but the cooperation of "those who work together in a common task – of college or factory or family" (Beveridge 1940: 25).

Beveridge in his 1940 work regards the concrete members of federation as west and north European countries and the members of the British Empire (except India). In other words, Britain, France, Germany, Denmark, Norway, Sweden, Finland, Belgium, Holland, Switzerland, Ireland, Australia, Canada, New Zealand, and South Africa. The limitation of areas is essential and leads to the institution being manageable. These members share a common culture and a similar standard of living, and also being firmly connected economically with one another. "The inclusion of Germany is essential to making the federation an organ of assured peace" (Beveridge 1940: 12). Present neutral nations are also necessary for power balance. The inclusion of the British Dominions is not essential, though highly desirable, which might be a first step to a unified government. "World federation is for the millennium" (Beveridge 1940: 23).

In summary, Beveridge points out a double, or reciprocal, structure: the seeds and the soil of war. The seeds include economic causes of war, but the most vital seed is the fear of war. The soil of war is international anarchy. To cut the reciprocal effects between the seeds and the soil, it is necessary to establish a federal union. Beveridge focuses less on the economic aspects of federalism,[10] and more on the international governance system. Around 1940, his emphasis was on limited members in the federation. He did not bring world federalism into view at that time.

## 4 Beveridge's motivation and methodology

Beveridge's federalism evolved from 1940 to 1945 on the background of his deep involvement in arguments on social security and full employment. After a frustrating time when he engaged in no responsible jobs in government for approximately two years since the outbreak of the war, in June 1941 Beveridge was finally appointed as chair for a committee on social insurance and allied services. The report of the committee (Beveridge 1942), published in December 1942, was enthusiastically welcomed by ordinary people as well as specialists (but not by the central organ of government at that time), and became a blueprint of the welfare state. However his thinking never stopped at one point. Before the report was officially made public, his interest had turned to one of its three promises: to abolish idleness, or to conquer mass unemployment. Then, he completed a second report in early 1944 with some young economists including B. Wootton and published it in November 1944, just after an influential white paper, titled *Employment Policy*, was published in May 1944. Again, his interest was turning to a third step: federalism afresh, and he published *the Price of Peace* (Beveridge 1945b).

At the third stage, Beveridge firmly connected the three reports as a trilogy.[11] The most important concept was 'security' for all the citizens. Among the Five Giants (want, disease, squalor, ignorance, and idleness), he explicitly tackled the freedom from want first and idleness second. Afterwards, he handled the whole premise of social security and full employment: freedom from war, or from the fear of war. He was very well aware of the different degrees of difficulty in solving them that he picked the easiest first, and the most difficult last.

The first step needs a comprehensive but only national programme. The aim of social security is to establish a *national* minimum by combining to some degree social insurance, *national* aid, and private savings. Every country could begin its programme at any given point in time. Likewise, the second step also needs a comprehensive *national* programme. Every nation could start its plans at any time, irrespective of other nations. However, the effects of full employment polices differ from those of social security ones for the following reasons. Full employment, according to Beveridge's interpretation of Keynesian theory, depends on the demand side of the economy. To stabilize the demand in one country it is necessary some control of production and prices of food and materials on an international level.[12] In particular, long-term collective contracts are necessary. To find and reorganize a new market in export products needs some public intervention. Full employment policies do not stand alone. There are countless areas that are necessary to intervene in for economic stabilization: international trade, industrial locations, financial networks, and the protection of consumers' rights. Depression in trade is infectious: it could easily spread from one nation to another. Beveridge pays special attention to the international aspects of full employment policies, whereas the white paper, he criticizes, lacks these international viewpoints.

Thus, to make these policies effective, the third step is necessary: coordination between independent nations. To be clearer, the creation of a coordinating organ is desirable. Federalism is a necessary condition to national policies on the one hand, while such polices could strengthen peace conditions by eradicating the fear of war and international anarchy on the other. Moreover, in a federal government, some powerful agents should handle discretionary policies: for Beveridge one of the agents should be an 'economic general staff'. He had virtually coined the term 'economic general staff' in 1923 (Beveridge 1923/24) and continuously demanded its establishment, even in the 1940s. The staff members are several public permanent servants, who can make full use of their economic expertise.

Nationalistic egoism (to raise the level of welfare in a singular country only) is not a proper remedy for abolishment of want as well as idleness. Consequently, Beveridge gradually shifted his position from a European federation into a worldwide federation. One of the possible reasons lies in the necessity of powerful coordinating agents (economic general staff) on a global level to accomplish their roles of dealing with social security and full employment even in a national sphere.

Just after the first report was published, Beveridge in January 1943 realized that maintaining productive employment and peace needed a similar approach, because they needed "planning of the use of all resources by a single authority, fluidity of labour and other resources, international co-operation, determination to find a solution at all costs"[13] and so on. Federation again entered his field of vision. Around the time when finishing the second report on full employment in April 1944, he expressed his ideal for world peace more explicitly:

> Social security is a thing that each country can organise itself, since in the main it means a redistribution of the income already in existence. Mass employment is not a thing that any country can plan for itself. It depends on international trade. . . . What we need is not merely collaboration between Britain and America. Collaboration with all the United Nations, including

particularly the Soviet Union and China, is as essential to success in peace as in war. Anglo-American understanding is only a beginning.[14]

In May 1944, he admitted that safety for small nations "means security – being without the fact or the constant fear of war . . . by placing international security in the hands of an international authority".[15]

The shift of opinion from regional to worldwide federalism is much more distinct in correspondence between the editor (F. L. Josephy) of the *Federal Union News* and Beveridge in September 1944. Beveridge replied to her letter just one day later:

> but on the whole, I am coming to feel that World peace is going to depend so much upon World organisation that Regional Federations are comparatively unimportant.[16]
>
> In November 1944, he specifically demanded the cooperation of the three great nations: "the United States of America, Soviet Russia, and the British Commonwealth."
>
> (Beveridge 1945a: 39)

Furthermore, the atomic bombing of Hiroshima and Nagasaki had a traumatic effect on Beveridge, and probably gave a lasting boost to his confirmation of the absolute necessity of a worldwide federation. On 14 August 1945, the day when Japan accepted the Potsdam Declaration, which meant she surrendered to the United Nations, Beveridge wrote a letter to the Editor of *The Times*, titled 'Atomic Bombs: The Logic of the Discovery, an Alternative to War'. He pointed out three characteristics that the two atomic bombs added to a history of wars: obliterating any distinction between military and civilians; relegating all other modern weapons obsolete, despite of the cheaper costs of developing nuclear fission for instance, compared to total war expenditure or the peace-time waste of unemployment; and increasing the price of peace. War itself had been expensive, while peace too could also be had, only at a price. Lasting peace after Hiroshima became worth a much higher price. Nevertheless, it was a price worth paying whatever the cost. It was true, Beveridge claimed, that the atomic bombs hastened the end of the war and saved countless other lives. Yet, the ultimate justification for using the bombs depended not on this argument, but "on its service in showing to humanity the danger to which we are all exposed if we allow war to recur. The decision has brought us to the necessity of abolishing war". He continued:

> [Abolition of war] depends upon finding a positive alternative to war as a means of settling disputes between nations. *This alternative method must be world-wide*; no nation can be content any longer to seek peace in its particular region and disregard the rest of the world. The only alternative method which can be world-wide is *compulsory arbitration by an impartial tribunal* applied to all disputes between all nations, *and backed by overwhelming*

*international force.* Only in this way can peace be reconciled with liberty and national self-government.[17]

In this way, after the end of World War II, Beveridge increasingly got involved in the world federation movement. As mentioned in Section 1, in 1946, the Federal Union called the first international conference of federalists in Luxembourg. At the other 1948 Luxembourg WMWFG Congress, Beveridge, as an elected Council member, delivered a closing address, titled 'Regional Federation and World Federation: Right and Left Arms of One Movement'. He preferred world to regional federation, although he admitted that the two directions pointed to the same goal: freedom from war.

Beveridge later got involved in the ONE WORLD Trust as one of the founder trustees "to build up a world conscience making for peace, social justice and freedom".[18] Its research aimed at studying the principles and methods of planning and organizing on a world basis. In the early 1950s, he frequently gave addresses on the subject of world federation. At every occasion, he stressed that "world government is possible so long as it does not limit the scale of national government",[19] and that "in order to make it easier to establish a World Government to make wars impossible, it was necessary to limit the powers of that authority to a minimum".[20]

Beveridge had been president of the Federal Union from 1948 until his death in 1963. In 1962 he signed a report, titled *Keeping the Peace*, calling for a permanent United Nations Force.[21] He still urged the putting of any armed forces under the control of law on a global scale. Peace had been his enthusiastic interest, and he devoted his last 25 years to this aim. Peace through a worldwide federation is, he believed, was the only ultimate measure to realize security and welfare for all citizens.

## 5 Summary and concluding remarks

Robbins and Beveridge have copious shared points in their proposals for federalism. Above all, the ultimate value to be protected was security for all citizens; and more generally, welfare or peace for all. Moreover, the ultimate cause of war is conflicts between separate national sovereignties (and the retaining of independent armed forces in particular). The seed of war apparently first emerges as the fear of war. This fear flourishes in the soil of international anarchy and accelerates due to greater economic intertwining, especially in an economic depression. War is a complex mix of political, economic, and psychological factors. To stop these negative chain effects, a powerful federation is necessary: a division of powers between nation states and a federal government. Every power that could cause conflicts between national interests should be transferred to the federation. Such powers include the armed forces, foreign policy, and, to some extent, economic elements (trade, migration, and currency). Advisory boards and courts of arbitration are also necessary.

Their ideas of federalism are well understandable by contrasting those of Hayek (or Mises). Hayek's priority was to establish liberty at all costs. He also joined the Federal Union movement, yet he also supported the abolition of national sovereignties because those were the root of all evil powers that intervene in the spontaneous order of the market.[22] As Masini (2015: 49) refers to, this is *instrumental* federalism. Federalism is merely the means to realize supreme liberty. By contrast, Robbins and Beveridge adhered to *constitutional* federalism. Their priority was peace,[23] or welfare. They always paid attention to arbitrating powers to arrange the external conditions outside the market.

Shared with the fundamental factors in federalism, Robbins and Beveridge had divisional cooperation. Robbins was a pioneer in examining the economic causes of war before the Federal Union movement arose. Beveridge then took the initiative about organizing proper groups, conceptualizing basic ideas, and publicizing their ideals, and so forth. Famous economists gathered under the leadership of Beveridge, including Robbins, Hayek, Plant, Meade, and Wootton. They elaborated more concrete and practical plans for a European federation. Among other things, Robbins and Meade fundamentally contributed to investigating the economic aspects of federalism, for instance, a unified currency versus changeable exchange rates in member countries. They collaborated well as a team.

The story does not end here; the two distinguished scholars had their own reasons to develop the ideas of federalism. Robbins, who had been defeated in the dispute over the diagnosis and remedy for mass unemployment with Keynes, attempted to take every opportunity to counter Keynes's 'insularity': an idea to assign, even if temporarily, higher priority to domestic equilibrium. Federalism was the best chance to contemplate international relations. In addition, it was the best example to apply his methodology in economics, which he expressed in Robbins (1932), to an urgent practical problem: to sharply distinguish economic theory and political economy, to reveal an economist's presuppositions, and to apply economic analysis to current issues on a criteria of *relevance* from comprehensive viewpoints.[24] Federalism was a natural result induced from Robbins's synthetic attitude as an economist.

The same is true of Beveridge. As a champion to promote essential liberty, it was natural for him to participate in the Federal Union movement around 1939. For him, war was the quickest way to destroy people's basic liberty, and the freedom from war, or from the fear for war, was by far the most important point. As in previous years, Beveridge and Robbins collaborated with each other, amplifying their strong points (grounded ideas and detailed analysis; judicial and economic approaches; and appeals to the public and specialists). However, the subsequent two reports on social security and full employment made Beveridge's federalism evolve further. Possibly inspired by Robbins's and Meade's arguments on the economic aspects of federalism, and definitely influenced by Keynes's and Meade's approach of effective demand,[25] Beveridge came to recognize the necessity of a competent worldwide federation to secure not only lasting peace on an international level but also maintaining full employment and high standard of living on a national level. For Beveridge, even the maintenance of national elements premised an international order. Finally, he recognized a trilogy of security for all citizens: freedom from want (Beveridge 1942), freedom from idleness (Beveridge 1944), and freedom from war (Beveridge 1945b). When finishing the second report of the trilogy in the early 1944, Beveridge perceived the necessity of an economic general staff on an international level. That was the worldwide federation to cease any economic and political conflicts. This is why he switched his position from a European federation around 1940, to a world federation after 1944 and up to the end of his life. One of the triggers for the shift was the atomic bombing of Hiroshima and Nagasaki. His shift was natural if one focuses upon his evolving thought process and grasping all his ideas on security.

There remain ideas on regional federation (the EU, for instance) and world federation (the United Nations in a wider sense), and various arguments based on economic and more constitutional aspects. If one understands well their collaboration and the natural processes of their own ideas in social science, it is acceptable to a large extent that Robbins and Beveridge, based on a renewed liberalism, contributed tremendously to the making of federal ideas in numerous spheres.

I would like to end my chapter with a quote from Beveridge's speech in the House of Lords in June 1962, just 9 months before his death:

> Our aim is war barred to great and small, and freedom secured equally to great and small. While war exists, neither equality nor freedom is possible in the world.[26]

## Notes

1 Regarding Keynes's liberal aspects and the diffusion of his ideas, see Biagini (2011) and Komine (2014).
2 *Federal Union News* (1939–1944) was a bulletin of the Federal Union, followed by *Federal News* (1944–1945) and *World Affairs* (1944–1955).
3 In 1941, they, under house arrest on the island, drew up a manifesto for a free and united Europe. See in detail Pinder ed. (1998).
4 See the following citations: "I hasten to say that I do not believe that the formation of a super-State or a federation on a world scale is within the bounds of practicability" (Robbins 1940: 46); "We cannot hope in our day to build a federation so wide that it embraces even a majority of the world's inhabitants" (Robbins 1941: 31).
5 It is a historical term: the New Liberalism claims that it is necessary to intervene in economic areas by a state in order to secure (or complete) liberty in a wider sense.
6 Robbins sent a mail to Lord Lothian on 24 May 1939 (Basco 1991: 26).
7 With regard to Beveridge's earlier ideas on unemployment, see Komine (2004).
8 In his eighties, Beveridge, who just returned from a 12-day stay in a hospital, was still undaunted by stating: "As long as I live I shall remain a firm Federal Unionist". BP, VII-66 (139), a letter from Beveridge to F. R. Rea (Secretary to Federal Union), 19 December 1960.
9 Beveridge pointed out like Robbins that "peace cannot be secured except by a radical change in the old conception of national sovereignty" (Beveridge 1945a: 38).

10 "Sir William said that in economics he doubted whether there was general need for a supra-national authority. The economic as distinct from the political relations of separate states could rest on contract, not on status". I MX 1335, 'Planning for Employment, the Editor of *Federal News* interviews Sir William Beveridge', *Federal News*, No. 117, November 1944.

11 Regarding another trilogy, replacing Beveridge (1945b) for Beveridge (1948), see Komine (2010).

12 "But international trade was essential for an adequate standard of life in Britain. Our objective must be to stabilise international demand as well as demand in this country. Stabilising overseas demand involved regulating production and prices of raw materials and food". I MX 1335, 'Planning for Employment, the Editor of *Federal News* interviews Sir William Beveridge', *Federal News*, No. 117, November 1944.

13 *The Observer*, 10 January 1943, page 4, 'The Pillars of Security: II – The Assumption of Victory, by Sir William Beveridge'.

14 I MX 1066, *Federal Union News*, No. 98, April 1943, 'Common Ends, by Sir William Beveridge'.

15 *The Observer*, 2 May 1943, page 4, 'A World Safe for Small Nations, by Sir William Beveridge'.

16 BP, VII-63 (147), from Beveridge to F. L. Josephy, 13 September 1944.

17 *The Times*, 14 August 1945, page 5, 'Atomic Bombs: The Logic of the Discovery, an Alternative to War, by W. H. Beveridge', emphasis added.

18 BP, VII-63, 'The ONE WORLD Trust: A Statement', n.d. [after 6 April 1951].

19 I MX 2456, *Federal News*, No. 201, January 1952, 'Beveridge says "W. G. is Possible"', also in BP VII-64.

20 I MX 2496, *Federal News*, No. 206, June 1952, 'The Hope for Humanity: 1500 Crowd Federal Union Meeting to Hear Yehudi Menuhin and Lord Beveridge'.

21 *The Times*, 22 March 1963, page 15, 'Obituary of Lord Beveridge, by M.M.W.'

22 Hayek concludes that "there would have to be *less* government all round if federation is to be practicable. Certain forms of economic policy will have to be conducted by the federation *or by nobody at all*" (Hayek 1948 [1939]: 266, emphasis added).

23 When he was asked by Lord Pekenham, who was once a key assistant to the Beveridge Report, "Would it be fair to ask whether peace is more important than Liberalism?", Beveridge replied: "Certainly it is more important than Liberalism". *Hansard*, HL Deb 24 March 1954, vol. 186, col. 668. See also *Manchester Guardian*, 25 March 1954, page 2, 'Peer Suggests All-in Security Treaty for Europe'.

24 Robbins admitted that he himself accepted "the historical association of English Economics with Utilitarianism" (Robbins 1932: 125), or "provisional utilitarianism" (Robbins 1938: 635).

25 Beveridge in December 1942 confessed that he did not know how to combat mass unemployment and he even did not know anybody else knew. *The Times*, 7 December 1942, page 2, 'Sir W. Beveridge on the New Britain: Need for an Economic General Staff'. It is obvious that he absolved Keynesian ideas during the creation of his second report on full employment.

26 *Hansard*, HL Deb 27 June 1962, vol. 241, col. 983. By contrast, Robbins only mentioned war in the following way in March 1982, just two years before his death: "In my judgment, short of nuclear war, disproportionate growth of population is the main danger to the human race in the next century". *Hansard*, HL Deb 3 March 1982, vol. 427, col. 1329. Even so, Robbins believed the power of thought: "our 'raison d'être' is the maintenance of the highest standards of thought and conduct" (Robbins 1976: 6). He claimed that, despite of "what there is of peace is the result of a balance of terror rather than mutual goodwill and understanding", "[s]uch an attitude is surely as illbased as nineteenth century complacency" (Robbins 1976: 5).

# References and further readings

## *Unpublished materials*

BP: The Beveridge Papers, Archives Section, British Library of Political and Economic Science, London School of Economics and Political Science.

## *Microfiche*

1 MQ 1–148, Federal Union Research Institute, *First Annual Report*, 1939–1940.
1 MX 1066, *Federal Union News*, No. 98, April 1943.
1 MX 1335–1336, *Federal News*, No.117, October 1944.
1 MX 741, *Federal Union News*, No. 31, April–May 1940.
1 MX 38–42, Beveridge, *Notes on Organisations of Federal Union*, 14 February 1940.
*Britain and Europe Since 1945*, Brighton: The Harvester Press, 1973.
I MX 2040–2041, *Federal News*, No. 163, October/November 1948.
I MX 2456, *Federal News*, No. 201, January 1952.
I MX 2496, *Federal News*, No. 206, June 1952.

## *Database*

*Daily Express, Economist, Guardian, Observer, The Times, The Times Literary Supplement*, among others.

## *General literature*

Basco, A. (1991). "Introduction", in P. Ransom (Ed.), *Towards the United States of Europe: Studies on the Making of the European Constitution*, London and New York: Lothian Foundation Press, 13–46.
Beveridge, W. H. (1923/24). "An Economic General Staff 1/2", *The Nation and the Athenaeum*, 29 December 1923, 485–486, and 5 January 1924, 509–510.
Biagini, E. (2011). "Keynesian Ideas and the Recasting of Italian Democracy, 1945–1953", in E.H.H. Green and D. M. Tanner (Eds.), *The Strange Survival of Liberal England: Political Leaders, Moral Values and the Reception of Economic Debate*, Cambridge: Cambridge University Press, 212–246.
Beveridge, W. H. (Ed.) (1931). *Tariffs: The Case Examined, by a Committee of Economists under the Chairmanship of Sir William Beveridge*, London: Longmans, Green & Co.
Beveridge, W. H. (1940). *Peace by Federation?* Federal Tracts: No. 1, London: Federal Union.
Beveridge, W. H. (1942). *Social Insurance and Allied Services*, Cmd. 6405, London: His Majesty's Stationery Office.
Beveridge, W. H. (1944). *Full Employment in a Free Society*, London: George Allen & Unwin Ltd.
Beveridge, W. H. (1945a). *Why I Am a Liberal*. London: Herbert Jenkins.
Beveridge, W. H. (1945b). *The Price of Peace*, London: Pilot Press.
Beveridge, W. H. (1948). *Voluntary Action: A Report on Methods of Social Advance*, London: George Allen & Unwin Ltd.

Burgess, M. (1995). *The British Tradition of Federalism*, London: Leicester University Press.

Cannan, E. (1927). *An Economist's Protest*, London: P.S. King & Son. Ltd.

Hayek, F. von (1948 [1939]). "The Economic Conditions of Interstate Federalism", reprinted in Individualism and Economic Order, Chicago: University of Chicago Press, 255–272. (First published in *New Commonwealth Quarterly*, 5(2): 131–149, September 1939.)

Howson, S. (2011). *Lionel Robbins*, Cambridge: Cambridge University Press.

Kimber, C. (1991). "Foreword", in P. Ransom (Ed.) *Towards the United States of Europe: Studies on the Making of the European Constitution*, London and New York: Lothian Foundation Press, 1–11.

Kimber, C. (2005). "The Birth of Federal Union", *The Federalist Debate*, 18(1), March. Available at http://www.federalist-debate.org/index.php/current/item/420-the-birth-of-federal-union).

Komine, A. (2004). "The Making of Beveridge's Unemployment (1909): Three Concepts Blended," *European Journal of the History of Economic Thought*, 11(2) Summer: 255–280.

Komine, A. (2010). "Beveridge on a Welfare Society: an Integration of His Trilogy", in R.E. Backhouse and T. Nishizawa (Eds.), *No Wealth But Life: Welfare Economics and the Welfare State in Britain 1880–1945*, Cambridge: Cambridge University Press.

Komine, A. (2014). *Keynes and His Contemporaries: Tradition and Enterprise in the Cambridge School of Economics*, Abingdon: Routledge.

Komine, A. (2016). "Beveridge and His Pursuit of an Ideal Economics: Why Did He Come to Accept Keynes's Ideas?" *International Journal of Social Economics*, 43(9): 917–930.

Komine, A. and Masini, F. (2011). "The Diffusion of Economic Ideas: Lionel Robbins in Italy and Japan", in H.D. Kurz, T. Nishizawa, and K. Tribe (Eds.), *The Dissemination of Economic Ideas*, Cheltenham, UK: Edward Elgar, 223–259.

Masini, F. (2009). "*Economics* and *Political Economy* in Lionel Robbins's Writings", *Journal of the History of Economic Thought*, 31(4): 421–436.

Masini, F. (2015). "European Integration: Contrasting Models and Perspective", in F. Fiorentini and G. Montanio (Eds.), *The European Union and Supranational Political Economy*, Abingdon, UK: Routledge, 44–64.

Mayne, R. and Pinder, J. (Eds.). (1990). *Federal Union: The Pioneers, A History of Federal Union*, London: Macmillan.

O'Brien, D.P. (1988). *Lionel Robbins*, London: Macmillan.

Pinder, J. (1995). "British Federalists 1940–1947: From the Movement to Stasis", in M. Dumoulin (Ed.) *Plans des Temps de Guerre pour l'Europe d'Apres-Guerre 1940–1947*, Bruxelles: Bruylany, 247–274.

Pinder, J. (Ed.) (1998). *Altiero Spinelli and the British Federalists: Writings by Beveridge, Robbins and Spinelli 1937–1943*, London: Federal Trust.

Robbins, L. (1932). *An Essay on the Nature and Significance of Economic Science*, London: Macmillan.

Robbins, L. (1934). *The Great Depression*, London: Macmillan.

Robbins, L. (1935). *An Essay on the Nature and Significance of Economic Science*, second edition, London: Macmillan.

Robbins, L. (1937). *Economic Planning and International Order*, London: Macmillan.

Robbins, L. (1938). "Interpersonal Comparisons of Utility: A Comment", *Economic Journal*, 48(192), December: 635–641.

196    *Atsushi Komine*

Robbins, L. (1939). *The Economic Causes of War*, London: Jonathan Cape.

Robbins, L. (1940). "Economic Factors and International Disunity", in *World Order Papers*, London: The Royal Institute of International Affairs, 23–47.

Robbins, L. (1941). *Economic Aspects of Federation*, Federal Tracts: No. 2, London: Macmillan.

Robbins, L. (1964). "A Comment on G. Myrdal's *Toward a More Closely Integrated Free-Word Economy*", in R. Lekachman (Ed.) *National Policy for Economic Welfare at Home and Abroad*, New York: Russell & Russell, Inc., 280–292 (Based on a conference at Columbia University, May 26–29, 1954)

Robbins, L. (1971). *Autobiography of an Economist*, London: Macmillan.

Robbins, L. (1976). *Graduation Address*, Alleo: University of Stirling.

Robbins, L. (1977). "Liberty and Equality", IEA Occasional Papers, No. 52, London: Institute of Economic Affairs.

Robbins, L. (1997 [1981]) "Economics and Political Economy", in S. Howson (Ed.) *Economic Science and Political Economy Selected Articles*, New York: New York University Press, 415–428 (First published in *The American Economic Review*, vol.71 Supplement, May 1981).

Sasazaki, Y. (2005). "Beveridge's Ideas for Federalism", 1–23, mimeo (in Japanese).

# 11 The wartime economy and the theory of price controls

*Paolo Paesani and Annalisa Rosselli*

## 1 Introduction[1]

One of the main economic lessons of the Second World War was that resources could be allocated in a reasonably efficient and equitable way, imposing strict regulations on markets without abolishing them. The success of these regulations depended greatly on cooperation between organised workers, producers and governments, and indeed on collaboration between nations. This was in sharp contrast with the inter-war period, characterised by mass unemployment, social unrest and fierce nationalism.

As the war was drawing to an end, a large group of economists and policy makers[2] – mainly in the Anglo-Saxon world – reflected on the possibility of preserving some of the measures that had been so successful during the conflict. This was justified by the desire to facilitate reconversion of the economy and permanently lock in some of the positive outcomes, in terms of price stability, full employment and social justice, achieved through wartime regulation. The proposals put forth in this context, utopian as they may appear today, reflected a certain scepticism about the "myth" of free markets and optimism about the possibility of reforming them. Inter-war studies on non-competitive market regimes and the direct observation of the harmful volatility of financial and commodity markets were particularly significant in this respect.

Price controls were one of the most controversial wartime measures discussed at the end of the conflict. There is little doubt that these controls were perceived as successful at the time. As the *Bulletin of International News* of the Royal Institute of International Affairs commented,

> The far greater success attained by many belligerents in this war, as compared with the last, has been largely due, not to any improvement in fiscal or monetary policy in the narrow sense [. . .] but to improvements in price-control and rationing.
>
> (A.J.B. 1945a: 15)

This success challenged the conventional idea that price controls were harmful and, moreover, would be inevitably confounded by the black market. At the same time, it encouraged those who supported continuation of some of the wartime controls to correct the inequitable and inefficient outcomes of competitive markets:

> The arguments *for* price controls have some weight. [. . .] Rising prices not only fail to provide satisfactory distribution of what is produced, but beyond some point lose any efficiency in attracting added resources into the production of these goods. Beyond this point, further price increases mean only "profiteering" for the resource owners lucky enough to be employed in these areas, creating social discord, and wage pressures likely to spread into other fields. Further, price controls tend to check hoarding of these goods.
>
> (Ackley 1951: 71–72)

Opponents of these views claimed that extending any price control to the peacetime economy would be politically impossible, administratively costly and economically useless, as containment of inflation – one of the main goals assigned to price controls – was best achieved through aggregate demand management.

> Controls are precarious; they are difficult to enforce, and, being unpopular when they are enforced, are liable to arouse political opposition and to be prematurely repealed. Moreover, controls can do no more than hold a potential inflation in check; they do not eliminate it.
>
> (Hawtrey 1948: 49)

In parallel with this debate, extensive discussion took place on rationing, as an alternative or complement to price controls. As Tobin wrote:

> The question becomes the more compelling because in some countries rationing is evidently more than a temporary wartime measure and because elsewhere emergencies that may give rise to rationing seem to be increasingly frequent.
>
> (Tobin 1952: 521)

Surveying the state of the theory, enriched by the contributions of some of the most eminent economists of the time,[3] Tobin (1952: 521) analyses the effects of rationing on individual choices and their impact on collective welfare compared with alternative measures of demand restriction.

These debates in the Anglo-Saxon world were part of a more general reflection on the appropriate role of the State in the economy against the background of the emerging conflict between US capitalism and Soviet collectivism:

> The basic principles of our economic policy are once more in the melting pot. Should we in peacetime continue a policy of economic planning? Or should we restore the working of the price mechanism? We have to resolve this issue both for the solution of the immediate and pressing problems of

the transition from war to peace and also for the construction of a more permanent and lasting economic system.

(Meade 1948: 1)

In this context, supporters of the command economy and complete deregula-
tion of markets were a minority with respect to a majority that shared a common
"Keynesian" theoretical framework. This framework assigned a positive role to
public intervention in fostering cooperation between economic agents, at the
national and global level, and in correcting market failures. This appeared to be
an appropriate framework to discuss two issues in particular: the prevention of
wage-price spirals in a full employment economy and the stabilization of commodity prices on the world markets.

At the start of the 1950s, the outbreak of the Korean War revived interest in price
and wage controls, especially in the USA, as epitomized by the publication of *A
Theory of Price Controls* by John K. Galbraith in 1952. Thereafter, as international
trade and economic growth picked up and inflationary pressures subsided, the need
(and advocacy) for price and wage controls gradually waned. They were debated
one last time in connection with the oil shocks of the 1970s and the inflationary
pressures that followed. Promotion of incomes policy and schemes to stabilize commodity prices at the supranational level, both supported by two die-hard Keynesians
like Richard Kahn and Nicholas Kaldor, was the last upshot of this debate. Thereafter, discussion on price and wage controls disappeared altogether, submerged by the
triumph of free market ideas, and the lessons of the war sank into oblivion. Interest
in the possibility of managing wages to combat deflation is re-emerging today, in
connection with doubts about the effectiveness of monetary policy in this respect.[4]

While several studies exist on the history of price controls, during and after the
war,[5] the aim of this chapter is to reconstruct and summarize the early phase of
the theoretical debate on this issue.

Our reconstruction yields three main findings. First, we show how the early
post-war debate on price controls emerged out of the theory of non-competitive
markets and the Keynesian theory of inflation as a consequence of excess demand.
Second, we find that the advocacy of price controls reflects conviction of the
impossibility of relying solely on market forces and competitive pricing to balance
supply and demand – especially in the case of major shocks affecting the markets
for consumer products and commodities. Third, we remark how considerations
of distributive justice form an integral part of analysis of price and production
controls and of the effects resulting should they be removed.

Based on these considerations, the structure of the chapter is as follows. Section 2 discusses wartime price controls and the problem of inflation. Section 3
explores early post-war theories of inflation and the main arguments for and
against price controls. Section 4 investigates the theory of price controls as developed by John K. Galbraith and its analytical background. Section 5 focuses on
the specific case of price controls as applied to agricultural commodity prices.
Section 6 concludes the chapter.

## 2 Price controls and the problem of wartime inflation

Historically, war causes inflation, which calls for the introduction of price controls. Wartime inflation develops through a process that consists of four stages.[6] In the first stage, demand for armaments increases, putting productive capacity under pressure. Existing plants are expanded and new plants are built, compatibly with physical limitations upon factory capacity, shipping facilities, raw materials and other needed factors. The second stage coincides with the increase in the demand for basic materials (e.g. lumber, metals, steel and chemicals) and with the need to boost capacity for their production. Initially, producers may be unwilling to do so, wary about running into over-capacity. Pushed up by government demand, the prices of raw materials and manufactured goods rise sharply, often overshooting their equilibrium level as a result of speculative purchases. This affects the cost of producing all other goods, while demand increases as civilians spend the increased money incomes received for defence work. Dealers bid to replace their stocks and speculative demand appears, pushing wholesale and retail prices further up (third stage). The fourth stage is marked by the emergence of a general demand for higher wages. Shortages in the labour market, especially shortages of skilled labour, reinforce this demand, leading nominal wages to rise and setting a wage-price spiral in motion. The process may be accompanied by strikes and protests disrupting production, further increasing the uncertainty that makes producers reluctant to create new productive capacity.

The expansion in private consumption, generated by rising employment and wages, competes with military demand while private producers may be reluctant to lose their regular markets to satisfy military requirements. The fact that inflation does not compress private demand sufficiently constitutes a major stumbling-block for reallocation of resources from civilian to military uses. Moreover, as usual, inflation has disruptive consequences on income and wealth distribution and the overall efficiency of the price mechanism. In this context, direct controls, on prices and quantities, appear to governments pressed by war needs as the most rapid means of intervention.[7]

> Direct controls may be classified roughly into three broad groups. The first includes all methods which apply direct action to channel and stimulate the flow of materials into military production [. . .] priorities, allocations, and rationing. The second broad group includes all devices which operate directly upon the price mechanism, such as fixing the prices of commodities and services, wage and interest rates, rents, real estate, and other capital values. The third group includes restrictions on bank credit and the flotation of new corporate securities.
>
> (Crum et al. 1942: 107)

The likelihood of price controls[8] being successful varies inversely with the degree of competitiveness prevailing in individual industries and the standardization of the different products. In general, control is easier for basic industrial materials where the number of producers is limited and heterogeneous quality is not a major issue. The opposite occurs in the case of foodstuffs and finished consumer goods where price controls are much more difficult to enact due to the presence of a high number of competing producers and/or to heterogeneity of goods produced. In this case, successful implementation of price controls requires the parallel introduction of rationing mechanisms (e.g. ration cards, specific taxes).[9]

While direct controls aim at preventing prices of specific goods or raw materials from rising, wage controls intervene to block the transmission of inflationary impulses to the cost of labour. The successful stabilization of nominal wages depends on the government winning the support of and coordinating the wage-setting process with trade unions and representatives of producers. If this is achieved, wage stability contributes to reducing inflation through the parallel containment of production costs and demand by consumers.

Two main policy implications emerge from this characterization of the inflationary process and controls. First, controlling wartime inflation means setting ceilings to all the elements of the price system (e.g. wages, interest, commissions, rents) rather than adopting a piecemeal approach.[10] Second, all types of price controls must be enacted simultaneously relying

> on direct controls and selective limitations on buying power in the areas of special scarcity, while imposing general limitations sufficient, if supplemented by informal pressures, to prevent serious increases of prices in the general field of miscellaneous consumer-products. [. . .] But unless some such division of the field can be worked out, the policy of preventing runaway prices will fail.
>
> (Clark 1942a: 21)

During the war, it was debated whether direct controls alone were the best means to achieve the twofold goal of price stability and efficient, equitable allocation. This debate related to a broader change in the underlying theoretical framework, highlighting the crucial role of aggregate demand in determining economic activity:

> This generation inherited a traditional economics in which the limits on wealth were thought of as the limits on physical power to produce it, while the money mechanism and the flow of money incomes could, in effect, be left to take care of itself. Since 1930 this economics of physical production has been dethroned by an economics in which the limits on wealth are thought of as residing in the flow of money incomes while the relation between this and physical production is, in substantial effect, left to take care of itself.
>
> (Clark 1942b: 13)

This framework offered the instrument of aggregate demand management to control wartime inflation caused by the conflict between growing private monetary incomes and a shrinking amount of goods available for civilian consumption. Based on this diagnosis, inflation control called for control of civilian expenditure, to be achieved by means of higher taxes or, alternatively, by introducing compulsory saving schemes, as notably advocated by Keynes (1972 [1940]) in *How to Pay for the War*. In the context of Keynes's plan, price controls on a limited number of consumption goods contributed to moderate requests for wage rises but played a secondary role with respect to deferred wages. The same was true of rationing, which Keynes favoured only in the case of few specific imported goods.

Keynes' opposition to universal price controls reflected his aversion towards "the abolition of consumers' choice in favour of universal rationing, a typical product [. . .] of Bolshevism" (Keynes 1972 [1940]: 410), capable of levelling down the differences between individual consumers. Keynes's opinion is indicative of a widespread hostility to price controls in the name of economic liberty and free choice. After the war, this constituted one of the main arguments against the continuation of price controls in peacetime, as discussed in more detail later.

In conclusion, this early phase of the debate related to a broader change in the underlying theoretical framework, characterised by:

- Emergence of the theory of non-competitive markets (supportive of price controls); wages determined by a bargaining process;
- Emergence of aggregate demand as the main determinant of economic activity and inflation;
- Demotion in the inflationary role of money.

## 3 Price controls and the theory of inflation: early post-war views

The end of the war saw the breakdown of the compromise between organised labour, manufacturers and agricultural producers that had kept inflation under control. The trade unions demanded wage increases after the prolonged wartime moderation. Producers, caught between difficult reconversion and uncertainty about future demand, acceded to these demands reluctantly, stoking up inflationary pressures (Dunlop 1947a: 156). In this context, economists and regulators discussed the possibility of maintaining price controls to contain these pressures.

Three main arguments were raised against this possibility. First, preserving price controls, which reflected the wartime allocation of resources, would hinder innovation and slow down the re-organization of economic activity.[11] Second, the revocation of costly administrative measures, such as priority systems, inventory controls and rationing, would make it difficult to maintain effective price controls, except in cases where large companies prevailed, sellers were few and excess shortages could be avoided (Wallace 1951). This was not the case of the agricultural markets and other wage goods (e.g. meat and clothing). Finally, price controls were increasingly regarded as incompatible with post-war liberal-ized economic systems (Eichengreen 2008: 61–62).

> Although virtually everyone is against inflation, many of the brakes on inflation encounter insuperable political obstacles. Any form of direct price control, for example, is out of question. So also is consumer rationing or increases in the personal income tax.
>
> (Slichter 1948: 4)

The actual removal of price controls contributed to the re-emergence of infla-tion in the US, in the UK and elsewhere. It was generally agreed that the main cause of inflation was the excess of aggregate demand over supply. This view was compatible with the prevailing Keynesian paradigm and had one major policy implication. In order to control inflation, governments should resort to fiscal and monetary restriction to restore macroeconomic equilibrium, leaving to market forces the task of setting individual prices.

> From different angles and with important individual variations Professor Jewkes, Mr. Harrod, Professor Meade and many others in this country and abroad, can be observed converging on the formula: "Equate aggregate demand to aggregate supply and set the price system free." Nor is this for-mula propounded on purely practical grounds. It is suggested that it repre-sents the fruits of the latest developments in abstract economic thought, the distillation of the genius of Lord Keynes, a profoundly thought-out synthesis of new facts and the wisdom of the ages, appropriate to the conditions of our time.
>
> (Henderson 1948: 471)

While it was generally agreed that inflation should be controlled by means of high taxes and monetary restriction, faith in the allocative power of the free markets was not unconditional, and arguments in favour of price controls or warnings against the negative consequences of their removal survived after the war. Our reconstruction indicates that there were two main lines of reasoning in favour of maintaining price controls after the war, one at the partial equilibrium level and one at the general equilibrium level.

At the partial equilibrium level, there are cases when price increases, caused by excess demand, feed on themselves, leading the market astray. On the supply side, exorbitant price rises, which generate large profit margins, may induce producers to limit their efforts and reduce supply instead of increasing it as expected under normal conditions. On the demand side, panicky buying, hoarding and specula-tion may accrue to the existing demand, exacerbating pressures on prices. In these cases, price controls can contribute to restoring equilibrium.[12]

At the general equilibrium level, the removal of price controls can immediately trigger a rise in inflation through its impact on wages and the cost of living. This reflects the strong bargaining power acquired by organised labour after the war through the trade unions and their political representatives. Recognition of the role of the trade unions in determining nominal wages contributed to the evolution of the post-war theory of inflation and price controls.

If all firms adopted competitive pricing and real wages were not staunchly defended by the trade unions, the inflation generated by excess demand (the inflationary gap) would be transitory. As nominal incomes lag behind prices and government revenues rise in real terms, falling purchasing power in real terms contributes to eliminating the inflationary gap, *coeteris paribus*. Increases in productivity, operating on the supply side, accelerate this process. If, on the contrary, we introduce the assumption that industrial prices are determined on the basis of mark-up pricing (and not only excess demand) and that hourly wages are determined so as to keep their real value constant in terms of a fixed-weight price index, then "inflation need not stop when excess demand is eliminated. If the wage-price spiral has not worked itself out, when the gap is closed prices may continue to rise" unless the bargaining powers of the trade unions are limited by emerging unemployment or demand for goods falls.[13]

Kalecki (1948) presents a very simple model that is useful to understand the interaction between wages and prices after the elimination of price controls on primary products. Kalecki models the economy as consisting of two sectors: the foodstuffs sector and the non-foodstuffs sector (manufacturing and services). Prices in the primary sector are determined competitively to equate demand and supply. Prices in the secondary sectors are mainly determined on the cost side (e.g. prices of durable consumer goods) and depend on wages, labour productivity and the pricing policies of the firms. Equilibrium in the foodstuffs sector is given by

(1) $\quad F_1 = S - F_2$

where $S$ is supply, $F_1$ is domestic consumption out of wages, salaries and government transfers and $F_2$ is the residual (domestic consumption by earners of incomes other than wage earners plus foreign consumption). Both S and $F_2$ are exogenous and inelastic to prices. Domestic demand for foodstuffs is equal to

(2) $\quad F_1 = m\dfrac{W}{p} + n\dfrac{q}{p} + A \qquad m,n>0$

where $W$ is the nominal wage rate (equal across sectors), $p$ is the cost of living index, $q$ is a price index of non-foodstuffs goods and $A$ is an exogenous component. Equation (2) treats $q$ as exogenous. *Coeteris paribus*, domestic demand for foodstuffs increases with the real wage (income effect) and with the relative price of non-foodstuffs (substitution effect). Equating (1) and (2) and isolating the price level $p$ we obtain

(3) $\quad p = \dfrac{mW + nq}{S - F_2 - A}$

Based on (3), Kalecki argues that the decontrol of prices and abolition of rationing releases pent-up demand, rising foodstuff prices. This triggers wage increases, reflecting pay-rise requests in both sectors of the economy, which leads both $q$ and $p$ to rise. Equation (3) clarifies the logic underlying the linkage between price and wage controls in a world where the prices of primary products are determined competitively by demand and supply while industrial prices are determined by the application of cost mark-up systems.

In the following years, the two-sector model became the standard tool to analyse price controls and inflation dynamics,[14] as exemplified by John K. Galbraith and his *Theory of Price Controls* (Galbraith 1952).

## 4 Galbraith's Theory of Price Controls

The outbreak of the Korean War in 1950 and the ensuing reintroduction of price controls in the USA revived interest in price and wage controls. Galbraith, who had served as deputy head of the Office of Price Administration between 1941 and 1943, took this opportunity to publish his views on the subject, developing previous research.[15]

Galbraith's theory is interesting for two reasons in particular. First, because it links the Keynesian theory of inflation as a consequence of excess demand to the interaction between price and wage setters in a full employment economy. Second, because it exemplifies how the economic lessons of WWII reverberated on the policy debate of the 1950s.

Galbraith's book presents one of the few attempts – the only one according to Milton Friedman (Friedman 1977) – to elaborate a systematic theory of price controls in peacetime.[16] Galbraith reconstructs the two main traditional arguments against price controls. First, there is the conviction that price controls prevent market-clearing and distort resource allocation.

> Freely moving prices, as the first textbook lessons tell, are the rationing and allocating machinery of the economy. They keep demand for goods equal to what is available; they guide resources from less to more important uses. Obviously if prices are fixed they can no longer perform these functions [. . .] At a minimum, the effect must be some malfunctioning of the economy; at a maximum it might be chaos.
>
> (Galbraith 1952: 2–3)

Second, there is the possibility that, as the regulatory authorities introduce price controls, coalitions of dissatisfied buyers and sellers emerge to sabotage them. In the case of excess demand, for example,

> If the price increase is arrested by authority, the action runs not only against the interest of sellers, but also against the interest of those buyers who are not able to satisfy all or substantially all of their wants at the fixed price. An incentive thus exists for a coalition on behalf of higher prices between

sellers and at least some buyers. This coalition is based on an equally rational interpretation of immediate self-interest on both sides of the market. [. . .] At some point, the price-fixing authority will surrender to the coalition against it.

(Galbraith 1952: 3–4)

The first argument reflects the traditional confidence in the idea that competitive pricing guarantees the efficient allocation of scarce resources. The second argument points to the likely failure of price-fixing schemes unless they take into account the needs of both producers and consumers. If prices are fixed below their equilibrium level, rationing reduces the number of potentially dissatisfied buyers, whose number depends positively on the elasticity of demand for a given supply.

Against these arguments, Galbraith offers the evidence of the success of price and wage controls during the Second World War, a unique case in history, which calls for an explanation. He finds it in the shift in markets structures from competition to oligopoly.

Prior to World War II there did not exist in economic history, so far as I am aware, an important experiment in the public regulation of prices or wages which, in the consensus of interpreters, was thought to be a brilliant success or even a success.

(Galbraith 1952: 3)

In a competitive market, the high number of anonymous market participants increases the costs of monitoring and the likelihood that price-fixing will fail, unless accompanied by rationing and other forms of direct control. In a monopolistically competitive/oligopolistic market, instead, especially if the number of sellers (and/or buyers) is low, trading is no longer anonymous and companies allocate among market participants based on their status, size and habitual presence in the market. Galbraith argues that this endogenous rationing is more efficient than any external control and less likely to lead to the emergence of coalitions of dissatisfied buyers and sellers capable of disrupting the market. In addition, a small number of sellers makes it easier to adapt regulation to their specific needs, to monitor prices and to enforce price controls. It also makes it easier for buyers to identify companies that infringe the regulations. Finally, sellers in monopolistically competitive markets control their prices and may choose to change them infrequently, to minimize the risk deriving from the reaction of competitors and disappointed customers to price changes. This fact, coupled with price adjustment costs, introduces a strong conventional element into price-making and contributes to the success of price-fixing schemes without the help of rationing.

Oligopoly [. . .] was no longer the exception [. . .] it was the rule. Where a few large firms dominated an industry, as they did steel, aluminium, oil, chemicals, pharmaceuticals and many other, prices were already controlled [. . .] these markets lend themselves to price regulation to a far greater extent than had been previously supposed.

(Galbraith 1981: 173)

While Galbraith was not the only one[17] to think that oligopolistic industries can adjust relatively easily to price controls whereas competitive industries do not, the novel element of his theory resides in the role he assigns to price controls relative to monetary and fiscal policy to keep inflation at bay in the case of full employment.

Like most other Keynesians, Galbraith regards excess demand as the main cause of inflation. Unlike them, however (e.g. Harrod 1947; Meade 1948), Galbraith is convinced that price stability and full employment cannot be achieved by monetary and fiscal policies alone without resorting to price controls. Indeed, the equilibrium between supply and demand at the aggregate level is neither a necessary nor sufficient condition for price stability. It is not necessary, because if price controls are in place, a limited condition of excess demand, as required by wartime mobilization,[18] will not generate any rise in prices. It is not sufficient, because in the absence of controls, the non-cooperative interaction between wage and price-setters in monopolistically competitive industries, converts any small rise in demand into a wage-price spiral. In this respect, price controls are not a substitute for but an essential adjunct of the monetary and fiscal measures that makes the economic system more resilient and less exposed to the risk of inflation and instability.

> Specifically, a simple choice has been assumed between a policy of maintaining an equilibrium of demand and supply at stable prices by use of appropriate fiscal and monetary measures – a policy that would employ no price and wage controls – and one of using controls to suppress an inflationary excess of demand. [. . .] The choice, in fact, is between three possible policies – an equilibrium without controls, a disequilibrium sustained by controls, and an equilibrium of demand and supply supplemented by controls.
>
> (Galbraith 1952: 62–63)

Galbraith's ideas did not have a significant impact on the profession. In particular, Galbraith's belief that the Second World War had shown that price controls were both possible and useful came in for criticism. On the one hand, it was argued that wartime price stability was due more to an increasing demand for money, which absorbed excess purchasing power, than to price and wage controls (on this see Bronfenbrenner 1954). The increase in the demand for money came from the widespread fear that the war would be followed by depression, as had happened at the end of the First World War, and from the expectation that postwar prices would fall. On the other hand, critics of Galbraith (e.g. Hildebrand 1952) argued that, unless monetary policy was accommodating, the economy would run no risk of incurring wage-price spirals. In addition, the usual warnings against the administrative costs and the risks of efficiency losses associated with extensive price controls were raised in opposition to Galbraith's proposals.

At the end of the 1950s, however, the idea of an inflationary process fuelled mainly by wage increases and their impact on monopolistically determined prices gained ground,[19] reviving interest in Galbraith's idea that aggregate demand management and price and wage controls could be coordinated to achieve the distinct goals of full employment and price stability. As Ackley (1959) argued, for example, the interaction between administered prices in the manufacturing sector and of competitive prices in the agricultural sector could generate a wage-price spiral. In the case of excess demand, the firms' endeavours to buy more raw materials drive their (demand-determined) prices upwards. As they do so, production costs rise directly and indirectly (via rising wages and possibly rising mark-up on the assumption that administered prices are determined by adding a mark-up or margin to unit costs), starting a wage-price spiral. Ackley interprets this process in administrative, that is, essentially political, terms, and on the price side as well as the wage side. One of the implications of this approach is that extensive controls can contribute to stabilizing the price level while the usefulness of monetary and fiscal policy in this respect is limited:

> Surely these instruments should be used [. . .] But we probably cannot count on them for complete stabilization of the price level. Rather, successful efforts to stabilize prices must more directly affect the crucial elements which determine the inflationary process; that is, the rate of increase of wage rates relative to living costs, the rate of increase of productivity, the level of business markups, and (at times) speculative movements of raw material prices.
>
> (Ackley 1959: 429)

With the disappearance of inflation between the end of the 1950s and the 1960s in the developed world, there was no longer any room in the agenda for the idea that inflation could be avoided and/or stopped by coordinated controls of wages, productivity and profit margins. The idea was revived in the 1970s, after the first oil shock, taking the form of incomes policy. This was the last attempt to achieve full employment and price stability simultaneously, evoking cooperation between workers, manufacturers and governments, which had been so successful during the war.

## 5  Price controls in practice: the case of agricultural prices and international commodity agreements

While the idea of extensive price controls began to be questioned immediately after the war, selective controls, on internationally traded agricultural commodities in particular, received more lasting attention and support. This reflected the experience of the previous decades.

In the inter-war period the collapse of commodity prices had thrown producers and dealers into distress. Governments had responded by adopting a mix of policy measures, ranging from quotas and subsidies to the signing of bilateral agreements between exporting and importing countries.[20] With war approaching the situation changed abruptly. Strategic stockpiling by governments, together with hoarding and speculative purchases, led to the emergence of shortages in many commodity markets. The ensuing inflationary pressures were kept at bay by combining rationing and price controls as documented above. As the war ended, price decontrol in the foodstuffs sector, coupled with persistent shortages due to the disruption of agricultural production in Europe and Asia and to the dislocation of international trade, contributed to stoking up inflationary pressures.[21] The main lesson to be drawn from this long period of volatility, which was particularly pronounced between the 1930s and the 1950s,[22] was that prices could be stabilized by resorting to *ad hoc* measures, and should be stabilized in the interests of both producing and consuming countries.

Various policies were devised to contribute to this end at the national level.[23] Measures aiming at boosting production and exports were the principal policies adopted in the US.[24] In continental Europe, the policy of high protective tariffs, first introduced in the 1920s, continued in combination with currency controls and import quotas designed to raise incomes for farmers. The UK, the major food importer at the time, combined policies to raise the income of agricultural workers (via high prices) with rationing (to limit imports in view of Britain's balance of payment difficulties) and long-term contracts guaranteeing cheap imports from Commonwealth countries. Exporting countries in Africa and Asia resorted to centralized trading and marketing boards to stabilize the income of producers and facilitate taxation. These policies contributed to reducing producer and consumer prices (subsidized to support domestic consumption) to levels below world market prices, limiting the incentives to increase production. Agriculture in the Communist Bloc was collectivized and agricultural prices fell relative to the prices of industrial goods. Initially, both measures depressed production and productivity.

While many of these measures had a strong protectionist tinge, other plans, more ambitious in scope and aims, were put forward in the aftermath of the war. These plans aimed at stabilizing commodity prices at the global level through supranational institutions, without resorting to artificial limitations of supply. Most attention focused on three types of international commodity agreements (henceforth ICAs) during the early post-war years: (1) international buffer stocks, (2) flexible multilateral bulk purchases, and (3) commodity reserve money. They were particularly suited to overcome the interwar segmentation of international commodity markets, reflecting one of the main economic lessons of the war as to the importance of market regulation and economic cooperation between countries.

> The principal feature, common to the three proposals, is the absence of any "restrictionist" provisions, such as quantitative limits on exports or the fixing of relative shares in the market. Moreover they cannot be branded as "producers' schemes": not only minimum but also maximum prices are fixed, and

thus they appear, at least *prima facie*, free from the shadow of the exploitation of the consumer.

(Tyszynski 1950: 439)

1    International buffer stocks were to be operated by supranational agencies standing ready to buy (sell) unlimited amounts of a given commodity whenever its price moved below (above) a pre-determined minimum (maximum) level. These agencies could be financed by resorting either to public transfers (from exporting and importing countries participating in the scheme or from supra-national institutions) or to private funds raised on the international money markets. Any profits made by the agency would contribute to covering the operating expenses of the buffer stock.[25]

2    Flexible multilateral bulk purchases were schemes under which importing (exporting) countries agreed to acquire (sell) a given amount of a specified commodity if its market price fell below (rose above) a pre-determined level. A dual price system would *de facto* be established with prices on guaranteed transactions contributing to stabilise the income of producers and consumers and prices on marginal transactions directing resource allocation.

3    Commodity reserve money schemes implied the possibility of issuing an international reserve currency backed by stockpiles of commodities and managed in connection with the stabilization of a commodity price index.[26]

Many of these schemes, which we discussed elsewhere (Paesani and Rosselli 2014), took into account the fact that commodity markets were intrinsically unstable and therefore in need of being regulated to reconcile price stability in the short-run with the re-allocation of resources in the long run. The intrinsic instability is mainly caused by low short-run price-elasticity of both demand and supply. Consequent upon these rigidities, unexpected and frequent shifts in either demand or supply lead to sharp price fluctuations and the rapid expansion or contraction of stocks. This, in turn, causes further disturbances of market equilibrium in later periods, magnified by delayed adjustments in productive capacity and speculation. The ICAs bore close resemblance to the measures adopted during the war to stabilize prices (see note 8); they proved successful and were to be agreed among the countries participating in the price stabilisation scheme. Prior agreement was recommended to avoid possible conflicts between exporting and importing countries.

Two main obstacles stood in the way of the successful implementation of the ICAs and in particular of buffer stocks – the most ambitious type of price stabilization scheme originally inspired by Keynes (Fantacci et al. 2012). The guarantee of a minimum price constituted a powerful incentive for producers to increase their supply and productive capacity as long as the guaranteed price covered their costs, regardless of the changing state of demand. Moreover, the presence of an institution endowed with limited funds to stabilize the price of one or more commodities at the global level could incite destabilizing speculation whenever doubts were raised about the financial solidity of the institution itself. This made it crucial to endow the agency with substantial funds, as Keynes advocated in 1943 (Fantacci 2012),

> Provided the Agency has sufficient funds it should always be possible to put a floor under the price of any storable commodity. [. . .] (M)uch will depend upon the ability of the Agency to inspire confidence. The greater the apparent strength, the less often will it be required to use it. The case is similar to the operation of the gold standard by the Bank of England in the latter part of the nineteenth century. Simply because the world had confidence in its strength and integrity it could operate with a relatively small gold reserve.
>
> (Porter 1950: 99)

The lack of adequate funds could be overcome to some extent by giving the agency a very flexible mandate, relying on the shrewdness of the agency managers to beat private speculators at their own game.

> The operations of an international buffer-stock agency would have some similarity to the operations of the private speculators. [. . .] (Both) tend to buy when prices are low and to sell when prices are high. If either of them succeeds in doing this, and if he abstains from creating abnormal conditions in the market [. . .], this will tend to facilitate the equation of supply and demand, over time, and to reduce the magnitude of short-term price fluctuations.
>
> (Zaglits 1946: 434)

Richard Kahn's analysis of the interaction between commodity price stabilisation and buffer stocks is consistent with these ideas.[27] Kahn agreed that the buffer stock should act as a speculator in the public interest and was convinced that the actions of the buffer stock should not be predictable. Kahn's position was motivated by two concerns. First, if the buffer stock was left no margins of discretion and was required to disclose its intentions and to follow a fully predictable strategy, this could open the way to destabilising speculation.

> It is bad enough if the market can guess which way the cat is going to jump if it jumps at all, it is fatal if they not only know this for certain but also how far it is going to jump and when.
>
> (Kahn quoted in Rosselli 2012: 216)

Moreover, if its resources were limited, to ensure financial viability for the ICAs in the long run the buffer stock would have to be left the autonomy to decide when and whether to intervene or to abstain from any intervention.

In spite of the efforts put by the supra-national institutions and individual economists into elaborating and promoting international commodity agreements, only five were launched for as many commodities, and only two of them in the 1950s.[28] Several reasons can be cited to account for this collective failure, including: lack of political support (from the US and the UK in particular), disappearance of the need to stabilize commodity markets in a context characterized by increasing prosperity, interference between national and international schemes to stabilize commodity markets, structural decline in the terms of trade of producers of primary products *vis-à-vis* the industrial countries, and *a priori* hostility towards price controls. The United Nations Conference on Trade and Development (UNCTAD), inaugurated in 1964, contributed to keeping the debate on international commodity agreements alive until the late 1970s. Thereafter, any residual interest in this subject disappeared altogether.

## 6 Conclusions

The Second World War held two main lessons for later generations of economists and policy makers. First, that it was possible to allocate resources efficiently, in view of crucial contingent objectives, imposing strict regulations on markets without abolishing them. Second, that the success of these regulations depended on mutual accord between workers, producers and governments and, at a higher level, on cooperation among nations.

Wartime regulatory measures contributed to the simultaneous attainment of full employment, price stability and a more equitable distribution of resources relatively to the pre-war period. Full employment, together with other factors of a social and political nature, significantly strengthened the bargaining power of organised labour. At the same time, organisations of producers, which had dealt directly with governments during the war, learned to "speak with one voice," acquiring a countervailing power with respect to that of the trade unions.

These developments had a significant impact on the plans formulated at the end of the war with a view to reconciling full employment, price stability and equity with the rapid reconversion of the economy. At the time, there was ample agreement between economists and policy makers on these objectives, and indeed on the possibility of attaining them by managing aggregate demand. This was coherent with the Keynesian paradigm then prevailing. Agreement on the usefulness of price controls was not equally unanimous, as our reconstruction suggests.

On the one hand, the majority of economists and policy makers were convinced that aggregate demand management was sufficient to attain the desired macroeconomic goals without resorting to price and wage controls, which they considered unnecessary, unless in very specific and transitory cases, if not actually harmful. On the other hand, a minority of economists and policy makers, famously represented by John K. Galbraith, took a different position.

Eager to maintain full employment and price stability and fearful of the ensuing risks of wage-price spirals, Galbraith and various other economists advocated a combination of policies: aggregate demand management to achieve full employment, and systematic price and wage controls, to maintain price stability and render the economy more resilient and less exposed to risks of inflation.

While the impact of Galbraith's theory of price controls was very limited, the idea that systematic control of prices and – more importantly – wages was instrumental to achieving full employment and price stability lived on. At the beginning of the 1970s, interest in this idea was revived in the wake of the oil shocks and the ensuing stagflation. This renewed interest in price and wage controls led to the formulation of incomes policies in many European countries and in the US between the end of the 1970s and the beginning of the following decade.

Raw materials, and agricultural commodities in particular, represented another field where the debate on price controls lived on. Historically, the commodity markets had been characterized by marked price and income volatility. This was caused by the competitive interaction between multitudes of atomistic buyers, sellers and speculators rather than by the exertion of market power by wage and price-setters, as in the case of manufactured goods. At the end of the war, many developed countries adopted measures to stabilize prices and incomes. These measures, together with the gradual integration of markets, resulting from the post-war liberalization of trade, rendered the stabilization of prices more difficult, calling for the formulation of ambitious plans for the establishment of comprehensive international commodity agreements.

Advocated with these plans was the creation of supranational agencies entrusted with the task of stabilizing commodity prices in the mutual interest of producing and consuming countries. This mandate reflected the principles of international cooperation which the Second World War had shown to be so important for the success of the war effort, and which had already led to the creation of the International Monetary Fund and the World Bank in 1944.

Later on, interest in incomes policies and the stabilization of commodity prices at the supranational level disappeared altogether from the agenda of economists and policymakers alike, due to a series of concomitant factors. Notable among these factors were the shift away from Keynesian ideas in the prevailing theoretical paradigm, renewed confidence in the allocative power of the markets and the long-run neutrality of money, perception of government failures, reduction in the bargaining power of organised labour and declining interest in equity seen as part of a trade-off with efficiency.

Interest in incomes policies and the possibility of managing wages to combat deflation is re-emerging today, in connection with growing doubts about the effectiveness of monetary policy in this respect.

## Notes

1 We wish to thank the participants in the Otaru ESHET-JSHET conference 2015 and in the session "Interwar period and beyond" (STOREP annual conference 2016) for their useful comments and an anonymous referee for his/her insightful comments and suggestions. The usual disclaimers apply.
2 A non-comprehensive list of British and American policy-makers and economists involved in this activity can be found in Gardner (1986: 22–23).
3 On this see, for example, Scitovsky (1942), Lerner (1944) and Kalecki (1947).

4 For a recent proposal by O. Blanchard and A. Posen to revive inflation in Japan by starting a managed wage-price spiral, see www.piie.com/publications/opeds/oped.cfm?ResearchID=2889).

5 On this see, for example, Dornbusch et al. (1993).

6 On this point, see Clark (1942a, 1942b) and Crum et al. (1942). For a contemporary account of wartime inflation, during the Second World War in the US, in the UK and in Germany see A.J.B. (1945b) among others.

7 As noted by Clark (1942a), other policy instruments that contribute to achieving price stabilisation include measures to increase the elasticity of supply (tax provisions favouring rapid amortization by private enterprises, public investment and building-up of stockpiles of critical and strategic commodities) and the centralisation of government purchases to avoid wasteful competition among public agencies.

8 Wartime price controls can be direct and indirect. Direct price controls can take different forms: (1) indication of maximum, minimum or average prices defined with respect to a given date or a given period of time (for one or more types of each good), (2) fixing markups or margins over cost, (3) rigid price fixing. In the case of indirect (or informal) price controls, "representatives of the industry concerned agree with price controls officials upon prices to be charged and impose upon themselves the enforcement procedure known as price discipline" (Crum et al. 1942: 114).

9 Tobin (1952: 538) finds straight rationing, as a form of demand restriction, superior to taxation on the ground of equity. However, he warns against the disincentive effect of rationing on production through its impact on the choice of individuals between consumption and leisure.

10 In the US, the proposal to introduce a comprehensive scheme of price controls had been famously advanced by Bernard Baruch, financier, political advisor, chairman of the War Industries Board during the First World War and advisor to the office of war mobilization during the Second World War. For reference on Baruch's proposal and his advocacy of the expediency of introducing price controls to restrain speculation, see Laguerodie and Vergara (2008) and the reference cited therein.

11 In response to this concern, it was suggested to adopt flexible price controls in terms of product standards and pricing formulas. A shift from comprehensive to selective coverage, abolition of ceilings (unless demand was clearly in excess of capacity or risks of speculation emerged) and/or adoption of controls on margins rather than prices might also be advisable. On this, see Wilcox (1945) among others.

12 On this see Ackley (1951), Henderson (1948) and Johnson (1951), among others.

13 On this see Duesenberry (1950).

14 Duesenberry (1950) reaches similar conclusions in a more complex two-sector dynamic model where nominal wages are adjusted with a one-period lag to changes in the consumer price index computed as a weighted average of industrial prices (set on the basis of mark-up pricing), agricultural prices (set on the basis of competitive prices) and administered prices (e.g. rents).

15 See Galbraith (1946) and Galbraith (1947).

16 On the theory of price controls elaborated by Galbraith see Colander (1984), Laguerodie and Vergara (2008) and the literature cited therein.

17 On this see Dunlop (1947b) and Lerner (1948) among others.

18 Galbraith refers to the imminent Korean War.

19 On this and on related aspects see Balogh (1958).

20 On this, see Rowe (1936).

21 The inflation subsequent to the phasing-out of controls in the U.S. was discussed by many economists, including Kalecki, Duesenberry and Ackley. On this, see also Davis (1948) and Heflebower (1948).

22 On this see Dwyer et al. (2011: 50–51).
23 See Ezekiel (1952). This section builds significantly on Paesani (2014).
24 On the evolution of the agricultural price support and adjustment programs in the US between 1933 and 1965, see Rasmussen and Baker (1974).
25 For a list of references on international buffer stocks, see Paesani (2014) and the literature cited therein.
26 On this see Ussher (2009) and the reference cited therein.
27 On Kahn's plans of buffer stocks see the reconstruction by Rosselli (2012).
28 The five commodities were: tin (ITA, 1954, buffer stock plus export control), sugar (1954, ISA, export control), coffee (ICoA, 1962, export control), cocoa (ICCA, 1972, buffer stock) and rubber (INRA, 1982, buffer stock). On the design and performance of the ICAs see Gilbert (1987); on the reasons leading to their end see Gilbert (1996).

# References

Ackley, G. (1951). "The Relation of Price and Production Controls," *American Economic Review*, 41: 70–73.
Ackley, G. (1959). "Administered Prices and the Inflationary Process," *American Economic Review*, 49: 419–430.
A.J.B. (1945a). "War-Time Inflation: I. What Is Inflation," *Bulletin of International News*, 22: 11–15.
A.J.B. (1945b). "War-Time Inflation: II. Some Outline Case-Studies," *Bulletin of International News*, 22: 102–109.
Balogh, T. (1958). "Productivity and Inflation," *Oxford Economic Papers*, 10: 220–245.
Bronfenbrenner, M. (1954). "Reviewed Work: A Theory of Price Control by J. Kenneth Galbraith," *Journal of Political Economy*, 62: 68–70.
Clark, J.M. (1942a). "Wartime Price Control and the Problem of Inflation," *Law and Contemporary Problems*, 6–21.
Clark, J.M. (1942b). "Problems of Price Control," *Proceedings of the Academy of Political Science*, 20: 11–22.
Colander, D. (1984). "Galbraith and the Theory of Price Control," *Journal of Post Keynesian Economics*, 7: 30–42.
Crum, W.L., Fennelly, J.F. and Seltzer, L.H. (1942). *Fiscal Planning for Total War*, NBER.
Davis, J.S. (1948). "Food Prices," *Review of Economics and Statistics*, 30: 8–10.
Dornbusch, R., Nölling, W. and Layard, R. (1993). *Postwar Economic Reconstruction and Lessons for the East Today*, Cambridge, MA: MIT Press.
Duesenberry, J. (1950). "The Mechanics of Inflation," *Review of Economics and Statistics*, 32: 144–149.
Dunlop, J.T. (1947a). "A Review of Wage-Price Policy," *Review of Economics and Statistics*, 29: 154–160.
Dunlop, J.T. (1947b). "Wage-Price Relations at High Level Employment," *American Economic Review*, 37: 243–253.
Dwyer, A., Gardner, G., and Williams, T. (2011). "Global Commodity Markets – Price Volatility and Financialisation," *Bulletin of the Reserve Bank of Australia*, June, 49–57.
Eichengreen, B. (2008). *The European Economy since 1945: Coordinated Capitalism and Beyond*, Princeton, NJ: Princeton University Press.
Ezekiel, M. (1952). "Price Policies and Trends in International Trade," *Journal of Farm Economics*, 34: 649–660.

Fantacci, L. (2012). "Keynes's Commodity and Currency Plans for the Post-war World," in M.C. Marcuzzo (Ed.), *Speculation and Regulation in Commodity Markets: The Keynesian Approach in Theory and Practice*. Rapporto tecnico, Dipartimento Scienze Statistiche, Sapienza No. 21, 177–206.

Fantacci, L., Marcuzzo, M.C., Rosselli, A. and Sanfilippo, E. (2012). "Speculation and Buffer Stocks: the Legacy of Keynes and Kahn," *European Journal of the History of Economic Thought*, 19: 453–473.

Friedman, M. (1952). "Price, Income and Monetary Changes in Three Wartime Periods," *American Economic Review*, 42: 612–625.

Friedman, M. (1977). *From Galbraith to Economic Freedom*, Occasional Paper 49. London: Institute for Economic Affairs.

Galbraith, J.K. (1946). "Reflections on Price Control," *Quarterly Journal of Economics*, 60: 475–489.

Galbraith, J.K. (1947). "The Disequilibrium System," *American Economic Review*, 37: 287–302.

Galbraith, J.K. (1952). *A Theory of Price Control*, Cambridge, MA: Harvard University Press.

Galbraith, J.K. (1981). *A Life in Our Times*, Boston, Houghton Mifflin Company.

Gardner, R.N. (1986). "Sterling-Dollar Diplomacy in Current Perspective," *International Affairs*, 62: 21–33.

Gilbert, C.L. (1987). "International Commodity Agreements: Design and Performance," *World Development*, 15: 591–616.

Gilbert, C.L. (1996). "International Commodity Agreements: An Obituary Notice," *World Development*, 24: 2–19.

Harris, S.E. (1948). "Ten Economists on the Inflation: Introduction," *Review of Economics and Statistics*, 30: 1–3.

Harrod, R. (1947). *Are These Hardships Necessary?* London: Rupert Hart-Davis.

Hawtrey, R.G. (1948). "Monetary Aspects of the Economic Situation," *American Economic Review*, 38: 42–55.

Heflebower, R.B. (1948). "Food Prices, Wage Rates, and Inflation," *Review of Economics and Statistics*, 30: 27–29.

Henderson, H.D. (1948). "The Price System," *Economic Journal*, 58: 467–482.

Hildebrand, G.H. (1952). "Review," *American Economic Review*, 42: 986–990.

Johnson, A. (1951). "To Check Inflation," Social Research, 18: 1–8.

Kalecki, M. (1947). "General Rationing", in *Oxford Institute of Statistics: Studies in War Economics*, Oxford: Blackwell, 137–141.

Kalecki, M. (1948). "Determinants of the Increase in the Cost of Living in the United States," *Review of Economics and Statistics*, 30: 22–24.

Keynes, J.M. (1972 [1940]). "How to Pay for the War," in D. Moggridge and E.A.G. Robinson (Eds.), *The Collected Writings of John Maynard Keynes*, Vol. IX, London: Macmillan.

Laguerodie, S., and Vergara, F. (2008). "The Theory of Price Controls: John Kenneth Galbraith's Contribution," *Review of Political Economy*, 20: 569–593.

Lerner, A.P. (1944). *The Economics of Control*, New York: Macmillan.

Lerner, A.P. (1948). "Rising Prices," *Review of Economics and Statistics*, 30: 24–27.

Meade, J.E. (1948). *Planning and the Price Mechanism*, London: George Allen & Unwin LTD.

Paesani, P. (2014). "International Commodity Agreements in the 1940s and 50s: Theoretical Underpinnings, Operational Implications and Policy Debate," Paper presented at the 16th ESHET Annual Conference, Lausanne.

Paesani, P., and Rosselli, A. (2014). "The Case for a Supra-National Control on Commodities in the Post WWII World: Novel Perspectives From FAO and Kaldor Archives," *History of Economic Thought and Policy*, 1: 5–30.

Porter, R.S. (1950). "Buffer Stocks and Economic Stability," *Oxford Economic Papers*, 2: 95–118.

Rasmussen, W.D., and Baker, G.L. (1974). "A Short History of Price Support and Adjustment Legislation and Programs for Agriculture, 1933–65," *Journal of Agricultural Economics Research*, 45: 92–101.

Rosselli, A. (2012). "Richard Kahn and the Stabilization of Commodity Prices," in M.C. Marcuzzo (Ed.), *Speculation and Regulation in Commodity Markets: The Keynesian Approach in Theory and Practice*. Rapporto technico, Dipartimento Scienze Statistiche, Sapienza No. 21, 207–223.

Rowe, J.W.F. (1936). *Markets and Men*, Cambridge: Cambridge University Press.

Scitovsky, T.D. (1942). "The Political Economy of Consumers' Rationing," *Review of Economic Statistics*, 24: 114–124.

Slichter, S.H. (1948). "The Problem of Inflation," *Review of Economics and Statistics*, 30: 3–5.

Tobin, J. (1952). "A Survey of the Theory of Rationing," *Econometrica*, 20: 521–553.

Tyszynski, H. (1950). "A Note on International Commodity Agreements," *Economica*, 17: 438–447.

Ussher, L. (2009). "Global Imbalances and the Key Currency Regime: The Case for a Commodity Reserve Currency," *Review of Political Economy*, 21: 403–421.

Wallace, D.H. (1951). "Price Control and Rationing," *American Economic Review*, 41: 60–62.

Wilcox, C. (1945). "Price Control Policy in the Postwar Transition," *American Economic Review*, 35: 163–174.

Zaglits, O. (1946). "International Price Control through Buffer Stocks," *Journal of Farm Economics*, 28: 413–443.

# 12 From barter to monetary economy

## Ordoliberal views on the post-WWII German economic order

*Raphaël Fèvre*

## Introduction

Keynesianism never actually took root in Germany. It had to wait for the late sixties to be given a partial tryout, only to be abandoned.[1] If "the triumphal march of Keynesianism came to a halt on the borders of Federal Germany" (Abelshauser 1992: 186), it was because another approach was preferred, namely ordoliberalism. Of course, there were certain institutional and contextual factors that had decisive impact, but the aim of the present article is to look into this particular phenomenon, starting from the following hypothesis: taking in the same intellectual ground as Keynesianism, the ordoliberal approach proved a formidable rival in Germany. But what exactly is that *ground*?

Historically, Keynesianism came in response to the *laissez-faire* crisis of the 1920s and 1930s. Ordoliberalism constituted a response to the crisis of Germany's planned economy[2] of the 1930s and 1940s. The debate that arose in consequence is generally passed over in studies on ordoliberal thought, the issue being the *transition* towards a competitive order (see Helmut 2001 as an exception). To this end, we will focus on a very limited but exceptionally eventful period, namely the early post-war years (1945–1950). One immediate concern for the ordoliberal literature at the time was to draw the lessons that could be learnt from the economy of the Third Reich. In particular, this article shows that, from the ordoliberal point of view, the problem was then seen to lie not so much in the fact that Germany had lost the war as in the perpetuation of an unsustainable economic order.

Turbulence is generated in the economy by a fundamental mechanism consisting in a pendulum motion, increasing in magnitude, from "repressed" inflation to planning activities (and vice versa). In this sense, the ordoliberal inflation phobia – echoes that still resound to our contemporary ears – has to do not only with conventional disturbance mechanisms but also with the way it nourishes planning velleities from the beginning: it eventually affects the economic but also the social and political orders of a nation as a whole.

Starting from a decidedly unfavourable situation in which, "politically, liberalism was weak and discredited in Germany after the war" (Nicholls 1994: 137), the influence exerted by ordoliberal thinking on political decisions in West

Germany, and particularly the veer towards the market economy, probably had to do with this work of assimilation. It was through this historical consideration that the issue of moving on to the competitive order could be performed. This move started in June 1948.

On the 20th and 24th of June 1948, monetary reform and a law liberalising prices marked the unexpected entry of West Germany into the market economy. Still under the control of the Allies, these reforms appear to have reflected what was expected of the Anglo-American Bizone, in keeping with their liberal principles while standing up to the rise of the Communist bloc. However, their sole direct concern was monetary reform. With the first steps of the Social Market Economy (*Soziale Marktwirtschaft*),[3] which saw Ludwig Erhard as figurehead at the political level, the ordoliberal authors appear, with the liberalisation of prices, to have won their first victory having long waited in silence during the National-Socialist[4] period (see Rieter and Schmolz 1993; later nuanced by Kurlander 2011).

The chapter is structured as follows. First, we show that Walter Eucken, Fritz Meyer, Wilhelm Röpke, and indeed Ludwig Erhard as well as Alfred Müller-Armack levelled their fire at the economic order in place as primary cause of West Germany's productive anaemia (both in productivity and total production). The old system of planning, and in particular price control, came in for severe criticism (Section 1). For ordoliberals, repressed inflation, which had already begun to spread into the economy before the war, eventually put the function of prices in channelling rare resources towards the best usage entirely out of action. They based their diagnosis on demonstration of a causal link between (repressed) inflation and planning, building on theoretical and historical considerations (Section 2). It was this circumstance that lay behind the current (1945–1948) disorder in the structure of trade coordination, perceived as a return to primitive forms of coordination such as black market, barter or personal production of means of subsistence. Black markets started to burgeon alongside the official channels, with barter economy and personal subsistence economy generating irrationality at the collective level (Section 3). At this point we will consider what lessons can be learnt from the issue of economic transition towards the market economy from an epistemological point of view (Section 4).

## 1 Germany's problem was not having lost the war: the issue of the economic order

The economic situation of West Germany emerging from the war appears paradoxical. Although the German cities, transport infrastructure and population had been so severely hit, historians[5] concur on the fact that Germany's productive potential remained at a level almost as high as prewar. For example, the capital stock (in billion *RM* of 1950 prices) goes from 51.8 in 1938 to 71.2 – its higher level – by the end of 1943, and terminates at 58.6 in 1946 (see Krengel 1963: 123, Table I).[6]

What was termed "zero hour" (*Stunde Null*) reflects a somewhat distorted view. Indeed, Germany found itself in a comparatively more favourable situation than that of the other European countries, especially thanks to a better "balance between wartime investment and destruction" (Carlin 1996: 463). And yet the German economy remained bogged down at an extremely weak production level (van Hook 2004: 187). Historians point at two major factors: first the Allies' determination to punish Germany, putting clamps on her economy; for instance by breaking industrial conglomerates and encouraging a pastoral turn (Allen 1989: 269). These adverse instructions against the German economy – namely the Morgenthau plan and JCS 1067 directive[7] – gradually weaken as from 1946.

The failure of Allies' economic planning undertaken on the basis of fixed prices and quotas before the war with the Nazi *Zwangswirtschaft* (command economy)[8] is the second main weakness argued by historians (Giersch et al. 1992: 19–23). It is this latter reason that interests us here, because ordoliberals will build their rejection on that *continuity*. Since the end of the war, Eucken (1946: 9) pointed out (to the eyes of the French zone) this very matter that he considers as an absurdity.

The Allies' pursuit of what van Hook (2004: 51) calls a "moderately socialist agenda", and Ptak (2009: 119) "comprehensive economic planning", rapidly proved to constitute a stumbling block in the coordination of productive forces. The Allies' planning is a really intricate system, mixing foreign officials with German administrative and political forces under the guidance of a bureaucratic military organization. It differs from one zone to another – jointly encouraging socialization and corporatism as a way to "democratize" the economy (Prowe 1985: 458). By promoting Länder's control, planning took a *local* face. It rested on new (and old) administrative bodies, but the fixed prices, and output/input objectives, as we noticed, persisted.

Although they attribute a major role to the disastrous effects of the Second World War, the ordoliberals point at the problem of the economic order as primary cause for the weakness of the German economy. Wilhelm Röpke (1947a: 123, italics added) deemed that behind the state of the post-war economy of the European countries (and of Germany in particular) lay two – almost independent – elementary reasons: "the war has destroyed so much, and *the economic process is in disorder*". The economic order emerged from the, necessarily manifold, forms[9] taken on by the structure coordinating exchange at a given moment in a given place:

> We know that at all times and in all places, everyday processes of the economy take place within the framework of particular forms. The economic order is the sum of the forms that are realized in a particular country and at a particular time.
>
> (Eucken 1949: 221)

According to Ludwig Erhard, the (political and economic) centralisation pursued with the merging of the British and American zones as of 1 January 1947 was also a major cause of constraints on production. Then chairman of the Special Department for Money and Credit (*Sonderstelle Geld und Kredit*) constituted in the Bizone, he made clear that "[w]ithout a centralized administration and its concomitant powers, for example, the deterioration of Germany's economy would never have assumed such pathological proportions" (Erhard 1947: 25).

Confidence in economic planning began slowly but surely to dwindle before the hardships experienced by the population, in particular after the terrible winter of 1946–1947 (Solchany 2003: 362). Like the German ordoliberals, Müller-Armack now came firmly down in favour of transition to a market economy:

> One of the beliefs which requires serious revision is, in my view, the assumption that in our present situation centrally planned economic management is the only path leading to a better future. [. . .] The opinion that a centrally planned economy is superior to a free market economy is now open to very serious doubts. A functioning economic order is the most fundamental economic basis which has to exist if we want to get the economy going at all. Whatever the actual shape of the system, we shall inevitably have to take step towards market freedom.
>
> (Müller-Armack 1947: 20)

In a special number of the *Annals of the American Academy of Political and Social Science* on "Postwar Reconstruction in Western Germany", Walter Eucken and Fritz Meyer (1948) addressed this issue. Their critical fire was now levelled at the "Evils of Planned Economy", which they attacked with a vocabulary redolent with warlike terms, referring to the administrative body in charge of planning as "this veritable *army* of officials", or "a whole *army* of officials" (Eucken and Meyer 1948: 53). In another context Walter Eucken observed that the figure of the entrepreneur (whose role is to respond to the needs of the consumers finding a way to meet them while still making a profit) disappears in an administered economy. The leading roles are taken over by technicians and statisticians through with administrative offices enjoying extraordinary importance:[10] "the tendency is increasingly to replace economic considerations by technical [ones]" (Eucken 1948c: 96).

The main consequence of economic disorder was to be seen in the price structure. Prices no longer had any real economic basis; they were "fictitious values" (Röpke 1947c: 247) having nothing to do with scarcity or need, and thus factors for inefficiency:

> The most important reason for the existing conditions is the reigning price structure. The prices simply do not make sense [. . .]. Wrong prices which do not reflect true scarcity are the first reason for the inadequate utilization of the productive capacity.
>
> (Eucken and Meyer 1948: 53)

Moreover, this problem of planning at the social level, making individual planning nugatory, was not confined to Germany. It was a difficulty for the countries of Europe as a whole, as was noted by Jacques Rueff, perhaps the most ordoliberal of French economists: "in practice, producers and consumers remain free to decide on the basis of the market prices, but they are not what they should be if the plan expectations were to be satisfied" (Rueff's remark in Perroux et al. 1949: 174).

In the course of his lectures in London,[11] Walter Eucken (1951: 81) stressed the tenuous connection between productive capacity, inflation and global coordination of the economy: "even existing possibilities of production were insufficiently exploited" at that time, because "[repressed] inflation had rendered the price system incapable of controlling the economy". Over and above the problem of monetary evaluation of goods and wages in a planned economy, there is the question of inflation, which is raised here. In the next section we will address the indissoluble link that Wilhelm Röpke and Walter Eucken sought to trace out between (repressed) inflation and planning.

## 2 Under planning, "money begins to smell": the case of repressed inflation

Inflationary pressures were nothing new in the post-war period, for they had been a cause of concern since the end of the 1920s. Indeed, looking to the post-conflict scenario, Ludwig Erhard (1944: 5) was already warning that "the real problem lies in the elimination of superfluous purchasing power from the economy". Inflation within the planned war economies constituted a generally recognised obstacle, proving, according to Gunnar Myrdal (1951: 35), "one main defect of [. . .] national planning". Wilhelm Röpke offered a pioneering study of this phenomenon, typical of a war economy, which he labelled as "repressed" inflation (as opposed to "open" inflation). For Röpke (1947c: 242), this is nothing less than "the great economic malady of our times":

> As a consequence of the war and of bad economic management after the war we observe almost everywhere a serious inflation in the sense of a great increase of the volume of money relative to a very slow recovery of production [. . .]. [Government] forbids the excess of demand to result in increased prices [. . .]. [T]here are now two sorts of pressure working against each other: the pressure of inflation driving prices, costs, and exchanges upward and the pressure of "control" which tries to neutralize that upward pressure. The question is how long the government can sit on the gusher of inflation, and what will happen as long as it is able to do so.
>
> (Röpke 1947c: 242)

If repressed inflation does not mean prices increase (as they remain fixed), in what sense is this inflation *at all*? In a nutshell, the fundamental mechanism can be summarized as follows:

> Wishing to achieve full employment, State planning results in an investment shock. The overabundant money supply, far in excess of the amount of available goods, sends prices rising. By definition, the clearing of markets through

prices (open inflation) is impossible. An excess of purchasing power follows and the authorities are forced to ration consumption, for instance with quotas or coupon allocations, in order to avoid massive shortages. People cannot obtain goods, therefore, the extra money becomes worthless and prices fail to function as relevant signals: money is no longer desired. The extra money results in forced savings. The only way out of this sequence is to stick to the available amount of purchasing power by increasing the volume of goods to bridge the gap. This latter solution comes in for logical and empirical opposition from an ordoliberal point of view.

Apparently, Röpke was the first to use the English expression "repressed inflation".[12] Hitherto a variety of terms had been used for the phenomenon, including "suppressed", "retarded" or "frustrated" (by Henry C. Simons or Frank Hahn) inflation. Röpke (1947c: 242) used the term "repressed" inflation, finding it both more appropriate and more expressive, notably being the first to apply it to the "measures of repression" (see below) perpetrated in the German economy. Albert O. Hirschman (1948: 599) observed that the concept "has since been widely used in the analysis of postwar monetary conditions", applying it himself to the situation in post-war Italy. Gottfried Haberler (1948: 11), Abba Lerner (1949: 195–196), and of course Walter Eucken (1948c: 79) were the first to discuss the term, and indeed Eucken adopted it to describe (in retrospect) the situation in Germany as from 1936.[13]

In doing so, Eucken implicitly left behind him the war/inflation connection to concentrate on a link that he deemed more fundamental, between planned economy and inflation. War has such an effect only insofar as the situation is one of planned economy. Röpke also stressed this necessary interconnection:

> First, repressed inflation is the monetary counterpart of collectivism because *all experiences bear out the well-founded assumption that collectivism leads invariably to inflation.* Secondly, as we saw, collectivism is connected with *repressed* inflation because *the measures of repression constitute what we call collectivism,* i.e. an economic system which replaces the spontaneous order of the free market by an order which some name "conscious" while, in fact, it is based on command and the sanctions assuring obedience.
>
> (Röpke 1947c: 243, italics added)

Röpke is arguing in terms of the empirical evidence; and then also as a logical tautology, pointing out the identity between the two terms. With a few years' hindsight, Walter Eucken was later to make of this connection the great lesson to be drawn from the economic experience of the Third Reich: planning feeds on monetary surplus. In his LSE talks of 1950, Eucken once again fostered the planning/inflation link, for instance by contrast with the opinion of "American" experts that German's inflations "were caused wholly and exclusively by two destructive wars which left the economy in monetary chaos" (Hansen and Musgrave 1951: 39).

What worried Eucken was not so much that inflation was a consequence of planning as, rather, the reverse, that is, inflation serving as precondition for planning tendencies to arise:

> Not only did the inflations destroy the price system and hence all free types of economic order, not only did *they engender or decisively foster the tendency to central planning*, but they were also *a precondition* of the existence of central planning. Appreciation of this *interconnexion* is one of the *most important fruits of German experience in the field of economic policy.*
>
> (Eucken 1951: 69, italics added)

Röpke makes the causal link clear, stressing the compensatory effect that comes into play between the two phenomena, one coming to the aid of the other and vice versa. It seems to him[14] that "collectivism serves just as well for an attempt to mitigate the open harms of inflation as inflation serves for an attempt to mitigate the open harms of collectivism" (Röpke 1947c: 244). Collectivism develops to curb inflation, and may justify its existence with this end; leading Röpke (1947d: 115) to the conclusion that "defense of controls rests on the assumption of inflation". At the same time, the greater circulation of money to some extent counterbalances disturbances in the production supply of certain goods. To some extent, the overabundant money supply feeds an ignis fatuus of prosperity and success.

The process rapidly enters into a circular, cumulative loop. In deciding to go on stepping up productivity given the impossibility of reducing the supply of money, and, above all, of fluctuating prices, they only delayed the reckoning:

> They set all their hopes on closing the gap between money and goods by increased production instead of first making an end to repressed inflation by mopping up the surplus of money and by a simultaneous abolishment of repression. But they fail to realize that it is exactly repressed inflation which is stifling production [because it deprives the economy of the required incentives], and that the longer we wait to break up the vicious circle the more illusionary becomes the hope that increased production might automatically solve the problem of a surplus of demand.
>
> (Röpke 1947c: 248)

In the final stage of open inflation, money loses its function both as a unit of account and as medium of exchange. On top of this, repressed inflation adds a disincentive to the maximum level of production and distribution, severely hitting the supply-side. By doing so, repressed inflation exacerbates the mismatch between the amount of goods and the quantity of money even more.

If the effects at the level of production are disastrous, criticism of this type of inflation eventually extended to matters of social justice:

> Under collectivism, it is no longer true that money embodies the liberty of choice and the freedom to buy under conditions equal to all. Collectivist

money means that money is next to worthless unless it is accompanied with rights and privileges accorded by the political authority. If the rationing is *equal* for all it is money *plus* ration coupons which decide its real value. If the rationing is *differentiated* according to a system of needs and merits defined by the government it is money *plus* ration coupons *plus* the social and political position of the owner which determines its ultimate value.

(Röpke 1947c: 245)

In a word, according to Röpke (1947c: 246), "under collectivism, money begins to smell". The value of money is no longer intrinsically guaranteed, but quite other factors, like the status or position in the hierarchy of the person holding it, become decisive in the purchase of goods and services. Moreover, its value abroad tends to plunge, encouraging the country to fall back on autarchy.

From an ordoliberal standpoint, the contradictions get so great that the planned economy system can no longer suffice to coordinate production and individual needs. Wilhelm Röpke was pessimistic about the prospects for Germany's post-war economy:

We are entitled to call this process *highly pathological* because it has the tendency to involve the national economy in progressive *disorder* and economic *paralysis*. [I]t is the case of Germany which allows us to follow up this process of repressed inflation to its very end of the *complete dissolution of the national economy*.

(Röpke 1947c: 246–247, italics added)

In a lecture called *Money and Economic Development*, Friedman appreciates the distinction between open and repressed inflation, referring to the German post-wars experiences. In accordance somehow with a Röpkean appraisal, Friedman (1973: 53) stresses that "repressed inflation is extremely harmful to efficiency, to development, and to *respect for the law*". Lastly, ordoliberals emphasize that the people of western Germany had, then, no other choice but to fall back on systems alternative to the official markets, which we will be looking into in the third section.

## 3 Neither planning, nor market economy: "no economic order at all"

As the ordoliberals saw it, the inflation fostered by the perpetuation of the planned economy imposed by the Allies came on top of the inflation stored from the Third Reich and war years. This accumulated (repressed) inflation brought the official economy to paralysis, and satisfying the primary needs of individuals consequently became an insurmountable problem:

If the system does not have a perfectly functioning "scarcity gauge", then although economic activity is still possible the lack of coordination will not be conducive to overcoming scarcity. The situation in Germany in 1946 and 1947 is an example of this.

(Eucken 1948a: 30)

The "scarcity gauge" Eucken refers to is the price system, suffering under the strain of rationing and price-fixing, but also troubled by serious monetary disequilibria. Given this, money could no longer fulfil its canonical functions (medium of exchange, unit of account and store of value), and a barter economy emerged – and with it the problem of the *twofold coincidence of needs* necessary for exchange: "a whole series of exchanges were sometimes necessary to obtain the desired commodity" (Lutz 1949: 122).

The official markets suffered from serious disproportions, and in particular severe shortages. When "[t]he direction of the economy by central administration broke down in 1946–47" (Eucken 1948c: 81), alongside these official channels emerged what we would now call an unofficial economy: black market obviously,[15] barter and a domestic self-sufficient economy. The ordoliberals pointed out that the economy bore such a complex system of coordination, spawning so much inefficiency, that it was impossible to identify it with either of the two major types of coordination hitherto known. From this point of view, Germany experienced "a border-line case [. . .] of particular interest" (Eucken 1951: 81), that finally lead "to a chaos where there is no economic order at all, be it collectivist or competitive" (Röpke 1947c: 247).

With the aim of raising the workers' productivity, but also of eluding the fixed ceiling set on wages, the firms introduced forms of "payment in kind" alongside monetary pay. Without affecting the level of production, according to Eucken and Meyer (1948: 53), these industries increased their wage bill to the detriment of the industries that did not practice such forms of remuneration. And even worse, it had the perverse effect of encouraging black markets (Röpke 1947c: 250).

Noting the same mechanism, Eucken and Meyer (1948: 53) point out the negative repercussions practices of the kind have on the secondary economy: "partial wage payments in kind, furthermore, have increased the turnover in the black market and in the barter deals". The consequent decline in productivity and total volume of production then enters into a vicious circle. Advantages offered by specialisation and division of labour are restricted and people turn to unofficial channels. In the ordoliberal analysis, then, as the division of labour declines to a more limited scale, "primitive" or "precapitalist" forms of organisation, including barter and domestic production of food, for example, are seen to develop (Eucken 1951: 69).

Eventually, faced with economic disorder, the people of West Germany turned to expedients that were rational at the individual level (taking on extra work, quests for black markets and exchange of goods, private market gardening economy) but led to increasing irrationality at the global level of the economy:

From the *economic point of view*, such extra work is *senseless waste*. From the point of view of the individual German, however, it is exceedingly important because *it saves him* from misery and frequently even from death by starvation. For that reason this extra work is also *more important to him* than the work at his job.

(Eucken and Meyer 1948: 53, italics added)

On way of reading these lines is to conclude that "the economic consequence of barter is 'misery' and risks 'death by starvation'" – as David Levy and Sandra Peart (2008: 689) in their entry on the "socialist calculation debate" in the *New Palgrave Dictionary of Economics* did. In this particular case, what Eucken and Meyer mean to stress is that resort to bargaining, rational at the individual level, was the only means for survival. Eucken makes the same point in another article.[16] Building on that, one might go even further.

Following the ordoliberal reading, barter is indeed an inefficient system, but it seems that Eucken and Meyer raise the issue not so much in deprecation as, rather, a signal pointing to spontaneous pressures for free exchange. In short, barter is approached as an additional argument in favour of reform in the direction of the market economy. Far from pointing the finger at individual behaviour or decrying the ill-will of the individuals involved, Eucken and Meyer bring discussion back to the field of economic systems analysis. Like Friedrich Lutz,[17] they find fault with the economic system itself, contravening the *invisible hand* mechanism, as read out in a contemporary way:

The economy was "organised" along lines such that the self-interest of individuals and firms was strictly opposed to the common interest. Working at a regular job was the least profitable occupation, and mere survival necessitated breaches of the law.

(Lutz 1949: 122)

Thus Lutz, too, argues along these lines: in the face of a chaotic economy, it had become indispensable for a great many of the workers to infringe the rule of law. The system undermined its own foundations.[18] Monetary reform became inevitable, and the Allies and German authorities were then faced with a choice between two paths: either to reinforce/improve planning, or to venture upon market economy. Here the ordoliberals were unanimous, urging a shock therapy,[19] which the authorities found premature at the time. What they called for was the simultaneous liberalisation of prices and wages (Röpke 1947c: 251).

Monetary reform alone would not save the German economy from inefficiency in an ordoliberal point of view. When they wrote the article, Eucken and Meyer (1948) were aware that a monetary and fiscal reform was imminent, but they did not know all the details. Their worries were about the other measures that were to accompany this reform:

The first and most important requisite for a reconstruction of the German economy is the introduction of a yardstick for economic calculations. [. . .] If an important part of the prices remains at a fixed level, the interaction of misorientation of the productive forces, formation of a new surplus of money, appearance of a black market, and the necessity of barter will begin again.

(Eucken and Meyer 1948: 61)

If there was nothing definite about the price reform that was to accompany monetary reform, a certain correspondence with the proposals of the ordoliberals was no mere chance: Ludwig Erhard had a particularly important role to play in the decision-making process.

## 4 Milestones of an ordoliberal economic system

Over and above the empirical observations, and well boosted by "the Ordo post-war propaganda campaign [which] succeeded in opening space for capitalism in the refined shape of the social market economy" (Ptak 2009: 122), the reforms were indeed a success in winning over the majority of the population and the political class to the cause, cementing national sentiment around a new social-economic project. As experienced here, gaining the support of public opinion is one of the overriding necessities in transition from one economic order to another.

Having crossed this brief period of German history throughout this study, what have we learnt about the *transitional* nature of ordoliberalism? To begin with, (1) the issue of the economic order eventually left behind the Manichaean opposition between exchange economy and centrally administered economy: Eucken and Röpke evidenced a more sophisticated comparative[20] institutional approach. They endorse a German thinking *leitmotiv*: in economics, history counts;[21] shrewd evaluation of concrete institutional factors previously experienced is a basic necessity. Furthermore, (2) it calls into question a fundamental issue in the contrast drawn between liberalism and planning, namely ownership of the means of production, pointing out the basic error of focusing on this issue.

1   The room given to experience and history, and a close connection with economic realities – "*die wirtschaftliche Wirklichkeit*" in Eucken and Böhm's (1948: vii) words – are among the defining elements of their approach. It is probably thanks to these qualities that their teaching finds application so readily in political action. Ordoliberal theory is a theory of economic policy.

We could and should leave the stage of speculation in order to enter the stage of experience-based economic policy. We can draw upon considerable experiences in the areas of monetary policies, crisis policies, agricultural policies, cartel policies, trading policies, tax policies and the like. Indeed these experiences ought to be exhausted; selective descriptions are not sufficient. (Eucken 1949: 219–220)

This is precisely what Walter Eucken (1946b: 1–5) warns the authorities of the French Zone about in his report, taking a few examples. In order to reach its goal, every measure of economic policy has to be conceived in relation to the historical situation as a primary step: if the aim is to realize a specific economic order these decisions should not be made in a vacuum.

In the literature, ordoliberal thought is implicitly taken to be built around the *exchange economy/centrally administered economy* dichotomy. Indeed these two (ideal) types are to be seen in the morphology of Walter Eucken's economic systems (1940: 117–177). However, just like Wilhelm Röpke (1944: 6), he actually maps out a scenario with finer distinctions between the various conceivable systems. In our case, we have seen that it is particularly useful to appreciate the concrete situation of an actual economy – the economy of West Germany – and thus offers an appropriate diagnostic basis. The same terms – money, above all (Röpke 1947c: 244), but also price, market, exchange and so forth – take on different meanings according to the coordination system in place: "with exchange replaced by allocations, all other economic institutions and procedures change their character, even though they do not change their names" (Eucken 1948c: 190).[22]

2   The second lesson that emerges from our study has to do with ownership of the means of production. Whether to privatize or nationalize is not the right question to address: the problem does not originate from the system of ownership, but from the type of coordination system in place, that is, the economic order. Is there a *complete* plan on the part of a central authority that is imposed on the individuals, or do *partial* plans enter into competition? For the latter method, and in the light of the points made in the first part (I): "in an exchange economy there must always be a *scale of calculation* (*Rechnungsskala*), or unit of account, according to which individual plans are adjusted" (Eucken 1940: 131). The criterion for "who" runs the *plan* and on what "scale" is the crucial issue. Walter Eucken's words are here particularly enlightening:

In Germany, the 1947 laws were passed providing for the dissolution of cartels and the breaking up of large companies in order to *distribute economic power more widely*. This occurred at a time when control of the economy was largely in the hands of government central departments. With an *economic system of this kind*, the dissolution of industrial mergers was bound to be *ineffective*. What changes take place in the supply of coal, steel, cement, leather et cetera, when the cartels or multi-corporations existing in these industries are dissolved? *None.* These products were distributed both before and after the law on dissolution was passed by government central departments. *Economic control remained essentially unchanged.* If, however, there had been a *different economic system* than there actually was in Germany in 1947, if central administrative departments had not carried out the control function and instead prices had served as regulators, then the antimonopoly law would have had *quite a different result.*

(Eucken 1948a: 43, italics added)

In 1946–1947 the Allied authorities of the military occupation endeavoured to deconcentrate German industries with the aim of thwarting German industrial potential, in accordance with the Potsdam agreements (Schwartz 1957: 642–648; Shapiro 1962: 4). For instance the Chicago economist Henry C. Simons stressed the imperative necessity of "dismantling" and "systematic industrial deconcentration and decentralization of enterprise control" in Germany during the war (see 1943: 444).

Wishing to weaken Germany, they could have promoted the foundation of a competitive setting, according to an ordoliberal viewpoint which precisely failed to take into account this issue of *transition*. Rightly, Walter Eucken dismissed the possibility that such laws could be effective: modification in the superstructure could only take effect following upon appropriate change in the infrastructure. In 1957, West Germany endowed itself with a special authority established to fight abuse and concentration with the famous Act against restraints of competition (*Gesetz gegen Wettbewerbsbeschränkungen*), which "reflect strong ordoliberal influence" (Gerber 1994: 65). And if that meant waiting until 1957, it was also because the conditions framing the production process were probably still too far from the competitive order for any such legislative measure to be susceptible to implementation.

Eucken put it more succinctly in another context: "there is little point in discussing private ownership and its economic and social functions without clearly specifying the economic system in which it operates" (Eucken 1948a: 41). To do so, or in other words to *historicize* liberal thought, as we saw in point (1), Eucken and Röpke availed themselves of the tools necessary to piece together a faithful picture of the national economy in all its immediacy.

The question of the rule of law – crucial in the Hayekian liberalist approach[23] (Hayek 1973: 87–174, 1993: 131–250) – arose here, at this particular stage, only as a secondary consideration: "to conclude that the law of property is unimportant for the economic system would certainly be mistaken. But the form of an economic system is not determined by the law of property" (Eucken 1940: 86). Having given due credit to Karl Marx for his insight in recognising the central problem of economic power, Walter Eucken took a different direction, observing that the 20th century had been marked by a misjudgement: collective appropriation of the means of production merely transferred economic power from the hands of private agents into the hands of the State:

> With a keen insight into economic forces of his epoch, he [Marx] grasped the full significance of economic power in an environment in which people enjoyed equal political status. The fact that private economic power often went hand in hand with private property did not escape his attention, either. To that extent, he was a realist. But he was ignoring the lessons of the past when he suggested that economic power could be eliminated by collective property. In that regard, he was a dreamer.
>
> (Eucken 1948b: 271)

According to the authors I am concerned with here, the fight against inflation, which is presented as a *leitmotiv* of up-to-date "ordoliberal Europe" and the policies of its Central Bank,[24] had its origins in a very particular framework of ideas. This article demonstrates that over and above the distortions in economic calculation and distribution (Helmut 2001: 337), inflation was seen by the ordoliberals as fundamentally dangerous since it paves the way to planning, with a potential assault on the competitive economic order. Despite the immensity of the task that remained to be performed if their ideal principles were to be followed through, the ordoliberals gave a truly enthusiastic reception to the reforms of June 1948. This particular period perfectly express ordoliberal policies in their relationship to history, that is, vigorous interventions in support of a perfect situation that will never be.

## 5  Conclusion

"Disorder", "complete dissolution" or "collapse" and "chaos" were some of the terms the ordoliberals used to describe the post-war situation. Although Germany's productive capacity remained considerable, the population were facing utter indigence. In their diagnosis the ordoliberals took this paradox as a key to analyse a condition they judged "highly pathological": the Allies were perpetuating a planning system much like that of the Third Reich. In other words, the problem of West Germany lay not in the defeat, but in a purely economic mechanism. The self-perpetuating, cumulative cycle between inflation and methods of control had driven the economic order back to primitive forms of trading such as barter. Inefficient as it was at the collective level, this (rational) individual behaviour gave spontaneous expression to the individual will to engage in free exchange. This theoretical reading is coupled with the use of a warlike lexical field,[25] with terms such as "army", "repressive", "command" or "obedience".

In the light of this observation, it was expedient to reintroduce a currency (monetary reform) that would serve for exchange but at the same time free prices (*Leitsäzegesetz*) so that they could reflect needs and scarcity. The 1948 reforms of ordoliberal inspiration had, then, to make it illegal what had been legal – the possibility for an agency to impose its choices on the others – and to legalize what had been illegal – the will to engage in free exchange among equals. Implemented in part, these principles did not free West Germany of all its economic difficulties; the period was notably marked by an increase in unemployment.

Drawing their lessons from the economic history of the Third Reich, the ordoliberals acquired the resources, not only intellectual but also political, to address the issue of institutional change in Germany. Simple as this response may seem, not so very many liberal authors appear to have opted to address the historical issue with such close attention. Following the theme of transition, the article has delved upstream a number of ordoliberal "recipes" generally stressed in the literature.[26] One of the keys for comparison with the methods of Keynes in inspiration comes into play here.

Ultimately, Walter Eucken, Wilhelm Röpke and the others found themselves formulating a "Listian argument" in reverse. Once again Germany had to follow its own particular path (*Sonderweg*): not that of protectionism in the face of *laissez-faire* liberalism, but of a *framed* liberalism that was to contrast with the triumphant rise of the British welfare state.

## Notes

1 Keynesianism is here merely understood as a practical economic policy consisting in demand management through public-works expenditures, wishing to achieve full-employment. On the fortunes of Keynesianism in Germany after WWII, as policy but also at the academic level, see the studies by Hagemann (2010, 2013) and those by Allen (1989, 2005) and especially the more nuanced light shed by Hesse (2012). German-speaking economists' "anticipations" of and reactions to Keynesian thought in Germany, before WWII, were investigated by Backhaus (1985), Klausinger (1999).

2 Both of these stream tried to pave a third way (*dritter Weg*), dismissing *laissez-faire* or collectivism. Ordoliberalism was built on study of the "social crisis" of the interwar period following upon critical appraisal of a process of massification (*Vermassung*) in all the spheres of society (Wörsdörfer 2014). However, there can be no getting away from the seminal importance of the critique of liberal capitalism: their interpretation is in terms of a causal relation between historical liberalism and planning (Fèvre 2015).

3 This concept, rather imprecise and shifting, was coined by Alfred Müller-Armack (1947, 1956, 1965, 1978). It shares with ordoliberal views some crucial philosophical bases, but also significant discrepancies (for example, strong social policies or countercyclical measures). For a historical outline of the concept, see Goldschmidt and Wohlgemuth (2008).

4 While they are usually viewed as fierce opponents of Nazism, the studies by Keith Tribe (1995) and Ralf Ptak (2009) make some very significant distinctions on the subject. Although Röpke and Rüstow, like Eucken, are above suspicion, certain ordoliberals, to one extent or another (Böhm, Müller-Armack and Ludwig Erhard in particular), yielded to the temptation to tailor their ideas in favour of an authoritarian state-controlled legal framework. For a more moderate position, see Commun (2003: 190–191).

5 See Braun 1990: 153; Nicholls 1994: 124–125; Sohmen 1959: 989; van Hook 2004: 9.

6 This is nuanced by Postan (1967: 24): "[t]rue enough, some of this productive capital was in the form of highly specialized munitions plants unsuited to peacetime employment".

7 The US authorities went furthest in German population culpabilisation (see Solchany 1997: 29–32).

8 As from 1936 the Nazi regime was based on Göring's "four year plan". Actually showing a certain affinity with a Soviet-type economy (Temin 1991), the plan relied on major investments (25 per cent of the overall amount), a drastic control of international trade especially in raw materials, and both prices (including wages) and output were set in key sectors. But the private ownership of enterprises was admitted on a very large scale, so planning was based on contracting (extremely imbalanced) through agencies, that is, a chain of command that went back to the highest authorities of the Reich (Tooze 2006: 106–108, 208–225).

9 Walter Eucken carried out a study on the different typologies the economic order could correspond to in his fundamental work of (1940), *Die Grundlagen der*

*Nationalökonomie* (literally Foundations of – Political – National Economy). Later, considering the case of Germany, Eucken (1948c: 79–80) pointed out that in 1932–33 the economy actually combined two forms of organisation – exchange economy (*Verkehrswirtschaft*) and centrally directed economy (*zentralgeleitete Wirtschaft*) – but as from 1936 the centrally administered economy began to dominate.

10 "By the 1940s Germany's statisticians were embarked on a minute enquiry into the structures of German industry, that would have satisfied even the most ambitious advocates of absolutist "police" (*Polizei*)" (Tooze 2001: 30). On the development of the statistical criterion in 20th-century Germany, see Adam Tooze (2001).

11 See *This Unsuccessful Age* (1951), published posthumously from a course of lectures at the London School of Economics in 1950.

12 Röpke first used the German term "zurückgestaute Inflation" in commenting on Jacques Rueff's *L'Orde social* (Röpke, 1947b).

13 Without any reference to Röpke's work, F.W. Paish's article (1953) and above all Harold K. Charlesworth's book (1956) provide the first systematic studies on this subject.

14 Or, in Eucken's (1951: 74) words: "planned economy [. . .] corelates with inflation".

15 The great extent of this phenomenon is borne out by the historians: "economic transactions reverted to a complicated form of barter plus a narrow black market" (Carlin 1996: 464, see also Rittershausen 2007: 20).

16

> For example, in Germany in 1946, although the workforce was occupied throughout the day, basic needs were not being adequately met owing to a badly organized or insufficiently developed division of labour. In struggling for their livelihood, those in charge of firms or households had to act in a way which did not accord with a rationally organized economy. One man worked in his garden instead of a factory in order to provide himself with food in place of almost useless money; another bartered his ration of tobacco for food instead of working in the factory.
>
> (Eucken 1948a: 43)

17 Friedrich Lutz, a former doctoral student of Walter Eucken, became his research assistant at Freiburg in 1929. He is the author of significant contributions in the field of monetary, interest and investment theory (see Dal-Pont Legrand and Hagemann 2013).

18 In some ways along the German methodological tradition, Ordoliberals provide us with economic relations challenging the dynamics of institutions like the State or the legal framework.

19 Later to be known as the "leap into cold water" (*Sprung ins kalte Wasser*), we find here an example of contrasting positions among German liberals, with Leonhard Miksch pressing for it in face of Müller-Armack's reluctance (Nicholls 1994: 184, 203, 206, 259)

20 Ananyin (2003: 6) places ordoliberalism, alongside the French regulation school (*l'école de la régulation*), within the strand of comparative economics, which he defines as "economics pursued from the viewpoint of the diversity of the real economies". A collection of essays (Labrousse and Weisz 2001) has, moreover, been dedicated to this methodological connection between ordoliberalism and the regulation school.

21 Of course this particular aspect is far from being an unprecedented component of ordoliberal thought, already visible in wartime with the major works of Eucken

(1940) or Müller-Armack (1941). But this present article does find a tangible example of making the theory/history link clearer and meaningful. In a study on Historicism and economic systems, Bertram Schefold (1995) provides insightful comparisons between the approaches of Marx, Roscher, Sombart Spiethoff and Eucken.

22 Even if his historical reading is different, in Human Action, Mises (1949: 718) also notes this epistemological shift: "This is socialism [the Nazi régime] under the outward guise of the terminology of capitalism. Some labels of the capitalistic market economy are retained, but they signify something entirely different from what they mean in the market economy".

23 On the Rule of Law in Hayek's thought, see, among others, Dietze (1977) or more recently Caldwell (2003: 287–320) and Shearmur (2006).

24 For a challenging view on the link between ordoliberals authors and the current practice of the European Central Bank, from the standpoint of the history of monetary thought, see Feldet al. 2015: 3–10.

25 Although in English, these specific words are of particular importance as they are directly addressed to the Allies, who still have the fate of Germany in their hands. Of particular interest are the numerous publications by Röpke in several British, American and French magazines. For instance, he frequently published in *Time & Tide* (11 articles between 1947 and 1951), a British weekly political and literary review magazine, founded by the feminist Margaret Lady Rhondda.

26 We may, for example, consider the principles that defined the field of Ordnungspolitik, developed in a work by Walter Eucken published posthumously, *Grundsätze der Wirtschaftspolitik* (1952). The organising principles aim at monetary stability (a), free access to the market (b), the right to private property (c), contractual freedom (d), and the civil and commercial liability of enterprises (e). The regulatory economic policy applies to control of firms acquiring a dominant position (1), a (re)distributive social policy (2), and, within the limits of the effects on investment, particular attention paid to externalities (3) and abnormal reactions of supply (4). Excellent discussion of these principles can be found in Grossekettler (1989, 1994) and at Vanberg (1998, 2005).

# References

Abelshauser, W. (1992). "Aux origines de l'économie sociale de marché état, économie et conjoncture dans l'Allemagne du 20e siècle," *Vingtième Siècle. Revue d'histoire*, 34(1): 175–191.

Allen, C.S. (1989). The Underdevelopment of Keynesianism in the Federal Republic of Germany. In P.A. Hall (Éd.), *The Political Power of Economic Ideas: Keynesianism Across Nations*, Princeton: Princeton University Press, 263–290.

Allen, C.S. (2005). Ordo-Liberalism Trumps Keynesianism: Economic Policy in the Federal Republic of Germany. In B.H. Moss (Éd.), *Monetary Union in Crisis: The European Union as a Neo-Liberal Construction*. London: Palgrave, 199–221.

Ananyin, O. (2003). "Comment intégrer l'économie comparative dans l'économie?" *Revue d'études comparatives Est-Ouest*, 34(2): 5–29.

Backhaus, J.G. (1985). "Keynesianism in Germany," in T. Lawson and H. Pesaran (Éds.), *Keynes' Economics, Methodological Issues*. London and Sydney: Routledge, 2009, 209–253.

Braun, H-J. (1990). *The German Economy in the Twentieth Century*, London ; New York: Routledge.

Caldwell, B. (2003). *Hayek's Challenge*, Chicago: University of Chicago Press.

Carlin, W. (1996). "West German Growth and Institutions, 1945–90," In N. Crafts and G. Toniolo (Éds.), *Economic Growth in Europe Since 1945*. Cambridge: Cambridge University Press, 455–497.

Charlesworth, H.K. (1956). *The Economics of Repressed Inflation*, London: Allen & Unwin.

Commun (2003). "La conversion de Ludwig Erhard à l'ordolibéralisme (1930–1950)," in P. Commun (Éd.), *L'ordolibéralisme allemand : aux sources de l'économie sociale de marché*, Cergy-Pontoise: CIRAC/CICC, 175–199.

Dal-Pont Legrand, M., Hagemann, M.D.-P.L. and Hagemann, H. (2013). "Lutz and Equilibrium Theories of the Business Cycle," *Oeconomia*, 3(2): 241–262.

Dietze, G. (1977). "Hayek on the Rule of Law," in F. Machlup (Éd.), *Essays on Hayek*, New York: Routledge, 2013, 107–146.

Erhard, L. (1944). "Kriegsfinanzierung und Schuldenkonsolidierung (War finance and debt consolidation)/The Economic Needs of Postwar Germany," in H.F. Wünsche (Éd.), D. Rutter (Trad.), *Standard Texts on the Social Market Economy: Two Centuries of Discussion*, Stuttgart: Gustav Fischer Verlag, 1982, 5–8.

Erhard, L. (1947). "Politischer Föderalismus und wirtschaftlicher Zentralismus (fédéralisme politique et centralisme économique)/The Functions and Limits of Central Economic Administration," in H.F. Wünsche (Éd.), D. Rutter (Trad.), *Standard Texts on the Social Market Economy: Two Centuries of Discussion*, Stuttgart: Gustav Fischer Verlag, 1982, 23–15.

Eucken, W. (1940). *Die Grundlagen der Nationalökonomie/The Foundations of Economics* (T.W. Hutchison, Trad.). London-Edinburgh-Glasgow: W. Hodge, 1950.

Eucken, W. (1946). "Über die Gesamtrichtung der Wirtschaftspolitik/Propos sur l'orientation générale de la politique économique," In W. Oswalt (Éd.), *Ordnungspolitik*, Münster: LIT Verlag, 1999, 1–24.

Eucken, W. (1948a). "Das ordnungspolitische Problem/What Kind of Economic and Social System ?" In A. Peacock and H. Willgerodt (Eds.), *Germany's Social Market Economy: Origins and Evolution [1989]*, London: Macmillan for the Trade Policy Research Centre, 27–45.

Eucken, W. (1948b). "Die Soziale Frage/The Social Question," In H.F. Wünsche (Éd.), D. Rutter (Trad.), *Standard Texts on the Social Market Economy: Two Centuries of Discussion*, Stuttgart: Gustav Fischer Verlag, 1982, 267-276.

Eucken, W. (1948c). "On the Theory of the Centrally Administered Economy: An Analysis of the German Experiment (Part I and II)," *Economica*, 15(58, 59): 79–100, 173–193.

Eucken, W. (1949). "The Competitive Order and Its Implementation," Reprinted in *Competition Policy International [2006]*, 2(2), 219–245.

Eucken, W. (1951). *This Unsuccessful Age: Or the Pains of Economic Progress*, London-Edinburgh-Glasgow: W. Hodge.

Eucken, W. (1952). *Grundsätze der Wirtschaftspolitik/Principes de politique économique* (E. Eucken and K.P. Hensel, Éds.) (7ᵉ éd.), Tübingen: Mohr Siebeck, 2004.

Eucken, W., and Böhm, F. (Éds.). (1948). "Vorwort – Die Ausgabe des Jahrbuchs," *ORDO: Jahrbuch für die Ordnung von Wirtschaft und Gesellschaft*, 1, vii–xi.

Eucken, W., and Meyer, F.W. (1948). "The Economic Situation in Germany," *Annals of the American Academy of Political and Social Science*, 260: 53–62.

Feld, L.P., Köhler, E.A., and Nientiedt, D. (2015). "Ordoliberalism, Pragmatism and the Eurozone Crisis: How the German Tradition Shaped Economic Policy in Europe," *CESifo Working Paper – Category [2] Public Choice*, 5368.

Fèvre, R. (2015). "Du libéralisme historique à la crise sociale du XXe siècle : la lecture de Wilhelm Röpke," *Revue économique*, 66(5): 901–932.

Friedman, M. (1973). *Money and Economic Development: The Horowitz Lectures of 1972*, New York; Washington; London: Praeger.

Gerber, D. J. (1994). "Constitutionalizing the Economy: German Neo-Liberalism, Competition Law and the 'New' Europe," *American Journal of Comparative Law*, 42(1): 25–84.

Giersch, H., Paqué, K.-H., and Schmieding, H. (1992). *The Fading Miracle: Four Decades of Market Economy in Germany*, New York: Cambridge University Press.

Goldschmidt, N., and Wohlgemuth, M. (2008). "Social Market Economy: Origins, Meanings and Interpretations," *Constitutional Political Economy*, 19(3), 261–276.

Grossekettler, H. G. (1989). "On Designing an Economic Order: The Contributions of the Freiburg School," In D. A. Walker (Ed.), *Twentieth-Century Economic Thought* (Vol. II, Aldershot Brookfield [Vt.]: Elgar, 38–84.

Grossekettler, H. G. (1994). "On Designing an Institutional Infrastructure for Economies: The Freiburg Legacy after 50 Years," *Journal of Economic Studies*, 21(4): 9–24.

Haberler, G. (1948). "Causes and Cures of Inflation," *Review of Economics and Statistics*, 30(1): 10–14.

Hagemann, H. (2010). "The Post-1945 Development of Economics in Germany," In A.W.B. Coats (Éd.), *The Development of Economics in Western Europe since 1945*, London: Routledge, 110–124.

Hagemann, H. (2013). "Germany after World War II: Ordoliberalism, the Social Market Economy and Keynesianism," *History of Economic Thought and Policy*, 1(1), 37–51.

Hansen, A. H., and Musgrave, R. A. (1951). *Fiscal Problems of Germany: A Report Prepared during the Summer of 1951*, Berlin: Druck.

Hayek, F. A. (1973). *Droit, législation et liberté – Règles et ordre* (R. Audouin, Trad.) (Vol. 1). Paris: PUF, 1983.

Hayek, F. A. (1993). *La Constitution de la liberté* (J. Garello and G. Millière, Trad.), Paris: Litec.

Helmut, L. (2001). "The Contribution of Neoliberal Ordnungstheorie to Transformation Policy," in A. Labrousse and J.-D. Weisz (Eds.), *Institutional Economics in France and Germany: German Ordoliberalism Versus the French Regulation School*, Heidelberg: Springer, 334–346.

Hesse, J-O. (2012). The 'Americanisation' of West German Economics After the Second World War: Success, Failure, or Something Completely Different?" *European Journal of the History of Economic Thought*, 19(1): 67–98.

Hirschman, A. O. (1948). "Inflation and Deflation in Italy," *American Economic Review*, 38(4): 598–606.

Hook, J. C. van. (2004). *Rebuilding Germany: The Creation of the Social Market Economy, 1949–1957*, Cambridge ; New York: Cambridge University Press.

Klausinger, H. (1999). "German Anticipations of the Keynesian Revolution? The Case of Lautenbach, Neisser and Röpke," *European Journal of the History of Economic Thought*, 6(3): 378–403.

Krengel, R. (1963). "Some Reasons for the Rapid Economic Growth of the German Federal Republic," *Banca Nazionale del Lavoro Quarterly Review*, 64: 121–144.

Kurlander, E. (2011). "Between Detroit and Moscow": A Left Liberal "Third Way" in the Third Reich," *Central European History*, 44(2): 279–307.

Labrousse, A., and Weisz, J.-D. (Éds.). (2001). *Institutional Economics in France and Germany: German Ordoliberalism Versus the French Regulation School*, Heidelberg: Springer.

Lerner, A. P. (1949). "Some Theoretical Aspects," *Review of Economics and Statistics*, 31(3): 193–200.

Levy, D. M., and Peart, S. J. (2008). "Socialist Calculation Debate," In S. N. Durlauf and L. E. Blume (Éds.), *The New Palgrave Dictionary of Economics* (2e éd.), Basingstoke: Nature Publishing Group, 685–692.

Lutz, F. A. (1949). "The German Currency Reform and the Revival of the German Economy," *Economica*, 16(62): 122–142.

Mises, L. von. (1949). *Human Action, The Scholar's Edition*. Auburn (Alabama): Ludwig von Mises Institute, 1998.

Müller-Armack, A. (1941). *Genealogie der Wirtschaftsstile: die geistesgeschichtlichen Ursprünge der Staats- und Wirtschaftsformen bis zum Ausgang des 18. Jahrhunderts*, Stuttgart: W. Kohlhammer.

Müller-Armack, A. (1947). "Die Wirtschaftsordnung, sozial gesehen (L'ordre économique, considération sociale)/The Social Aspect of the Economic System," In H. F. Wünsche (Éd.), D. Rutter (Trad.), *Standard Texts on the Social Market Economy: Two Centuries of Discussion*, Stuttgart: Gustav Fischer Verlag, 1982, 9–22.

Müller-Armack, A. (1956). "Soziale Marktwirtschaft/The meaning of the Social Market Economy," in A. Peacock and H. Willgerodt (Eds.), *Germany's Social Market Economy: Origins and Evolution [1989]*, London: Macmillan for the Trade Policy Research Centre, 82–86.

Müller-Armack, A. (1965). "The Principles of the Social Market Economy," In *The Social Market Economy*, Berlin & Heidelberg: Springer, 1998, 255–274.

Müller-Armack, A. (1978). "The Social Market Economy as an Economic and Social Order," *Review of Social Economy*, 36(3): 325–331.

Myrdal, G. (1951). "The Trend Towards Economic Planning," *The Manchester School*, 19(1): 1–42.

Nicholls, A. J. (1994). *Freedom With Responsibility: The Social Market Economy in Germany, 1918–1963*, Oxford: Clarendon Press.

Paish, F. W. (1953). "Open and Repressed Inflation," *Economic Journal*, 63(251): 527–552.

Perroux, F., Tinbergen, J., Rueff, J., Domar, E. D., Lundberg, E. F., Kalecki, M., . . . Dalal, K. (1949). "The Practice of Economic Planning and the Optimum Allocation of Resources: Discussion," *Econometrica*, 17: 172–178.

Postan, M. M. (1967). *An Economic History of Western Europe 1945–1964*, London: Routledge, 2013.

Prowe, D. (1985). "Economic Democracy in Post-World War II Germany: Corporatist Crisis Response, 1945–1948," *Journal of Modern History*, 57(3), 451–482.

Ptak, R. (2009). "Neoliberalism in Germany," in P. Mirowski and D. Plehwe (Eds.), *The Road From Mont Pèlerin: The Making of the Neoliberal Thought Collective*, Cambridge, London: Harvard University Press, 98–138.

Rieter, H., and Schmolz, M. (1993). "The Ideas of German Ordoliberalism 1938–45: Pointing the Way to a New Economic Order," *European Journal of the History of Economic Thought*, 1(1): 87–114.Rittershausen, J. (2007). "The Postwar West German Economic Transition: From Ordoliberalism to Keynesianism", Discussion Paper 2007/1, IWP.

Röpke, W. (1944). *The Moral Foundations of Civil Society [Civitas Humana]*, 2nd Revised ed. New Brunswick: Transaction, 2002.

Röpke, W. (1947a). "Marshall Plan and Economic Policy (reprinted and translated from the Neue Zürcher Zeitung, November 23, 1947)," in *Against the Tide*, Chicago: H. Regnery, 1969, 123–132.

Röpke, W. (1947b). "Offene Und Zurückgestaute Inflation," *Kyklos*, 1(1): 57–71.

Röpke, W. (1947c). "Repressed Inflation," *Kyklos*, 1(3): 242-253.

Röpke, W. (1947d). "'Repressed Inflation': The Ailment of the Modern Economy (reprinted and translated from the Neue Zürcher Zeitung, June 14–15, 1947)," in *Against the Tide*, Chicago: H. Regnery, 1969, 111–122.

Schefold, B. (1995). "Theoretical Approaches to a Comparison of Economic Systems From a Historical Perspective," in P.D.P. Koslowski (Éd.), *The Theory of Ethical Economy in the Historical School*, Berlin Heidelberg: Springer, 221–249.

Schwartz, I. E. (1957). "Antitrust Legislation and Policy in Germany: A Comparative Study," *University of Pennsylvania Law Review*, 105(5): 617-690.

Shapiro, D. (1962). "The German Law Against Restraints of Competition," *Columbia Law Review*, 62(1): 1–48.

Shearmur, J. (2006). "Hayek's Politics," In E. Feser (Éd.), *The Cambridge Companion to Hayek*, Oxford: Cambridge University Press, 148–170.

Simons, H. C. (1943). "Postwar Economic Policy: Some Traditional Liberal Proposals," *American Economic Review*, 33(1): 431–445.

Sohmen, E. (1959). "Competition and Growth: The Lesson of West Germany," *American Economic Review*, 49(5): 986–1003.

Solchany, J. (1997). Comprendre le nazisme dans l'Allemagne des années zéro: 1945–1949, Paris: Presses universitaires de France.

Solchany, J. (2003). *L'Allemagne au XXe siècle: entre singularité et normalité*, Paris: Presses universitaires de France.

Temin, P. (1991). "Soviet and Nazi Economic Planning in the 1930s," *Economic History Review*, 44(4): 573–593.

Tooze, J.A. (2001). *Statistics and the German State, 1900–1945: The Making of Modern Economic Knowledge*, Cambridge: Cambridge University Press.

Tooze, J.A. (2006). *The Wages of Destruction: The Making and Breaking of the Nazi Economy*, London: Allen Lane, Penguin Press.

Tribe, K. (1995). *Strategies of Economic Order: German Economic Discourse, 1750–1950*, Cambridge; New York: Cambridge University Press.

Vanberg, V. (1998). "Freiburg School of Law and Economics," In P. Newman (Éd.), *The New Palgrave Dictionary of Economics and the Law*, Vol. 2, London: Macmillan, 172–179.

Vanberg, V. (2005). "Market and State: The Perspective of Constitutional Political Economy," *Journal of Institutional Economics*, 1(1): 23–49.

Wörsdörfer, M. (2014). "The 'Societal Crisis of the Present' as a Neoliberal Leitmotif," *History of Economic Thought and Policy*, 3(2): 77–109.

# 13 The transformation of Kenneth Arrow's attitude toward war

*Nao Saito*

## Introduction

The aim of this chapter is to clarify the transformation that came about in Kenneth Arrow's attitude toward war.

Arrow is famous for his general 'impossibility theorem' (hereinafter, Arrow's theorem). His book *Social Choice and Individual Values* (hereinafter *SCIV*), which presents Arrow's theorem, includes both technical and philosophical aspects. With regard to the technical aspect, Arrow provides formal proof of the *collective-choice rule*, which derives social ordering from individual ordering adopting an axiomatic approach. Formally, the book presents proof of this collective-choice rule, that is, the *social welfare function*, which satisfies certain desirable conditions. The social welfare function is the mapping of all logically possible combinations of individual orderings of given alternatives into one social ordering. Arrow's theorem demonstrates the logical impossibility of such mapping, satisfying these desirable conditions.

This theorem is interpreted as proving the impossibility of a democratic collective decision process. He formulated the idea for this theorem in the 1950s during a visit to the RAND Corporation, an organization that focuses on military matters in the United States. In this organization and others, many scholars studied the Cold War using game theory and considered the Cold War itself to be an example of the prisoner's dilemma. Thus, these studies did not analyze the domestic decision process because they regarded the state as a rational actor. Arrow noted this point and was specifically interested in the following question: how does the democratic mechanism decide a nation's actions (e.g. its attitude towards war)? Arrow is said to have tackled this question by formulating his theorem.[1]

If we focus specifically on this aspect of the topic, we see that what matters to Arrow is only proof of the social decision process and that given the normative desirability of the conditions of the collective-choice rule, there is no philosophical question in *SCIV*. On the other hand, Arrow inherits the philosophical question, 'What is social welfare?', stating that individual and social ordering are operational terms standing in for individual and social welfare, respectively. Thus, his theorem is interpreted as proving the impossibility of a social welfare criterion.

Thus, Arrow's theorem has a philosophical aspect as well. However, Arrow initially intended to clarify the decision process scientifically. Therefore, he considered that he could scientifically operationalize such philosophical problems. His intention was backed by the trend of new welfare economics at that time. This type of economics had identified itself as a social science and had been value-neutral when Arrow published his theorem. Although the scope of his theory is broader than the new welfare economics, he still took the concept of scientific objectivity seriously (Amadae 2003; Saito 2016). However, Arrow gradually came to take the philosophical question, 'What is social welfare?' more seriously in the 1960s because he thought that such a value-neutral approach restricted the scope of his theory. After seeing the results of social choice theory and discussing them with others, the philosophical aspect of the issue became more important. As a result, in the 1990s and 2000s he came round to interpreting social ordering as value judgment but not always as a social welfare criterion.

Accordingly, his theoretical transition affected his attitude towards war. When he initially analyzed the Cold War structure, he was interested only in scientifically clarifying the nation's collective decision process (Arrow 2016, 32–33; Amadae 2003). In other words, he was not interested in the value of the consequences of a social decision (e.g. the negative effects of war on social welfare). However, he gradually came to analyze the effects and considered the meaning that he had regarded consequence of democratic decisions on war as a criterion of social welfare. This means, for example, that if the people decided to start a war, such a decision would improve social welfare. However, he changed his position and noted that disarmament theoretically improves social welfare, regardless of the consequence of democratic decisions. He concluded that if a nation decides to engage in war, due to the will of the majority, such a decision does not necessarily improve social welfare. In other words, he gradually came to judge the value of war by a theoretical standard of social welfare that was independent of the consequences of social choice.

This chapter seeks to clarify this transformation in Arrow's ideas and, hence, his attitude toward war.[2] First, we provide the background of Arrow's theorem (section 1). Then we go on to discuss the controversy between Arrow, Ian Little and Abram Bergson (section 2). It is shown that Arrow sought to establish a scientific theory by considering that, in his theorem, economic decision-making and political decision-making are formally the same. However, Arrow later changed his position and attached importance to the difference between the two (section 3). Over time, he came to believe that the consequence of a social decision is a value judgment, but he also realized that this is not always a criterion of social welfare. He then considered whether an armament policy improves social welfare, eventually concluding that it does not. Thus, he was against armament policies, regardless of the consequence of the social decision (section 4).

## 1　*SCIV* and its era

In this section, we clarify the two different backgrounds of Arrow's theorem: the academic background and the political background.

## 1.1 Science and ethics in welfare economics before SCIV

First, we review the treatment of the philosophical problem of 'what is happiness or social welfare?' in welfare economics before *SCIV*.

Arthur Cecil Pigou, a founder of the old welfare economics, searched for the way to improve social welfare, and then evaluated individual utility in cardinal numbers. When an individual utility is evaluated by a cardinal number, the philosophical problem of whether happiness is countable is raised. Lionel Robbins argued that the cardinal number of an individual utility was unscientific. He claimed that economics should be a science without ethical judgments (Robbins 1932: Chap. 6). In response to Robbins' criticism, the new welfare economics, which evaluates an individual utility only by an ordinal number, was founded. As Paul Samuelson argued, the new welfare economics contended that '[a]n ethical conclusion could not be drawn by the same method as a scientific hypothesis being reasoned or being proved' (Samuelson 1983: 220). Samuelson thought that welfare economics can establish the standard of value in the ordinal number, without asking the ethical contents of social welfare. From this position, Samuelson and Bergson created the Bergson-Samuelson social welfare function. Arrow derived the problem of 'what is social welfare?' from this function.

In recent years, the Bergson-Samuelson's social welfare function has been formalized as a real valued function that makes utility correspond to the social ordering by which the Pareto principle holds. Although Bergson and Samuelson thought that a social welfare function fulfilled the Pareto optimality, they believed that the contents of social welfare came from outside economics. On this point, Samuelson argued that a value judgment should be excluded from science. Arrow inherited the philosophical problem of 'what is social welfare?' from Bergson and Samuelson; however, as we have argued, he did not consider that a value judgment should be excluded from economics. He added the new problem of drawing social welfare from the individual welfare of the members of society. Arrow considered this problem as the problem of the social decision process.

## 1.2 The relationship between the social decision process and social welfare in SCIV

In general, Arrow's theorem is thought to prove the logical impossibility of a collective-choice rule that satisfies the four desirable conditions for such rules in a democratic society.

This theorem is proven by the *axiomatic approach*, by which one deduces the theorem from some axioms that are desirable conditions for a collective-choice rule under some assumptions. First, Arrow assumed that the members of society are *rational*; in other words, an individual has a ordering of given alternatives. *Ordering* is defined as a preference that satisfies the conditions of *completeness* and of *transitivity*. The condition of completeness means that for all $x, y \in X$, one prefers $x$ to $y$ or $y$ to $x$. The condition of transitivity means that for all $x, y, z \in X$, if one prefers $x$ to $y$ and $y$ to $z$, then one must prefer $x$ to $z$. Social ordering satisfies the same two conditions. The social welfare function is the formal way of deducing social ordering from the individual orderings of the members of a society.

Four conditions are imposed on this social welfare function: *unrestricted domain*, the *Pareto principle, independence from irrelevant alternatives*, and *non-dictatorship*. Unrestricted domain means that social ordering has to be derived from all logically possible sets of individual orderings. The Pareto principle means that if all members of society prefer one alternative to another, society has to prefer the former to the latter. Independence from irrelevant alternatives signifies that individual orderings against alternatives that are out of the opportunity set cannot influence social orderings against some alternatives that are in the opportunity set. Non-dictatorship signifies that there is no one whose ordering will be the social ordering, regardless of the orderings of other members. Arrow's theorem implies that a social welfare function that satisfies the four conditions cannot logically exist.

The technical aspect of Arrow's theorem is closely related to the philosophical aspect. Arrow's social welfare function is considered to be one way of characterizing Bergson-Samuelson's social welfare function, that is, the criteria of social welfare. Arrow argues for a relationship between his social welfare function and Bergson's economic welfare function (Arrow 1963: 22–24; Bergson 1938). Bergson's economic welfare function aimed to clarify the criterion of economic welfare as a function of several variables, such as the number of products, the amount of leisure and so on (Bergson 1938: 311). According to Arrow, his social welfare function can specify the most suitable function that meets Arrow's four conditions in Bergson's economic welfare functions. Therefore, it is clear that he took over the problem of the criterion of social welfare function from Bergson.

However, Arrow's conception of *social welfare* is different from Bergson's conception of *economic welfare*. First, Bergson's conception of economic welfare includes only economic elements. On the contrary, Arrow's conception of social welfare includes non-economic elements (Arrow 1963: 23–24).[3] Second, Bergson noted that economists could formulate the criterion of social welfare, but they could not determine it (Bergson 1938); however, Arrow considered social ordering a criterion of social welfare. For Arrow, individual ordering is an 'operational' idea of individual welfare, as is social ordering with regard to social welfare (Arrow 1963: 107). This means that theorists like Arrow can specify the criterion of social welfare because social ordering is determined to some extent by the desirable conditions of the social decision process that he fixed. In other words, he considered that the criterion of social welfare could also be operationalised scientifically by using his theory. The clarification of the idea of welfare is a philosophical problem; for this clarification to be scientific, one must translate it into formal terms. Thus, the problem of deriving social preference is the technical solution to the philosophical problem, 'What is social welfare?'

Let us summarize the discussion in this section. In *SCIV*, the social welfare function is the rule of the social choice process that aggregates individual orderings and is manifested in the real world. Moreover, the consequence of social decisions, social ordering, presents the criteria of social welfare.

## 1.3 The Cold War and Arrow's theorem

The political background of the 1950s in the United States influenced Arrow's theorem. The 1950s was the Cold War era. Arrow had visited RAND, a research institute of military affairs, before publishing his theorem. It is said that he was interested in analyzing how a state decides to act in the Cold War structure (Kelly 1987; Amadae 2003: Chap. 2).

In the 1950s, many researchers tried to analyze international affairs by assuming that each state is a rational actor. In particular, the Cold War structure was interpreted as a version of the prisoner's dilemma where neither utility nor social utility can be maximized in a Nash equilibrium (Plous 1993). However, such studies were limited. Although it is assumed that each state is a rational agent, and that its actions are decided by the distribution of utilities of all states and by making predictions regarding other states, each state must be a collective body. Moreover, if the state is democratic, its members must decide its actions by a democratic decision process. Studies such as those noted earlier did not account for this fact (Arrow 2016: 32–33).

Arrow focused on the fact that the state is a collective body and assumed that it makes a decision by aggregating the will, or individual orderings, of its members. For him, the democratic decision process should derive the social ordering from individual orderings. However, there is a famous problem of aggregation, illustrated by the well-known 'paradox of voting' (Arrow 1963: 2).

Moreover, the Cold War structure impinged on his way of thinking that scientific objectivity is important. It is believed that Arrow initially intended to establish a scientific theory of a capitalist democracy that satisfied conditions of scientific objectivity in order to counter the threat of socialism (cf. Amadae 2003, 2005). In the 1950s, capitalists and socialists argued over which system satisfied scientific objectivity and therefore, could be called a scientific theory. From the 1920s to the 1940s, there was an economic calculation controversy over the feasibility of the socialist market.[4] In short, the two backgrounds of Arrow's theorem are assumed to have influenced Arrow's idea of the importance of scientific objectivity.

# 2 The controversy between Arrow and the new welfare economists

Soon after Arrow published his theorem, it was both praised and criticized by many economists and philosophers. The criticisms can be grouped into two categories. The first focused on the theorem's mathematical aspects, while the other focused on its philosophical assumptions and background.[5] We will discuss the latter in this section.

## 2.1 Some criticism against Arrow

As mentioned earlier, Arrow wanted to prove the existence of a social decision process and to clarify scientifically the criterion of social welfare. However, his aims appeared to contradict themselves, because he seemed to make his theory as value-free as science but he also made it address the problem of using value as the criterion of social welfare. In other words, he not only proved the logical impossibility of a social decision process that satisfies desirable conditions, but also regarded its real consequences as an operational idea of the social welfare of a real society. On this point, many researchers criticized that a theorist such as Arrow should not clarify the criterion of social welfare because to do so is against the neutrality of value. Consequently, his theorem was criticized by many researchers, including Bergson, Little and Samuelson, who did not believe that Arrow's social ordering should be the criterion of social welfare (Herrade 2016). This criticism was backed by the inclination toward a scientific and value-free interpretation of the new welfare economics at the time.[6]

Little and Bergson criticized Arrow's philosophical assumption that social ordering is the criterion of social welfare. According to them, social ordering does not imply such a social value judgment. If social ordering is the criterion of social welfare, social action is interpreted as a desirable action from the viewpoint of social welfare. For example, if a state prefers starting a war to being against war, such a decision is considered desirable.

According to Little, Arrow's position in *SCIV* can be interpreted as such a case. Arrow used the term 'social welfare function' to refer to the collective decision process. Such terminology leads readers to believe that social ordering is the system of ethical judgment that society embraces. However, Little refutes Arrow's position, stating that an individual has his/her own preferences. According to Little,

> [T]o interpret it as a social welfare function is to give a nonsensical interpretation. [. . .] It is clear that this person (= the individual who calls the machine a social welfare function) must be contradicting himself unless the 'master'-order (= social ordering) coincides with his own value ordering.
>
> (Little 1952: 427, parentheses added)

In short, if the social ordering is different from the individual ordering and the social ordering should be accepted as a value judgment, an individual contradicts him/herself. Thus, such a social ordering cannot be accepted as a value judgment. In his words,

> In a given community, or committee, as many value orderings as there are individuals may coexist. On the other hand, as between two alternatives there can be only one effective decision. Thus we may all have our conflicting opinions as to whether we ought to go to war or not. [. . .]
>
> Thus an individual will often be prepared to accept a decision which goes against him, because the same decision-making process [. . .] will be used for making many other decisions between other alternatives, some of which will go in his favour.
>
> (Little 1952: 430–431)

Nevertheless, it is not because an individual accepts Arrow's conditions of decision-making process, or social ordering as a value judgment. If Arrow assumes that a social ordering is a value judgment, he should explain why an individual should accept it (Little 1952: 429–430).[7]

Moreover, according to Bergson, an economist like Arrow cannot judge that social ordering is desirable. Only the members of society can judge because it is a matter of their value judgment (Bergson 1954: 237–243). On the other hand, if social ordering does not imply such a value judgment, then it is only a guide to act. An economist should regard social ordering as a guide and should not estimate it at all. In other words, economists can formulate the social welfare function logically, but cannot specify the content of social welfare.

In short, Little and Bergson criticized Arrow's position because, while analyzing the collective decision process can be a scientific problem, the value judgment of social welfare is a philosophical problem. According to Little and Bergson, these two problems cannot mingle. In short, Arrow tried to solve the problem of the criterion of social welfare by defining it as social ordering deduced from individual orderings. However, Little and Bergson considered Arrow's approach to be unscientific.

## 2.2 Arrow's reply

Arrow accepted Little's criticism and clarified his position in the 1950s. Arrow explained that his position is in fact similar to Little's. According to Arrow, only an individual ordering entails an ethical judgment. An individual ranks different social states, such as military expansion or social services, by judging which is more desirable for the individual or society. Therefore, 'the ordering, for an individual, represents his entire social ethic' (Arrow 1983: 49). Thus, Arrow agrees with Little that a social ordering is only a guideline for social action, and does not reflect interpersonal ethics (Arrow 1983: 50).

It should be noted that although Arrow notes that an individual ordering entails ethical judgment, this does not mean that the individual obeys common social ethics when forming his/her individual ordering. Within Arrow's framework, any pattern of individual ordering can be accepted because of the condition of the unrestricted domain. In Arrow's words,

> I should like to emphasize that the decision as to which preferences are relevant and which are not is itself a value judgment and cannot be settled on an a priori basis. From a formal point of view, one cannot distinguish between an individual's dislike for having his grounds ruined by factory smoke and his extreme distastes for the existence of heathenism in Central Africa. There are probably not a few individuals in this country who would regard the former feeling as irrelevant for social policy and the latter as relevant, though the majority would probably reverse the judgment. I merely wish to emphasize here that we must look at the entire system of values, including values about values, in seeking for a truly general theory of social welfare.
>
> (Arrow 1963: 18)

Thus, Arrow's interpretation of 'social ethics' is the subjective ethics or faith according to which an individual acts. For example, even an individual preference for a warlike and criminal society over a peaceful society can be accepted. Similarly, if the individual's ethics dictate that social states should be ranked for his/her own sake, he/she will do so.

Moreover, according to Arrow, an individual ordering is 'observable'. This can be seen in voting. In the 1950s and 1960s, the theory of revealed preference was developed (Arrow 1963: 120n.72). According to this theory, economists can reconstruct a person's individual ordering by observing the person's action in the market. It appears that Arrow applied an idea of this theory to his theorem to make it scientific. Theorists can observe people's voting behaviours and can assume their individual orderings. Therefore, he did not judge individual orderings ethically and objectively; instead, he only observed them. It is true that Arrow regarded social ordering as a criterion of social welfare. However, he only regarded it as an operational idea of social welfare. In other words, he did not value its ethical meaning from a theoretical point of view.

In short, in the 1950s, Arrow wanted to analyze the actions of individuals and states scientifically and, therefore, did not consider that social ordering entails an ethical judgment. He thought that it was a scientifically and value-neutrally operational idea of social welfare. This means that if a state decides to start a war or to maintain a Cold War structure, such a decision does not imply any ethical judgment.

## 3 The relationship between political decision and economic decision

After publishing his theorem, however, Arrow changed his position. Arrow's change can be classified into two parts. The first is the relationship between economic decision-making and political decision-making. The other is the ethical meaning of the consequences of a political decision. This section examines the former.

### 3.1 The similarity between economic decision and political decision

As noted earlier, Arrow intended to make his theory scientific (Arrow 1951c). Arrow applied consumer choice theory to his theory, assuming that the rational consumer creates his/her preference for goods to maximize his/her utility. However, Arrow's theory excluded the assumption of an individual's utility function, in order to make the individual preference more general. A person creates his/her ordering according to his/her criterion of individual welfare, but it does not have to be directly related to consumption. As a result, an individual ordering is regarded as the informational basis of the collective decision process. To formalize this informational basis, Arrow used the axiomatic approach to generalize economic decision-making and political decision-making and to create a general theory. To make economics scientific, the economist only uses a rational analysis that can create a general theory and observable data (Arrow 1951c).[8]

It is clear that Arrow thought that his theory met this requirement by offering scientific proof of the existence of the collective decision process (Saito 2016).[9] He focused on the general collective decision process, and not economic or political decisions, in order to make his theory general. Arrow did not insist that economic decisions and political decisions were the same. Instead, he extracted the common character of these two decisions (Arrow 1963: 5) and did not take the difference between these two seriously in the 1950s.

However, first, his idea of the relationship between economic and political decisions gradually changed. Second, his idea of the meaning of a political decision also changed. We will explain these points step by step.

## 3.2 Market failure

Arrow mentions that some scholars consider the state to be a system of individual agencies whose actions can be analyzed using an analogy with the price system. Furthermore, such scholars think that these two systems contain the same individuals, with the same motivations (Arrow 1970: 18).

Arrow criticizes this view, believing that the motivations of these two systems differ. On the one hand, in an economic decision, like consumption, it is assumed that an individual acts according to his/her own utility. On the other hand, in a political decision like voting, it is assumed that he/she acts according to social good or moral obligation. The reasons for this may be twofold. The first reason involves the scale of the political decision. If an individual considers only his/her utility, he/she should not vote because the expected utility of the influence of his/her vote is smaller than his/her opportunity cost. Since many people actually vote, it is natural to assume that they vote according to some social obligation that cannot be reduced to their profit.[10]

The second reason involves the imperfection of the price system. According to Arrow, one merit of the price system is that the participant does not need to know much about the influence of his/her action. He/she may only know his/her own desire, and need not be concerned about the social influence or consequences of his/her action. This is true because he/she pays a price to the extent that he/she influences others and, therefore, does not need to be concerned about his/her influence on others beyond that price (Arrow 1974: 12). Moreover, individual selfish action is recommended in order to maximize social utility. Hence, it is assumed that he/she does not need to act according to others' interests.

In fact, the price system is not perfect and there are many beneficial social actions without a price. For example, the establishment of a relationship of trust does not have a price and may be broken if one is not concerned about others. As this example suggests, a person must consider his/her influence on others when acting outside of the market. In other words, one must act according to one's conscience and consider one's influence on others when making a political decision.

In short, Arrow clarified the difference between economic decisions and political decisions after publishing his theorem. He became aware that an individual must choose politically according to social ethics, and that his/her motivation to vote must be ethical. He concluded that political decisions, rather than economic decisions, entail social ethics. Moreover, the term 'social ethics' does not have the same meaning as that mentioned earlier. It is not merely subjective faith, but it must satisfy some conditions (e.g. to take care of the influence of others beyond his/her interest). He observed that 'the market is one system; the polity another. [. . .] Looking at policy issues from the point of any one system is likely to lead to unsatisfactory conclusions somewhere' (Arrow 1997: 765). Arrow understood the diversity of social decisions in the real world, and came to accept it.

## 4 Theoretical change of Arrow's idea of the ethical meaning of social ordering

The next question is whether the consequence of a political decision could be the criterion of social welfare.

### 4.1 Arrow in the 1950s

As noted earlier, when Arrow published his theorem in the 1950s, he stated that individual ordering involves ethical judgment. However, he did not state that social ordering involves ethical judgment. Moreover, whether such ethical judgment is selfish or undesirable from an objective standpoint is not a problem because of the condition of the unrestricted domain. Arrow only insisted that his theory can deal with subjective ethical judgment.

### 4.2 Arrow from the 1960s to the 1970s

However, Arrow changed his position in the second edition of *SCIV*, published in 1963. Little had criticized Arrow's statement that social ordering does not involve ethical judgment. In reply, Arrow noted that the evaluation of the collective decision process contributes to the evaluation of the concept of social welfare. In other words, he changed his position, and insisted that social ordering is not only an 'operational' idea but also a value judgment of social welfare. In his words,

> Little has argued cogently that a rule for social decision-making is not the same as a welfare judgment. [. . .] This distinction is well taken. I would consider that it is indeed a social decision process with which I am concerned and not, strictly speaking, a welfare judgment by any individual. That said, however, I am bound to add that in my view a social decision process serves as a proper explication for the intuitive idea of social welfare.
>
> (Arrow 1963: 106)

Arrow quoted Karl Popper's *The Logic of Science Discovery* (Popper 1959) and mentioned that one can deal with a philosophical problem by rational analysis.

Moreover, after publishing the second edition of *SCIV*, Arrow replied to Little's other criticism, in which he asks why an individual accepts a social ordering as a value judgment when it stands in opposition to his/her individual ordering. According to Arrow, the individual obeys the social ordering as an obligation because this is better than not obeying and creating a lack of consensus. The best situation for the individual is to become a dictator and to decide to act alone. In this situation, social ordering accords with his/her individual ordering. However, one cannot be a dictator in a democratic society. Hence, one adopts the second best measure and considers that it is better to make a compromise with others than to decide to take no social action. Thus, one agrees with the social ordering even if it stands in opposition to his/her individual ordering, and is obliged to obey a social agreement. Society is perpetuated by people's protection of such an agreement. However, this agreement does not last long, and can change in tandem with the environment and the individual's ordering (Arrow 1983: 78–79).[11]

In short, in the 1960s, he changed his position as follows. As mentioned earlier, soon after he published his first edition of *SCIV* (Arrow 1951a), Little criticized Arrow in 1952 (Little 1952). At that time, in 1951, Arrow indirectly replied to and accepted Little's criticism (Arrow 1951b). However, in his second edition of *SCIV* (Arrow 1963), he changed his position. He replied to Little's criticism again and regarded social ordering as a criterion of social welfare. Moreover, in 1974, he insisted that obeying a social agreement is a moral obligation, even if it is temporary. For example, a state might decide to start a war, through a democratic decision process, while an individual might prefer a more peaceful solution. In this case, the individual must accept the state's decision to start a war if he/she prefers this to having no plan at all (e.g. not adopting any security measures). Once one accepts the decision, one is morally obligated to obey it. If one prefers no plan at all over starting a war, one has no reason to obey the social ordering.

In the 1970s, Arrow still took individual welfare seriously, though he emphasized more generally than before that obeying the social ordering was a moral obligation for individuals, especially to maintain society. Arrow insisted upon the necessity of agreement for social stability. This is required for the following two reasons. First, it is required to compensate for market failure and to improve economic efficiency. According to Arrow, a person acts individually in the market, but cannot deal with all socially necessary things by doing so. It is also necessary to act collectively in various ways. The most typical example of collective action is a state's action. The state provides public services (e.g. public goods), which the market cannot distribute to individuals. However, it is a mistake to consider the state's action alone as a necessary collective action. More invisible collective actions include norms of social behaviour and ethical or moral codes. Such social norms can also compensate for market failure. In such a case, society imposes norms as a moral code on the individual (Arrow 1974: Chap. 1).

Mutual agreement is necessary to execute such non-market collective action. Some customs and norms, such as the ethical importance of a relationship of trust, provide commodities that the price system cannot adopt. A relationship of trust is also necessary to improve economic efficiency because it reduces transaction costs. This can be interpreted as an agreement to improve the economic efficiency of the market.

It clearly, however, costs too much to form such an agreement and to persuade those who enter society to accept it. Voting is one way to form the agreement, but the voting mechanism has its difficulties, and the larger its scale, the greater its costs. Therefore, as an alternative plan, society tacitly forms such an agreement by making it inherent in individuals. By doing so, society cuts the cost and can develop (Arrow 1974: 20).

Such an agreement can change as individual preferences change because they obey the agreement for their own sake. However, it costs a lot to form and modify such an agreement, even tacitly. The cost of modification is particularly high because people obey it tacitly. Therefore, even if such a modification is necessary from the viewpoint of compromising each individual's interest, people sometimes maintain the status quo. In particular, some people keep the agreement by using the technical ethical code for their own sake. In other words, some use such codes as an excuse for a monopoly or dictatorship (Arrow 1970: 20).

It is usually so difficult to change an agreement that it can continue to rule individuals, even if their preferences change, because of a sense of commitment to a past purpose. Arrow referred to an example from ancient Greece, when Athens was unable to stop a war because she insisted on observing a past promise. Arrow mentioned that Athens should have stopped the war immediately if the present purpose was different from the past purpose. That is to say, one should always leave room to decide whether to start a war or to finish it (Arrow 1974: 19–28).

The second reason why an agreement is necessary to social stability is that this is required to harmonize individual desire with social requirements in the individual's mind. According to Arrow, individual desire always conflicts with social requirements. It is essential to compromise with others who have different values and to form an agreement that is an abstraction of common elements. Thus, society requires individuals to protect social rules. For example, observing the law restricts individual freedom from a standpoint of individual desire, but it also protects the freedom of others. This means that individuals should agree to restrict individual desire in accordance with social requirements. Society cannot be stable without such an agreement which means that individuals should obey a social ordering revealed by a collective decision, such as voting.

In short, according to Arrow, it is true that social agreements create social norms. Such norms or morals are mutual compromises to increase each individual's interests, and technical ethics are merely tools by which a person maintains his/her interest.[12] An agreement is necessary to improve social welfare and to harmonize individual desires with social requirements. Therefore, it is our moral obligation to obey the social ordering, although we can change our social ordering or agreements if our individual orderings change.[13]

This summary of Arrow's statements sheds light on the following two aspects of his thought. First, he considered that obeying a social ordering meant obeying a social requirement, which is a moral obligation for individuals. Second, the purpose of this social requirement is to improve economic efficiency or to merge individual interests. Therefore, if individual preferences change, the requirement can change. Arrow admitted that individual orderings are variable, and insisted that a social ordering should always be modified. Such a social ordering is sometimes a tacit consent, and is revealed by a vote.

However, in the 1970s, Arrow changed his thinking, and began to consider moral obligations more seriously. Arrow mentioned this in his paper criticizing John Rawls's *A Theory of Justice* (Rawls 1971), as follows. Rawls assumed that the individual has a moral personality. However, Arrow adopted a more neutral position on individual preferences. By accepting any pattern of individual preference in his framework, Arrow was able to analyze a more general social decision process than that of Rawls (Arrow 1983: 97).

Arrow also opposed Rawls's idea that the will of the majority is not just. Arrow insisted that it is necessary to express individual will by voting; otherwise, a public officer cannot know whether social policies contribute to the social good. According to Arrow, maximizing the social good is one aim of justice:

> I would hold that the notion of voting according to one's own beliefs and then submitting to the will of the majority represents a recognition of the essential autonomy and freedom of others. It recognizes that justice is a pooling of irreducibly different individuals, not the carrying out of policies already known in advance.
>
> (Arrow 1970: 109)

Thus, Arrow considered obeying a social ordering as a moral obligation, even if it is neither a person's preference nor part of his/her compromise plan.

In any case, from the 1960s to the 1970s, Arrow thought that obeying the social ordering, whether or not it was a compromise, was a moral obligation which is important because it contributes to the stability of society. It is clear that Arrow thought that one should obey a social decision to start a war as a moral obligation, even if one does not agree with the decision.

### 4.3 Arrow from the 1980s to 1990s

In the 1980s and 1990s, however, Arrow seemed to have a positive attitude toward liberalism that does not regard the consequence of social process as ethically important. First, in 1985 Arrow agreed with Rawls that a standard of justice can be deduced from an agreement in hypothetical original position (Arrow 1985). Second, he admitted that social norms accept racial discrimination in some eras and in some areas, even though almost no philosopher in the 1990s supported it ethically. Arrow also refused it ethically (Arrow 1998). From this, it is clear that he was aware that real social norms sometimes stand in opposition to intuitive morality. It is also clear that Arrow became aware that technical ethics is not only an excuse used by some people to protect their interests, but also a fair tool to protect one's rights. Moreover, Arrow did not maintain that people should obey social norms such as racial discrimination as a moral obligation.

Third, Arrow insisted that the consequence of a vote must not violate certain individual rights. In Arrow's words, 'Judicial decisions and votes are not to go to the highest bidder. Individuals cannot waive certain legal rights' (Arrow 1997: 765). Arrow referred to child trafficking as an example, insisting it violates the rights of a child. This makes it clear that Arrow in the 1990s believed that if the consequences of the market or a vote go against people's rights, the consequences should become null, and people should not obey them.

According to Margaret Radin (1996), the market should not set any price on goods related to the violation of an individual's personality. Nevertheless, it does sometimes set the price of such goods, such as child trafficking and prostitution. Such goods 'contest' the setting of any price, and this is a market failure (Radin 1996; cf. Arrow 1997). Arrow partly agreed with this opinion, but he did not clarify the reason. However, it can be interpreted that he considered that there are two types of goods, only one of which should be purchased in the market, but individuals and the market sometimes mistakenly confuse the two. Hence, the individual mistakenly prefers one social state that sells goods that should not be purchased, to another that refrains from doing so. Then, he/she may form an individual ordering as such. Therefore, a social ordering, which is an aggregation of individual orderings, is not always considered to have ethical meaning.

In the 1960s and 1970s, Arrow accepted the condition of an unrestricted domain and regarded the consequences of a social decision as an ethical judgment. Therefore, if most individuals judge child trafficking to be ethically acceptable, Arrow may have admitted this ethical judgment. However, in the 1990s, Arrow rejected some types of individual ordering on ethical grounds, for example preference for child trafficking.[14]

### 4.4 Arrow in the 2000s

In the 2000s, Arrow proposed a disarmament policy, from the viewpoint of its economic effect.

At the practical level, Arrow was involved in the founding of the Economists Allied for Arms Reduction (ECAAR), and was appointed as the first chairman with Lawrence Klein of Pennsylvania University.[15] This is an international organization that aims to analyze the negative impact of military expenditure on the economy. According to Arrow, the end of the Cold War structure made it possible to advance international disarmament, and economists therefore had to seek a strategy for this.

According to Arrow, any increase in governmental expenditure, including increases in military expenditure, means an increase in national income. Hence, a disarmament policy reduces national income. Arrow referred to the cynical joke that the Cold War activated the economic systems of both the United States and the Soviet Union (Arrow 2000: 13–16).

However, war has huge costs that reduce social welfare. For example, about 60 per cent of national income was accounted for with military outlay during World War II in the United States. Moreover, most of the production created by the war was destroyed by the war. This problem is not peculiar to World War II. For example, Arrow mentioned that the Gulf War cost member nations of the United Nations about 70 billion dollars.

Arrow analyzes the negative cost of war from two perspectives. One is the model of general competitive equilibrium, and the other is new growth economics. According to the model of general competitive equilibrium, reducing one dollar of military expenditure means increasing one equivalent degree of social welfare. Thus, we have to promote disarmament projects to increase social welfare. Moreover, military expenditure is covered by taxes which cost the economy much more than the revenue from those taxes. For example, the economic cost of one dollar income tax is 1.25–1.75 dollars in the United States. Reducing military expenditure by one dollar means increasing social welfare by 1.25–1.75 degrees. Next, according to new growth economics, military affairs need 10 times more human resources for technological innovation than are needed in other fields. If disarmament is advanced, the technological innovation of private industry will advance, because many engineers who are involved in military affairs will become involved in other fields (Arrow 1994b).

On the other hand, it is true that reducing military expenditure causes a negative economic effect for part of the population. The utility of those with specific roles, such as those who serve in the military or are arms dealers, may decrease with a reduction in military demand. Many people oppose disarmament policies for this reason. However, according to Arrow, such people may not understand that they can efficaciously channel their talent and resources into other fields. Moreover, disarmament causes a positive economic effect for other parts of the population by enabling them to obtain necessary public services.

Therefore, disarmament policy may not result in Pareto improvement in an economic sense, but the lost utility of some workers can be cancelled out by the gain of many other people and, thus, the policy contributes to improving social welfare. Accordingly, Arrow suggested that disarmament policy contributes to transforming potential Pareto efficiency into real Pareto efficiency. He referred to unemployment policy in this context (Arrow 2000: 22). He does not make it clear whether this potential Pareto efficiency implies the compensation principle. However, Arrow's idea is similar to the Kaldor-Hicks criterion (Kaldor 1939; Hicks 1939).

Arrow also failed to mention the relationship between the consequence of social choice and disarmament policy, although military expenditure in the United States was increasing when Arrow published his paper on disarmament policy. It appears that he did not consider the consequences of democratic decisions as having ethical value.

Arrow's doubt about the ethical value of the consequence of democratic decision can be clearly seen in a recent interview. Arrow mentions that he was opposed to the Iraq War because there were no weapons of mass destruction in Iraq. Furthermore, he criticised Donald Trump severely, saying that 'his politics does not even meet the first test for rationality. It's crazy' (Arrow 2016: 181). He added that 'what we are seeing now is not restricted to the United States. Democracy is going crazy' the world over (Arrow 2016: 180). He said that it was his very core value that things should be decided democratically, but 'Obviously there are situations in which it's clear to me that I don't care what the majority says. [. . .] I don't have a consistent answer' (Arrow 2016: 112). This means that Arrow admits that his core value is now shaken.

In summary, after publishing his theorem, Arrow gradually admitted the moral obligation to respect the social ordering. However, after the 1980s, he admitted that social ordering is not always the objective criterion of social welfare. In the 1990s and 2000s, Arrow proposed a disarmament policy using a theoretical criterion of social welfare that was independent of social ordering. Although the cause of his theoretical change is unknown, the theoretical development of social choice theory, like the studies showing that there is no ideal collective decision process (Riker 1982; Suzumura 2006), may have influenced him.

## Concluding remarks

In this study, we traced Arrow's theoretical change from the 1950s to 2000s. Arrow's change of attitude towards war prompts us to consider whether economists should analyse social affairs such as war scientifically and in a value-neutral way, if they should accept a social decision as criterion of social welfare, or if they should propose positive policies that, theoretically, improve social welfare. Moreover, it shows that scientific analysis and policy proposals for improving social welfare are seldom compatible with each other. At first, the aim of Arrow's theorem was to clarify the social decision process scientifically and did not regard the consequences of a social choice, such as whether or not to start a war, as an ethical judgment.

However, Arrow gradually came to admit that social ordering is not only a guideline for state action, but also a value judgment, and insisted that people should respect it as a social norm and obeying it is a moral obligation. According to this idea, if a state decides to start a war, an individual should obey the decision as a moral obligation.

He later changed his position again, this time insisting that social ordering is not always the criterion of social welfare. Thus, respecting the social ordering is not always a moral obligation. The reason why he changed his position lay in the realisation that it sometimes clashes with intuitive moral sense. It seems that Arrow searched for a theoretical way to improve social welfare. As an example, Arrow suggested disarmament in the 2000s because it would increase social welfare according to the theoretical criterion. At that time, military expenditures in the United States were steadily rising. Thus, we find Arrow contesting the consequences of a real democratic decision process at that time. Although Arrow is famous for his early theoretical achievement, his later works also teach us another way to improve social welfare.

## Notes

1 In an interview, Arrow mentioned his argument with Olaf Helmer. Helmer said that economists like him assume that a state is a rational actor when it analyses the Cold War structure. However, he asked Arrow how a democratic state can decide its attitude toward war. Arrow stated that in his attempt to answer Helmer's question, he started creating his theorem (Arrow 2016, 32–34).
2 Well-known previous studies of the philosophical aspect of Arrow's theorem include Mackay (1980), Riker (1982), Pildes and Anderson (1990), Amadae (2003), Amadae (2005), Mackie (2003), and Pattanaik (2005). However, these studies do not analyze the theoretical change in Arrow's view of democracy and his attitude toward war, on which this paper focuses.
3 However, Samuelson generalized Bergson's economic welfare function and redefined it as the Bergson-Samuelson social welfare function (Samuelson 1983: Chap. 8).
4 The debate in the 1950s traced their roots to these famous arguments. Arrow took up this argument in *SCIV* between Maurice Dobb, a socialist, and Lerner, a capitalist. He defended Lerner, and so defended capitalism against Dobb (Arrow 1963: 84–85). Although Arrow's theorem is interpreted as the impossibility of capitalist democracy, it also created its logical foundation, and we can justify capitalism if we can solve Arrow's theorem. In that sense, a defense of capitalist democracy against socialism was included in the initial aim of Arrow's theorem (Amadae 2003: Chap. 2).
5 James Buchanan in particular criticized Arrow as being against individualism, because he assumed that society is a single rational agent. According to Buchanan, an individual does not make collective decisions in the market. Moreover, even if such a collective decision exists, the assumption that society has its own preferences means that the substance of society exists beyond individuals. Such an assumption is against an individualistic view, which holds that only the individual can be a rational agent. In short, Arrow tried to analyze the actions of the state by regarding it as a rational agent and collective body, while Buchanan criticized the view that such a collective body can have its own preferences (Buchanan 1954).
6 Samuelson admitted, however, that new welfare economics has some normative assumptions. He listed them and mentioned that they are not controversial and can be accepted in general. Therefore, according to Samuelson, it is important for new welfare economics not to be value-free, but to minimize its normative assumptions (Samuelson 1983: 243, 249).
7 Bergson also criticized Arrow for this reason (Bergson 1954). However, Bergson and Little did not clearly mention political decisions regarding war. They simply mentioned the more general issues of social decision-making.
8 This also means that the assumption of rationality satisfies the requirement of science and prediction and, therefore, represents real action better than other assumptions do. Accordingly, Arrow's theory overlooked the irrational character of political decisions.
9 This can be controversial, because Arrow's theorem includes four normative conditions. Therefore, it cannot be value-free. I think that Arrow's position is similar to that of Samuelson. Though Arrow's theory cannot be totally value-free, it can be scientific by minimizing its normative assumption.

10 It is worth noting that this position is not contradicted by Arrow's theorem, according to which it is assumed that an individual will vote according to faith or values because of the condition of an unrestricted domain.

11 Arrow also replied to Bergson's criticism in the second edition of *SCIV*.

12 The term 'technical ethics' means ethics that a moral philosopher theoretically advocates.

13 See for example Arrow (1967b).

14 However, he mentioned this in 1974. Therefore, we cannot separate Arrow's thought in the 1970s and 1990s clearly. Moreover, it is uncertain whether or how the anti-war movement against the Vietnam War in the 1970s and the end of the Cold War structure in the 1990s influenced Arrow's thought.

15 ECAAR began as Economists for Peace and Security (EPS) (ECAAR 2016).

## References

Amadae, S. (2003). *Rationalizing Capitalist Democracy: The Cold War Origins of Rational Choice Liberalism*, Chicago: University of Chicago Press.

Amadae, S. (2005). "Arrow's Impossibility Theorem and the National Security State," *Studies in History and Philosophy of Science* Part A, 36(4): 734–743.

Arrow, K. (1951a). *Social Choice and Individual Values*, New York: Yale University Press.

Arrow, K. (1951b). "Little's Critique of Welfare Economics," *American Economic Review*, 41(5): 923–934.

Arrow, K. (1951c). "Mathematical Models in the Social Science," in D. H. Lerner and D. Lasswell (Eds.), *The Policy Science*, Stanford, CA: Stanford University Press, 129–154.

Arrow, K. (1963). *Social Choice and Individual Values*, 2nd ed., New York: Yale University Press.

Arrow, K. (1967b). "The Place of Moral Obligation in Preference System," in S. Hook (Ed.), *Human Values and Economic Policy*, New York: New York University Press.

Arrow, K. (1970). "Political Economic Evaluation of Social Effects and Externalities," NBER Chapters, in *The Analysis of Public Output*, National Bureau of Economic Research, Inc., 1–30.

Arrow, K. (1974). *The Limits of Organization*, New York: Norton.

Arrow, K. (1983). Collected Papers of Kenneth J. Arrow: Social Choice and Justice, Cambridge, MA: Harvard University Press.

Arrow, K. (1985). "Distributive Justice and Desirable Ends of Economic Activity," in G. Feiwel (Ed.), 1965 *Issues in Contemporary Macroeconomics and Distribution*, Albany: State University of New York Press, 134–156.

Arrow, K. (1994a) "Individualism and Social Knowledge," *American Economic Review*, 84(2): 1–9.

Arrow, K. (1994b) "Some General Observations on the Economics of Peace and War," ECAAR Japan.

Arrow, K. (1997). "Invaluable Goods," *Journal of Economic Literature*, 35(2): 757–765.

Arrow, K. (1998). "What Has Economics to Say About Racial Discrimination?" *Journal of Economic Perspectives*, 12(2): 91–100.

Arrow, K. (2000). "The Basic Economics of Arms Reduction," *Peace Economics, Peace Science, and Public Policy*, De Gruyter, 6(3): 1–17.

Arrow, K. (2016). On Ethics and Economics: Conversations With Kenneth J. Arrow, New York and London: Routledge.

Arrow, K., and Debreu, G. (1954). "Existence of Equilibrium for a Competitive Economy," *Econometrica*, 22: 265–290.

Bergson, A. (1938). "A Reformulation of Certain Aspects of Welfare Economics," *Quarterly Journal of Economics*, 52: 310–334.

Bergson, A. (1954). "On the Concept of Social Welfare," *Quarterly Journal of Economics*, 68: 233–252.

Buchanan, J. (1954). "Social Choice, Democracy, and Free Markets," *Journal of Political Economy*, 62(2): 114–123.

ECAAR (2016). "Welcome to ECAAR.ORG." Available at www.ecaar.org/. Accessed 02/10/2016.

Herrade, I. C. (2016). "The Death of Welfare Economics: History of a Controversy," CHOPE Working Paper No. 2017–03.

Hicks, J. (1939). "The Foundations of Welfare Economics," *Economic Journal*, 49(196): 696–712.

Kaldor, N. (1939). "Welfare Propositions in Economics and Interpersonal Comparisons of Utility," *Economic Journal*, 49(195): 549–552.

Kelly, J. S. (1987). "An Interview With Kenneth J. Arrow," *Social Choice and Welfare*, 4(1): 43–62.

Little, I. (1952). "Social Choice and Individual Values," *Journal of Political Economy*, 60(5): 422–432.

Mackay, A. (1980). *Arrow's Theorem: The Paradox of Social Choice: A Case Study in the Philosophy of Economics*, New Haven, CT: Yale University Press.

Mackie, G. (2003). *Democracy Defended*, Cambridge: Cambridge University Press.

Pattanaik, P. K. (2005). "Little and Bergson on Arrow's Concept of Social Welfare," *Social Choice and Welfare*, 25: 369–379.

Pildes, R., and Anderson, E. (1990). "'Slinging Arrows at Democracy: Social Choice Theory, Value Pluralism, and Democratic Politics," *Columbia Law Review*, 90: 2121–2214.

Plous, S. (1993). "The Nuclear Arms Race: Prisoner's Dilemma or Perceptual Dilemma?" *Journal of Peace Research*, 30(2): 163–179.

Popper, K. (1959). *The Logic of Scientific Discovery*, New York: Basic Books.

Radin, M. (1996). *Contested Commodities*, Cambridge, MA: Harvard University Press.

Rawls, J. (1971). *A Theory of Justice*, Cambridge, MA: Harvard University Press.

Riker, W. (1982). *Liberalism Against Populism: A Confrontation Between the Theory of Democracy and the Theory of Social Choice*, San Francisco, CA: W. H. Freeman.

Robbins, L. (1932). *An Essay on the Nature and Significance of Economic Science*, London: Macmillan.

Saito, N. (2016). "Arrow's Social Preference as the Moral Rule," *The History of Economic Thought*, 57(2): 68–88 (Japanese).

Samuelson, P. (1983). *Foundations of Economic Analysis*, Cambridge, MA: Harvard University Press.

Suzumura, K. (2006). *The Foundation of Welfare Economics*, Toyo Keizai Press (Japanese).

# Index

Note: Page numbers in italics indicate a table on the corresponding page.

For Product Safety Concerns and Information please contact our EU
representative GPSR@taylorandfrancis.com
Taylor & Francis Verlag GmbH, Kaufingerstraße 24, 80331 München, Germany

www.ingramcontent.com/pod-product-compliance
Ingram Content Group UK Ltd.
Pitfield, Milton Keynes, MK11 3LW, UK
UKHW021009180425
457613UK00019B/871